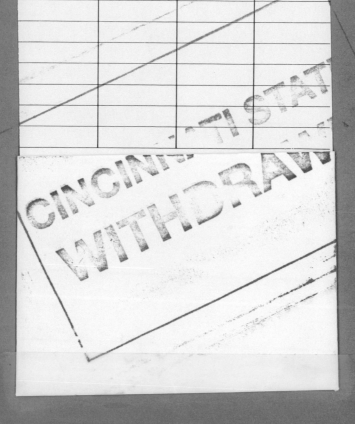

THE GASTRONOMY OF
SPAIN
and
PORTUGAL

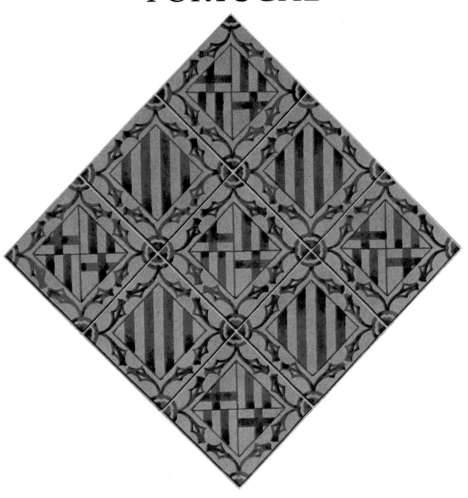

THE GASTRONOMY OF
SPAIN
and
PORTUGAL

MAITE MANJON

 PRENTICE HALL

New York London Toronto Sydney Tokyo

PRENTICE HALL PRESS
15 Columbus Circle
New York, NY 10023

PRENTICE HALL PRESS and colophon are registered
trade marks of Simon & Schuster, Inc.

Library of Congress Card Number: 89–045886

ISBN 0–13–347691–X

Typeset by Area Graphics Ltd,
Letchworth, Hertfordshire
Manufactured in Portugal

10 9 8 7 6 5 4 3 2 1

First Prentice Hall Press Edition

To my husband Jan
who helped so much

CONTENTS

LIST OF COLOR PAINTINGS

ACKNOWLEDGMENTS

I should first of all like to thank the various Spanish and Portuguese government bodies which have helped me to write this book, both by arranging visits to study the wines and food and in providing information.

My husband and I have gone to Spain many times at the invitation of Wines from Spain in London and are particularly indebted to its Director of Public Relations, Mr David Balls. Mr Graham Hines and Mr Bryan Buckingham of the Sherry Institute have often encouraged us to visit Jerez de la Frontera, where Sr. Bartolo Vergara Vergara of the Sherry Exporters Group has been the most attentive of hosts. Miss María José Sevilla of Foods from Spain, another branch of ICEX (the Spanish Promotion Center), has been a fund of information about Spanish food. Some few years ago the then Spanish Ambassador in London, Don Manuel Fraga Irribarne, lent his support to a book on the Spanish Paradores, and the Ministerio de Información y Turismo, as it then was, despatched us on a six week tour of the Paradores, which proved invaluable in allowing me to investigate the cooking from every corner of the country.

The Portuguese authorities have been similarly hospitable. A first visit was arranged by Sr. Jorge Dias, when Director of the Portuguese National Tourist Office in London, and since then successive members of the London Trade office, including Dr. Domingos Simões, Sr. Luis Charters and Sr. João Henriques, have organized extended research trips allowing for detailed study of the regional cooking as well as the wines.

I can thank only a few of those who have been so generous with recipes and advice. Lalo Grosso de Macpherson, who bears the titles of *Cocinera del Rey* ('Royal Cook') and *Cocinera del Jerez* ('Cook of Jerez'), is an old and dear friend and I learned a great deal in the course of translating her invaluable *Los vinos de Jerez en la cocina universal* into English. Those who have invited me into their kitchens range from masters like Luis Cruañas of the Elorado Petit in Barcelona, Jamie Subirós of the Hotel Restaurant Ampurdán in Figueras and Gonzálo Córdoba of El Faro in Cádiz to Loly of the tiny Bar Restaurant Conchita in Cenicero, who makes the best *pochas riojanas* (bean stew) in the Rioja, and the redoubtable Petri, cook at the Marqués de Riscal, with whom I have spent many busy mornings planning menus to set off vintage wines from the "Catedral" or roasting sackfuls of red peppers for preserving. Don Manuel Domecq Zurita, well known in Jerez for his knowledge of all things gastronomic, introduced me both to some of the best restaurants in the area and drew my attention to a number of very well worthwhile books. At the other end of Spain, Don Miguel A. Torres and his wife Walla performed a similar service in Cataluña, while Don Antonio and Da. Africa Mascaró, and Don Mariano and Da. Teresa Fuster have taken me to many of the most interesting restaurants in Barcelona and around.

In Portugal, special thanks go to Dña M.A.F. de Souza, the gifted cook and hostess of the Quinta das Torres in Azeitão, to Dña Rosa Marques da Cunha Ferreira of the Estalagem Dom Duarte in Viseu, who alas has died, to Sr. Anibal Soares of the Hotel Mirassol, Praia de Miramar, and to Dña Angela Pombo, cook with one of the lightest hands in the country at the uniquely beautiful Quinta Palacio da Bacalhoa near Setúbal, where we were recently privileged to be the guests of Mr Tom Scoville. Mr Noel Cossart has kindly allowed me to reproduce his mother's recipe for *bolo de miel* – Madeira cake as made on the Island – from his book, *Madeira – the island vineyard*. Other good friends who have regularly helped and guided me in Portugal are Mr and Mrs David Delaforce, Sr. Jorge Ferreira of *A.A. Ferreira sucrs.* and Sr. Antonio d'Avillez of João Pires.

I must thank Mr Noel Treacy and Mrs Juliet Pierce of the Hispanic Council Library for their prompt and unfailing help in meeting my insatiable demands for books. I have not been accompanied on my journeyings by a secretary or consultant cook, but am most grateful to my husband, Jan Read, for his help in preparing the book for press and over the notes on wines, and also to Miss Liz McEwan of Canon (Scotland), without whose computer programming skills, the thousands of entries would never have appeared in the right order!

INTRODUCTION

Writers, other than the Spanish and Portuguese themselves, make great play of the adjective "Iberian", thereby suggesting a basic similarity between Spain and Portugal, whatever the subject under discussion. Until the beginning of the twelfth century there was, in fact, no distinction between the two countries, but with the Reconquest of the Peninsula from the Moors, they increasingly followed separate paths. In a book covering the gastronomy of both countries the question at once arises as to what extent the cuisines are comparable.

Both Spain and Portugal are fortunate in retaining a splendid range of regional dishes, and both countries make extensive use of olive oil, garlic and wine. What emerges is that the Portuguese and Spanish, working with more or less identical raw materials (though varying, of course, from north to south and from the seaboard to the common border) have sometimes gone their own ways and in other cases produced, for example, similar roasts of suckling pig, baby lamb and kid; *gazpachos* or *gaspachos*; *cocidos* or *cozidos*, stews made with beans, vegetables and meat; a great variety of grilled and fried fish; wonderful *mariscos* (shellfish); a range of cured hams and *chorizos* or *chouriços*; and egg sweets, such as the *tocino de cielo* or *toucinho de ceu*, which are basically the same. Spanish and Portuguese cooking is at its most similar in the far north, in the Portuguese Minho and in Galicia, the areas least affected by the Moorish occupation, where the *caldeiradas* (fish stews) and other dishes are identical.

On the other hand, there are striking differences. The Spanish make far greater use of that ubiquitous blend of tomatoes, peppers and onions, known as *sofrito*, than do the Portuguese of the rather similar *refogado*. The Portuguese have frequent recourse to the spices introduced to Europe from the Far East by their mariners, especially in marinating fish and meat, and serve vegetables together with a main dish instead of separately for a starter, as do the Spanish. And there are, of course, dishes entirely typical of each country, such as *paella*, *riñones al Jerez* and *zarzuela* from Spain or *caldo verde*, *carne de porco à alentejana* and *tripas à moda do Porto* from Portugal.

As regards wines, the two countries have little in common apart from the young *pétillants* wines of the Minho and Galicia. Port and Madeira are as unique and typical of Portugal as is sherry of Spain. There is, in fact, less similarity between Dão, the best-known of the Portuguese table wines, and Rioja than between Rioja and claret.

While regional dishes continue to be served at home and in the smaller

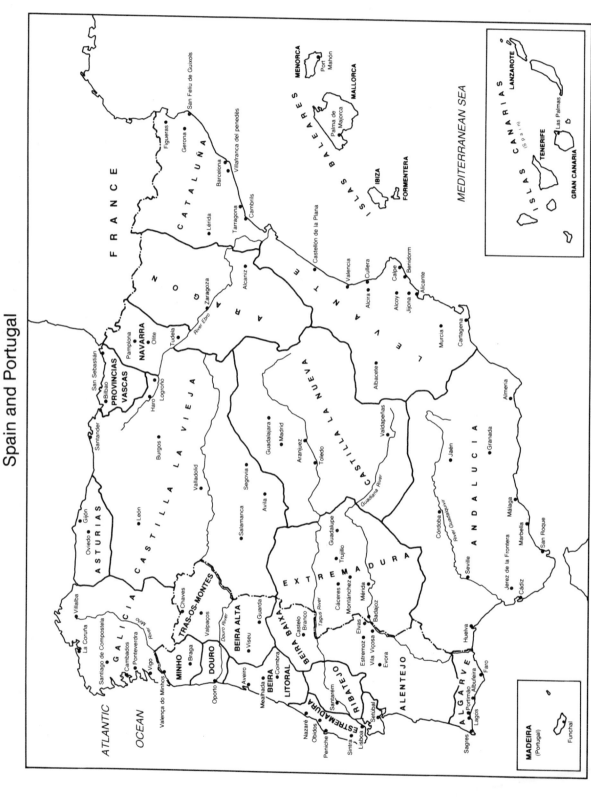

Spain and Portugal

restaurants of both countries, the larger and more sophisticated restaurants, especially in Cataluña and the Basque country in Spain, have been influenced by the *nouvelle cuisine*. Mercifully, the vogue for tiny plates of assorted steamed vegetables and minuscule helpings is on its way out, and there is now an emphatic return to robust traditional cooking. In the Basque country the movement sparked off the *nueva cocina vasca*, far from a slavish imitation of the original, which in the hands of chefs like Arzak and Subijana, has resulted both in a refinement and lightening of heavier dishes and in ingredients cooked to bring out their natural flavors to the full. It need hardly be added that the large resort hotels, as everywhere, provide "international cooking" and that to sample the traditional dishes one must choose one's restaurant; some of the best are listed in the entries for the different regions and cities.

As to my own initiation into cooking, I must confess that I did not tiptoe into the kitchen at an early age, nor did my mother have much to do with such matters, apart from discussing the day's menus with our cook. At that time, Spanish girls like myself were expected to be proficient in needlework and embroidery and to acquire the social graces, and it caused a major family ruction when I insisted on studying medicine at Madrid University – and even more so when I departed unchaperoned to London to learn English and very shortly married an English writer. At that point I frankly admit that my husband had to show me how to turn on a gas stove and he did most of the cooking. He did, however, have a housekeeper with a real flair for good English cooking, who taught me a lot. Similarly my mother-in-law's "treasure" in Scotland was an unsung genius in preparing Scottish food. She herself was a Yorkshirewoman and a dab hand at baking and the annual rituals of making Christmas puddings and jams from the fruit in the garden. I learned a great deal from both of them.

I did not acquire a knowledge of Spanish and Portuguese cooking by undertaking a journey of thousands of kilometres and transcribing recipes at well-known restaurants (although we did once travel the whole of Spain at a stretch in aid of a book about the Spanish Paradores). Over the years I have profited from the advice of much better cooks than myself in Spain and Portugal, but this was a gradual business, starting in the days when we hired houses in Spain for my husband to write film scripts and I cooked for the family and guests. The time came when I felt that it would be helpful to share my experience with visitors catering for themselves in Spain – hence the title of my first book, *Spanish Cooking at Home and on Holiday*. Since those days, I have spent a great deal of time in Spain and Portugal helping my husband, Jan Read, to research his wine books (and contributing gastronomic notes to them). I have also become increasingly fascinated with the historic origins of Spanish and Portuguese cooking, and have found a great wealth of published material, in Spanish,

Portuguese and English, both historical and practical, as will be apparent from the bibliography.

I have tried to keep the recipes as simple and economical in time as possible. I myself am not prepared to begin the preparation a day or a couple of days beforehand – and think that few people are. I, therefore, see little point in reproducing complicated recipes from restaurants calling for, say, meat stock or fish *fumet* plus assorted sauces – these things are ready to hand in restaurants, but not at home. I have made suggestions for substitutes where the Spanish or Portuguese ingredients are not readily available abroad, but only in so far as they will not affect the quality of the dish. There are certain dishes, such as the famous *urta a la roteña*, made from a fish feeding on shellfish in the Bay of Cádiz, which cannot be prepared abroad and it is profitless to offer alternatives. I hope that readers will enjoy browsing over the descriptive and historical notes about ingredients, history and wines, but the recipes are definitely for using!

MAITE MANJON

HOW TO USE THE GASTRONOMY OF SPAIN AND PORTUGAL

Three basic forms of cross-reference are used to make the information easily accessible in *The Gastronomy of Spain and Portugal*.

Firstly, the Spanish and Portuguese languages, though linguistically very close, often use different words to describe subjects. A boxed S or P indicates the origin of each recipe. In the majority of cases the entry has been put under its Spanish name in the alphabetical ordering with a corresponding cross-reference in Portuguese elsewhere in the text to lead the reader to the main commentary. When the term refers mainly to a Portuguese food, wine or dish, there is a Spanish cross-reference. Certain dialect words are also cross-referred to main entries. This is designed to help the reader, particularly when abroad, to consult the *Gastronomy* when only the Spanish or Portuguese term is known.

Secondly, certain words have been CAPITALIZED within the body of the text. This indicates that they are separate entries, where you will find an explanation of their meaning and additional details about their background or uses. However, terms or ingredients with their own entries are not capitalized wherever their meaning is self-evident or their usage so frequent that you will quickly become familiar with them. Full details are given in the entries for terms like these, but they are so essential to Spanish and Portuguese cooking that their presence in *The Gastronomy of Spain and Portugal* needs no greater emphasis.

CAPITALIZED cross-references have not been used within the recipes themselves. Where a Spanish or Portuguese ingredient or term is unfamiliar, a bracketed translation is provided. Where a recipe is important, but does not have an introductory entry of its own, it is highlighted with a main entry heading within the recipe box.

Finally, there is a second form of cross-reference underneath the main text, at the foot of some pages, which refers English terms to their Spanish and Portuguese equivalents, for example: Almond: see almendra. This supplements the English translations to the entry headings in the margins.

In addition, the comprehensive index at the end of the book is arranged by types of food – meat, fish, soups, cakes – cooking methods and terms, kitchen equipment and other subjects.

a la brasa
COOKING METHOD

To broil (see A LA PARRILLA) over a bed of glowing charcoal.

a la parrilla
COOKING METHOD

To cook meat or fish on a grid placed over a charcoal fire. The bars of the best *parrillas* are stout, and the grid must be kept very hot so that the juices do not drip from the meat or fish. For the same reason meat or fish must not be pierced with a fork and should be turned only once, using two wooden forks.

Meat for the *parrilla* should be cut rather thick (about 1 inch); it should be cleaned of sinews and any skin around the edges removed so that it does not shrink during cooking. Never try to flatten it with a cleaver. The addition of salt during cooking results in the loss of juices. leaving the meat

Broiling meat on a parrilla

dry, so it should be seasoned afterwards. See also PARRILLADA DE MARISCO.

a la plancha
COOKING METHOD

Most roasting in Spain and Portugal (see ASAR) is done on a grid over a charcoal fire or *a la plancha* – on a hot plate. A *plancha*, or large flat metal griddle, is to be found in most Spanish and Portuguese kitchens and also in CAFETERIAS and bars, where it is also used for making toasted sandwiches.

For cooking meat, the griddle is made as hot as possible and the meat brushed with olive oil to prevent it sticking. Butter is never used for this since it burns at high temperatures and gives the meat a bad flavor. To test whether meat cooked on the *plancha* is ready, press lightly with the fingers; if elastic to the touch it needs more time and should be cooked until firm. As with the *parrilla* (see A LA PARRILLA), use tongs or wooden forks and turn only once during cooking to retain the juices.

For cooking fish, see MARISCADA A LA PLANCHA CON SALSA ROMESCO.

à padeira
COOKING METHOD

Padeiro means "baker" in Portuguese, and it is the custom in country districts of taking dishes to be baked to the hot brick oven of the village baker after the day's bread-making (see ASAR, COCHINILLO). The term *à padeira* is, therefore, used to describe roasting in a hot oven in an earthenware casserole.

Academia Española de Gastronomía
SPANISH ACADEMY OF GASTRONOMY

Rafael Ansón, the noted gastronome and writer, Secretary General of the Academy, defines its aims as: "The investigation of the origins of our diet and the study of our traditional recipes to evaluate their merits, eliminate their defects and make them more attractive, so that hispanic cooking may occupy the place which rightfully belongs to it, not in a spirit of competition with that of other countries, but as a complement to the gamut of world cuisines." In pursuit of these aims, the Madrid-based Academy, founded in 1979, lends its support to publishers, both in reprinting classical texts and in publishing innovative new books.

🅿 *açafrão*

Saffron; see AZAFRAN.

🆂🅿 *acaramelar*

COOKING METHOD

To coat a cooking vessel with caramel (see JARABES) so as to give a gloss and color to the food cooked in it. See also FLAN DE HUEVOS and FLAN DE MANZANAS.

Opposite: Spain has always possessed abundant supplies of fruit and vegetables. This 17th century still life captures some of that natural wealth, with its tantalizing depiction of grapes, pears and apples taken from the surrounding countryside

🆂 *aceite de oliva*
🅿 *azeite de oliva*

OLIVE OIL

The olive tree is the most common in Spain as a whole, where over 3,900 square miles are dedicated to olive growing, and in the south of Portugal in the province of the ALENTEJO. It grows best in poor and barren, chalky soils. In the province of Jaén in ANDALUCIA – the largest grower in Spain, followed by Córdoba, SEVILLA and Badajoz – whole valleys and hillsides are clothed with the gnarled trees and grey-green foliage.

Some 92 percent of the Spanish olive crop is used for making olive oil, the rest being used for preserved olives. For making olive oil the fruit is picked just before it is fully ripe either by hand or by shaking it down with poles. Both are labor-intensive operations which account for its high cost in comparison with substitutes such as corn, sunflower, rapeseed and peanut oils.

There are three types of olive oil: *extra virgin olive oil* which is obtained by cold pressing of the pulp from the fruit and which is a perfectly natural oil retaining all the aroma and flavor of the olive; *virgin olive oil* which is made by refining both extra virgin oil and oil obtained by a second and firmer pressing of the pulp – it is blander and lacks the fragrance of the extra virgin oil; *pure olive oil* which is a blend of the first two types and which represents a half-way stage in taste.

This is to put matters in the simplest possible terms since in Andalucía alone, which accounts for some 20 percent of world production of olive oil, there are 156 varieties of olives – of which the Picual, Hojiblanca and Léchin of Sevilla make up 75 percent – all with their subtly different flavors. To take account of this, the Spanish Ministry of Agriculture has demarcated the virgin oils from four regions: Baena in the province of Córdoba, Sierra de Segura in the province of Sevilla, and Borjas Blancas and Siurana in CATALUÑA. As the broadest of generalizations, the Catalan oil is lighter and drier in taste than the sweeter and fruitier Andalucian oil, and is, therefore, particularly suitable for making SALSA VINAGRETA, SALSA MAHONESA or for smearing on to bread for the famous *pan con tomate* (country bread smeared with olive oil and rubbed with fresh tomato), a specialty of the region.

The virtues of olive oil were first recognized by the Greeks, but it was the Romans who introduced it to the Iberian Peninsula.

Olive branch

In the latter days of the Roman Empire, a long and pleasant life was popularly held to be dependent upon two fluids: "wine within and oil without". Many centuries later it has been recognized that olive oil is perhaps one of the healthiest of all for culinary purposes. Unlike animal fats such as butter or lard with a content of up to 55 percent of saturated fatty acids, it contains 90 percent of polyunsaturated fatty acids and is less likely to cause heart disease.

Olive oil is used both as an ingredient in its own right and as a base for cooking other ingredients. Its pleasant and aromatic smell and flavor for both purposes set it apart from cheaper substitutes with their pungent odors which pervade a house from one end to the other. The Spaniards, at any rate, recognize this and the average household uses about 1 quart per week.

As an ingredient it is essential in making ALIOLI, *salsa vinagreta* and *salsa mahonesa*. It is also used in a wide variety of dishes such as the GAZPACHOS of Spain and *gaspachos* of Portugal, and in making sauces generally.

The refined and pure (*puro*) oil possesses many virtues as a cooking medium for frying (see FREIR). It may safely be heated to higher temperatures than animal fats without burning. If the flavor of butter is required in a particular dish, a good tip is to mix it half and half with olive oil, remembering, however, to cook it at a lower temperature.

Imported in small bottles, olive oil is ridiculously expensive, and if you use it at all regularly, the best buy is a reliable Spanish brand such as "Carbonell" or "Musa" in gallon cans.

aceitunas azeitonas
OLIVES

Both in Spain and Portugal, olives (see also ACEITE DE OLIVA) are produced on a large scale for use as hors d'oeuvres.

Green olives are picked unripe, treated in hot alkaline lye to remove the bitter taste and then pickled in spiced brine. Among the most delicious are *aceitunas rellenas*, from which the stones are removed and the olives stuffed with anchovies or pimentos.

Black olives are picked ripe and do not require the alkali treatment. They are, however, thoroughly washed before being pickled in olive oil containing flavorings such as thyme, cumin, oregano, rosemary and vinegar, all carefully chosen to suit the individual type of olive.

Apart from being bottled, olives are also pickled in bulk and make a colorful display when the new season's crop appears in the open markets of Spain and Portugal just before Christmas.

acelgas
SWISS CHARD

A winter vegetable with dark green leaves resembling spinach, popular in Spain and used in dishes such as MENESTRA A LA RIOJANA.

acelgas con pasas y piñones
SWISS CHARD WITH RAISINS AND PINE NUTS

A vegetable dish popular both in CATALUÑA and the ISLAS BALEARES, eaten as an appetizer and made by boiling ACELGAS and adding pine nuts and raisins.

Opposite: Chilis and onions; two ingredients in Spanish and Portuguese cuisine

Swiss chard

P *acepipe*
APPETIZER

The Portuguese enjoy a large range of delicious and often unfamiliar appetizers including *croquetes* (croquettes of ham, kid, PRESUNTO, veal etc); *limões de pescador* (scooped-out lemons filled with mashed tuna or salmon); MANTEIGAS COMPOSTAS; RISSOIS; *tomates recheados* (stuffed tomatoes) – and many others.

P *açorda*
A BREAD SOUP

A substantial soup made from a variety of ingredients, but always containing bread. The best known is the *açorda alentejana* from the ALENTEJO in the south of Portugal, containing garlic, eggs, potatoes and slices of bread. Made from inexpensive ingredients most readily to hand, it was created to satisfy the needs of peasants who had done a hard day's work on the land. When served as a soup before a main course, it blunts rather than stimulates the appetite and may more appropriately be taken as a meal in itself.

Other variations are *açorda de alhos* (garlic soup with bread and sometimes eggs) from the Baixo Alentejo; *açorda de coentros e* *poejos* (bread, cilantro and mint soup); *açorda de marisco* (shellfish bisque) from Cascais; and *açorda de sável* (a soup made with shad and bread) from the RIBATEJO and ESTREMADURA.

Açorda de marisco

P *açúcar*

Sugar; see AZUCAR.

S P *adobar*
TO MARINATE

To marinate meat or fish (see BOQUERONES EN ADOBO) by steeping it in a liquid such as wine, olive oil and/or vinegar containing herbs and condiments. The object is to impregnate the food with the flavor of the condiments and also to soften the fibers.

---

adobo a la madrileña (S)
marinade for prime cuts of pork

1 clove garlic, crushed
pinch of salt
pinch of paprika
⅓ cup olive oil
⅓ cup dry white wine
2 tbsp vinegar
bay leaf, chopped
pinch of oregano
pinch of black pepper

Make a paste by crushing and blending all the ingredients in a mortar and pestle or a food processor. Transfer to a dish, cover and chill in the refrigerator for at least 4-5 hours. Use sparingly; the above quantities are sufficient for about 2 lb meat.

S P *agua*
WATER

"The Iberians," wrote Richard FORD, "are decided water drinkers. The vinous Greek Athenaeus was amazed that even rich Spaniards should prefer water to wine; and to this day they will just drink the wine that grows nearest, while they look about and enquire for the best water . . . . Properly to understand Solomon's remark, that cold water is to a thirsty soul as refreshing as good news, one must have experienced what thirst is in the exposed plains of the calcined Castiles, where *coup de soleil* (sunstroke) is rife, and a gentleman on horseback's brains seem to be melting like Don Quixote's when Sancho put the curds into his helmet . . . . The common form of praise [even today] is *agua muy rica* – very rich water, [and] Ferdinand the Catholic, on seeing a peasant drowned in a river, observed that 'he had never before seen a Spaniard who had had enough water.' "

The water in Spain and Portugal is alas no longer what it was when the Moors constructed their elaborate irrigation channels fed by fresh springs and rivers from the hills. It is safe enough in any of the large places in both countries, though it may taste strongly of chlorine, and it is always pleasanter to drink *agua mineral, con gas* (bubbly) or *sin gas* (still) in Spain, or *com gás* and *sem gás* in Portugal.

ᵃ *aguacate*
AVOCADO

This tropical fruit has been acclimatized in Spain and is now grown all year round in favorable spots in the province of Granada and also around Málaga and in the Islas Canarias. With their high vegetable oil content, avocados were used by the Aztecs both as a food and as a beauty aid. They are popular nowadays because they contain potassium, iron, calcium and vitamin E, and it is claimed that their natural oils prevent the skin tissues from drying out, thus helping to rejuvenate them, and also that they are an aphrodisiac.

ᵖ *aguardente*
BRANDY

Brandy is called *aguardente* or *aguardente de vinho* in Portugal to distinguish it from the popular *aguardente de bagaceira* or *marc*, which is usually known simply as BAGACEIRA. Most Portuguese brandy is made by the continuous distillation of wine in tall steam-heated columns, but the better brands are made by the traditional Charentais process in small pot stills.

ˢ *aguardiente*
GRAPE SPIRIT

A potent and popular Spanish spirit, distilled like the French *marc* or Portuguese BAGACEIRA from the skins and seeds left over after making wine. There is a Spanish saying which suggests that it requires three men to the glass – one to drink it and two friends to carry him home!

ˢ *ajo*
ᵖ *alho*
GARLIC

Garlic has been used both as a flavoring and for medicinal purposes from the earliest times. The ancient Egyptians made a poultice from the crushed heads of garlic as a remedy for the bite of an asp; and it has since been recommended for the treatment of rheumatism, arthritis and high blood pressure. It is an excellent diuretic and intestinal antispasmodic and is said to reduce the risk of heart disease.

In Spain it is grown mainly in the south and southeast in the provinces of Cuenca, Valencia, Alicante, Albacete, Murcia, Granada and Córdoba, but the so-called "Capital del Ajo" is the village of Las Pedroñeras near Cuenca and the surrounding area. These account for some 70 percent of all exports of Spanish garlic, of the best purple variety. Spain is the fourth largest producer of garlic in the world, and a large-scale exporter, although 80 percent is consumed at home.

Garlic should be hard and plump and the cloves should not be shrunken within the paper-like sheath. Avoid soft or discolored garlic, which not only smells bad but ruins any food cooked with it. In early summer the new season's garlic, if harvested too young, tends to have a somewhat rank, but not unhealthy, flavor.

In Spain and Portugal, garlic is, of course, the most universal flavoring, used in large amounts for dishes such as the Portuguese AÇORDAS. For less avid garlic lovers the secret of cooking with it is moderation. When properly used, it enhances the taste of the food without overpowering it. When using garlic in salads, it should be crushed in a mortar – garlic squeezers give it a somewhat metallic taste – and a simple Spanish method is to crush a clove under the flat of a kitchen knife before chopping it. *One* crushed clove is ample for a vinaigrette dressing. Chopped garlic should be fried only briefly because it rapidly burns and blackens; if adding crushed garlic to, say, *sofrito* (see REFOGADO), do so shortly before removing the pan from the heat. The other method of cooking with garlic is to add the whole cloves earlier in the cooking and to remove them with a spoon afterwards. Again, be sparing with it and use too little rather than too much – one medium-sized clove goes a long way.

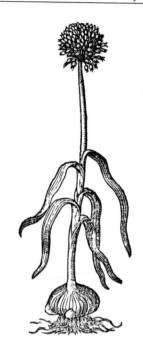

---

ajo blanco con uvas de Málaga (S)
cold grape soup from Málaga

Serves 4

1 cup almonds, blanched and skinned
½ cup pine nuts
3 cloves garlic
salt
1 tbsp olive oil
1 tbsp white wine vinegar
2½ cups cold water
½ lb white grapes, peeled and seeded
1 cup fresh breadcrumbs, soaked in water and squeezed dry
ice cubes

Pound the almonds and pine nuts in a mortar and pestle with the garlic and salt to taste. Alternatively, this may be done in a blender or food processor. Stir in the oil gradually, mix well and then add the vinegar. Transfer to a soup tureen and add the water, grapes and breadcrumbs. Cover the dish with plastic wrap and cool in the refrigerator for about an hour before serving with an ice cube in each bowl.

S *ajoarriero*

COUNTRY-STYLE BACALAO

Arriero means "muleteer", and this salt cod dish is a creamy, country-style *bacalao* (see BACALHAU) cooked with garlic, eggs and potatoes.

S *ajos tiernos*

GARLIC SHOOTS

When you see *tortilla de ajos revueltos* on the menu of a Spanish restaurant, it is not an ordinary garlic omelet but is delicately flavored with chopped young garlic shoots. The season is short but they can be bought in cans.

🇪 albahaca

Basil; see MANJERICÃO.

🇪 albaricoque
🇵 alperce
APRICOT

Spain is the largest supplier of apricots to Europe. Grown in the provinces of Murcia, VALENCIA and Zaragoza, they are thought to contain more vitamin A than any other fruit. They are often used for decorating fruit desserts and confectionery, but the Spanish and Portuguese prefer to eat them fresh. I myself think that the dried variety has more flavor. Soaked in liqueur overnight, they make wonderful tarts or, in purée form, ice cream. See also SONHOS DE ALPERCE.

🇪 albóndigas con salsa rubia
MEATBALLS IN SAUCE

Serves 4

1 lb cooked veal or pork, or a mixture, ground
½ lb cooked ham, ground
1 onion, finely chopped
salt
1 egg, beaten
2 tsp fresh breadcrumbs
1 clove garlic, crushed
1 tbsp chopped parsley
⅓ cup flour, to coat
½ cup olive oil

Sauce
1 onion, finely chopped
2 tbsp olive oil
1 heaping tbsp flour
2 tbsp fino sherry
1¼ cups chicken stock
salt and pepper

Put the ground meat and the onion into a bowl and season with salt. Mix thoroughly with the egg, breadcrumbs, garlic and parsley. Shape into balls with your hands, then dredge in flour and fry for 5 minutes in hot olive oil over a high heat until golden brown. Remove the meatballs with a slotted spoon and set aside.

To make the sauce, sauté the onion for 10 minutes in hot olive oil, then pour off the excess oil. Add the flour and stir in the sherry and stock. Simmer for a few minutes until well blended, and season with salt and pepper.

Transfer the sauce to a casserole, add the meatballs, cover and simmer gently for 30 minutes until cooked through.

🇵 Alcántara, Monasterio de
ALCANTARA, MONASTERY OF

The monastery of Alcántara lay in the path of General Juno's invasion of Portugal during the Peninsular War (1806–1814). He sacked it and ordered all but one of its precious manuscripts to be used for making cartridges. With Gallic interest in gastronomy, he preserved the monastery's recipe book which he sent to his wife, the future Duchess of Abrantes. She reproduced parts of it in her *mémoires*, and Escoffier was later to comment that "It was the major trophy, the only positive advantage that France reaped from that war." The remark was justified because the centuries-old manuscript contained the first known references to *consommé* (under the names of *consumado* or *consumo*), directions for the use of truffles and a recipe for *pâté de foie gras*.

S *alcaparras*
CAPERS

Capers are the flower buds, preserved in vinegar, of a thorny shrub (*Capparis spinosa*) that grows wild in southern Europe. Since the 1960s they have been farmed in ANDALUCIA, the ISLAS BALEARES and Murcia and their labor-intensive cultivation and picking have done much to stimulate employment. With 30 square miles under cultivation, Spain is the largest producer in the world and exports to Switzerland, Britain, Italy and Germany.

The ancient Greeks were very aware of the medicinal properties of capers, and used them for treating stomach complaints. Modern research has shown that they are particularly rich in vitamin P – also known as citrin. The Greeks also knew that the buds developed into beautiful pink flowers which in turn bear a fruit rather larger than capers. These are known in Spain as *alcaparrones* and are delicious served with sherry or other apéritifs.

S *alcaparrones*

Capers; see ALCAPARRAS.

P *Alcobaça*
A CHEESE

A semi-hard ewe's milk cheese with a fat content of 55 percent from the ESTREMADURA, north of LISBOA. It resembles the better-known *queijo da* SERRA, but is pure white inside.

> *The index, in English, is arranged by types of food — eggs, cheese, fish — kitchen equipment, cooking terms and other subjects. Consult it for recipes that make use of particular ingredients.*

S *Alella*
DEMARCATED WINE REGION

The smallest of the demarcated regions in Spain, Alella, on the northern outskirts of BARCELONA, has been making wines since Roman times. It is celebrated for its fruity white wines, of which the best known are from the old-established cooperative and labeled "*Marfíl*" ('Ivory'). More recently a very light, fragrant "Marqués de Alella", made by cold fermentation in stainless steel tanks, has come on the market.

Alentejo
PORTUGUESE REGION

The immense southern province of Alentejo, stretching from the Atlantic to the Spanish border for much of its length, occupies about a third of the total land area of Portugal. Its wide, undulating plains are carpeted with grey-green olive groves shimmering in the heat and with darker cork oaks. In spring there are drifts of pink almond blossom (see ALMENDRA) and the long, straight roads are hedged with dazzling yellow broom and flanked with rolling expanses of fresh green wheat, for this is Portugal's grain producing region.

Among historic and interesting places to visit in the Alentejo are Vila Viçosa with its great ducal palace, once the seat of the Bragança family (where there is, incidentally, a huge kitchen, complete with spit, sixty-foot chimney and batteries of copper cooking vessels), and Evora, predominantly

Moorish in character, but walled since Roman times with the pillared temple of Diana at the center. The POUSADA of Dos Loios, installed in an old monastery, is among the most attractive in the country; but of greater interest gastronomically is that of Elvas, another historic old town on the Spanish frontier, whose cooking is famous. Specialties include BACALHAU A LISBONENSE, *lulas recheadas* (stuffed squid), *arroz de pato à pousada* (baked duckling on rice), *cericia com ameixas de Elvas* (sponge cake with a sauce of the celebrated Elvas plums), and CARNE DE PORCO A ALENTEJANA. This original blend of pork and clams, together with the AÇORDAS, are the most significant of the Alentejo's contributions to Portuguese cooking.

The region produces some good and sturdy red wines from Borba, Reguengos and Vidigueira, near the Spanish border, but in the Alentejo as a whole, the vines were uprooted in Moorish times and never replanted so that it does not constitute a great reservoir of drinking wine as do the somewhat similar regions of VALDEPEÑAS and LA MANCHA in Spain.

🅿 *aletria*
A PASTA

A fine pasta akin to vermicelli (thin spaghetti or angel hair pasta).

🅿 *aletria doce*
SWEET VERMICELLI

Vermicelli cooked with egg yolks and sugar, and flavored with cinnamon and lemon zest. This dish is a Christmas specialty (see NAVIDAD).

> CAPITALIZED *words within entries refer the reader to more information on the same subject.*

Algarve
PORTUGUESE REGION

The Algarve, the southernmost province of Portugal, took its name from the Arabic *el-gharb*, meaning "west", as it was the most westerly point in the Iberian Peninsula occupied by the conquering Moors. It was at Sagres, at the far tip of the Algarve overlooking the ocean, that HENRIQUE O NAVEGADOR established his Nautical School. Here he gathered around him the cartographers and mariners whose studies made possible the voyages of discovery which, among other things, resulted in the introduction of many exotic spices and fruits to Europe.

With its pretty beaches and coves and resorts such as Faro, Albufeira and Lagos, the Algarve is now one of Europe's favorite vacation playgrounds – and it is to the credit of the Portuguese that they have not turned it into a concrete wilderness, as have the Spanish much of the Costa del Sol. Back from the coast the geraniums, camellias and oleanders grow alongside cotton, rice, figs and almonds, carob, sugar cane and lemon, with villages of white-washed houses set in this near idyllic garden.

Of the towns, Portimão preserves perhaps as much character as any, and its burgeoning market overflowing with fish, vegetables and flowers is certainly worth a visit, while in the streets back from the front you

of the better-known Portuguese dishes such as the ubiquitous CALDO VERDE or (with a little luck) CARNE DE PORCO A ALENTEJANA. The shellfish is magnificent (though expensive) wherever you eat it, and charcoal-grilled sardines are to be found at outside stalls by any of the beaches. For more typical dishes, such as *cataplana de amêijoas* (cockles cooked in CATAPLANA), *mexilhões a marinheira* (wine-steamed mussels), *perdices com amêijoas* (partridge with clams) or *ensopado de cabrito* (kid stew), it is best to visit the smaller restaurants of a place like Portimão.

The Algarve has inherited from the Moors (see MOROS, LOS) a multiplicity of confections, usually made with egg yolks, sugar, almonds and spices. Often made by nuns, they are sold in the PASTELARIAS and include specialties such as BOLOS DE D. RODRIGO, *duquesas* ("duchesses"), *bolinhos de S. Bras* ("fritters of S. Bras") and *tutano celeste* ("marrow from heaven").

will find the old-fashioned *ferrageio* (ironmonger), who will sell you a hand-made CATAPLANA.

The cooking of the large resort hotels is "international" in style, modified by some

---

P *Algarve*

DEMARCATED WINE REGION

Almost all the wine that comes from this popular Portuguese vacation spot is an undistinguished cooperative-made red, acceptable for everyday drinking.

P *alho*

Garlic; see AJO.

S *Alicante*

DEMARCATED WINE REGION

The area in the hills behind the city of Alicante produces both full-bodied red wines that are high in alcohol and also some light and refreshing rosés.

S *Alicante*

A CHEESE

A goat's milk cheese made around Alcoy in the hills behind Alicante. Cylindrical in shape, white and soft, with a fat content of 37 percent, it is eaten fresh.

S *Alimentaria, Salón Internacional de*

A FOOD FAIR

This biennial food fair held in March in the exhibition halls of Montjuich in BARCELONA is one of the largest international events of its type, with thousands of exhibitors from all over the world displaying food, wine and catering equipment. It is also the venue of authoritative seminars on food and wine technology.

The seal for the Alicante demarcated wine region

Opposite: In modern Spain, vegetables are grown all year round under huge plastic greenhouses which often cover many acres

Pages 30-31: Farm workers harvest saffron crocuses; only the dried stigmas are used

Page 32: Garlic and peppers; two of the ingredients of a refogado or sofrito

S *alioli*
GARLIC SAUCE

Used since Roman times, this classic Catalan sauce corresponds to the *aïoli* (garlic mayonnaise) of Provence and is served with grilled or roast meat, fish and vegetables.

---

alioli (S)
garlic sauce

Makes about ⅔ cup

3 cloves garlic
salt
2 tbsp chopped parsley
⅔ cup virgin olive oil
a little lemon juice

Crush the garlic in a mortar and pestle with a little salt and the parsley. Drip in the olive oil little by little, stirring all the time with a wooden spoon, then add the lemon juice and continue stirring until the sauce thickens like a mayonnaise. This may also be done in a blender or food processor. A variety of other ingredients such as an egg yolk, chopped walnuts, almonds may be added. Creamy cheeses are also sometimes incorporated in the basic recipe.

S *Almansa*
DEMARCATED WINE REGION

Centered on the town of Almansa, with its storybook castle, the region lies on the east of the great central wine producing area of LA MANCHA. It produces mainly full-bodied red wine, most of which is sold in bulk for blending.

S *almejas*
CLAMS

Clams are often eaten in Spain like oysters with a squeeze of lemon juice. They are also cooked all over the country *a la marinera* (*marinière*) in a white wine sauce. To clean and open clams, see MEJILLONES.

---

almejas a la marinera (S)
clams marinière

Serves 4

1 onion, chopped
4 tbsp olive oil
1 tsp paprika
4 tomatoes, peeled, seeded and chopped
2 lb clams or mussels, in shell, well scrubbed
    and washed in cold water
¼ cup dry white wine
salt and pepper
1 tbsp chopped parsley
1 lemon, cut into wedges

Sauté the onion in hot olive oil for 10 minutes, then add the paprika and tomatoes, reducing the heat to avoid burning them. Stir in the clams, wine and a little salt and pepper, and cook over a high heat until the clams open. Sprinkle with parsley and serve with lemon wedges.

---

see also   **All Saints' Day:** *see Los Santos*

S *almendra*
P *amêndoa*

ALMOND

The almond tree was introduced to Spain and Portugal by the Moors. There is a charming story as to how they were planted around Córdoba. The poet king al-Mu'ta-mid, who succeeded to the throne of Sevilla in 1090, married a captivating and willful slave girl, Rumaykiyya. One day in February, looking out from the window of the palace at Córdoba, she saw the whole plain covered with a sparkling white mantle of snow. It was an unaccustomed sight, and she turned to her husband, reproaching him that he never took her to the countries of the north where she could see it more often. Al-Mu'tamid promised to grant her wish – and planted the whole Córdoban plain with almond trees so that she could enjoy the sheets of blossom each spring.

Almonds are widely grown in ANDA-LUCIA, in the Portuguese ALGARVE and ALENTEJO, and in Majorca (see ISLAS BALEARES). Here, the harvest starts toward the end of August. With the drift of younger people to Palma, the whole remaining population of the villages, including old women and children, is pressed into service. The fruit is first shaken down onto large canvas sheets, the tough green skin is then cut off and the nuts are left to dry in the sun before being dispatched in sacks for cracking, roasting or milling. The female kernels, which occur in pairs, are usually ground for confectionery, while the larger male nuts are roasted or salted.

The range of cakes and sweetmeats, first made by the Moors and later by the nuns in their *conventos,* largely from almonds and

Almond tree

egg yolks, is still available in the PASTELAR-IAS of Portugal and CONFITERIAS of Spain. See also BOLOS DE D. RODRIGO.

S *almendras garrapiñadas*

SUGAR-COATED ALMONDS

These pink, sugar-coated almonds are popular in Spain. They are made on the spot in every village at fiesta time and are also generally available in CONFITERIAS.

S *almuerzo*
P *almoço*

Lunch; see HORAS DE COMIDA.

P *alperce*

Apricot; see ALBARICOQUE.

S *alubia*

Dried white beans; see FABADA ASTURIANA.

> *If Spanish and Portuguese terms differ from each other, the entry in Portuguese, in the majority of cases, is referred to its Spanish equivalent, where you will find information relevant to both countries.*

see also   **Almond:** *see almendra*   **Almond sauce:** *see salsa de almendras*

amêijoas

COCKLES

Amêijoas, larger than English cockles and sometimes translated as clams, are one of the few inexpensive shellfish available at any Portuguese market. Some of the best come from the lagoon of Santa Maria near Faro and are so thin-shelled that very little heat is needed to open them. If you are prepared to invest some time in preparing them, they are delicious. I therefore make no apology in giving a number of recipes from different regions of the country which may also be used for clams.

Where a recipe calls for removal of the shellfish from the shells, the variety bottled in brine may be used. These are often smaller than the Portuguese, and if, for

example, you are frying them in batter, you should coat two or three of them and fry them together.

---

amêijoas à espanhola (P)
cockles or clams
Spanish style

Serves 4

⅓ cup olive oil
3 onions, cut up coarsely
2 cloves garlic, chopped
1 bay leaf, coarsely chopped
2 large red or green peppers, broiled or roasted, peeled, seeded and cut into strips
3 large tomatoes, peeled and seeded
4½ lb cockles or clams, in shell, well scrubbed and washed in cold water
salt and freshly ground pepper

Heat the olive oil in a large frying pan and cook the onions until they begin to color. Remove the oil and keep in a clean jar for further use. Now add the garlic, bay leaf, peppers and tomatoes. Cook for 10 minutes, then add the cockles or clams, season with salt and pepper, cover with a lid and shake the pan over heat until the shellfish open (in about 8 minutes).

The same recipe can be used for mussels.

---

amêijoas à moda de Portimão (P)
cockles or clams
Portimão style

Serves 4

4½ lb large cockles or clams, in shell, well scrubbed and washed in cold water
2 green peppers, seeded and coarsely chopped
a little olive oil
2 cloves garlic, crushed
salt and pepper
1 tbsp chopped parsley

Put the cockles or clams into a saucepan, cover with a lid and shake the pan over heat until the

shellfish open. No water is necessary. Alternatively, cook in a cataplana (see page 94).

Meanwhile, sauté the peppers in hot olive oil for 15–20 minutes, adding the crushed garlic toward the end. Add the cockles or clams, salt and pepper to taste, then cover the pan with a lid and cook for a few minutes longer to encourage any shellfish that remain closed to open. Sprinkle with chopped parsley before serving.

amêijoas à Nazaré (P)
cockles or clams Nazaré style

Serves 4

4½ lb large cockles or clams, in shells, well
　scrubbed and washed in cold water
½ cup dry white wine
2 shallots or 1 onion, finely chopped
½ cup fish stock
a little lemon juice, to taste
salt and freshly ground pepper
1 tbsp freshly chopped parsley

Put the cockles or clams into a pan with the
wine and bring to the boil, keeping the pan
covered. Turn off the heat and leave to open.
Remove from the cooking liquid and separate
the halves of the shells, keeping the part with
the shellfish attached and discarding the empty
half. Strain the wine into a clean pan, add the
shallots or onion, reduce for 5 minutes, then
push through a sieve or purée in a blender or
food processor. Return the shellfish to the pan,
add the shallots or onion, fish stock and lemon
juice, season and warm up by shaking the pan.
Sprinkle the parsley on top and serve.

amêijoas fritas (P)
fried cockles or clams

large cockles or clams
lemon juice
white wine
salt and pepper
chopped parsley
massa vinhe (batter)
olive oil

The Portuguese usually open amêijoas by
leaving them in the oven in a closed saucepan.
The following method is equally effective.
　Choose large cockles or clams and wash them
well. Put them into a saucepan, cover with a lid
and shake the pan over heat until the shellfish
open. (This will happen without the addition of
water, which is unnecessary.) Remove the
shells and marinate the fish for 30 minutes in a
mixture of lemon juice and white wine, seasoned with a little salt, pepper and chopped
parsley. For every 2 lb shellfish, use the juice of
1 lemon, ¼ cup wine and 1 tbsp chopped
parsley. Drain and coat with massa vinhe
(batter), using the amount given on page 189
for 2 lb of fish. Deep fry in hot olive oil and
serve accompanied by molho de tomate and
fried parsley.

P ameixa

PLUM

The Portuguese often preserve their small
green plums in syrup, draining them and
packing them in small wooden boxes. They
are a speciality of the old town of Elvas on
the Spanish frontier, also known for the
good cooking of its POUSADA. See also
ALENTEJO.

CAPITALIZED words within entries refer
the reader to more information on the
same subject.

ameixas com canela em vinho do porto (P) plums with cinnamon and port wine	*Serves 4* *2 cups port wine* *1 tbsp ground cinnamon* *1–2 tbsp sugar or honey to taste* *12–16 plums, skinned and pitted* *For the decoration* *½ cup heavy cream* *1 tbsp tawny or good quality ruby port* *a little lemon zest*	*Heat the port, cinnamon and sugar or honey for a few minutes until thoroughly dissolved to make a light syrup. Pour over the plums and leave to cool. Decorate with heavy cream stiffly whipped and flavored with port, and finally decorate with the lemon zest. Chill in the refrigerator before serving.*

ameixas recheadas com nozes

STUFFED PLUMS

A dessert from the BEIRA BAIXA, in which pitted plums are stuffed with walnuts.

amêndoa

Almond; see ALMENDRA.

Ampurdán-Costa Brava

DEMARCATED WINE REGION

The region lies back from the Gulf of Rosas and the holiday coast and is located in the foothills of the Pyrenees. Its best-known winery, the Castillo de Perelada, makes a good CAVA by the Champagne method, and its associated company, Cavas del Ampurdán, makes a range of very drinkable red and white wines including the popular white "Pescador". The Castle of Perelada incorporates an interesting wine museum, a fine library and a casino. Ampurdán-Costa Brava is also making young red *vi novell* (new wine) in the manner of Beaujolais Nouveau.

The seal for the Ampurdán-Costa Brava demarcated wine region

ananás

PINEAPPLE

Portugal grows exceptionally tender, juicy and sweet pineapples, especially in the Azores where they are ripened in greenhouses with a whiff of wood smoke to flavor them and sometimes crystallized in slices as *rodelas de ananás cristalizadas*. See also PATO CON ANANAS.

ancas de rana

FROGS' LEGS

One of the largest sources of frogs in Spain is the rice fields of VALENCIA, but I have seldom seen frogs' legs in restaurants, and they are mostly eaten at home. This is perhaps because of the lengthy cleaning and soaking which is necessary. They should be soaked in changes of cold water for 2–3 hours.

---

ancas de rana rebozadas (S)
fried frogs' legs

Serves 4 as an appetizer

24 frogs' legs
salt and pepper
flour
3 eggs, beaten
olive oil or pork fat for frying
1 parsley sprig

It is usual to buy frogs' legs ready for cooking; otherwise they must be cleaned. First skewer the legs, then skin them and immerse them in cold water for 2–3 hours, changing it every hour or so until the meat is tender and white. They are now ready for cooking.

Dry the legs and season with salt and pepper. Dredge them in flour, shake off the excess and dip in beaten egg. Fry in hot olive oil or pork fat until golden, and garnish with parsley. Serve very hot.

S *anchoa*
P *anchova*
ANCHOVY

Anchovies are the preserved fillets of the small fry of a herring-like fish known in Spain as BOQUERONES and in Portugal as *biqueirões*. The preservation of anchovies in salt along the coasts of Biscay, particularly in the small ports of Santoña, Laredo and Colindres, dates from the 16th century. The industry still flourishes, although the anchovies are now canned in olive or other vegetable oils, and Spain accounts for 5 percent of world production, the bulk coming from Latin America and Morocco.

In the Ampurdán area of CATALUÑA, *anchoas enteras* (whole anchovies) are preserved whole and unfilleted by seasoning with thyme and leaving between layers of salt for a year. They are then soaked in milk, filleted and served as an appetizer. The middle bones are then soaked in milk, tossed in flour and fried until crisp. Served separately as *raspas de anchoa*, they are an appetizing delicacy.

P *anchova*

Anchovy; see ANCHOA.

Andalucía
SPANISH REGION

Andalucía takes its name from al-Andalus, the southern part of Spain occupied for so many centuries by the Moors, and embraces the eight provinces of Almería, Jaén, Granada, Córdoba, Málaga, SEVILLA, CADIZ and Huelva. Quite apart from the great vacation resorts of the Costa del Sol, it is everybody's idea of "sunny Spain", with its shining white houses, sparkling fountains and secret patios, olive and almond groves and sherry vineyards, flamenco and *cante jondo*, and the Easter processions in Sevilla. The cities of Andalucía are historically and artistically among the most memorable in Spain: Córdoba with its great mosque, now the cathedral; Sevilla with its great cathedral, royal palace and old Jewish quarter; Granada, where the many-fountained Alhambra

Córdoba

---

see also   *Anchovy: see anchoa, boquerones*

was the last refuge of the Moors; the great seaport of Málaga; and Cádiz islanded by the sea, a shimmering white citadel looking over towards Africa.

Many Andalucían dishes are inherited from the Moors, including perhaps the most famous, the GAZPACHOS or cold soups. These are made from a variety of ingredients including ground almonds and fresh grapes as well as the more familiar tomato and cucumber. In Spain, Andalucía is known as the *zona de los fritos*, "region of fried food". Among the best of such dishes

are the crisply fried CHANQUETES, similar to smelt, SARDINAS, CALAMARES (squid) and BOQUERONES or a combination of assorted fried fish, known as a *parrillada* (see PARRILLADA DE MARISCO). In addition, the different areas of Andalucía have their own specialties. Cádiz is famous for the magnificent variety of fish and shellfish from its bay; in Jerez, as might be expected, great use is made of sherry in cooking, as in the RIÑONES AL JEREZ. A favorite dish from Córdoba is the *rabo de toro* (stewed oxtail) while the gypsy-inspired *tortilla al Sacromonte* from Granada is a substantial version of the Spanish omelet containing brains.

The wine *par excellence* of Andalucía is, of course, SHERRY. The light, dry *fino* is, in fact, drunk right through a meal as is the rather similar MONTILLA in Córdoba. The sherry region is now producing some refreshing white table wines, but the other famous wine from Andalucía is the rich dessert Málaga.

There are many good restaurants serving regional food. Outstanding among them is El Faro in Cádiz, the place for the fascinating variety of fish from the Bay, and El Caballo Rojo in Córdoba, famous throughout Spain for its oxtail. The Costa del Sol boasts some of the most sophisticated (and expensive) restaurants in the country. Notable among them are La Fonda, La Hacienda and La Meridiana in Marbella, and Los Remos in San Roque near Gibraltar, which provide food to the highest international standards and also serve some beautifully prepared regional dishes.

S *anguilas*

Large eels; see ANGULAS.

S *angulas*

ELVERS

Angulas are baby freshwater eels, or elvers, a great delicacy in the Basque region. One of the first mentions of them is in a book written in 1778 by José María Busca Isusi, who comments on the excellence of those fished around BILBAO.

They are spawned in the distant Sargasso Sea and, after swimming for almost 2 years, flood into the rivers of the Spanish north coast between November and January. The

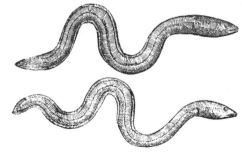

see also   *Angler fish: see rape*

fishermen catch them at night using lights and metallic nets, some working from small boats and others from the shore.

Those that survive grow into large eels (*anguilas*) reaching a length of about 6 feet, living between 10 and 20 years and return-ing to the spawning grounds in the Sargasso Sea.

It is simplest to try *angulas* in a restaurant, since they must be cleaned with black tobacco to release the mucilage, but if you wish to cook them fresh, proceed as follows:

---

angulas en cazuela (S)
freshwater eels in individual dishes

For each serving

⅓ lb baby eels
1 tbsp olive oil
1 clove garlic, chopped
½ small chili pepper, seeded

To prepare the baby eels for cooking, stir 2 tbsp of the loose black tobacco used in Spain for rolling cigarettes into water. Add *angulas* and stir with a wooden spoon until free of mucilage, then drain and rinse thoroughly in cold water.

Meanwhile, bring 2 quarts salted water to the boil in a large saucepan. Add the baby eels and stir vigorously to prevent them sticking together. Remove the pan from the heat, leave for 45 minutes, then drain in a colander. The fish is now ready for use.

Heat a little oil in individual earthenware cazuelas or ovenproof dishes, sauté the garlic briefly without browning it, and add the chili pepper. Stir in the baby eels and cook for exactly 1 minute and no more. Cover, serve piping hot, and eat with a wooden fork accompanied by warmed bread for dipping.

P **anho**

LAMB

Lamb is less popular in Portugal than kid (see CABRITO ASADO) because sheep are reared for their wool and milk rather than for meat.

S **anís**

A SPIRIT

Like anisette, *anís* is made by blending grape spirit with an extract of aniseed. One of the best brands, "Chinchón", is made in the picturesque little town of that name, southeast of Madrid.

It was a 17th century Marquesa of Chinchón, wife of a governor of Peru, who in 1638 discovered the medicinal properties of quinine and gave her name to the tree from whose bark it is extracted.

Aragón and Navarra

SPANISH REGION

Kingdoms in their own right in medieval times, Aragón and Navarra lie side by side bordering France to the north. In both, the land falls from the sudden heights of the Pyrenees to the placid Ebro basin further south, a region of wheat fields, vineyards, orchards and vegetables such as peppers, beans, artichokes and the wonderful asparagus.

Aragón centers on Zaragoza, dominated by a massive cathedral at the end of a long Roman bridge across the Ebro. The capital of Navarra is Pamplona, a mountain town with a fine medieval cathedral, famous for the bull-running in the streets that is vividly described by Ernest Hemingway in *The Sun Also Rises*.

In gastronomic terms, Aragón is some-times described as the *zona de los Chilindrones* in reference to its famous CHILINDRON sauce. Also popular are MIGAS or savory fried breadcrumbs, humble enough country fare, but traditionally a favorite not only of James the Conqueror of

---

see also   **Appetizer:** *see acepipe, banderilla, tapa*   **Apple:** *see manzana*
                      Apricot: *see albaricoque*

CATALUÑA and that scourge of the Moors, El Cid, but also of the legendary Lovers of Teruel, the ancient city in the south of Aragón, unfortunately damaged during the Spanish Civil War. The mountainous north produces excellent lamb, the young animals

being cooked as *Tres Madres* ("Three Mothers") or *espárragos montañeses* ("mountain asparagus" – in fact, stewed lambs' tails) in Aragón, and COCHIFRITO in Navarra. The CHULETAS DE PALO O DE COSTILLA cooked Navarra-style in a sauce of onion, tomato and ham, and garnished with CHORIZO, are delicious. Navarra has some excellent vegetable dishes including the soup, *garbure*, also made on the French side of the Pyrenees, and the *menesta de habas de Tudela*, containing fresh fava beans, garlic, mint, saffron, almonds, artichoke hearts, boiled eggs, white wine, thyme and seasoning. The town of Tudela on the Ebro is also famous for its large and juicy asparagus, served either on its own or within an omelet.

Navarra makes good wines, especially rosés and reds, while Aragón is best known for its sturdy red Cariñena (see NAVARRA and CARIÑENA, demarcated wine regions).

The four PARADORES in Aragón, at Bielsa in the Pyrenees, in Sos del Rey Católica, Alcañiz and Teruel, all serve some regional dishes, as does the particularly attractive Parador Nacional Príncipe de Viana installed in the restored palace of the Kings of Navarra in Olite. The most sophisticated restaurant in the region is Josetxo in Pamplona, particularly well known for game such as *codorniz con uvas* (partridge with grapes), *jabalí con salsa de castañas* (wild boar with chestnut sauce) and *conejo con caracoles* (rabbit with snails).

🔊ℙ *arenque*

HERRING

Herring are not as plentiful in Spain and Portugal as they are in the USA.

They are eaten both fresh and marinated,

and especially salted. In this form they are sold from small barrels, decoratively packed in fan shapes.

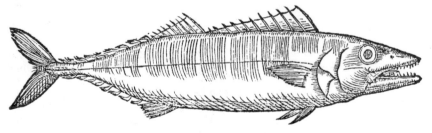

🔊 *Armada*

A CHEESE

This is also known as *Sobado* and *Calostro*. It is made in the province of León from the milk obtained from ewes after lambing and is a curious cheese, both in its triangular

shape and somewhat bitter taste. White and semi-hard, containing 69 percent dry extract, the cheeses weigh from about 3 to 6½ lb and are matured for 2 months.

P *arraia*

Skate; see CALDEIRADA.

S P *arroz*

RICE

Rice, which probably supports a greater number of human beings than any other cereal, was introduced to Spain and what is now Portugal by the Moors (see MOROS, LOS) soon after their invasion of the Iberian Peninsula in 711. It flourishes in warm swampy areas such as the lagoon of the Albufera outside VALENCIA or in those up and down the west coast of Portugal.

The common type is a short-grained variety, particularly suitable for PAELLAS in Spain, but there is also longer-grained rice which absorbs less water and is used for garnishes or for stirring into soups.

In Spain, rice is classified as: *Categoría Extra* (red label), containing 95 percent whole grains; *Categoría 1* (green label), containing 87 percent whole grains; *Categoría 2* (yellow label) with only 80 percent whole grains.

It is important to choose the right type of rice since broken grains cook faster than whole grains and produce something akin to rice pudding. Cooked properly at the right temperature and with the correct amount of water, rice should swell to 2 or 3 times its volume. When rice is over-cooked the grains burst lengthwise and become mushy.

I measure rice in a teacup that is roughly equivalent to ¾ cup in a standard American measure. In fact, any teacup may be used, the important point being that two of the same size cupfuls of water or stock are used. The rice is cooked as follows: bring the rice and liquid to the boil, then simmer uncovered for 18 minutes. Cover the rice and leave for 10 minutes. It will absorb all the water and be beautifully cooked with the grains unruptured and separate.

S *arroz a la catalana*

CATALAN RICE

A Catalan rice dish in the style of PAELLA, incorporating BUTIFARRA, the white sausage from the region, pork ribs and snow peas.

S *arroz a la cubana*

CUBAN RICE

A dish originating in Spanish America, in which the rice is served with fried bananas and eggs.

S *arroz abanda*

FISH WITH RICE

A dish made with rice and fish, served separately and almost as popular in VALENCIA as PAELLA.

The index, in English, is arranged by types of food — eggs, cheese, fish — kitchen equipment, cooking terms and other subjects. Consult it for recipes that make use of particular ingredients.

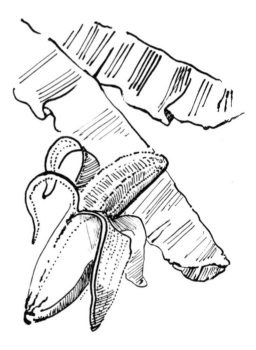

Bananas give arroz a la cubana its exotic taste and appearance

arroz abanda (S)
fish with rice

Serves 4–6

Fish stock
2 lb fish heads and trimmings
2 cloves garlic
1 small onion, halved
2 quarts water
bouquet garni
1 tsp freshly ground salt
few black peppercorns
squeeze of lemon juice

Fish
2 scampi (langoustines) per person
1 lb halibut, cut into thick pieces, skinned and
*   boned*
1 lb monkfish, cut into thick pieces, skinned and
*   boned*

2 tbsp olive oil
1 onion, finely chopped
4 large tomatoes, peeled, seeded and chopped
salt
2 cloves garlic
few strands of saffron
¾ cup per person Spanish or Italian short-
*   grain rice*

To make the fish stock, bring all the ingredients to the boil in a large pan. Skim until the stock is clear, then simmer gently for 30 minutes. Strain and set aside.

To prepare the fish (if not already cooked), poach the scampi and white fish in a little of the reserved fish stock for 5 to 10 minutes. Remove carefully and arrange in a serving dish.

To complete the dish, heat the olive oil in a paellera or large frying pan, add the onion and cook for a few minutes until soft but not brown. Add the tomatoes and a little salt to taste and keep on a low heat. Meanwhile, crush the garlic and saffron together in a mortar and pestle, dissolve with a teaspoonful of hot water, then transfer the paste to the sauce. Add the rice to the pan and sauté until golden.

Add fish stock equivalent to double the volume of the rice, made up with water if necessary to the mixture, check the seasoning and simmer gently for 18 minutes until all the stock has been absorbed. Do not stir but simply shake the uncovered pan, finally covering it with a lid or clean dish towel and leaving the contents to rest for 10 minutes. Serve the rice and fish separately accompanied by ALIOLI.

Any shellfish (including lobster) and any firm white fish may be used for this recipe, and if preferred the rice may be cooked in a preheated oven (325°F) for 30 minutes in a covered dish.

Arroz abanda

arroz canario (S)
Canary style rice

Serves 4

¾ cup olive oil
1½ cups chopped onions
1 lb pork loin, cubed
½ lb peeled tomatoes, seeded and chopped
3 cups short-grain Spanish or Italian rice
salt
6 cups chicken stock
4 small bananas, cut lengthways
flour, for coating
1 egg, beaten
additional olive oil for frying
4 eggs

Heat the oil in a deep casserole and sauté the onions until soft but not brown. Add the meat and cook for a further 10 minutes, then add the tomatoes, and cook for a little longer. Mix well, add the rice and cook together for about another 5 minutes. Season with salt, stir in the chicken stock and simmer gently, uncovered, for about 18 minutes until the stock has been completely absorbed.

Cover with a clean dish towel and leave for 10 minutes.

Meanwhile, dredge the bananas in flour and egg, fry them in the additional oil until golden brown, then transfer them to a plate. Next fry the eggs, one at a time, in the same oil. Arrange the bananas around the rice and serve it topped with the eggs.

S *arroz con costra alicantino*

RICE WITH CRISP TOPPING

A rice from Alicante taking its name from the fluffy egg with which it is topped. It contains meatballs, chicken, sausage and chickpeas.

S *arroz con leche a la asturiana*

RICE PUDDING

A creamy rice pudding from ASTURIAS with a generous amount of milk, flavored with cinnamon, lemon, ANIS and brandy, and topped with caramel.

The index, in English, is arranged by types of food — eggs, cheese, fish — kitchen equipment, cooking terms and other subjects. Consult it for recipes that make use of particular ingredients.

---

arroz con riñones María (S)
María's rice with kidneys

Serves 4

1 lb lambs' kidneys, cleaned and sliced
4 medium onions, sliced
1 clove garlic, crushed
salt and ground black pepper
juice of 1 lemon
¼ cup fino sherry
1 tbsp chopped parsley
1¼ cups short-grain rice
4 tbsp olive oil
½ lb cooked ham, chopped

Put the kidneys in a shallow dish with half the onions, the garlic, salt, pepper, lemon juice, sherry and parsley. Marinate for 1 hour.

Meanwhile, boil the rice in salted water for 18 minutes, then drain and leave for 10 minutes in a low oven. Sauté the remaining onions in hot olive oil until tender, then drain well. Add the kidneys and the marinade, together with the ham, and cook for a further 10 minutes until the kidneys are just cooked. Take the rice out of the oven and pour the mixture over it.

arroz de bacalhau com coentros

RICE WITH BACALHAU AND CILANTRO

A version of BACALHAU from the ALENTEJO, cooked with rice and cilantro.

Cilantro

arroz de Cabidela

CABIDELA RICE

A dish of rice and chicken from the BEIRA ALTA, cooked with onions, garlic, parsley, bay leaves and herbs.

arroz de lampreia

RICE WITH LAMPREY

A dish of rice and lamprey from Monção in the MINHO, cooked with onions, parsley, white wine and CHOURIÇO.

---

arroz de manteiga (P)
buttered rice

Serves 4 as a side dish

6 tbsp butter
1½ cups short-grain Spanish or Italian rice
3 cups water or stock
salt and pepper
1 onion, halved
1 parsley sprig

Melt half the butter in a saucepan, add the rice and cook for a few minutes until glazed but not browned. Add the water or stock, a little salt and pepper, and when the water begins to boil, add the onion and sprig of parsley. Cook slowly for 18 minutes, uncovered, by which time all the water will have been absorbed. Remove from the heat and leave for 10 minutes, keeping the lid on the pan. Beat in the remaining butter with a fork and transfer to a warm serving dish.

---

arroz de polvo

RICE WITH OCTOPUS

There are different versions of this dish from the BEIRA LITORAL and ALGARVE. Both are cooked with garlic and onion, but the Algarve version is spicier as it also contains tomatoes, red peppers, ground pepper and PIRI-PIRI.

It is often cooked on Christmas Day by families in Coimbra.

arroz de sarrabulho

SARRABULHO RICE

A most substantial rice dish from the MINHO containing, for example, beef and boiling fowl or stewing chicken and rib, loin and collar of pork, as well as CHOURIÇO and pig's blood together with parsley, onion, bay leaves and olive oil.

arroz doce bairradinho

CREAMY RICE PUDDING

A rice pudding from the BAIRRADA made with a large number of egg yolks and flavored with lemon zest and cinnamon.

P *arroz dos casamentos*

RICE FOR WEDDINGS

This so-called "Rice for Weddings" is a dessert from the ESTREMADURA and is made with sugar, lemon, milk and egg yolk. It is served to the bride and groom and guests of honor and is often decorated with suitable motifs such as hearts or intertwined initials.

The other guests are served with a less rich rice pudding containing fewer egg yolks. A typical rice pudding for 15 to 20 persons might be made with 1 lb rice, 2 lb sugar, a lemon, 1½ quarts milk and 25 egg yolks!

S *arroz en caldero a la murciana*

RICE IN POT
MURCIAN STYLE

In its native Murcia this dish was traditionally cooked in a kettle hung over an open fire. The rice is cooked with fish and shellfish, dried and fresh red peppers, garlic in abundance and tomatoes, and is served with ALIOLI.

If Spanish and Portuguese terms differ from each other, the entry in Portuguese, in the majority of cases, is referred to its Spanish equivalent, where you will find information relevant to both countries.

S *arroz murciano*

RICE WITH PORK
MURCIAN STYLE

A dish from the seaport of Murcia, south of Alicante on the Mediterranean and home of one of the most famous of Spanish regional restaurants – the Rincón de Pepe.

---

arroz murciano (S)

rice with pork
Murcian style

Serves 4

1 lb lean pork, cut into small pieces
½ cup olive oil
2 cloves garlic
3 red peppers, seeded and cut into strips, or 6 canned pimentos
1 lb tomatoes, peeled and seeded
a little parsley, chopped
few strands of saffron
salt and pepper
2¾ cups short-grain rice

Sauté the pork in hot olive oil for a few minutes until browned, then remove it with a slotted spoon and reserve. Using the same pan, sauté a whole clove of garlic until golden, then remove and discard it.

Add the peppers and tomatoes, and cook until soft. Grind the other garlic clove with the parsley and saffron in a mortar, dissolve in a little warm water, then stir the paste into the vegetables in the pan. Add a little water, season with salt and pepper and simmer for 15–20 minutes or less until all the water has evaporated. Now add the rice and cook until well blended with the mixture, stirring all the time with a wooden spoon.

Measure out 5½ cups of water, pour it into the pan, and as soon as the contents begin to boil, transfer them to a hot ovenproof dish. Stir in the pork and cook in a moderate oven (350°F) for 1 hour until the liquid has been absorbed.

S *arroz negro con calamares*

RICE WITH SQUID

This "black rice" takes its color from the ink sacs of the squid with which it is cooked, together with red wine, fish stock, onion, tomato and PIMIENTO.

Arzak, Juan María

A CHEF

Arzak, who runs the restaurant of the same name in SAN SEBASTIAN, consistently rated one of the best if not *the* best restaurant in Spain, was one of the founders of the NUEVA COCINA VASCA. His devotion to inherent flavor is typified by the Case of the Disappearing Pea. His suppliers insisted on selling him a variety which looked well in a tastefully arranged "vegetable garnish" in the manner of the NOUVELLE CUISINE, but tasted of nothing. On investigating, he found that local farmers were planting a high-cropping pea from Madagascar, and he is now campaigning for a return to the native variety.

asar
assar

ROASTING

In Spain and Portugal, it is unusual to roast large pieces of meat except on special occasions. When it is a question of roasting, say, a suckling pig (see COCHINILLO), this is often taken to be cooked in the oven of the local bakery. The way in which the baker distinguishes one roast from another at festive seasons remains a secret of the trade! Frying and stewing (see FREIR and ESTOFAR) are the commonest cooking methods, and when meat is roasted, it is usually A LA PARRILLA or A LA PLANCHA as fillets, chops or steaks. See also CABRITO ASADO.

assadeira

COOKING PAN

A large roasting pan used in Portugal for roasts, turkey etc.

assar

Roasting; see ASAR.

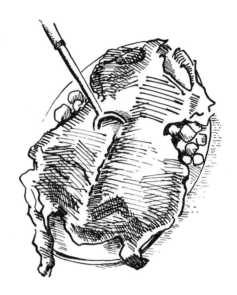

A large joint of roasted meat for a special occasion

Asturias and Galicia

SPANISH REGION

Asturias and Galicia are situated in the far north-west of Spain. Asturias, with its apple orchards, chestnut forests and lush pasturages, is a green strip between the north coast with its secluded beaches and coves and the massive Cordillera Cantábrica, one of the highest mountain ranges in Europe. Over the mountains lies Galicia with its granite-strewn hills covered with flowers in spring and its eucalyptus and pine groves. To the west lie the RIAS BAJAS which indent the coast like the fjords in Norway and whose deep, dark blue waters are the source of much of Galicia's magnificent shellfish. A well-known Galician dish, CONCHAS DE PEREGRINO, commemorates the scallop shells worn as a badge by medieval pilgrims to the shrine of St James the Apostle at Santiago de Compostela. Another emotive name is that of La Coruña, scene of the British evacuation during the Peninsular War and the death of Sir John Moore, commander of the British expeditionary force.

From a culinary angle, Asturias is best known for its vegetables and fish, its most famous dish being FABADA A LA ASTURIANA, a rich garlicky stew made with butter beans, CHORIZO, MORCILLA and pork. Fish dishes include *ventesco de bonito con tomate* (fresh tuna in tomato sauce), *pixin con salsa verde* (monkfish in green sauce) and the delicious *crema de andaricas* (cream of crayfish). Its apples are put to good use in many other fish dishes such as the sumptuous *merluza a la sidra* (hake in a sauce made from cider, brandy, mussels, flour, hard-boiled eggs and red bell peppers).

The best known of Spanish veined cheeses, the blue CABRALES, is from Asturias.

Even Alexandre DUMAS, generally so scathing about Spanish cooking, was most

---

see also   **Asparagus:** *see espárragos*

enthusiastic about fish from Galician waters, singling out the fresh cod, eels from the rivers and sea, lamprey, octopus, clams and oysters. He even went so far as to take the recipe for *caldo gallego,* a rich meat and vegetable soup, back to France.

With superb vegetables, fish, meat and dairy products, rivalled perhaps only by the Basque country, Galicia does, in fact, boast a formidable culinary repertoire. Shellfish, including lobsters, scallops, scampi, cockles, prawns, langoustines, spider crabs, PER-CEBES and SANTIAGUIÑOS may all be sampled at the *marisquerias* (shellfish bars), where they are usually priced by weight. To meet the demand by top Spanish restaurants, Galician shellfish is flown overnight to MADRID and other large cities.

Many Galician dishes bear a strong re-semblance to those from the neighboring north of Portugal: *caldereta de pescado* (a rich fish stew) is virtually the same as CALDEIR-ADA; *caldo a la gallega* has a strong affinity with the famous CALDO VERDE of the MINHO; and the highly spiced *callos a la gallega* (tripe) is served with haricot beans in the same way as the renowned TRIPAS A MODA DO PORTO. Other typical dishes are EMPANADA GALLEGA; LACON CON GRELOS and *filloas* (cream-filled pancakes cooked in liqueur).

Asturias makes no wine but produces the best Spanish cider (see SIDRA). Galician wines, typically bone dry and *pétillant,* resemble the Portuguese VINHOS VERDES (see also RIBEIRO and VALDEORRAS). The very best of them are made, however, from the white Albariño grape in the newly demarcated region of Rias Bajas. Of the Albariño from Fefiñanes near Pontevedra, Xosé Posada, an expert on Galician wines, writes in his authoritative book, *Os Vines de Galicia,* of a friend "who married in Cambados so as to have better opportunities of drinking them", adding "I think the sacrifice was well worthwhile!"

The PARADORES in Asturias and Galicia are to be recommended for their regional food, notably those in Gijón, Villalba, Cam-bados and Pontevedra, also the palatial Parador Nacional de Gondomar at Bayona on the coast with its huge grounds and *marisquerías.* Among many good res-taurants, a few of special interest are Las Delicias in Gijón, Trascorrales and La Goleta in Oviedo, Chocolate near Cambados, and Vilas in Santiago de Compostela.

Opposite: A roast is removed from the oven
Pages 50-51: Two large besugos, or sea bream,
from an 18th century kitchen scene
Page 52: Two classic fish dishes; a paella (top)
and monkfish with capers (bottom)

atadito de hierbas aromáticas

Bouquet garni; see RAMO DE CHEIROS.

atascaburras
RABBIT STEW

A dish originating in La Mancha. The rabbit is dredged in flour and browned briefly in olive oil. It is then put into a large CAZUELA and stewed with heads of garlic, onions and herbs including bay leaf, thyme, oregano and cinnamon, plus tomatoes and wine.

atum

Tuna fish; see ATUN.

---

atum à Algarvia (P)
tuna Algarve style

Serves 2

1 lb fresh tuna, soaked, skinned, boned and cut into steaks
salt and pepper
a little lemon juice
1 tbsp chopped parsley
1 bay leaf, chopped
flour
olive oil
1 onion, chopped
2 tbsp tarragon vinegar
few strands of saffron, crushed

Sprinkle the fish with salt, pepper, the lemon juice, half the chopped parsley and all the chopped bay leaf. Leave for 30 minutes, then dredge in flour and cook in hot olive oil until golden. Drain well and keep hot. Reserve oil.

Sauté the chopped onion in the remaining oil until brown, then add the vinegar, crushed saffron and remaining parsley. Cook together for a few minutes more, stirring until well blended. Pour the sauce over the fish and serve.

If fresh tuna is unavailable, use monkfish or other firm fish.

---

atún
atum
TUNA FISH

This large game fish (*Thunnus thynnus*) can grow to about 10 feet in length and 650 lb in weight. Fished commercially in the Mediterranean, it is very popular in Spain and Portugal, eaten either fresh, canned or salted, or dried and sold as *mojama* or *cecina de atún*.

Until recent years, tuna fish has been most widely available in the United States in cans. Now, however, it is possible to buy

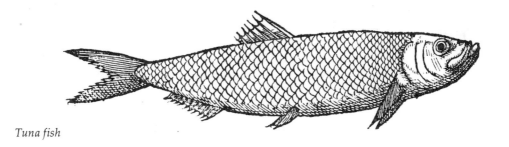

Tuna fish

fresh tuna from specialized fishmongers, and in large supermarkets.

Fresh tuna may be left in cold water for about 30 minutes to soak the blood out of the fish; it can then be cut into steaks. Since it is a very dry fish, it is usual in Spain and Portugal to moisten it thoroughly during cooking, e.g. with tomatoes, white wine and onions. It may also be marinated in wine or vinegar and herbs, and then cooked in a casserole or served as an appetizer like *atum* de escabeche (marinated tuna) from MADEIRA. In the latter case it is first simmered with garlic, parsley and salt, then dressed with oil, vinegar and chopped garlic, sprinkled with pepper and left to rest until the next day.

Tuna is also used to stuff eggs and as an ingredient in salads and omelets. See also ENSALADA MANCHEGA and TORTILLITAS DE BONITO CON TOMATE Y BESAMEL.

---

atún valenciano (S)
Valencian tuna

Serves 6

6 fresh tuna steaks, about ¾ in thick, skinned and boned
freshly ground salt and pepper
flour for coating
olive oil for frying
1 medium-sized onion, chopped very finely
2 cloves garlic
1 tbsp minced parsley
few strands of saffron
½ cup dry white wine

Sprinkle the fish with salt and pepper and dredge in flour. Heat some olive oil in a frying pan and cook the fish on both sides until golden, then transfer to a casserole. In the oil remaining in the pan sauté the onion for 10 minutes until golden, then drain and transfer with a slotted spoon to the casserole. Pound the garlic, parsley and saffron in a mortar, stir in the wine and pour this over the fish. Place the casserole over medium heat, bring to the boil and simmer for about 20 minutes or a little longer, until the fish is cooked through.

S *avellana*

HAZELNUT

The hazel was introduced to Spain by the Greeks. According to Christian legend, the tree once gave shelter to the Virgin in a violent storm and for this reason it can neither be struck by lightning nor lodge snakes!

Spain, in particular Tarragona, is among the major European producers of hazelnuts, which are eaten as an appetizer and also used in making TURRON and chocolates.

S *azafrán*
P *açafrão*

SAFFRON

A spice that was introduced to Spain and Portugal from Asia Minor by the MOORS, it is prepared by drying the stigmas of the saffron crocus, which flowers in purple sheets in the autumn in CASTILLA LA VIEJA and other parts of Spain. Some 4,000 flowers must be picked to make 1 oz. Weight for weight it is more valuable than gold and is

Saffron crocus

---

see also　　　***Avocado:*** *see aguacate*

---

expensively sold, a few filaments at a time, in small packets.

In medieval times saffron was used for medicinal purposes but it is now used only as a coloring and flavoring agent, as for example, in PAELLA. The filaments must first be crushed in a mortar and pestle with the addition of a little hot water.

A so-called "saffron powder" is available much more cheaply than the real thing, but this confers only a yellow color without the authentic flavor.

azahar
ORANGE OR LEMON FLOWER WATER

A flavoring used in confectionery.

azedos
SAUSAGE

From the DOURO, this is made with ham, CHOURIÇO, salt pork, hot peppers and spices. *Azedos* are eaten both thinly sliced as an appetizer or cut into chunks for cooking.

Azeitão
A CHEESE

These are small cream cheeses with a fat content of 45 percent, made from ewe's milk in the Setúbal Peninsula south of LISBOA. They are left to ripen for 3 to 4 weeks before being sold, and are often served as an appetizer.

azeite de oliva

Olive oil; see ACEITE DE OLIVA.

azeitonas

Olives; see ACEITUNAS.

Trays of ripe Azeitão cheeses

azúcar
açúcar
SUGAR

Sugar cane was first introduced to Spain by the Moors in 755, when they began planting it in the conquered territories along the Mediterranean coast of the LEVANTE. However, it remained an expensive commodity throughout the Middle Ages and honey was the usual sweetening agent until the 19th century.

Soon after the discovery of MADEIRA in 1419 by an expedition despatched by HENRIQUE O NAVEGADOR, cuttings of sugar cane from Sicily were planted by the early colonists, and the crop began to thrive. The Portuguese later introduced it to Brazil, and there was a lucrative trade in Brazilian sugar through the Lisbon market until it was undercut by exports from the new British colonies in the West Indies.

The Portuguese still have a *very* sweet tooth, using three packets to a cup of coffee or heaping it onto ripe fruit.

ⓢ *bacalao*

Salt cod; see BACALHAU.

---

bacalao a la vizcaína (S)
bacalao Biscay style

Serves 4

2 lb salt cod, cut into 1 in pieces, prepared by the second method on page 57
1 tbsp flour
¼ cup olive oil
2 dried chili peppers (optional), soaked for 2 hours and seeded
2 cloves garlic, peeled
½ in slice bread fried in butter
1 cup salsa de tomate (tomato sauce)
2 red peppers, seeded and cut into strips
1 tbsp chopped parsley
1 cup fresh breadcrumbs

Dredge the fish in flour, then fry in hot olive oil until golden. Put to one side.

Pound the chili peppers, garlic and fried bread in a mortar. Add to the salsa de tomate (tomato sauce), stir well and pour half the mixture into a shallow ovenproof dish. Lay the pieces of fish in the sauce and pour the remainder over them. Garnish with the peppers, and sprinkle with a mixture of parsley and breadcrumbs. Cook in a fairly hot oven, 375°F, for 15 minutes until tender.

---

bacalao al ajoarriero (S)
country-style bacalao

Serves 4

1 lb salt cod, prepared by the second method on page 57
2 lb freshly boiled potatoes, diced
1¼ cups salsa mahonesa (mayonnaise) made with 2 cloves of garlic instead of 1
1 tbsp flat parsley, minced

Mix the bacalao (salt cod) with the potatoes while they are still hot, then add the salsa mahonesa (mayonnaise), stirring it in well. Garnish with the parsley and serve cold.

Ⓟ *bacalhau*
ⓢ *bacalao*

SALT COD

Bacalhau (or bacalao in Spanish form) is immensely more popular in Portugal and Spain than fresh cod. In Portugal, where it is said that there is a different recipe for every day in the year, it is more or less the national dish.

Down Portugal's long seaboard, fish has always been the staple diet and not long after Columbus's discovery of America, the Portuguese were fishing for cod in the Grand Banks of Newfoundland. Another commodity of great importance in medieval times was the sea salt produced in pans around Setúbal, south of LISBOA, and elsewhere. It was, therefore, natural that the Portuguese should take to salting fish, and the demand for salted cod was consequently so great that the salt exported to their English allies was in part shipped back in the form of cod, plentiful in the cold northern waters and salted on board ship.

In Spain, the Basques took to bacalao rather later, towards the beginning of the 17th century, much of it coming from

Norway. In a fervently Catholic country and in the days when transport to the interior was by mule or wagon, *bacalao* became established as the staple diet for Fridays and Lent (see Cuaresma).

Bacalhau is salted at sea and then dried ashore. The large, mummified slabs can be seen hanging in Portuguese and Spanish *bacalerias*, market stalls and grocers. Little hint is given of the succulence and flavour of the fish when soaked and cooked with the appropriate accompaniments. The choicest part of *bacalhau* is the middle cut: the *lombo* (or *lomo* in Spanish).

To prepare *bacalhau* for cooking, soak the dry fish for 24 to 48 hours, changing the water occasionally, then remove the bones and skin. Alternatively, soak it overnight and next morning discard the water. Cover it with fresh cold water in a saucepan, bring to the boil and again discard the water. Repeat twice, leaving the fish to cool in the water the second time. Strain, then remove the skin and bones.

One or other of these procedures must be followed before using it for any of the recipes in this book.

bacalhau à biscainha
BACALHAU BISCAY STYLE

This is a Portuguese variant of a style popular all along the Biscay coast.

---

bacalhau à biscainha (P)
bacalhau Biscay style

Serves 2

½ lb salt cod, prepared by the second method above
3 onions, chopped
4 tbsp olive oil
1 clove garlic, peeled and chopped
1 tsp chopped parsley
4 potatoes, parboiled for 10 minutes
3 tomatoes, peeled, seeded and chopped
2 whole red peppers, coarsely chopped
salt and pepper

Put the prepared salt cod into an ovenproof dish.

Make the refogado: sauté the chopped onions for 10 minutes in hot olive oil, then add the chopped garlic and chopped parsley.

Meanwhile, slice the potatoes and place them, together with the tomatoes and red peppers, on top of the fish. Season with salt and pepper, then add the refogado from the frying pan and bake in a preheated oven, 375°F, for 15 minutes, until cooked.

---

bacalhau à lisbonense
BACALHAU LISBON STYLE

At that most beautiful of Portuguese ESTALAGENS or inns in the Setúbal peninsula, the Quinta das Torres, housed in a small Italianate-style palace, this dish appears on the menu as *bacalhau dourada*.

The index, in English, is arranged by types of food — eggs, cheese, fish — kitchen equipment, cooking terms and other subjects. Consult it for recipes that make use of particular ingredients.

---

bacalhau à lisbonense (P)
bacalhau Lisbon style

Serves 4

2 onions, finely chopped
olive oil
1 lb salt cod, prepared by the second method on page 57 and flaked
4 potatoes, cut into matchsticks as for straw potatoes
4 eggs, beaten
salt and pepper
1 tsp chopped parsley

Sauté the chopped onions in hot olive oil until golden, then add the flaked salt cod and cook for a further few minutes.

Fry the uncooked straw potatoes in ⅔ cup olive oil in a separate pan until tender. Remove them before they become golden; it is most important that they should not be crisp. Drain and add them to the salt cod, then mix thoroughly with the beaten egg, and season with salt and pepper.

Continue cooking just long enough for the egg mixture to achieve the bright yellow colour and consistency of creamy scrambled eggs (do not allow them to set). When turned onto a serving dish, sprinkled with chopped parsley and served immediately, this is a food fit for the gods.

P bacalhau à transmontana

BACALHAU
TRANSMONTANA
STYLE

Distant as it is from the sea, even this mountainous region (see TRAS-OS-MONTES) has its special method of cooking BACALHAU.

bacalhau à transmontana (P)
bacalhau transmontana style

Serves 2

2 onions, chopped
3 tbsp olive oil
100 g (4 oz) toucinho or salt pork, coarsely chopped
chopped parsley
2 cloves garlic, peeled and chopped
1 bay leaf, chopped
1 lb salt cod, prepared by the second method on page 57 and flaked
salt and pepper

Sauté the chopped onions in hot olive oil for 10 minutes, then add the toucinho, parsley, garlic and bay leaf, and continue cooking for a few minutes more until the toucinho is pale brown. Stir in the flaked salt cod, season to taste and leave over a low heat until heated through and the fish has taken on the color of the other ingredients in the pan. Serve hot with boiled potatoes.

P bacalhau nas brasas com batatas de borralho

CHARCOAL-GRILLED
BACALHAU

Charcoal-grilled BACALHAU with potatoes baked in the hot ashes, from the DOURO.

bagaceira
GRAPE SPIRIT

A clear white spirit distilled from *bagaço*, the grape skins and seeds left over from winemaking. It is even more popular in Portugal than brandy and is made all over the country. Some of the best and freshest, fruity in nose and smooth in flavor, is from the BAIRRADA. It is a fairly potent spirit, and a good tip is to serve it in a brandy glass after dinner with a lump of ice, when it makes a delicious *digestif*.

Bairrada
DEMARCATED WINE REGION

Although this region, flanking the Atlantic and extending from just south of OPORTO to near Coimbra, has a history of viticulture as long as any in Portugal, it was demarcated only as recently as 1979. It makes intensely fruity but very tannic red wines from the Baga grape, requiring long years to mature. It is also here that most of the sparkling wines (*espumantes naturais*) are made by the Champagne method.

banderilla
AN APPETIZER

The first meaning of the word *banderilla* is the decorated dart plunged into the neck of the bull at a *corrida* (bullfight). Because of the similar colorful appearance, it is also used to describe an appetizer made by skewering on a stick pieces of CHORIZO, JAMON SERRANO, cheese, tuna, stoned olives, asparagus tips, which is then laid on top of a slice of bread.

A still for making the grape spirit bagaceira

banha
LARD

This rendered pork fat is used extensively as a cooking vehicle in Portugal, especially in the north, sometimes in conjunction with the more expensive olive oil or butter. It tastes more definitely of pork than does the more highly refined American lard.

banho maria

Bain-Marie (water bath); see BAÑO-MARIA.

baño-maría
banho maria
WATER BATH

This is a bath of hot or boiling water in which a smaller pan containing sauces or other delicate food is immersed so that they can be cooked more gently than over direct heat. The *baño-maría* was introduced to Spain and Portugal by the Moors.

> CAPITALIZED *words within entries refer the reader to more information on the same subject.*

see also   **Bakery:** *see panadería*   **Balearic Islands:** *see Islas Baleares*
Banana: *see plátano*

Ⓢ *barbacoa,* Ⓟ *grade para assar*

BARBECUE

Barbecued food is popular in Spain and Portugal, especially the wonderful sardines and prawns sold in the seaside resorts along the Atlantic coasts of both countries. See also A LA PARRILLA.

Barcelona

SPANISH CITY

The second city of Spain, Barcelona is a great deal more than a regional capital. Founded by the Phoenicians, it took its name from the Barca dynasty of Carthaginia. During the Middle Ages it was queen of the Mediterranean, the heart and mainspring of the Catalan-Aragonese Empire; and today its autonomous parliament, the Generalidad, has been restored.

In culinary matters, as in others, Barcelona is the capital of CATALUÑA; and it was the proud boast of the noted Spanish epicure, Luis Antonio de Vega, writing in the 1960's and 1970's that you could walk into any of its small restaurants with your eyes shut and not be disappointed.

These smaller restaurants continue to serve traditional Catalan fare, and in the port area you will find large places like Casa Costa, which offer a truly magnificent range of fish dishes such as *parrilladas* (see PARRILLADA DE MARISCO), ZARZUELA and BULLABESAS.

The sophisticated restaurants have been much influenced by NOUVELLE CUISINE. This has, however, been taken on mainly to lighten the sometimes heavy Catalan dishes, to simplify sauces and to bring out to the full the flavors of the excellent local ingredients. Leading exponents are the Belgian Jean Louis Neichel, who runs the elegant restaurant of the same name, James Bagués, who at Jaume de Provença serves in parallel Catalan and *nouvelle cuisine* dishes, and Luis Cruañas of Eldorado Petit in San Felíu de Guixols and Barcelona, rated among the top restaurateurs in Spain.

The index, in English, is arranged by types of food — eggs, cheese, fish — kitchen equipment, cooking terms and other subjects. Consult it for recipes that make use of particular ingredients.

The steeples of Gaudi's unfinished cathedral in Barcelona

---

see also   **Bar:** *see cervecería, cervejaria*   **Barbecue:** *see barbacoa*
Basil: *see manjericão*   **Basque omelet:** *see piperada vasca*

Bardají, Teodoro

EARLY 20TH-
CENTURY CHEF AND
WRITER

At the turn of the century when, at the tender age of 14, Teodoro Bardají arrived in MADRID from his native Huesca to serve his apprenticeship as pastry cook and chef, it was fashionable to denigrate the native Spanish cuisine at the expense of the French. Bardají subsequently spent 40 years as chef de cuisine for the Dukes of Infantado. He acquired an international reputation as a chef and published a series of scholarly books. Publication of the first, *Indice culinario*, an invaluable collection of authentic Spanish recipes, was halted in midstream, and it appeared only in a limited and numbered edition in 1915.

La salsa mahonesa (1928) is a critical enquiry into the historical origins of mayonnaise, often attributed to the French, in which Bardají quotes convincing evidence that it was first used in Minorca, taking its name from Port Mahón. Bardají enjoyed a long career. His magnum opus, the encyclopedic *La cocina de ellas*, which, for example, gives no less than 49 different ways of cooking potatoes, was written at the advanced age of 74.

bartolillos

CUSTARD-FILLED
PASTRIES

A specialty of MADRID, the pastry is made with flour, olive oil, milk and lemon zest, then rolled out into rectangles, filled with CREMA PASTELERA and fried before being dusted with sugar and cinnamon.

batata

Potato; see PATATA.

baunilha

Vanilla; see VAINILLA.

Beira Alta

PORTUGUESE
REGION

The Beira Alta and BEIRA BAIXA to its south are among the most mountainous regions of Portugal and an extension of the high central plateau of Spain to the east. Except for a gap to the west near Coimbra in the Beira Litoral, the Beira Alta is shut off from the rest of Portugal by mountains, bounded to the south by the Serra da Estrela and to the north by the Caramulo mountains and Serra de Montemuro. In between lies the basin of the Mondego River, a patchwork of vineyards, arable land and pasturage, broken by outcrops of naked granite and splashed by dark belts of pine.

BEIRA ALTA

• Viseu

• Guarda

---

see also   **Basque Provinces:** *see Provincias Vascas*   **Batter:** *see massa vinhe*
                   Bay leaves: *see hojas de laurel*   **Beef:** *see bife, carne de vaca*

The granite-built villages and fortified towns towards the Spanish frontier are a legacy of the intermittent wars between the two countries. The Roman town of Viseu, which lies at the center of the DÃO wine region, is an important agricultural center with a fascinating open market.

The Beira Alta probably makes the best of Portuguese cheeses, the *queijo da* SERRA from the Serra da Estrela. Local dishes are typically of the sturdy peasant variety like *feijão con carne de porco*, in the style of a boiled dinner and made with dried white beans, CHOURIÇO, *toucinho* (see TOCINO), pork, cab-

bage and carrots. The locals eat COZIDOS such as this as two courses: *first* the meat and *then* the soup. Viseu was for centuries a stronghold of the Moors (see MOROS, LOS), and at a local PASTELARIA I once encountered no less than eight varieties of Moorish-inspired confections, now made by nuns from egg yolks, almonds, chestnuts, sugar and spices: *Castanhas* ("chestnuts"), *Papos de anjo* ("angel puffs"), *Ouricos* ("hedgehogs"), *Pingos de Tocha* ("candle drippings"), *Principes* ("princes"), *Fios* ("threads"), *Celeste* and *Tamaras* ("dates").

Beira Baixa

PORTUGUESE
REGION

The physical and geographical characteristics of the Beira Baixa are very similar to those of the BEIRA ALTA. It is crossed by two mountain ranges, the Serra da Gardunha and the Serra da Lousa, between which lies the wide valley of the River Zezere, a tributary of the Tagus. Its principal town is Castelo Branco, a pleasant enough place trading in cheese, honey and olive oil. It suffered greatly from the bloody wars between Portugal and Spain, and even more so from the devastation wreaked by Napoleon's army during the Peninsular War, and little of historic interest remains.

The region draws on the same ingredients as the Beira Alta, and its cooking is very similar. Typical dishes are *sopa de lebre à provinciana* (a hare soup); *cabrito assado de Castelo Branco* (roast kid); *batatas da vindimia* (new potatoes boiled without peeling and heated again with onion and tomato sauce); ALETRIA DOCE and AMEIXAS RECHEADAS COM NOZES.

Beira Litoral

PORTUGUESE
REGION

This low lying coastal area stretches along the Atlantic southwards from OPORTO. It takes in the wine-growing area of the BAIRRADA and Coimbra, the first capital of Portugal and home of its oldest university, romantically built up a hillside and overlooking the Mondego River. Near the northern extreme of the province is Aveiro on its great salt water lagoon, surrounded by marshes, paddy fields, canals and salt pans. Until a great storm closed the lagoon in 1575, Aveiro was a deep sea port and a base

for fishing cod off Newfoundland. It still lives by fishing sea-eels and sea perch from the lagoon, sardines and skate from inshore, and cod from further afield, much of it canned in the town. Inland, the Beira Litoral grows olives, fruit, wheat and maize as well as vines.

As might be expected, there is a great choice of seafood: *sopas de caldeirada* (thick fish soups); *canja de enguia* (eel broth); CALDEIRADA DE ENGUIAS; BACALHAU and skate in regional versions and many others.

Of meats, CHANFANA A MODA DA BAIRRADA is a favorite at weddings, but quite the most famous, renowned throughout Portugal, is the *leitão assado* (roast suckling pig) cooked in the brick ovens of Mealhada, north of Coimbra, and most famous of all, that from the ovens of Pedro dos Leitões served on scrubbed wooden tables accompanied simply by freshly baked bread and BAIRRADA wine.

Near Mealhada is the magnificent Palace Hotel with its beautiful *azulejos* (tiles) and grand stone staircase. The restaurant is noted for its quite outstanding BUÇACO wines. These are set off by the sophisticated cuisine, the set menu including consommés and game soups; a first-rate BACALHAU A LISBONENSE; roast duck and of course *leitão assado* (roast suckling-pig) and *cabrito asado* (roast kid), excellent desserts and a good selection of Portuguese cheeses.

berenjenas
EGGPLANT

Eggplants are plentiful and very much used in Spain. They are stuffed and fried (see BERENJENAS MAITE), baked, broiled and also made into a paste known as *caviar de berenjenas* (eggplant caviar).

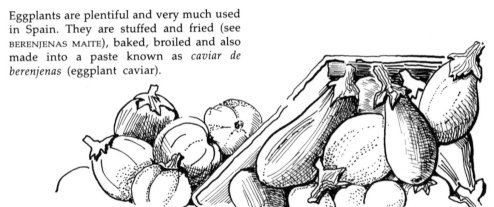

---

berenjenas Maite (S)
eggplant Maite

Serves 4

4 small eggplant, peeled and cut into rounds
2 tbsp flour
1 tbsp water
½ tsp vinegar
1 egg, beaten
salt
¼ lb chorizo sausage, thinly sliced
olive oil

Soak the eggplant rounds in salted water for 1 hour, then drain well. Make a batter with the flour, water, vinegar, egg and a little salt. Sandwich the slices of chorizo between the rounds of eggplant, repeating until all the eggplant has been used. Coat the rounds with the batter and fry in hot olive oil until golden.

S *besugo*

SEA BREAM

Besugo *(Pagellus cantabricus)*, the handsome grey and white striped sea bream, is much esteemed in Spain. In books of US origin, it and URTA are mistakenly translated as Porgy *(Pagrus pagrus)*, which whatever its merits, will not double up for either fish, though mackerel may sometimes be substituted for *besugo*. It is eviscerated and scaled by the fishmonger. All that need be done at home is to wash it well under cold running water and dry it with a clean cloth.

S *besugo a la madrileña*

SEA BREAM MADRID STYLE

Sea bream cooked in white wine and tomato sauce — a traditional favorite at Christmas (see NAVIDAD).

---

besugo al horno (S)
baked sea bream

Serves 2

2 potatoes, cut into rounds, 2 in thick
½ cup olive oil
1 bream of about 2 lb, cleaned
1 lemon
salt and pepper
2 tbsp fino sherry or dry white wine

Fry the potato rounds in the oil until crisp, then reserve. Make two slits in the upper side of the fish without cutting through and insert a slice of lemon in each. Line the base of an oven proof dish with the fried potato rounds and place the fish on top. Squeeze the juice from the rest of the lemon over it, season with salt and pepper, and add the sherry or white wine. Bake in a fairly hot oven, 375°F, for about 30-45 minutes until the skin is crisp.

---

besugo con almendras a la castellana (S)
sea bream with almonds

Serves 4

1-2 bream of about 4½ lb total weight, cleaned
1 lemon, sliced
6 almonds, blanched, skinned and split in half
1 large onion, sliced
2 tbsp chopped parsley
1 tbsp olive oil
salt and pepper
1 tsp cornstarch
¼ cup dry white wine

Make a few slits in the sides of the fish without cutting through it and insert the lemon slices and split almonds. Place in an ovenproof dish, cover with the sliced onion and parsley, pour on the oil, season with salt and pepper to taste, and bake uncovered in a moderate oven, 350°F, for about 1 hour or until well cooked.

Transfer the fish to a hot serving dish. Sprinkle the cornstarch into the pan juices, add the wine and cook for a minute or two until blended, then pour over the bream.

bife, bifes
BEEF

Except in expensive restaurants and hotels, the beef in Portugal is not good and is, in fact, often a tough cut from a cow (see also CARNE DE VACA). *Bifes* are steaks of beef, pork, lamb and even tuna.

Bilbao
SPANISH CITY

Bilbao, in the region of Viscaya, bestrides the dark flow of the River Nervión and has been described as the gastronomic capital of Spain. As far as the north of Spain is concerned, the Spanish epicure Luis Antonio de Vega puts it on a par with Vigo. The outlying Santurce is famous for its fish market and grilled sardines, but the single most famous delicacy from the Bilbao region is the ANGULAS or baby eels. It is also renowned for its *bacalao al pil pil* (one of the versions of salt cod); *merluza a la bilbaína* (hake Bilbao style) and for *besugo* (sea bream). There are many first-rate restaurants such as Guria and Goizeko Kabi, but the seriousness with which the Bilbaínos take their cuisine is proved by the numerous SOCIEDADES GASTRONOMICAS.

biqueirões

Fresh anchovies; see BOQUERONES.

biscoitos
COOKIES

Despite the profusion of desserts and small cakes, cookies are not much made in Portugal except for religious festivals – most especially Easter (see PASCOA) when half-a-dozen different varieties are made.

---

biscoitos de Lamego (P)
Lamego cookies

Serves 6-8

3½ cups self-rising flour
1 cup sugar
⅔ cup butter
2 eggs, beaten
3 egg yolks, beaten

Heap the flour on a table top or pastry board, make a well in the center, add all the ingredients except the beaten yolk in the order given. Work the dough with your fingers – if it is too thick, moisten with as little milk as possible to make it bind – then put it into a bowl and leave to rest for 1 hour, covered with a dish towel.

Dust the table or pastry board with flour and roll out the dough to a thickness of about ⅛ inch. Brush with the beaten egg and then cut it into strips about ¼ inch by 2 inches. Place these, with a little space between them, on a baking tray previously sprinkled with water, and score a criss-cross pattern on top. Preheat the oven to hot, 425°F, turn it down to 375°F, and bake the cookies until golden.

---

bistec, bife
A CUT OF BEEF

A Spanish corruption of the English "beefsteak", this is a cut from inside the sirloin bone, usually of cow beef, also known as SOLOMILLO. It is cooked A LA PLANCHA or A LA PARRILLA.

CAPITALIZED *words within entries refer the reader to more information on the same subject.*

S *bizcochos borrachos*

TIPSY CAKES

These small cupcakes from CASTILLA LA NUEVA are made by beating egg yolks with sugar, stirring in flour, then folding in the beaten egg whites. The mixture is spooned into into small, greased muffin pans. They are baked in a hot oven, then left to cool before a syrup of sugar and Málaga wine is poured on to them, followed by a sprinkling of ground cinnamon.

S *blanco y negro*

Coffee sorbet; see LECHE MERENGADA.

S *blanquear*
P *branquear*

TO BLANCH

To boil food for a few minutes so as to eliminate blood and make it white; generally, to put food in boiling water.

S *bocadillo*

SANDWICH

This resembles a "poor boy" more than a traditional sandwich. Made from a *barra* (baguette) of crusty Spanish bread, it may contain JAMON SERRANO, JAMON DE YORK, CHORIZO or cold *tortilla* (see TORTILLA ESPAÑOLA), and is what the shepherds and agricultural workers take to the fields with a BOTA of wine, for their midday meal. An interesting idea for a picnic.

A Spanish sandwich or Bocadillo

P *bocheiras*

SAUSAGE

A highly spiced sausage made with pig's heart and beef.

P *boi de páscoa*

Loin of ox; see PASCOA.

P *bola de carne*

MEAT PIE

Savory pie from the MINHO and DOURO made with yeast-raised dough, and filled with either rabbit, partridge, boiling fowl or veal and CHOURIÇO, PRESUNTO and onion, and baked in the oven. Alternatively, two kinds of game or fowl are mixed with veal, together with the chouriço and presunto.

P *bola de sardinhas de Lamego*

LAMEGO SARDINE PIE

A bread dough filled with sardines and onions, flavored with parsley and baked in a hot oven.

If Spanish and Portuguese terms differ from each other, the entry in Portuguese, in the majority of cases, is referred to its Spanish equivalent, where you will find information relevant to both countries.

S *bolets*

WILD MUSHROOMS

Boletus mushrooms *(porcini)*, from CATALUÑA, often cooked on a charcoal grill with garlic and parsley. See also SETAS.

---

see also   **To boil:** *see blanquear*

bolo de mel

MADEIRA CAKE

What is generally known as "Madeira cake" is unknown on the island itself. The following recipe for true rich and spicy Madeira cake, which goes well with any of the wines, is reproduced by kind permission of Mr Noel Cossart from his book *Madeira – the island vineyard* (Christie's Wine Publications, London, 1984) and is the one used by his mother.

---

bolo de mel (P)
Madeira cake

Makes 10 small cakes

4 lb flour
6 tbsp granulated sugar
⅓ cup butter
¼ cup lard or shortening
½ tsp ground cinnamon
1 tsp ground aniseed
½ tsp ground cloves
5 cups molasses
1½ tbsp candied citrus peel, chopped
½ cup ground almonds
½ cup ground walnuts
½ tsp soda
2 oz compressed yeast

Combine butter, lard, molasses and sugar and stir over gentle heat. Mix other ingredients and add yeast. Pour together and stir well until completely mixed. Leave mixture in earthenware bowl covered with a cloth in a warm place for two days to rise. Divide into ten flat cakes and bake in a moderate (350°F) oven for about 20 minutes.

---

bolo de páscoa

Meat loaf; see FOLAR GORDO.

bolo-rei

Twelfth Night cake; see ROSCON DE REYES.

---

bolos de amor (P)
loving cakes

Serves 6–8

½ lb butter, softened
1 cup + 2 tbsp sugar
grated zest of ½ lemon
1 pkg active dry yeast
2 large eggs, beaten
milk, equal in volume to the eggs
3½ cups self-rising flour
1 egg yolk, beaten

In a warm bowl mix the butter, sugar, lemon zest and dissolved yeast (following the instructions on the package). Add the 2 beaten eggs little by little, beating well with a wooden spoon, then add the milk (warmed if necessary in cold weather or if taken straight from the refrigerator), and the flour. Dust the table or pastry board with flour and work the dough with your hands, finally shaping it into a ball.

Cut up the dough, shape it into small rounds and place them on the floured surface separated from each other. Brush with the beaten egg yolk, cover and leave for 30 minutes to allow the yeast to work. Bake the cakes in a hot oven (425°F) until golden.

P *bolos de canela*

CINNAMON CAKES

Use the recipe for BOLOS DE AMOR, substituting a dusting of ground cinnamon for the beaten egg yolk.

P *bolos de D. Rodrigo*

CANDY

One of the best-known Moorish-inspired candies (see MOROS, LOS), now frequently made by nuns.

It is made with ground almonds and filaments of egg, prepared by dripping beaten egg in a fine stream into boiling syrup. There are now special funnels for doing this, but the original method of the nuns was to use an eggshell which was pierced at the bottom with a pin.

P *bolos de figo*

FIG AND ALMOND CANDY

This may be made either with fresh or dried figs, but the hard stalks must be first removed.

---

bolos de figo (P)
fig and almond candy

Serves 6–8

1⅔ cups shelled almonds
grated zest of 1 orange
11 oz figs, fresh or dried
2½ oz semisweet chocolate, chopped
4 tbsp water
1 cup sugar

Heat the almonds in the oven until brown, then peel them. Mince the orange zest, figs, chocolate and almonds in a food processor or blender. Boil the water and sugar until thick and syrupy, then add the other ingredients. Allow the mixture to cool on a plate, then shape it into small balls and roll them in sugar. Serve with coffee.

S *bonito*

ATLANTIC BONITO

Very similar to ATUN, this is a smaller fish with dark stripes on the head and body and much whiter meat. It is cooked and prepared the same way.

S *boquerones*
P *biqueirões*

FRESH ANCHOVIES

A silvery fish of the herring family (*Engraulis encrascholus*), about the size of a sardine and equally delicious broiled or fried. The fillets of the young fish are canned as anchovies. They are cleaned by removing the guts but not the backbone.

The index, in English, is arranged by types of food — eggs, cheese, fish — kitchen equipment, cooking terms and other subjects. Consult it for recipes that make use of particular ingredients.

Opposite: Chili peppers, used in many Spanish and Portuguese dishes, were introduced from South America by the Conquistadores in the 16th century.

Pages 70-71: Spices on sale at a village market. While the Conquistadores were exploring the west, Henry the Navigator and Vasco da Gama discovered the sea route to the east. The resulting trade, particularly with the East Indies, brought many of the spices seen here, nutmeg, cloves, cinnamon, to the Iberian peninsula for the first time and added a new dimension to the region's cooking.

boquerones en adobo (S)
marinated fresh anchovies

Serves 6 as an appetizer

*2 lb fresh anchovies or very small smelts,
    cleaned, backbone removed and opened
    lengthwise*
salt
1 tbsp minced parsley, flat leaf if available
2 cloves garlic, finely chopped
1 tbsp sherry vinegar
2 tbsp virgin olive oil

Put the fish in a large oval glass dish and sprinkle with the salt, parsley, garlic, vinegar and oil. Cover with plastic wrap and keep in the refrigerator for 2 days before serving.

borrego assado com hortela

ROAST BABY LAMB
WITH MINT

Borrego means baby lamb and I am grateful to J.M. da Fonseca Internacional (see ESTRE-MADURA) for this way of roasting it.

borrego assado com hortela (P)
roast baby lamb with mint

Serves 8

3 heads garlic, peeled and chopped
1 sprig fresh mint
1 sprig parsley
salt
few drops piri-piri
1 tsp colorau (hot paprika)
a little olive oil
1 cup dry white wine
1 baby lamb

Mix all the ingredients and leave the baby lamb in this marinade for 24 hours, spooning it over at intervals. For the meat to be pink, roast in a preheated oven (375°F) for 20 minutes per 1 lb plus 20 minutes more, if you like the meat well done.

bota

LEATHER WINE
BOTTLE

Not so long ago no Spaniard would travel without his *bota* of wine, of which Richard FORD wrote that it "is always near every Spaniard's mouth who can get at one, all classes being ever ready, like Sancho Panza, to give 'a thousand kisses', not only to his own legitimate *bota*, but to that of his neighbor, which is coveted more than wife . . . The way to use it is thus – grasp the neck with the left hand till the wine, in obedience with hydrostatic laws, rises to its own level, and keeps always full in the cup without trouble to the mouth . . . No drop of the divine contents is wasted, except by some newly-arrived bungler, who, by lifting up the bottom first, inundates his chin."

Today, agricultural workers and shepherds still go out to work with their *bota* and refresh themselves from it during their midday break.

Opposite: A selection of nuts; walnuts were first planted in Spain and Portugal by the Romans and hazelnuts by the Greeks

see also   **Bouquet garni:** *see ramo de cheiros*

P *branquear*

To blanch; see BLANQUEAR.

S *brasear*
P *refogar*
TO BRAISE

To braise, by simmering meat, fish or vegetables in a small amount of liquid in a tightly covered pan. The food may first be browned to seal and add flavor.

S *brazo de gitano*
A DESSERT

Literally "gypsy's arm", this is a dessert popular in ANDALUCIA, made with eggs, flour and jam, and resembling a jelly roll.

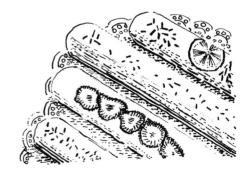

Brazo de gitano

P *broa*
A BREAD

This robust cornmeal bread from the MINHO in northern Portugal is baked in flat rounds and may also contain barley and alfalfa flour.

P *Buçaco*
A WINE

Tucked away in the forests of the Buçaco mountains – the "damned long hill" where Wellington defeated Marshal Masséna in 1810 – is a former royal hunting lodge, now the Palace Hotel. Here are made and bottled perhaps the best of all Portuguese table wines. In the catalog of the sale held at Christie's in 1986 to celebrate the 600th anniversary of the Anglo-Portuguese Alliance, Michael Broadbent, Master of Wines, wrote of the red 1959, "I put it on a par with a great vintage of Lafite."

P *Bucelas*
DEMARCATED WINE REGION

The white wines from this tiny region, covering less than a square mile just north of LISBOA, were popularized in England by the officers of Wellington's army returning from the Peninsular War. It was one of the first Portuguese regions to be demarcated, in 1911. All its dry white wines are now made by one firm, Caves Velhas. When young, they are light, delicately perfumed and slightly acid, and go very well with fish.

P *bucho de porco recheado*
STUFFED BELLY OF PORK

A haggis-like dish from the BEIRA LITORAL made with rice, belly, loin and head of pork, garlic and herbs.

> CAPITALIZED *words within entries refer the reader to more information on the same subject.*

S *budín*
TERRINE

A dish in which ground meat, poultry, fish and sometimes vegetables are incorporated in SALSA BESAMEL. This is then mixed with eggs beaten separately as for a soufflé and is always cooked in a BAÑO-MARIA. It may be eaten hot or cold.

S *bullabesa*
FISH STEW

The famous *bouillabaisse* (fish soup), or *bullabesa* in its Spanish form, was introduced to southern France from CATALUÑA. The word simply means *hierve bajo* or *bouillir bas* – "to boil slowly" – and in both forms the name is a corruption of the original and very similar Catalan or Languedoc dialects.

---

see also

Brains: see sesos   **To braise:** see brasear   **Brandy:** see aguardente, coñac
Bread: See pan, pão   **Bread pudding:** see pudim de pão

---

buñuelos
FRITTERS

A Manchegan and Andalucían variant of CHURROS, in which yeast is mixed with the dough; it is consequently lighter and emerges as a hollow tube. Like *churros*, *buñuelos* are becoming increasingly difficult to find.

buñuelos de bacalao (S)
fish fritters

Serves 4

¼ lb salt cod, prepared by the second method on page 57 and flaked finely
1 cup freshly made mashed potato
2 eggs, separated
1 tbsp chopped parsley
2 cloves garlic, crushed
1 cup flour
salt
nutmeg
olive oil, for deep frying

Mix the fish with the mashed potato in a bowl, then add the egg yolks, parsley, garlic, flour and a little salt and nutmeg, mixing together well. Beat the egg whites until stiff, then fold into the mixture. Shape the fritters with two tablespoons and fry in hot olive oil about 1 inch deep until browned. Drain on paper towels and serve the buñuelos piping hot.

buñuelos de San Isidro
CREAM-FILLED FRITTERS

These cream-filled BUÑUELOS are traditionally made for the fiesta of San Isidro, the patron saint of MADRID, in May, also the occasion for a full week's bull-fighting.

buñuelos de viento
SWEET FRITTERS

Light as air, as the name implies, these are tiny BUÑUELOS eaten as part of the celebration of All Saints' Day (see LOS SANTOS), an important date in the Spanish religious calendar. There are many recipes, but I prefer the one which follows.

buñuelos de viento (S)
sweet puff fritters

Serves 8–10

2½ cups flour
pinch of salt
¼ cup olive oil
¼ cup dry white wine
1⅓ cups cold milk
1 tsp active dry yeast
olive oil, for deep frying
confectioners' sugar

Put the flour and salt into a large bowl, make a well in the center and add the olive oil and wine. Now add the milk, stirring slowly until a creamy consistency is obtained. Allow the dough to rest for 30 minutes, then add the yeast, dissolved in a tablespoon of water.

Heat olive oil about 1 inch deep in a frying pan, and drop teaspoonfuls of mixture into the hot oil, frying until they are golden and puffed up. Drain on paper towels and sprinkle the buñuelos with confectioners' sugar.

S *Burgos*
A CHEESE

One of the best known Spanish cheeses, this is made from ewe's milk with 18 to 20 percent dry extract fat. The cheese is mild and white with a hint of saltiness, and it must be eaten fresh within 2 days of making. It is often sprinkled with sugar or served with honey and eaten as a dessert.

S *butifarra*
CHARCUTERIE

A delicate white Catalan sausage made from ground pork, spices and a little of the blood, filled into sausage skins, cooked and hung up to dry (see also EMBUTIDOS and LA MATANZA). *Butifarra* may be eaten without further cooking, but is also used in stews of which the best known is *butifarra amb mongetes*, made with a local dried white bean. Some of the best of this sausage is from the old cathedral town of Vich in the foothills of the Pyrenees, but it is also popular in Majorca where the rich and self-important are scathingly known as *butifarrones*.

see also   **Butcher's shop:** *see carnicería*
                  Butter: *see mantequilla*

cabello de ángel
ANGEL'S HAIR

A sweet topping for pastries in the form of golden-colored filaments, popular in Spain and made by heating the pulp of pumpkin or squash with sugar, lemon zest and spices. See also ENSAIMADA.

Cabrales
A CHEESE

The most famous Spanish blue-veined cheese containing 44 percent of dry extract fat. It is made in the mountain farms of ASTURIAS from cow's milk, sometimes mixed with ewe's or goat's milk. Reminiscent of Roquefort, Cabrales is indeed so fully flavored that there is a saying that it is matured in heaps of manure! The curd is, in fact, first skimmed from the whey with a hollow circle of bark like that used by the Homeric Greeks and then dried in front of a fire. It is subsequently transferred to an HORREO. When the blue mould appears, the cheeses are taken to the famous cave of Jouz del Cuevu to complete their maturation among the great stalactites, and must be eaten within 3 to 5 weeks of being removed from the cave.

Cabreiro
A CHEESE

A smooth white cheese made with mixed goat's and ewe's milks from Castelo Branco near the Spanish frontier of Portugal. It is eaten fresh or may be ripened in brine.

🅿 *cabrito*
KID

Goats thrive in barren areas without much grass such as the ALENTEJO in Portugal and LA MANCHA and ESTREMADURA in Spain. Baby, milk-fed kid is popular both in Spain and Portugal and is usually roasted in the same way as COCHINILLO and CORDERO.

---

cabrito asado (S, P)
roast leg of kid

Serves 6–8

1 leg of kid or lamb (6½ lb)
1–2 cloves garlic
salt
2 tbsp olive oil or 4 tbsp lard
1 small glass brandy

Put the leg in a roasting pan, rub it with garlic, season with salt and moisten with oil or dot lard on top. Roast in a preheated moderately hot oven (375°F) for 20 minutes per 1 lb.

Halfway through cooking, pour the brandy over the leg; this will give it a rich color and improve the flavor.

When the meat is done, place on a serving dish and keep warm in the oven. Meanwhile, skim off the fat from the juices in the roasting pan. To make a gravy for serving with the roast, add a little more brandy to the juices, heat gently, and stir well with a wooden spoon until smooth.

P *cabrito assado com arroz de açafrão*

ROAST KID WITH SAFFRON RICE

Roast kid Minho-style with saffron rice. The leg of kid is marinated overnight in white wine, salt and black peppercorns, then put into an *assadeira de barro* (earthenware dish) with partially cooked onion, PRESUNTO, stoned olives and lemon juice, and basted from time to time during roasting. The rice is cooked separately in the same oven.

In the MINHO, the whole kid is often cooked in a baker's oven with saffron.

P *caça*

Hunting; see CAZA, LA.

S *cacao*

Cocoa bean; see CHOCOLATE Y COCOA.

If Spanish and Portuguese terms differ from each other, the entry in Portuguese, in the majority of cases, is referred to its Spanish equivalent, where you will find information relevant to both countries.

P *cação em vinho tinto*

DOGFISH IN RED WINE

A dogfish stew from the DOURO cooked with red wine and herbs and served in a rich, thick sauce.

S *cachelos*

SPICY RED POTATOES

These are served in the Guadarrama Mountains north of MADRID in the cold winters. They go well with boiled ham.

---

cachelos (S)
spicy red potatoes

Serves 4

2 lb potatoes, peeled
2 tbsp olive oil
2 cloves garlic, peeled and chopped
2 tbsp pimentón picante (hot paprika)

Boil the potatoes in salted water for 20 minutes. Meanwhile, heat the olive oil and sauté the garlic until brown, being careful not to burn it. Remove from the heat and stir in the pimentón. Drain the potatoes and return to the pan and pour the mixture over them while still hot. Keep on a low heat for 2-3 minutes, shaking the pan, until the potatoes turn a deep red.

Cádiz

SPANISH CITY

The seaport city of Cádiz, standing at the tip of ANDALUCIA and connected with the mainland only by a narrow causeway, was founded by the Phoenicians. It has often been razed and rebuilt, and its present elegant white houses and domed churches date from the last of such destructive raids when the place was destroyed by the English in 1596.

Apart from its other attractions, this is *the* place to visit to enjoy fish and shellfish – many of the varieties from the Bay of Cádiz are unknown elsewhere. One such fish is the carnivorous, shellfish-eating URTA from nearby Rota used for the famous URTA A LA ROTEÑA. Other fish that I have not come across elsewhere are *acedías* (*Gadus pollachius*) resembling a baby sole; *barbujitos* (tiny fresh anchovies, usually fried); CAÑAILLAS DE LA ISLA: *puntillitas* (tiny local squid) and *cazón* (baby shark, usually marinated in vinegar with red paprika).

Cádiz can be said to be the original home of the fish and chip shop, though its FREIDURIAS are a great deal more sophisticated. Fish and shellfish of many different sorts are fried individually to perfection in olive oil, either to take away or to eat on the premises. El Faro is one of Spain's outstanding seafood restaurants. Gonzalo Córdoba, owner and head chef, buys from fishermen who use rod and line, and offers fish, like some of those mentioned above, not available in the markets. Among his specialities are an *urta* soup, DORADA A LA SAL and *tortillas de camarones* (shrimp fritters), which melt in the mouth.

Cádiz
A CHEESE

A firm pale cheese with mellow taste made from goat's milk in the southerly province of Cádiz. The interior is light yellow with a fat content of 28 to 30 percent and the cheeses are pressed into braided *esparto* baskets, which leave their pattern impressed on the golden rind.

▣ *café*
COFFEE

Of some 25 varieties of coffee, the original and best is *arábica*, which originated in Ethiopia or the Yemen but which has subsequently been grown in almost every country with a suitable tropical climate. The former Portuguese colonies of Angola and Timor, and also, of course, Brazil, grow some of the world's finest coffee beans, as do Colombia and other countries that once comprised Spain's extensive South American empire. In more recent times Spain still produced coffee in Fernando Po, an offshore island of the former Spanish Guinea.

In Spain and Portugal, coffee is made stronger than in the US. In Spain there are three types: *solo* (black), *con leche* (with milk or cream), and *cortado* (expresso coffee with just a little milk). In Portugal, *bica* is the ultra strong variety served in the demi-tasses of coffee houses; *café* is the ordinary brew; *carioca* is half and half *café* and hot water, corresponding more to North American coffee; while *galão* is a strong filter coffee served with hot milk in a glass.

cafetería
CAFETERIA

People in big cities are notoriously in a hurry and, especially in MADRID, the tradition of quick service survives in the crowded and popular *cafeterías*. Their staples, served either at the counter or a table, are substantial toasted sandwiches or PLATOS COMBINADOS.

calamares lulas
SQUID

In Spain and Portugal squid is enormously popular. However, until recently in North America, the fishermen used to throw it back into the sea. Along the Cantabrian coast, where the tiny squid are known as *chipirones*, the Basques go to the trouble of catching them by rod and line. They are stewed in a rich, blue-black sauce made from their ink. Alternatively, cut into rings and fried until crisp, they are a favorite TAPA in Spanish bars; they also lend a particularly good flavor to PAELLA.

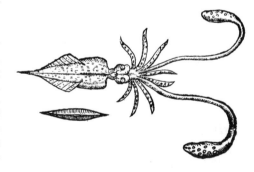

Choose small or medium-sized squid. To clean them, first pull away the body from the head and tentacles. Cut the tentacles from the head (they are the tenderest part of the fish) and discard the rest of it with the attached gut. Pull the flat spine from the body and strip away the thin, outer membrane. Wash the body well, then turn it inside out, wash again and cut into rings.

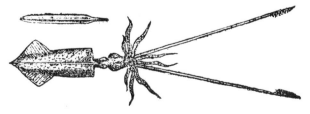

S *calamares al Jerez*

SQUID IN SHERRY SAUCE

An Andalucían way of cooking squid with a sauce containing sherry, ground almonds and saffron, but not the ink.

---

calamares en su tinta (S)
squid in their ink

Serves 4

2 lb squid
4 tbsp olive oil
2 medium onions, chopped
2 tomatoes, peeled and chopped
1 clove garlic, peeled and chopped
1 tbsp chopped parsley
1 tbsp fresh breadcrumbs
2 tbsp brandy
salt

Clean the squid as described on page 79 and reserve the small ink sacs, putting them in a little water so that they do not dry out.

Sauté the onions in hot olive oil until golden, then add the tomatoes and cook gently for another 10 minutes. Stir in the prepared squid rings and tentacles, add the garlic, parsley, breadcrumbs, brandy and salt, and simmer for about 15 minutes until tender (do not overcook them or they will become tough). Now, through a strainer and with the help of a wooden spoon, squeeze the ink from the sacs into a cup, mix with a little water and add to the sauce; this will immediately turn a deep blue-black if sufficient ink is used. If not, the flavor will still be good but the color will not be as dark. (In Spain and Portugal you can ask the fishmonger for the ink sac from a large squid; it is then easier to make a really black sauce.)

Serve the squid, together with the sauce, on a bed of boiled white rice.

---

calamares fritos a la romana (S)
fried squid

Serves 2 (or 4 as an appetizer)

1 lb squid
2 tbsp self-rising flour
2 tbsp milk
1 egg, separated
2 tsp olive oil, plus more for frying

Clean the squid as described on page 79, then dry thoroughly using paper towels.

Make the batter 30 minutes before it is needed by mixing the flour, milk, egg yolk and oil until creamy. Just before using it, fold in the stiffly beaten egg white. (This same thin batter is also ideal for frying other shellfish.)

Coat the rings and tentacles with the batter, fry briefly in hot olive oil until golden-brown, drain on paper towels and serve immediately.

S *calamares rellenos*

STUFFED SQUID

In this method of cooking squid, the fish is cleaned in the usual way but the body is left whole instead of being cut into rings. It is filled with a cooked mixture of the chopped tentacles, ham and onion before being cooked in a tomato sauce.

S *calcotada*

GRILLED SCALLIONS

This is made in CATALUÑA in the spring by slicing young scallions in half, grilling them over a wood fire and serving them with a sauce such as SALSA ROMESCO.

caldeirada

FISH STEW

This substantial fish stew from northern Portugal and Galicia, somewhat akin to the French *bouillabaisse*, is one of the best fish dishes from either country. It is prepared in different ways up and down the Atlantic coast and, as with *bouillabaisse* or the Spanish ZARZUELA, it is important to include a broad selection of fish.

In Portugal this might comprise *safio* (conger eel), *arrais* (skate), *ruivo* (gurnet), *chocos* (cuttlefish), *tamboril* (frog fish) and *lulas* (squid). At home, choose from halibut, bream, hake, eel and mullet. As with the Spanish PAELLA, squid contributes much to the flavor. Soft fish with small bones are not suitable. Clams and mussels are an inexpensive, flavorful and decorative addition, and other shellfish such as shrimp and scampi are all most welcome – it is a question of how much you wish to spend.

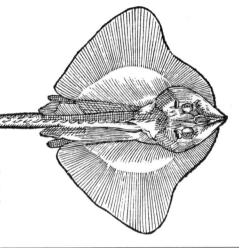

caldeirada de enguias

EEL STEW

A fish stew from the BEIRA LITORAL along the lines of *bouillabaisse*, but made with eels, potatoes, bread, onions, garlic, bay leaves and herbs.

---

caldeirada estilo Nazaré (P)
fish stew from Nazaré

Serves 6

2 tbsp olive oil
3 onions, chopped
8 oz canned pimentos, drained and cut into
    strips
1 lb tomatoes, peeled and chopped coarsely, or
    1 lb canned tomatoes
⅔ cup dry white wine
1 bay leaf
1 clove garlic, crushed
salt and pepper
few strands of saffron, crushed
1 tbsp chopped parsley
4½ lb mixed firm white fish
bouquet garni
shellfish as available

To make the refogado, heat the olive oil in a pan and sauté the chopped onions and pimento strips slowly for 10 minutes until soft. Add the tomatoes and continue cooking for 5 minutes before mixing in the white wine, bay leaf, crushed garlic, salt and pepper and saffron and finally the chopped parsley.

Meanwhile, remove the heads, and skin and bone the fish. Cover with water in a large saucepan and simmer for 20 minutes with a little salt and a bouquet garni, skimming the foam. Drain and reserve the stock. If you are using shellfish, which will naturally add to the richness of flavor, boil them separately in some of the same stock. Cut the fish into chunks. Arrange in one layer on top of the refogado in a large ovenproof dish. Cover with the reserved fish stock, put the dish in a moderate oven (350°F) and cook for 30 minutes until the fish is well done. It is also possible to use a fish poacher but in this case cook over a very low heat for about 15 minutes, shaking the pan occasionally.

Finally, transfer the caldeirada to a serving dish, arrange boiled potatoes around the side and garnish with shellfish, if using.

S P *caldo*

SOUP

A clear broth or *consommé* as distinct from thick soup.

---

caldo de perro gaditano (S)
fish soup Cádiz style

Serves 4

1½ lb hake, cod or other white fish, cut up coarsely
coarse salt
2 cloves garlic, peeled
4 tbsp olive oil
1 large onion, finely chopped
1 quart boiling water
juice of 2 Seville oranges

Put the fish in a bowl, sprinkle with coarse salt and leave for 1 hour. Fry the whole cloves of garlic in hot olive oil, discarding them when brown. Cook the onion in the oil until soft but not crisp.

Add the fish to the boiling water in a deep saucepan, simmer for 15 minutes, then lift out and remove the skin and bones. Return to the broth in the saucepan with the cooked onion and orange juice, let stand for 5 minutes to allow the flavors to mingle, then heat through. Season and serve hot.

P *caldo verde*

SOUP OF GREENS

There is no adequate translation for this, the best known soup of Portugal. It originated in the north, but is served everywhere – in restaurants and at home. It takes its name from the tall, dark green *couve* or Portuguese cabbage from which it is made, often grown beneath the trellised vines in the MINHO.

When making *caldo verde* outside Portugal, turnip greens or kale are the best substitute, but usually it will prove necessary to fall back on ordinary cabbage. It is important that this should be finely shredded and cooked very briefly to prevent it becoming flabby. In Portugal, *caldo verde* is eaten with PÃO DE BROA, a bread baked with mixed rye and wheat flours.

---

caldo verde (P)
soup

Serves 6

5 cups chicken stock
1 onion, coarsely chopped
1 lb potatoes, peeled and sliced
½ cup light cream
salt and pepper
¾ lb greens, kale or cabbage, shredded
few slices chouriço, cut up coarsely
1 tsp chopped parsley

Heat the chicken stock in a saucepan. Add the onion and potatoes, cook for 20 minutes until tender, then pass through a sieve or purée in a blender or food processor until smooth. Return to the saucepan, add the cream and season with salt and pepper. In a separate pan, boil the greens briskly in salted water for just 5 minutes, keeping the pan uncovered to preserve the fresh color. (Some recipes do not recommend cooking the greens at all, in which case it is essential that it should be shredded extremely finely, preferably in one of the machines specially used for this purpose in Portuguese markets.)

Drain the greens, if boiled, and stir into the purée. Ladle the soup into bowls and sprinkle with a little chopped chouriço and parsley before serving.

---

callos

Tripe; see TRIPAS and DOBRADA.

---

callos a la madrileña (S)
tripe Madrid style

Serves 4

2 lb tripe, cleaned, washed and cut into strips
1 pig's foot, blanched
2 tbsp olive oil
1 medium onion, chopped
¼ lb cooked ham, diced
¼ lb chorizo, diced
2 tbsp tomato paste
2 tsp flour or arrowroot
2 chili peppers, seeded and chopped finely
salt, freshly ground white pepper
1 tbsp chopped parsley

Put the tripe and pig's foot into a heavy casserole, cover with water and bring to the boil. Skim off the foam, then cover and cook slowly for 1–2 hours or until tender. Remove the pig's foot with a slotted spoon, take out the bones and return to the casserole.

Heat the olive oil in a skillet and sauté the onion for about 10 minutes until soft but not brown, then add the ham, chorizo and tomato paste and cook together for a few minutes more. Combine the flour or arrowroot with a little of the broth from the tripe and add. Stir well with a wooden spoon and pour the mixture into the casserole. Add the chili peppers and a little salt and pepper. Cook together very slowly for 15 minutes until very tender and sprinkle with chopped parsley before serving.

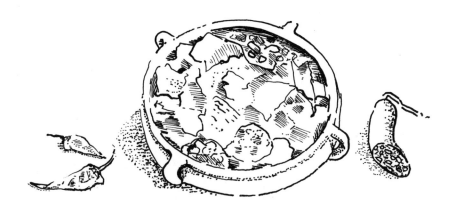

Calostro

A cheese; see ARMADA.

Camerano

A CHEESE

A mildly acid and very soft goat's milk cheese with a fat content of 45 percent from the Sierra de Cameros in the famous wine region of the RIOJA. The rind is thin and smells of the willow baskets in which the cheese is molded. It is usually eaten within the week, but there are those who prefer to let it dry, when the flavor becomes much more intense.

S *Campo de Borja*

DEMARCATED WINE REGION

Named after the Borgia family, whose ancestral castle survives in the Aragonese town of Borja, this region makes full-bodied red wines.

S *cañaíllas de la Isla*

SEA SNAILS

These large sea snails are typical of the Bay of Cádiz. They are lightly boiled and eaten cold, the sharp tail of one being used to extract the meat from the others, which, although a little rubbery, tastes of the whole wide Atlantic. Before the introduction of synthetic dyes, it was from this shellfish (*Murex brandaris*) that the costly Tyrian purple of the ancients was obtained.

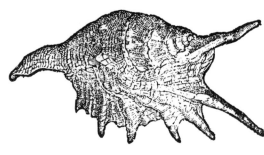

S *canalones*

STUFFED PASTA

Spanish cannelloni are better for weight watchers than the normal Italian variety because they are thin rectangles rather than thick corrugated tubes and are little more than an excuse for wrapping up the savory filling. There are two types: one requires boiling, and the other is simply soaked in cold water.

canela rellenos (S)
stuffed pasta

Serves 6

24–30 Spanish canalones
1 large onion, finely chopped
olive oil
2 lb ground pork, veal, chicken livers and
    chopped bacon or ham, mixed
salt
3 tbsp fresh breadcrumbs
1 egg, well beaten
2 tbsp fino sherry
1 tbsp minced parsley
2½ cups salsa de tomate (tomato sauce)
pinch of grated nutmeg
½ lb inexpensive liver pâté
2½ cups salsa besamel (white sauce), made
    with the addition of 4 oz Parmesan cheese,
    grated (about 1 cup)
4 tbsp butter
4 oz Parmesan cheese, grated (about 1 cup)

Soften the canalones according to the instructions on the package, either by boiling them or
soaking in cold water for 1–2 hours. (I use the
type soaked in cold water and give them about
2 hours.)

Meanwhile, sauté the onion in a little olive
oil for about 10 minutes until soft, but not
brown. Add the mixed pork, veal, chicken livers
and bacon or ham, and cook uncovered over
medium heat for 15 minutes longer, seasoning
to taste. Remove with a slotted spoon and purée
in a food processor or mince finely to obtain a
thick and very smooth mixture. Transfer mixture to a large bowl and add the breadcrumbs,
egg, sherry, parsley, 2 tbsp of the salsa de
tomate (tomato sauce), the nutmeg and liver
pâté. Mix thoroughly until smooth. Cover the
bowl with plastic wrap and cool in the refrigerator. (It is easier to fill the canalones
when the stuffing is cold and it may be kept in
the refrigerator until the following day. The
tomato sauce may be made the day before.)

Place a clean cloth on a large working
surface, remove the canalones from the water
and lay out the squares in rows, drying them
carefully by blotting with another cloth. Using
a tablespoon, put some filling in the center of
each square and roll the pasta around the filling
to form tubes.

Pour half the salsa besamel (white sauce)
into a large flat ovenproof dish or baking pan.
On top of this arrange the canalones in rows,
separating them by spoonfuls of salsa besamel
(white sauce) and covering with a layer of salsa
de tomate (tomato sauce). Decorate with a little
of the salsa de tomate (tomato sauce) poured in
a thin stripe between the canalones. Dot with
butter and sprinkle with the grated cheese. Bake
in a hot oven (425°F) for about 20 minutes, or
until bubbling and brown on top.

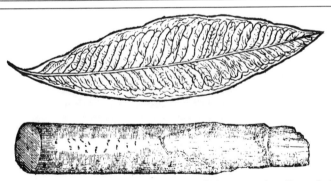

S P canela

CINNAMON

Cinnamon is made from the bark of a tree
grown in Ceylon, and was first introduced
to Europe by the Portuguese – it is said that
Vasco Da GAMA was paid enough for one
boat load to meet the entire cost of the
expedition to the East Indies (see also
ESPECIARIAS). Cinnamon, either as a powder
or in sticks, is used very widely in Portugal
and Spain to flavor sweets, custards, creams
and puddings – especially rice.

see also

Canary Islands: see Islas Canarias

P *canja*
A CONSOMMÉ

A clear chicken broth, sometimes containing rice or pasta.

S *caños*
SALTWATER FISH PONDS

Fish from the shores of ANDALUCIA are still sometimes caught in traditional fashion by allowing them to swim into *caños* (pools), which are then dammed up. During the year the salinity of the water increases because of evaporation, and when the fish have grown and multiplied, the pool is emptied and the owner and his friends gather to scoop them out by hand. Their long sojourn in the salty water gives them an especially good flavor. A somewhat similar custom prevailed along the shores of Huelva, where the fish pools were the perquisite of the Dukes of Osuna.

S *cantelo*
A BREAD

A bread in the shape of a ring specially baked for weddings in ASTURIAS. Here it is customary for the bread to be broken up and for the pieces to be given to the guests by the bride and groom, accompanied with a glass of wine.

S *carbón de leña (carbón vegetal)*
P *carvão de lenha*
CHARCOAL

Charcoal was formerly used widely for firing kitchen stoves, but has largely been replaced by electricity and butane gas. However, with the revival of charcoal grills and barbecues, charcoal cooking survives in the wooded country districts of Spain and Portugal. See also A LA PARRILLA.

P *Carcavelos*
DEMARCATED WINE REGION

The output of this tiny region near LISBOA, now swamped by urban development, is minuscule. The wine, when you can find it, is dryish and topaz-colored with a flavor of almonds and is drunk cold either as an apéritif or with a dessert.

S *cardo*
CARDOON

A plant belonging to the same family as the artichoke. With its curly leaves and thistle-like appearance, cardoon was a favorite subject of early Spanish painters in their *bodegones* or still lifes. A salad prescribed for the ailing Martín the Humane of Aragón (d. 1410) by the royal doctor has passed into medical history. It was prepared by making four criss-cross cuts in a raw white Aragonese cabbage and inserting into them the cut leaves of the cardoon.

Cardoons must be cleaned and boiled before cooking. Remove and discard the prickly leaves and hard outer stems. Cut the tender stalks into lengths of 4 inches, discarding any stringy parts. Cut the heart into 4 inch lengths and rub them with a lemon half to prevent discoloration.

To a large saucepan of water add 1 tbsp

A cardoon plant

see also   *Capers: see alcaparras*

flour and a little salt, both dissolved in a little cold water. Bring to the boil, add the pieces of cardoon and continue to cook gently for 1 to 2 hours until soft, then drain and use as required.

Cardoons are cooked with SALSA BESAMEL, to which grated cheese is added, and baked in the oven as *cardo en salsa blanca* (cardoon in white sauce). It can also be served with SALSA VINAGRETA (vinaigrette), garnished with hard-boiled eggs and chopped parsley. Another method of using it is as *puré de cardo* (cardoon purée), which is made by passing the cooked cardoons through a sieve, mixing it with mashed potato and grated cheese, and baking this in the oven.

cari

Curry powder; see CARIL

caril
CURRY POWDER

Curry powder has been available in Portugal and much used in its cooking since Vasco da GAMA's voyages of discovery to the spice islands of the East. There is no standard recipe for curry powder. The yellow color derives from turmeric, while other common ingredients are black pepper, cayenne, cloves, cinnamon, coriander, cumin, curry leaves, ginger, mace, nutmeg, mustard and poppy seeds. Rather than using it for making meat or chicken curries in the Indian fashion, the Portuguese add it in smaller amounts to give zest to soups or stews, or in dishes such as the famous TRIPAS A MODO DO PORTO. Curry powder, known as *cari*, is not much used in Spanish cooking.

Cariñena
DEMARCATED WINE REGION

This largest and best known of the wine-growing regions of Aragón centering on the area just south of Zaragoza, makes strong, deep red wines sold up and down Spain in litre bottles for everyday drinking. The largest of the wineries, the co-operative of San Valero, ages the best of its red wines in oak casks and also makes fresher and lighter wines, such as its "Percebal" rosé by temperature-controled fermentation in stainless steel tanks.

The seal for the Cariñena demarcated wine region

Carlos V, Emperador
16TH-CENTURY MONARCH

Charles, the grandson of the Catholic Monarchs, Ferdinand and Isabel, became King of Castile and Aragón in 1516 and was crowned Holy Roman Emperor in 1520. He was a renowned gourmand and had VALDEPEÑAS wines transported across Europe on muleback during his campaigns in the Low Countries. After his abdication in 1555, he spent his last years at the Monastery of Yuste north-west of MADRID, where, according to the 19th-century Spanish politician and historian Emilio Castelar, "Valladolid presented him with eel pies, Zaragoza with veal, Ciudad Real with game, Gama with partridge, Denia with sausages, Cádiz with anchovies, Sevilla with oysters, Lisbon with sole, the Extremadura with olives, Toledo with marzipan and Guadalupe with stews provided by its numerous and inventive chefs." To deal with this mountain of provisions, a stove of huge dimensions was installed in the monastery, and all sixty of the Emperor's servants were able to gather round it and warm themselves at it.

see also   **Cardoon:** *see cardo*

P *carne de porco*

Pork; see CERDO.

P *carne de porco à alentejana*

FRIED PORK WITH CLAMS

This most original combination of meat and shellfish originated in the ALENTEJO, in the far south of Portugal, but is now served throughout the country.

---

carne de porco à alentejana (S)
fried pork with clams

Serves 4–5

2 lb pork loin, cut into ¾ inch cubes
2 tsp white wine vinegar
1⅓ cups dry white wine
2 cloves garlic
1 bay leaf
1 tbsp chopped parsley
1 onion, finely chopped
1 carrot, grated
few strands of saffron, crushed
1 sprig cilantro
2 tbsp banha (lard) or olive oil
2 lb clams, well scrubbed and washed in cold
　　water
2 tsp tomato paste
salt, pepper
cilantro or parsley, chopped
lemon slices

Leave the meat cubes for 24 hours in a marinade made by mixing the vinegar, wine, garlic, bay leaf, parsley, onion, carrot, saffron and coriander sprig.

Remove the pieces of meat from the marinade with a slotted spoon. Heat the banha (lard) or olive oil in a pan or cataplana and fry the meat over high heat for 10 minutes. Add the clams, the liquid from the marinade and the tomato paste. Season to taste. Put the lid on the pan – this is important because it encourages the clams to open more quickly and dependably – and continue cooking over a reduced heat. Once the shellfish are open, the dish is ready to eat. Garnish with the cilantro or chopped parsley and serve with lemon slices.

S P *carne de vaca*

BEEF

The best beef, especially for roasts, is from 5 to 6-year old grass-fattened bulls. In Spain and Portugal, beef is almost always the meat of a cow. It is not of the same standard as prime beef in Britain or the USA, although a superior *carne de buey* is available in Spain after bullfights. See also CORTES DE CARNE and under individual cuts, e.g. ENTRECOTE, SOLOMILLO etc. (see index).

P *carneiro*

MUTTON

Mutton is eaten more widely in Portugal than lamb, sheep being bred for their wool and milk and used for making cheese rather than for meat.

Carneiro is usually stewed and occasionally roasted. For the delicious *carneiro frito com tomate* (fried mutton with tomato), the meat is cut into small pieces and marinated overnight with white wine, a little vinegar, chopped garlic, cloves, bay leaves and parsley. Next day the meat is dried and dusted with flour and fried in BANHA before being served with small potatoes cooked in the same fat and accompanied by *molho de tomate* (tomato sauce).

---

see also   **Carrots:** *see cenouras*

carnero
MUTTON

This is not as much eaten in Spain as the CARNEIRO in Portugal.

carnicería
BUTCHERS SHOP

The typical Spanish butcher shop presents a somewhat barren appearance, but this is because most of the supplies are kept in the refrigerator.

A price list is displayed on the wall – and prices can be high for items in short supply, such as steak. Veal, lamb, pork and chicken are the best buys.

Cartagineses, Los
CARTHAGINIANS

The Carthaginians were among the early invaders of the Iberian Peninsula and had made determined inroads on the interior before they were driven out by the Romans after the second Punic War in 201 BC. On the culinary front their achievements are largely unknown, but they did introduce the GARBANZO or chickpea, a source of merriment to Plautus and writers after him but a staple of many COCIDOS, *cozidos* and RANCHOS cooked all over Spain and Portugal.

carvão de lenha

Charcoal; see CARBON DE LEÑA.

castaña castanha
CHESTNUT

On the night of 11 November, the Galicians and Catalans celebrate Martinmas by roasting the first chestnuts. On the following day they are on sale at the little *estufas callejeras* (street braziers) all over Spain.

In *The Bible in Spain* George Borrow, who in the early nineteenth century traveled Galicia by foot and on horseback for the British Bible Society, wrote feelingly of the quagmires and the thunderstorms and of the chestnut forests and the rain "ceaselessly pattering among the broad green leaves." During the Roman occupation of Spain the legions of Augustus were no strangers to the nutritive value of chestnuts and a staple ration was the *bullote* made with chestnut flour.

Chestnuts provide more than 100 calories per ounce and they still form an essential element of the diet of the peasantry in Galicia and neighboring Portugal. There is a traditional dish of *mayugues* (dried chestnuts) which is made by boiling them and then dressing them with olive oil or, in the past, with pork fat.

At the other end of the scale are *marrons glacés*. Even Alexandre DUMAS wrote of those produced in Galicia that they were "the most exquisite confection known to the civilized world." The only manufacturer in Spain (and probably the largest in the world) is Cuevas y Cía in Orense, which out of an intake of 3,000 tons of chestnuts produces only about 15 tons of *marrons*, the end product of a rigorous selection of the fruit and the elaborate processes of cooking and glazing it which are carried out by hand by women who are forbidden to wear perfume for fear of spoiling the flavor. See also TURRON DE CASTAÑAS and TORTA DE BURZAGO.

castanha

Chestnut; see CASTAÑA.

Castelo Branco
A CHEESE

A cheese made of ewe's milk (sometimes mixed with goat's milk) from Castelo Branco near the Portuguese frontier with Spain. It contains small holes and is semi-hard with a 45 percent fat content. The cheese may be eaten fresh or left to ripen for 3 to 4 weeks, when it develops a strong peppery flavor.

---

see also

Carthaginians: see Cartagineses, Los
To carve: see trinchar

🅿 *Castelo de Vide*

A CHEESE

A soft and creamy Portuguese cheese made in small quantities near the Spanish frontier and rather similar to *queijo da* SERRA.

Castilla la Nueva

SPANISH REGION

Between them, Castilla la Nueva and CASTILLA LA VIEJA occupy most of the great central plateau of Spain. The area north of MADRID was the first to be recaptured from the Moors and is, therefore, known as Castilla La Vieja; Castilla La Nueva, with Madrid at its northern end, stretches in the other direction as far as the Sierra Morena, which divides it from ANDALUCIA. Its limit-less, undulating plains, given over to wheat and vines, are bitterly cold in winter and pitilessly hot in summer. Richard FORD, who rode them on horseback, describes how "the heavens and earth are on fire, and the sun drinks up the rivers at one draught, when one burnt sienna tone pervades the ground, and the green herb is shrivelled up into black gunpowder, and the rare pale ashy olive trees are blanched into the livery of the desert."

With its windmills on the skyline and distant villages, a line of whitewashed houses strung along a dusty road, this is Don QUIXOTE country, and when Cervantes described his diet as "an *olla* (stew) contain-ing more cow's meat than mutton, scratch fare most nights, grief and bickering on Saturdays, lentils on Fridays and perhaps a pigeon on Sundays," it is, with a few additions, what the country folk still eat today.

Most famous of its dishes is the OLLA PODRIDA or COCIDO CASTELLANO, a substan-tial boiled dinner in which broth, veget-

ables and finally meat are served separately. The Don's pigeon was no doubt the fruit of a hunting expedition (see CAZA), which still on Sundays yields rabbits, partridge and quail. Other specialties are the cold *gazpacho manchego* (made with breadcrumbs, olive oil, garlic, peppers, tomatoes and finely chopped onions that are added at the last moment). In summer, there is PISTO and *mojete,* resembling the French *ratatouille,* and the thick round TORTILLA ESPANOLA made with potatoes and onions. There are splendid melons in the autumn, and the best known of Spanish cheeses, the ewe's milk QUESO MANCHEGO, is from these parts.

LA MANCHA produces more white wine than red; most of it is made in large cooperatives, and thanks to cold fermentation, much of the wine is now light and refreshing. The best of the reds are from VALDEPEÑAS.

Apart from those in Madrid, there are few sophisticated restaurants in the region except in Toledo, once the capital of Spain and a fascinating old city with a beautiful cathedral and associations with El Greco. Here the best restaurant is perhaps the Hostal del Cardenal, whose specialties are roast suckling pig and baby lamb roasted in wood-fired ovens, stewed partridge in season and strawberries and asparagus from Aranjuez.

Castilla la Vieja

SPANISH REGION

Castilla la Vieja, stretching from north of MADRID to Santander on the Atlantic coast and westwards to the Portuguese border, is the heartland of Catholic Spain. It has given its name to the Spanish language, and it was from here that the Reconquest of the country from the Moors was begun and that El Cid Campeador set out to conquer VALEN-

CIA. Its cities such as Salamanca, Valladolid, Segovia, Burgos and León are among the most beautiful in Spain and its ochre expanses are variegated in spring by the fresh green of the wheat and in autumn by groves of dazzling yellow *chopos* (Lombardy poplars) and the purple fields of the saffron crocus.

The cuisine has a good deal in common with that of CASTILLA LA NUEVA: COCIDOS are typical of both areas. Great use is made of the GARBANZO bean or chickpea and there is lamb from the rolling plains, partridge and other game, and trout from the cold mountain streams, a good Castilian version being *truchas a la montañesa*, cooked with white wine, bay leaves and onions. Castilla la Vieja is, however, most famous for its roasts of lamb, suckling pig and kid, and is, in fact, known as the *zona de los asados* (the region of roasts). The RIOJA, famous for its wines, also has a well-developed and individual cuisine. Specialties include CORDERO LECHAL ASADO; CHULETAS DE CORDERO; PATATAS RIOJANAS; PIMIENTOS RELLENOS A LA RIOJANA; POCHAS RIOJANAS; MENESTRA A LA RIOJANA; and *melocotones en almíbar* (the fat local peaches preserved in syrup).

Much of the best Spanish table wine is from Castilla La Vieja; its demarcated regions are LA RIOJA, RIBERA DEL DUERO, RUEDA and Toro in the west of the area towards the Portuguese frontier. Worthwhile undemarcated wines are the light reds from Cigales north of Valladolid and the red wines from León, especially those from El Bierzo to the north of the city. Cebreros, between Madrid and Avila, produces gutsy red wine, often sold in litre bottles in Madrid.

There are a great many good restaurants in such a large area. A very personal list includes Terete in Haro for its superb *cordero lechal*; La Merced in Logroño, quite the most elegant of Riojan restaurants with cooking to match the surroundings; El Molino near Santander, the creation of Víctor Merino, one of the founders of the NUEVA COCINA VASCA and mentor of a whole generation of young chefs; the ever-popular if showmanlike Mesón de Cándido in Segovia for its COCHINILLO; and the Mesón de la Villa in Aranda de Duero with its annual *Semana del Cordero* or "Lamb Week".

Castro y Serrano, José

19TH-CENTURY WRITER

From the time when the first of the Spanish Bourbons, Philip V, left France to be crowned King of Spain in 1700, a thoroughgoing feeling of inferiority about the national cuisine vis-à-vis the French spread downwards from court circles. The long and uphill task of reviving pride in the native cuisine was begun in 1885, when Mariano PARDO DE FIGUEROA and José Castro y Serrano published a series of articles under the pseudonyms of *El doctor Thebussem y un* *cocinero de S.M.* (Dr Thebussem and a cook of His Majesty). It was followed by a rash of cookbooks, written in haste and without knowledge, indiscriminately mixing Spanish recipes with others copied from abroad, and it was only during the first decades of the present century that skilled and informed chefs, such as Ignacio DOMENECH and Teodoro BARDAJI, produced large compilations of genuine Spanish recipes.

Cataluña

SPANISH REGION

In gastronomy, as in other matters, Cataluña is one of the richest and most individual regions of Spain. During the Middle Ages, Aragón-Cataluña under the Counts of Barcelona was, after all, the most powerful state of the Mediterranean, and the cuisine benefited from Catalan maritime expansion and the large-scale importation of spices from the East.

The terrain is exceptionally varied, with the great mountain spurs of the Pyrenees descending to the coastal plain of the Mediterranean and the Ebro delta, so that livestock, freshwater and saltwater fish, vegetables and fruit abound. It is divided into four provinces: Gerona, Lérida (or, in Catalan, Lleida), Tarragona and Barcelona. The cities of Gerona, with its fine cathedral,

and Tarragona, with its extensive Roman remains, are fascinating, but in many ways BARCELONA, the second city of Spain, *is* Cataluña. It was certainly here that a renaissance of Catalan cooking began, triggered by the NOUVELLE CUISINE in France.

Spanish food writers constantly return to a magic figure of some hundred different regional specialties and stress that each small locale has its individual way of preparing traditional dishes. One might start with the five basic Catalan sauces: ALIOLI; PICADA; *chanfaina*, akin to the CHILINDRON sauce of Aragón; *sofrito*, made of chopped and fried vegetables (see REFOGADO); and SALSA ROMESCO, named after the small, hot, dried red peppers used to make it. Popular starters are *pan con tomate y jamón* (country bread smeared with olive oil and rubbed with fresh tomatoes and garlic, then sometimes served with cured ham); *espinacas a la catalana* (boiled spinach with pine nuts and raisins); CALCOTADA and *habas a la catalana* (fresh fava beans with black sausage and other ingredients). Fish dishes abound, among them *parrilladas* (mixed grills of

fish); LANGOSTA A LA CATALANA; *rape a la Costa Brava* (monkfish cooked with fresh peas, red peppers, mussels, saffron, white wine, garlic, parsley and lemon); BULLABESA,

akin to the French *bouillabaisse,* and the famous ZARZUELA. A substantial and thoroughly traditional meat dish is the ESCUDELLA I CARN D'OLLA. Favourite desserts are CREMA QUEMADA A LA CATALANA, *mel y mato* (cream cheese with honey) and POSTRE DE MUSICO.

Cataluña makes some 99 per cent of Spanish sparkling wine – see CAVA – and also a wide range of first-rate table wines (described under the demarcated regions of ALELLA, AMPURDAN-COSTA BRAVA, PENEDES, PRIORATO and TARRAGONA). Best known abroad are those from the family firm of

TORRES, which also makes excellent brandy or *coñac,* as it is colloquially known in Spain. Raimat, an undemarcated area in the province of Lérida, is also producing good wines, among them a delicate Chardonnay and fruity and well-balanced Cabernet Sauvignons.

Barcelona is a paradise for diners-out, and its restaurants are separately described. Others of note outside the capital are Eldorado Petit in San Felíu de Guixols, the Hotel-Restaurant Ampurdán near Figueras, Ca'n Gatell and Casa Gatell in Cambrils, and Sol Ric in Tarragona.

P *cataplana*
COOKING UTENSIL

The *cataplana* is a cooking utensil entirely typical of the ALGARVE, the resort coast of southern Portugal. It may be bought in the ironmongers or tinsmiths of places like Portimão away from the seafront and souvenir shops.

It is made in various sizes and has been described as a precursor of the pressure cooker, consisting as it does of two metal halves, shaped like very large and deep saucers, and fitting tightly together. The Portuguese use it for cooking fish, especially for the clams, cockles and mussels so abundant along the Algarve coast. See AMEIJOAS A

MODA DE PORTIMÃO and PEIXE NA CATAPLANA.

The *cataplana* is used on top of the stove and heated directly over the flame rather than in the oven. It is turned at intervals without being opened, thus ensuring even cooking of the contents.

In recipes calling for a *cataplana* you may use a saucepan with a tight fitting lid – as is, in fact, done in other parts of Portugal – although, of course, it is impossible to turn it over and thus to achieve quite the same even cooking; the pan should, therefore, be placed in a hot oven and not on top of the stove.

S *catavino*
A GLASS

A special tulip shaped glass used for tasting wines.

S *cava*
SPARKLING WINE

When Don José Raventos of the old family firm of Codorníu began making the first Spanish wine by the Champagne method, it was known as *champaña.* In deference to the producers in Rheims the description has long been prohibited, but the *cava* wines (some 99 percent from CATALUÑA and 80 percent from its PENEDES district), though

made from different grapes, are produced by exactly the same method with a long second fermentation in bottle in cool cellars. The best of them, like Codorníu, Freixenet, Castellblanch, Segura Viudas and Juvet y Camps, are fruity and refreshing with good mousse and are very reasonably priced.

S P *caviar*
CAVIAR

Caviar was known in Spain as long ago as the sixteenth century, since in Chapter 54 of Don QUIXOTE, Cervantes writes: "They also put before them a black-colored delicacy called 'cabial', made from fish roes." During the years after the Bolshevik Revolution in 1917, caviar was no longer obtainable from

Russia. In the 1920s a small manufactory was started in the Gironde by a Czarist refugee while another was started in SEVILLA by the brothers Nicolás and Jesús de Ibarra y Gómez Rull, who engaged a Rumanian technician to supervise production. It drew on sturgeon from the waters of the Guadal-

---

see also   **Catalan sauce:** *see picada*   **Cauliflower:** *see coliflor*   **Caviar:** *see caviar*

quivir below Sevilla, whose roes had formerly been fed to the pigs. They were, however, judged to be of such interest by 1929 as to merit a monograph commissioned by Dirección General de la Marina Civil y Pesca. The Ibarra factory produced good quality caviar in sufficient quantity to supply the domestic market and to export small amounts. In 1954 the catch of sturgeon from the lower Guadalquivir was 400, but by 1964 it had been so diminished by pollution of the river that the factory closed.

caza, la
caça, la

GAME HUNTING

In Spain, "hunting" is of two kinds. *Caza mayor* refers to the hunting of stags, deer and wild boar in wild districts such as the mountains of ASTURIAS, the Sierra de Gredos west of MADRID or the Sierra de Ronda in ANDALUCIA. *Caza menor* is a much more widespread activity. Along the dusty side roads of the country districts there are signs at every turning labeled *coto privado* (hunting reserved). The Sunday silence of the rolling sierra is punctuated by the crack of guns, and towards evening, as in the days of Don QUIXOTE, the little groups of hunters return with their pouches full of rabbit, hare, quail, woodcock, partridge and pheasant. Grouse is not known in Spain.

The Portuguese are equally keen on rough shooting and hunting (*caça*). Friends of mine regularly cross the border into Spain at weekends for the privilege of shooting in the country on the Spanish side of the border where game is abundant.

cazuelas de barro

EARTHENWARE
CASSEROLES

Cazuelas in all depths and sizes, from the small, shallow dishes used for making HUEVOS A LA FLAMENCA and ANGULAS EN CAZUELA to pots large enough to make a stew for a family of 12, may be bought in shops and markets all over Spain. Inexpensive as they are, it is certainly worth bringing home a set (if weight is no problem when traveling). Apart from their decorative appearance and heat retaining properties, they are excellent cooking utensils since they preserve the flavor of ingredients better than metal pots and pans and can be carefully heated directly over a gas flame.

To prevent a new *cazuela* from cracking over the fire, rub the unglazed base with two or three cloves of garlic and, when the juice has been absorbed, pour in some water and bring it slowly to the boil. Discard the water, and the *cazuela* is ready for use.

Similar earthenware vessels are much used in Portugal, where they are known as TACHOS DE BARRO.

P *cebola*
S *cebolla*

ONION

The onions most often seen in great piles in the open markets of Spain and Portugal are large and hard although smaller onions and scallions – *cebolinhas* in Portugal, and *cebolletas* in Spain – are also available. They are much used in both countries, raw and sliced in salads, in stews or in bases such as the REFOGADO of Portugal and *sofrito* of Spain. Like garlic, onions are widely held to reduce the risk of thrombosis or coronary disease.

P *cebolinhas*

Scallions; see CEBOLA.

S *cebolla*

Onion; see CEBOLA.

S *cebolletas*

Scallions; see CEBOLA.

If Spanish and Portuguese terms differ from each other, the entry in Portuguese, in the majority of cases, is referred to its Spanish equivalent, where you will find information relevant to both countries.

S *Cebrero*

A CHEESE

In common with most Galician cheeses, *Cebrero* is made with cow's milk. It has a most unusual shape resembling that of a very thick-stalked mushroom with a hollow in the top. This is because the cheese, before being pressed in a wooden mold, is enveloped in gauze which is then tied into a knot, leaving the small hole at the center. The interior is creamy and close-textured and fairly sharp in taste, has a fat content of 50 percent, and ripens in 3 to 4 days.

S *cecina de atún*

Dried salted tuna fish; see ATUN.

S *cena*

Evening meal; see HORAS DE COMIDA.

P *cenouras*
S *zanahorias*

CARROTS

Carrots, boiled or sautéed, are a favorite accompaniment to meat in Portugal; they are so sweet that they are also boiled and made into a marmalade.

S *centolla*
P *santola*

SPIDER CRAB

The most common type of crab in Spain and Portugal, the spider crab (*maia squinada*), differs from a larger-bodied type in having a flatter, almost round body and long legs, and in lacking the claws. It is often cooked by removing the top shell, then cooking the meat with white wine before replacing the shell.

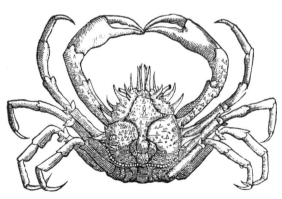

Spider crab

cerdo
carne
de porco
PORK

Pork is the favorite meat in Spain. Every part of the pig is put to good use in making cured meats and sausages (see EMBUTIDOS) as it is in Portugal, and the prince of Spanish pigs is the *cerdo ibérico*, which provides *pata negra* ("black foot"), the most sought-after JAMON SERRANO.

Richard FORD had much to say about these "greyhound-looking animals" fed on acorns (also, as he comments, constantly eaten by ladies of high rank at the Madrid opera) and shut up by the Duke of Arcos "in places abounding in vipers, on which they

fattened". They are, he continues, "the pets of the peasants; they are brought up with their children . . . they are universally respected, and justly, for it is this animal who pays the 'rint'."

Fresh pork is extremely popular in Portugal, as in CARNE DE PORCO A ALENTEJANA, *leitão* (see COCHINILLO) and *bifes de lombo de porco* (small tenderloin escalopes of pork). Examples of Spanish recipes are COCHINILLO ASADO, *lomo de cerdo asado* (roast loin of pork) and *chuletas de cerdo con salsa de tomate* (pork chops with tomato sauce).

cerdo
ibérico

Spanish pig; see CERDO.

Cervantes

16th-century novelist; see QUIXOTE, DON.

The index, in English, is arranged by types of food — eggs, cheese, fish — kitchen equipment, cooking terms and other subjects. Consult it for recipes that make use of particular ingredients.

cervecería
BAR

Cerveza means beer, and a Spanish *cervecería* is a bar, usually with outdoor tables in summer, serving mainly light lager-style beer in *cañas*, but also other drinks and light refreshments.

cervejaria
BAR

The Portuguese equivalent of the Spanish CERVECERIA, serving beer, wine, port, brandy, coffee and soft drinks as well as sandwiches and snacks such as omelets.

Cervera
A CHEESE

Also known as *queso fresco valenciano*, this is a fresh white ewe's milk cheese with a fat content of 67 percent. It is made in the Valencian area and is very similar to Queso de Burgos. It should be eaten immediately.

cerveza

Beer; see CERVECERIA.

chá
TEA

The somewhat unlikely Portuguese word for tea. Served mostly in PASTELARIAS or hotels, it is, as in Spain, usually made with tea bags. In the *casa de chá* or *salões de chá* (tea rooms) fashionable with Portuguese ladies there is, however, no shortage of fine, aromatic teas from the east.

Chacolí
A WINE

The only wine to be made in the wet Basque provinces of Spain. *Chacoli* is a young, fragrant and rather acid wine with a slight bubble, and contains only 9° to 11·5° (percent by volume) of alcohol. Most of it is white and it is drunk locally as an apéritif or with the excellent shellfish from the region.

S *champiñones*

EDIBLE FUNGI

One of the most widely eaten forms of mushrooms. Nowadays *champiñones* are often of the cultivated type and available all year round. See also SETAS.

---

champiñones con ajo y perejil (S)
mushrooms with garlic and parsley

Serves 4 as an appetizer or side dish

1 lb mushrooms
4 tbsp butter
2 cloves garlic, peeled and crushed
3 tbsp chopped parsley
salt and pepper

Sauté the mushrooms gently in the butter until cooked but not overdone. Add the garlic and parsley and season to taste. Serve hot.

P *chanfana à moda da Bairrada*

KID OR LAMB IN RED WINE

From the region north of Coimbra, this dish, like the famous *leitão* (see COCHINILLO) was traditionally cooked in a baker's oven, and the wine reduces to a rich and pungent sauce.

---

chanfana à moda da Bairrada (P)
kid or lamb in red wine

Serves 4

2 lb leg of lamb, boned and cut into large cubes
2 large onions, cut into rings
3 large cloves garlic, finely chopped
pinch of freshly ground black pepper
pinch of ground cloves
1 tbsp chopped parsley
½ lb bacon, chopped
pinch of salt
⅓ cup olive oil
1¼ cups Bairrada or other full-bodied red wine

Put the meat into an earthenware or ovenproof dish, cover with the other ingredients except for the wine, and marinate for about 2 hours, turning occasionally. Pour the red wine over the marinated meat and cook in a fairly hot oven (400°F) for about 1½ hours, tasting from time to time, making sure that the wine has not all evaporated and adding more if necessary. Serve with arroz de manteiga.

S *changurro*

SPIDER CRAB

Basque name for CENTOLLA.

CAPITALIZED *words within entries refer the reader to more information on the same subject.*

chanquetes
TRANSPARENT GOBY

A tiny fish (*Aphia minuta*), very pale pink in color, almost transparent and never more than 2 or 3 inches in length. After being dusted with a mixture of half flour and half breadcrumbs, they are fried in deep oil until crisp.

Along the Costa Brava, a net was traditionally towed out and parties of villagers would then haul it up on to the beach by the two ends, sharing out the great pile of tiny fish – but *chanquetes* have been overfished and there are now very stringent restrictions on the catch.

charcutaria
PORK BUTCHER'S SHOP

A Portuguese shop selling the many varieties of cured ham and sausages such as CHOURIÇOS, EMBUTIBOS, FIAMBRE and PRESUNTO.

Chartreuse
A LIQUEUR

Many well-known French liqueurs are made under licence in Spain, but Chartreuse is a special case. In 1903 the anticlerical policies of the French government resulted in the monks from La Grande Chartreuse transferring lock, stock and barrel to TARRAGONA, where they set up a new distillery. With its palm trees and courtyard fragrant with the smell of herbs, it is still operative (and may be visited) today, though the monks returned to France in 1940. Only three share the secret of compounding the herbs for the famous liqueurs (130 for the green variety and rather fewer for the yellow) and they divide their time between Tarragona and La Grande Chartreuse.

There is no distinguishable difference between the Chartreuse made in France and that made in Spain.

P Châteaubriand
A CUT OF MEAT

This is a French term used in sophisticated Spanish restaurants for porterhouse steak from the sirloin. It is the best cut of beef for cooking A LA PARRILLA. A large fillet taken from the middle of the loin weighs about 1-1½ lb and should be cooked on the hot grid, smeared with olive oil, for about 6 minutes on each side, then rested for 5 minutes before serving.

See also SOLOMILLO.

chilindrón
A SAUCE

This famous spicy, orange-coloured sauce from ARAGON is made with tomatoes, peppers, onions and garlic. It may accompany either chicken or lamb (see CORDERO EN CHILINDRON).

chines
STRAINER

A conical fine mesh strainer much used in Portugal for making vegetable purées etc. Known as *chino* in Spain.

chino

Strainer; see CHINES.

> The index, in English, is arranged by types of food — eggs, cheese, fish — kitchen equipment, cooking terms and other subjects. Consult it for recipes that make use of particular ingredients.

---

see also

Cheese: *see queijos, quesos*   **Chestnut:** *see castaña*
Chicken: *see pollo*

S *chipirones*

Cantabrian squid; see CALAMARES.

S *chirimoya*

A FRUIT

Also known as custard apple, this exotic South American fruit was brought to Spain, not by the CONQUISTADORES, but much later by Spanish emigrants returning from the Andean countries and the Caribbean. Like many other tropical fruits such as kiwis, lichees, pineapple and yucca, it has flourished in the fertile valleys descending from the Sierra Nevada above Granada.

The fruit looks somewhat like a large yellow avocado. Here the resemblance ends, since it is peeled, the large seeds are removed, and it is then cut like a pineapple into thick, juicy slices. Its flavor is rather similar to that of a pineapple, though more delicate.

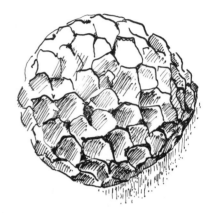

Chirimoya

S *chocolate y cacao*

CHOCOLATE AND COCOA BEANS

The cocoa bean, from which chocolate is prepared, was widely cultivated in Mexico when the first of the CONQUISTADORES under Hernán Cortés invaded the country in 1519. So highly was cocoa appreciated that the beans were used as currency, and it is on record that the city of Tabasco paid the Emperor Montezuma an annual tribute of three "xipuipil" or 24,000 fruit – enough to ensure him his 30 cups of chocolate a day and another 2,000 for his courtiers. Cocoa as drunk then and long afterwards was, however, made by blending the cocoa powder with herbs or honey rather than with sugar.

It is said that Columbus first brought back cocoa beans to Spain, but it was not until Cortés began sending regular supplies after 1519, and in the face of initial opposition, especially from the Church, that chocolate drinking became fashionable. Thereafter, the export of cocoa to other countries was forbidden, although the precious beans formed part of the dowry of Spanish princesses marrying foreign royalty. Indeed MARIA TERESA DE AUSTRIA, daughter of

see also   **Chili:** *see pimenta da Guiné*   **Chocolate:** *see chocolate y cacao*

Philip IV of Spain, was laughed to scorn at Versailles for her black teeth, attributed to her predilection for chocolate (though it appears that chocolate had been introduced to France some 7 years earlier via Italy, where a chocolate factory was established about 1600).

Even the demanding Alexandre DUMAS comments on the excellent breakfast chocolate in Spain, though complaining that it was served in thimblefuls rather than cups. Richard FORD, writing earlier in the 19th century, reported that there was prolonged theological controversy as to whether chocolate did or did not break a fast, and that when it was decided that it did not, "it was made just liquid enough to come within the benefit of clergy, that is, a spoon will almost stand up in it."

Chocolate is still drunk at breakfast in Spain, though generous cupfuls have replaced thimbles, and it is often accompanied by CHURROS.

Hand-made Spanish chocolates of dark, bitter chocolate are also first-rate.

---

chocolate (S)
drinking chocolate

Serves 2

4 oz semisweet chocolate
1¾ cups boiling milk

Using a double boiler, break the chocolate into the inner pan. When it begins to melt, add a little of the boiling milk, stirring with a wooden spoon until the chocolate becomes pasty. Now whisk in the rest of the milk until frothy.

Chocolate should never boil and it is best made the day before use, as the consistency is better if it is left overnight.

---

chocolatería

CHOCOLATE SHOP

When the consumption of drinking chocolate became widespread in Spain in the 18th and 19th centuries, *chocolaterías* serving it made their appearance in MADRID and stayed open all night for the benefit of travelers and the homeless. It was they which first introduced CHURROS.

chocos

Cuttlefish; see CALDEIRADA.

chorizo

SAUSAGE

A spicy, orange-colored, cured sausage, made all over Spain (see also EMBUTIDOS and La MATANZA). It consists of chopped pork mixed with paprika, spices, herbs and garlic. This mixture is put into casings (cleaned intestines of the pig), and the sausages are hung up to dry for a long period. Cut into thin slices, *chorizo* is eaten as an appetizer and also as a piquant ingredient in dishes such as HUEVOS A LA FLAMENCA. Of the many different varieties, three are *chorizo de Pamplona*, made with finely chopped pork;

Two gentlemen drink hot chocolate in a chocolatería

chorizo de Salamanca, containing bigger chunks of pork loin, coarser in texture and concentrated in flavor; and *chorizo de Cantimpalos*, which comes in strings of smaller sausages and is often used for cooking.

Chorizo can be made in a large country kitchen. Follow the instructions for CHOURIÇO, substituting paprika for PIRI-PIRI.

P *chouriço*
SAUSAGES

The best of the Portuguese *chouriços* come from Lamego and the mountainous Chaves with its chestnut forests, across the frontier from the EXTREMADURA, where the Spanish make many of the best of their very similar CHORIZOS. Of the two best-known types of *chouriço*, LINGUIÇA contains finely chopped or ground pork and is most used in *cozidos*, although it may be eaten uncooked. PAIO is a bigger sausage containing larger pieces of pork loin and much resembling LOMO embuchado, a thick Spanish sausage made with pork loin.

To make either of these *chouriços*, the procedure is as follows. First buy the sausage skins or casings. In Portugal, these are available either in markets as dried yellow bundles of gut or at a pork butcher. Wash the skins several times in water with lemon juice, adding a little AGUARDENTE (or brandy) for the last wash. Turn them inside-out and leave to dry. Use the smaller intestines for *linguiça* and the larger ones for *chouriço*.

Grind or chop pork tenderloin and pieces of pork fat, and marinate for 2 or 3 days in an earthenware pot with sweet paprika, garlic, salt and PIRI-PIRI. Transfer to another pot and cover the mixture with white wine (village folk in Portugal use red wine to give the *chouriço* a darker color and a more intense flavor). Leave it to marinate for another 2 or 3 days; in hot weather the period should be reduced. Taste the mixture at this point, first frying a little in hot olive oil to see whether more paprika, garlic, salt and piri-piri are needed. Fill the prepared skins using a funnel of suitable size and tie the sausages at intervals with thread. Finally, hang up the *chouriços* to dry and mature in a kitchen with a wood fire.

S *chufa*
TIGER NUT

The small and wrinkled root of a tuber, resembling a truffle and used for making the refreshing summer drink HORCHATA VALENCIANA.

S *chuleta de buey sin hueso*
P *costeleta de vaca*
A CUT OF MEAT

A slice of meat from the COSTILLA, taken from between the ribs of beef.

> CAPITALIZED *words within entries refer the reader to more information on the same subject.*

S *chuletas de palo o de costilla*
A CUT OF MEAT

Lamb rib chops. They are often cooked A LA PLANCHA, but are especially delicious in the *bodegas* (wineries) of the RIOJA when grilled A LA PARRILLA over the glowing embers of dry grapevines.

P *churrasco*
GRILLED FOOD

Charcoal-grilled meats and chicken are popular in northern Portugal. The restaurants, known as *churrasqueirias* in which they are served, often belong to emigrants who have returned from Brazil, where *churrascos* are a national institution.

---

see also   **Christmas:** *see Navidad*

---

churros

DOUGHNUTS

"Doughnut" is as close a translation as there is. *Churros* are, in fact, golden brown fingers or loops. Made of a dough cooked in smoking hot olive oil, they are popular all over Spain for breakfast or a MERIENDA. They are made fresh every morning in *churrerías*, which later in the day produce potato chips – large, crisp, thick and of a flavor lost in the packaged variety – served in the bars and CERVECERIAS. Until the 1940s and 1950s there

was a *churrera* (*churro* seller) on every street corner in MADRID in the early morning, when the servants emerged to buy their wares for the household. Although Spain, like other countries, is turning to convenience foods such as the packaged "Bimbo" toast, some hotels will still produce *churros* for breakfast if you insist (though they are likely to be a prefabricated frozen variety, deep-fried).

churros (S)
doughnuts

Serves 6

2½ cups slightly salted water or half water and milk
3¼ cups cake flour, sifted
2 eggs
olive oil, for deep frying
confectioners' sugar for dusting

Bring the liquid to the boil in a saucepan over a high heat, add the flour and beat vigorously with a wooden spoon, stirring until the dough no longer sticks to the sides of the pan. Remove
from the heat, add the eggs and continue to stir until the dough is completely smooth.

Now put the dough into a pastry bag fitted with a wide fluted nozzle, heat the oil in a deep frying pan until it smokes, then pipe the mixture into it in dollops shaped like a loop. Fry the churros until golden-brown, then remove them with a slotted spoon, drain them on paper towels to absorb excess oil and transfer to a serving dish. Dust them with sugar before serving.

cilantro

Coriander; see COENTROS.

clavos

Cloves; see CRAVINHOS.

---

see also   **Cider:** *see sidra*   **Cinnamon:** *see canela*   **Clams:** *see almejas*

S *clementina*

CLEMENTINE

A small, sweet, seedless variety of tangerine, grown around VALENCIA and Castellón de la Plana and exported to Japan for crystallizing (see also NARANJA).

S *Club de Gourmets*

A MAGAZINE

Well known and handsomely produced Spanish gastronomic magazine, which organizes an annual spring Salón or food fair in MADRID.

S *coca mallorquina*

SAVORY TART

This Majorcan specialty resembles an Italian pizza and is made from a substantial dough filled with slices of onion, pepper and tomato, sometimes with the addition of anchovies, sardines or tuna and also cooked spinach. It was traditionally, and still is, cooked by country people in their outdoor ovens of stone or brick. The oven is fired with wood or almond shells and allowed to heat until the black deposit of carbon is burnt off the domed roof. The fire is then raked out, the trays of *coca* are slid in, the arched aperture at the front is stopped up

Opposite: Fishermen at Nazaré, Portugal (top) and a market in Castellón, Spain (bottom)

Pages 106-107: The Quinta das Torres in Azeitão, Portugal: this estalagem or inn is renowned for its high standard of cuisine

Page 108: A traditional Valencian kitchen

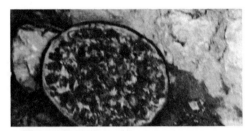

and the *coca* baked for an hour or two until ready. It makes an excellent picnic dish, and portions may be bought at any CONFITERIA to take away.

---

coca mallorquina (S)

savory tart

Serves 4

Pastry
1 oz compressed fresh yeast, or 1 pkg (½ oz) active dried yeast
3 tbsp lukewarm milk
4 tbsp pork fat or lard
⅓ cup olive oil
1 lb all-purpose flour, sifted

Topping
3 red or green peppers, seeded and cut in strips
3 scallions or 1 large onion, chopped
3 medium tomatoes, peeled and sliced
1 clove garlic
1 tbsp chopped parsley
salt

Dissolve the compressed yeast in the milk in a large bowl or if using dried yeast, follow the instructions on the package. Leave for 5 minutes, add the pork fat and oil and then the flour, little by little, kneading the dough with the fingers until it no longer sticks to the sides of the bowl. Shape the dough into a ball, and leave it covered for 1 hour to rise.

Roll out the pastry on a floured surface, then spread it in a rectangular baking pan so that it forms a sheet about ⅜ inch thick. On this, spread out the peppers, onion and tomatoes, finally crushing the garlic onto them, sprinkling on the parsley and seasoning with salt. Bake in a moderate oven (350°F) for 20–30 minutes until the top is golden brown. Eat hot or cold.

Canned sardines or tuna, cut into pieces of suitable size, and also cooked spinach are often added to the layer of vegetables to give additional flavor.

---

see also   *Clementine: see clementina*   *Cloves: see cravinhos*

cochifrito
BRAISED LAMB

Navarra and the Spanish Pyrenees produce a particularly tender milk-fed lamb, known as *Tres Madres* ("Three Mothers") and this is the traditional way of cooking it.

---

cochifrito (S)
braised lamb

Serves 4

4 tbsp olive oil
2 lb milk-fed lamb, cut in large cubes
1 onion, chopped
1 clove garlic, chopped
1 tsp paprika
freshly ground white pepper
1 tbsp chopped parsley
juice of 1 lemon
salt

Heat the oil in a heavy casserole, brown the pieces of lamb and add the onion, garlic, paprika, white pepper, parsley and lemon juice, together with a little salt. Cover and cook slowly over moderate heat for about 1 hour until tender — milk-fed lamb will require less time than meat from an older animal.

Serve from the casserole accompanied by fried potatoes.

---

cochinillo
leitão
SUCKLING PIG

The milk-fed piglets in Spain and Portugal are smaller and more tender than those usually available abroad; they are cooked in a baker's oven.

In Spain, both Avila and Segovia are renowned for their *cochinillo*. Some of the best may be eaten at the Mesón de Cándido, a venerable establishment in the shadow of the great Roman aqueduct in Segovia, founded by a retainer of Henry IV in the 15th century. Here, the meat is so tender that Cándido López cuts it in person at the table with the edge of a plate.

In Portugal, the region best known for its suckling pig is the Bairrada northwest of Coimbra. The capital of the *leitões* is the village of Mealhada on the main road to OPORTO where, at the restaurant of Pedro dos Leitões, the crisply roasted, golden-brown suckling pig of unforgettable tenderness is served straight from the baker's oven on plain wooden tables.

The following Spanish recipe is for special occasions such as Christmas. Ask the butcher to prepare the pig — and give him the measurements of your oven! The piglet may be roasted plain or stuffed.

cochinillo asado (S)

roast suckling pig

Serves 8–10

1 suckling pig, about 6½–9 lb
4 tbsp olive oil
coarse salt

Stuffing
¼ lb sausage meat
½ lb cooked ham, chopped
liver from the piglet, chopped
½ lb mushrooms, chopped
1 medium apple, grated
6 shallots, chopped
2 eggs, beaten
2 tbsp fino sherry
2 cups fresh breadcrumbs
1 tbsp chopped parsley
salt and pepper
1 tsp mixed dried herbs
2 tbsp brandy

Gravy
2 tbsp Málaga wine or oloroso sherry

Garnish
1 small apple

If unstuffed, score the skin of the piglet, rub with oil and salt, and place pieces of foil around the mouth and ears to prevent them blackening during roasting. If it is to be stuffed, do this after sewing it up.

To make the stuffing, mix together all the ingredients, then stuff the mixture into the cavity and sew up with a strong needle and thread.

Place the piglet on an oven rack in a roasting pan, opening it out if unstuffed. Put it in a hot oven (425°F) and roast for 20 minutes basting frequently. Now reduce the heat to fairly hot (375°F) for 20 minutes and lower it to warm (325°F) until the piglet is tender. The total cooking time is about 2½ hours, or a little longer if the piglet is stuffed.

Make the gravy by skimming the fat from the cooking juices in the roasting pan and stirring in the Málaga or sherry; heat until blended. Garnish with an apple in the piglet's mouth.

S *cocido*
P *cozido*

MEAT AND
VEGETABLE STEW

Very similar stews of meat, vegetables and beans are found in France (*pot-au-feu*); in Italy (*bolliti*); and in Spain where they are known as *cocidos*, OLLAS and PUCHEROS, and in Portugal as *cozidos*. Local variants in Spain are the *cocido andaluz*, rich in vegetables and colored with peppers and saffron; the Catalan ESCUDELLA I CARN D'OLLA; and the Galician *pote gallego*, containing a variety of pork meat and white beans. The most famous is the COCIDO CASTELLANO. This noble and substantial stew, a variant of the OLLA PODRIDA beloved by Don QUIXOTE, constitutes a whole meal and is served as three separate courses.

cocido castellano (S)
Castilian meat and vegetable stew

Serves 6–8

1 lb brisket of beef, cut into large pieces
2 marrow bones
1 pig's foot or ham hock, blanched
11 oz dried chickpeas, soaked overnight with a
    pinch of salt and baking soda, then drained
salt to taste
5 oz back bacon, cut into large pieces
1 turnip, cut up coarsely
3 leeks, split lengthways
2 carrots, split lengthways
2 oz estrellita (fine Spanish pasta) or vermicelli
1 lb potatoes, peeled and halved
5 oz chorizo sausage, skinned and cut into
    chunks
5 oz loop of morcilla sausage, pricked

Meatballs (Rellenos)
2 cups fresh breadcrumbs
1 tbsp chopped parsley
1 clove garlic, crushed
salt
3 eggs, beaten
4 tbsp olive oil

Cabbage
2 lb cabbage, cut up coarsely
2 tbsp olive oil
1 clove garlic, chopped

Put the brisket of beef, the marrow bones and pig's foot or ham hock into a large stewpot with a good quantity of water, and bring to the boil over a high heat. Skim off the foam as it boils until the water is clear. Tie the chickpeas in a muslin bag so that they do not distintegrate during cooking and add to the pot, together with a little salt. Reduce the heat, cover and cook gently for 2 hours. Add the back bacon, the turnip, leeks and carrots, and simmer covered for another 30 minutes until the meat is tender. If necessary add a little boiling water during this time to replace any that has evaporated.

Half an hour before serving the cocido, remove a quantity of broth from the stewpot to make the soup. Transfer it to a saucepan, add the estrellita or vermicelli and cook for 10 minutes until al dente, check the seasoning and keep hot.

Meanwhile, make the meatballs by mixing together the breadcrumbs, parsley, garlic, salt and beaten egg. Shape them with the hands into 1½ inch balls and fry in hot olive oil until golden. Transfer to a plate and put to one side.

Add the potatoes, chorizo and morcilla to the stewpot, cook for 5 minutes, then add the meatballs, and cook covered for a further 15 minutes until extremely tender.

In a separate saucepan, boil the cabbage in salted water for 15 minutes, then drain and put to one side. Heat the oil in a pan, sauté the garlic and then add the cabbage, stirring well until glazed. Finally cover to keep it hot.

Serve the different components of the cocido separately, as follows:
1. The soup
2. The chickpeas, removed from the muslin bag and surrounded by the other vegetables including the cabbage.
3. The meat, meatballs, chorizo and morcilla sausage.

cocina

Kitchen; see COZINHA.

cocochas

FISH

Also known as *kokotxas* in the Basque country, where they are considered a great delicacy, these are strips of glandular tissue from the lower part of the hake's jaw. They are fried briefly in olive oil with a little garlic and parsley in the earthenware CAZUELA in which they are served.

see also

Cockles: see améijoas

S P *codornices*

QUAIL

Popular in both Spain and Portugal, *codornices* are delicate birds which are usually marinated and cooked before being preserved in glass jars. This must be done as soon as possible after they have been shot.

They are often cooked in wine and herbs before being wrapped in vine leaves. It is important not to overcook them. I usually allow 20 to 30 minutes for a large bird.

---

codornices al nido (S)
quail in nest

Serves 4

4-8 quail, trussed
½ lb back bacon, cut into strips
⅓ cup pork fat or lard
salt and freshly ground pepper
straw potatoes

Put the quail in a roasting pan and cover the breasts with the strips of back bacon. Melt the fat and pour it on top, then season with the salt and freshly ground pepper. Roast in a preheated moderate oven (350°F) for 20–30 minutes until golden-brown.

Serve in a nest of straw potatoes.

P *coelho*
S *conejo*

RABBIT

Rabbit is popular in Portugal and Spain and features largely in the bag of the rustic weekend hunting parties (see CAZA, LA). The meat of rabbits less than 3 months old is insipid and indigestible; the ideal is a rabbit of between 4 and 12 months. Here are a few Portuguese recipes.

> CAPITALIZED *words within entries refer the reader to more information on the same subject.*

---

coelho à caçadora (P)
hunter's rabbit

Serves 4

2 young rabbits
salt and pepper
olive oil
2 onions, chopped
¼ lb toucinho or bacon, chopped
⅓ lb cooked ham, chopped
1 clove garlic, crushed
1 small glass brandy
⅔ cup dry white wine
1 lb tomatoes, peeled and chopped or 1 lb
   canned tomatoes
fresh thyme
10 oz mushrooms, chopped
4 slices bread

Cut up the rabbits and season with salt and pepper. Heat a little olive oil in a pan and fry together the chopped onion, toucinho and ham for about 10 minutes until the onion is golden, adding the garlic toward the end. Remove with a slotted spoon and keep on a plate.

Sauté the pieces of rabbit in the oil left in the pan until they are browned. Drain off any remaining oil with a spoon, and pour the brandy and white wine over the meat.

Transfer the contents of the frying pan to a saucepan, add the tomatoes, thyme, a little more salt and pepper and the refogado of onion, toucinho and ham. Cover the saucepan and simmer for 1 hour until tender, adding the mushrooms 15 minutes before cooking is finished.

Cut each slice of bread diagonally in four. Fry in hot olive oil until golden brown. Transfer the rabbit and its sauce to a serving dish and arrange the fried bread triangles around it.

coelho à moda de Ranhados

RABBIT IN RED WINE

A highly seasoned rabbit stew from the Douro made with red wine, garlic, parsley, rosemary, pork and small potatoes.

coelho à transmon-tana

RABBIT STEW

Another version of stewed rabbit, made by cooking the cut-up rabbit slowly in a covered pan with onions, parsley, olive oil, BANHA and white wine.

The index, in English, is arranged by types of food — eggs, cheese, fish — kitchen equipment, cooking terms and other subjects. Consult it for recipes that make use of particular ingredients.

coelho guisado com arroz (P)

stewed rabbit with rice

Serves 4

2 young rabbits
1⅓ cups dry white wine
2 onions, chopped
1 carrot, grated
fresh thyme
salt and pepper
4 tbsp banha (lard)
2 cloves garlic, crushed
5 oz chouriço, sliced
4 tomatoes, peeled and chopped
1¼ cups short-grain rice

Cut the rabbit into small pieces and marinate for 30 minutes in a mixture of the white wine,

one chopped onion, the grated carrot, thyme and a little salt and pepper. Transfer to a large saucepan and cook slowly for about 1 hour until the rabbit is tender.

Twenty minutes before the rabbit is done melt the banha (lard) in a large pan and cook the second chopped onion for 10 minutes. Add the crushed garlic, the chouriço, chopped tomatoes, salt and pepper. Measure 2½ cups of water or meat stock and pour into the pan. Now add the rabbit and the rice. Stir well and cook together for 18 minutes until the rice has absorbed all the liquid.

coentros

CORIANDER

In Portugal coriander is the most widely used of all herbs. The leaves and flowers are available all year round. Widely sold in Portuguese markets, they are much used for flavoring vegetable dishes, soups and fish stews. Chopped and used with restraint they give these foods delicious overtones of flavor. The seeds, with their orange-like flavor, employed so lavishly in Middle Eastern and Indian cookery, are not, however, much used in Portugal. Coriander is known as *cilantro* in Spain.

cofradías

Gastronomic societies; see SOCIEDADES GASTRONOMICAS.

cogumelos

Mushrooms; see SETAS.

---

see also   **Coffee:** *see café*

P *Colares*

DEMARCATED WINE REGION

The classic red wines of Colares are made from vines planted deep in the dune sands of the Portuguese coast west of the historic old town of Sintra. For this reason the plants were among the few in Europe never to be attacked by that destructive pest, the phylloxera bug, and are to this day grown ungrafted. The region is small and shrinking and its red wines, tannic and astringent when young, require long years in cask and bottle to emerge at their glorious best.

S *coliflor*
P *couve-flor*

CAULIFLOWER

In Spain, cauliflower is used largely for salads, and the cooked florets are dressed with SALSA VINAGRETA while still hot. Another popular method is to fry the florets as COLIFLOR FRITA. In the Portuguese version of this dish, *couve-flor frita*, the cooked and cut-up cauliflower is dredged in MASSA VINHE and the pieces are then fried in hot olive oil.

In modern Spanish cooking, cauliflower is also served in SALSA BESAMEL to which almonds or pine nuts have been added.

---

coliflor frita (S)
fried cauliflower

Serves 4 as a side dish

1 cauliflower, trimmed
salt
1 egg, beaten
seasoned flour
olive oil

Cook the cauliflower in salted water for 15 minutes. Drain and cut into florets, then dredge in beaten egg and flour and fry in hot olive oil until golden brown.

P *colorau*

HOT PAPRIKA

Made by grinding dried red peppers, *colorau* corresponds to the Spanish PIMENTON *piquante*. It is used extensively in Portuguese cooking to lend piquancy and color to the dishes. Like PIMENTON *dulce, colorau doce* is a sweet paprika.

S *Comida*

Lunch; see HORAS DE COMIDA.

P *cominho*

Cumin; see COMINO.

S *comino*

CUMIN

The cumin plant, an annual with pink flowers, grows wild near the Nile and is mentioned in the Bible. It was introduced to southern Europe in the Middle Ages, and the aromatic fruits, improperly called seeds, are used to enhance salads, breads, cakes and pastries, and GAZPACHOS.

S *coñac*

SPANISH BRANDY

Much to the annoyance of the French producers, this is what most Spaniards call Spanish brandy. Unlike cognac, the bulk of it is made from grape spirit continuously distilled from surplus grapes up and down Spain in large, steam-heated columns in the manner of grain whisky. It is then transported to Jerez de la Frontera and aged by the SOLERA system, like SHERRY. Some of the

Catalan brandy, notably the TORRES "Black Label" and Mascaró, is made by double distillation in small Charentais-type stills, like cognac, but the typical Spanish brandy is darker and a little sweeter than cognac.

conchas de peregrino
FRIED SCALLOPS IN TOMATO SAUCE

A specialty from Galicia prepared by frying scallops briefly in olive oil and flavoring them with parsley, thyme, salt and pepper. They are then flamed in brandy, put into their original shells or into individual CAZUELAS, topped with SALSA DE TOMATE and browned in the oven for 10 minutes.

Condado de Huelva
DEMARCATED WINE REGION

Huelva, in the far southwestern corner of Spain, has been known for its sherry-like wines since Chaucer wrote of their "fumosi-tée" in his *Pardoner's Tale*. Much of the better wine was, in fact, sent to Jerez for blending with SHERRY. The region also produces white wines, and determined efforts are being made to publicize and export them.

conejo

Rabbit; see COELHO.

The seal of the Condado de Huelva demarcated wine region

confitería
CONFECTIONER'S SHOP

In addition to selling cakes and candies, many of them of Moorish origin, and made from almonds and eggs – such as YEMAS DE SANTA TERESA, *yemas de coco* (coconut candies), *bocadillos de monja* (almond and egg candies), *melindres de yepes* (marzipan candies) — and marzipan generally, the Spanish *confitería* also sells a wide range of brandies and liqueurs.

Conquista-dores

After the discovery of America by Columbus in 1492, the Conquistadores moved in to explore the vast New World and to appropriate it for Spain. Hernán Cortés occupied Mexico, Francisco Pizarro, Peru, and Pedro de Valdivia, Chile. With a handful of troops and with horses that terrified the Indians, who had never seen them before, they rapidly conquered a continent. Their epic exploits, insatiable demand for gold and silver, and missionary zeal resulted in the brutal overthrow of the ancient civilizations of the Aztecs and the Incas. On the credit side, they brought back to Spain a wealth of new plants for culinary purposes. The kitchens of Western Europe

remained innocent of such present-day staples as potatoes, tomatoes, PIMIENTOS and chocolate until they were acclimatized and grown in Spain and elsewhere. For example, potatoes were first grown in Europe in the area around Málaga at the suggestion of the Catholic Monarchs, Ferdinand and Isabel.

> CAPITALIZED *words within entries refer the reader to more information on the same subject.*

---

see also

Confectioner's shop: *see confitería, pastelaria, pastelería*
Cooker: *see fogón*   **Cookies:** *see biscoitos*

P *coração*

Heart; see DESPOJOS.

P *corar*

Sauté; see SALTEAR.

S *corazón*

Heart; see DESPOJOS.

S *cordero*

LAMB

Lamb is popular in Spain and eaten more than in Portugal. See also CHULETAS DE PALO O DE COSTILLA and COCHIFRITO.

---

cordero en chilindrón (S)
lamb in chilindrón sauce

Serves 4

4 tbsp olive oil
1 onion, coarsely chopped
3 cloves garlic, chopped
1 parsley sprig
4 large tomatoes, peeled and chopped
3 oz bacon, finely chopped
2 lb lamb rib chops
6 canned red peppers (pimentos), drained and cut into strips
salt and pepper
2 tbsp chopped parsley

Heat 2 tbsp of the oil in a frying pan and add the onion, 1 chopped garlic clove and the parsley. Cook slowly for 5 minutes, then stir in the tomatoes and continue cooking for another 10 minutes until the flavors are well blended.

Heat the rest of the oil in a casserole and add the bacon and the lamb. Brown the meat, then add the remaining garlic, the contents of the frying pan and the red peppers. Season with salt and pepper, cover and cook slowly for 1 hour or until the meat is tender. Sprinkle with chopped parsley before serving.

---

cordero lechal asado (S)
roast baby lamb

Serves 4-6

½ baby lamb (lechazo) or 1 leg of spring lamb
2 to 3 cloves of garlic, crushed
salt and pepper
5 tbsp dry white wine

Season the lamb with the garlic, salt and pepper, put it in a roasting pan with the wine and leave to marinate for 1–2 hours. Roast in a fairly hot oven (400°F) for 20 minutes, then reduce the temperature to moderate (250°F) for

the remainder of the time, cooking it a total of 15–20 minutes per pound until the lamb is browned on the outside and pink inside. Baste from time to time with the meat juices. To make a gravy, skim off the fat from the juices in the roasting pan, add a little more wine, and heat gently, stirring well, until blended.

Serve with mashed or fried potatoes.

S **P**

carne

CUTS OF MEAT

The Spaniards and Portuguese cut meat more in the style of the French than do the British or Americans. Details will be found under individual cuts of meat, for example CHULETAS, MEDALLONES, etc (see index).

---

see also **Corn:** *see* maíz

P *costeleta*

A CUT OF MEAT

A cutlet or chop, usually boneless. *Costeletas de porco à alentejana* are marinated for 24 hours with garlic, salt, pepper, white wine and red *pimentón* (paprika). They are then dredged in beaten egg, fried until crisp and served with slices of fresh orange.

S *costillas*

A CUT OF MEAT

Spare ribs of pork or fore ribs of beef. In Spain, these are mainly fried until crisp or grilled over charcoal.

> *The index, in English, is arranged by types of food — eggs, cheese, fish — kitchen equipment, cooking terms and other subjects. Consult it for recipes that make use of particular ingredients.*

P *couve*

Portuguese cabbage; see CALDO VERDE.

P *couve-flor*

Cauliflower; see COLIFLOR.

P *cozido*

Meat and vegetable stew; see COCIDO.

P *cozido à portuguesa*

MEAT AND VEGETABLE STEW

This dish has been known from the earliest times and was originally, like the famous stew from La Mancha (OLLA PODRIDA), called *olha podrida*. There are numerous different versions: *cozido do Minho* contains boiling fowl, PRESUNTO, cow's meat, pig's ear, *toucinho* (bacon), CHOURIÇOS of different types, cabbage stalks, carrots and potatoes; *cozido de Tràs-os-Montes* is made with pig's ear, snout, feet and tail, leg of ham, *toucinho*, ham bones, veal, chicken, cured sausage and *chouriços*, cabbage stalks, carrots, turnips and potatoes; *cozido das Beiras* has a smaller variety of meat than that from TRAS-OS-MONTES, but includes the SALPICÃO sausage; *cozido alentejano* (also known as *cozido de grão con vagens*) contains no cow's meat, but includes baby lamb, *toucinho*, LINGUIÇA and FARINHEIRA, together with chick-peas, *vagens* (green beans) and pumpkin. There are two types of *cozido de Algarvio*. The first, *cozido de grão*, is made with chick-peas, mutton, *linguiça*, *toucinho*, green beans, pumpkin and potatoes. The second, *cozido de repolho*, contains tight cabbage, accompanied by *chouriço*, ribs of pork, *toucinho*, kidney or butter beans, potatoes and sweet potatoes.

The recipe that follows is for a hearty meat stew from the mountainous north of Portugal, more appropriate for a cold winter's day and large family appetites than for a dinner party. The more varied the meat, the better the dish will be.

---

cozido à portuguesa (P)
meat and vegetable stew

Serves 8–10

2 lb stewing veal, cut into pieces
1 lb chicken, cut into pieces
1 lb fresh brisket of beef (in Portugal, use carne de vaca), rolled in one piece
1 pig's foot, blanched
1 ham bone (optional) to enrich the flavor
½ lb presunto or ham, coarsely chopped
½ lb chouriço sausage
2 turnips, coarsely chopped
2 carrots, coarsely chopped
4 potatoes, coarsely chopped
2 onions, coarsely chopped
6 oz green beans, coarsely chopped
1 cup short-grain rice
fresh mint
salt

Leave the veal, chicken, beef, pig's foot, ham bone and presunto (ham) in cold water for 30 minutes so as to soak out any blood, then rinse and bring to the boil in cold water, covering the meat. Skim off the white foam with a spoon and simmer gently until all the meat is tender. The time that this requires will depend upon the meat, but 1–2 hours are usually sufficient, if the pieces are not too big. After cooking 1 hour, add the chouriço and all the vegetables except the rice and mint and continue simmering gently for 30 minutes longer until very tender, then season to taste.

Remove 2 cups of the broth and use it to cook the rice, together with the mint and a little salt, for 18 minutes, then allow to stand for 10 minutes.

Serve the stew in a large dish with the meat in the middle and the vegetables arranged around it. Slice the chouriço and place on top of the rice, which is served separately.

Any broth that is left can be used for making other soups.

P *cozinha*
S *cocina*
KITCHEN

Fine examples of traditional Portuguese kitchens on the grand scale are those of the Royal Palace in Sintra with its huge conical chimney, the Ducal Palace in Vila Viçosa with its dazzling copper utensils, and the monastery of Alcobaça where a stream runs through the center (see also CUARESMA).

There is a splendid reconstruction of a typical tiled Valencian kitchen, complete with utensils, in the palace of the Marqués de dos Aguas in VALENCIA, now a magnificent museum of ceramics.

Today's kitchens in Spain and Portugal are equipped, as elsewhere, with refrigerators, freezers and food processors, etc. In Spain there are also earthenware CAZUELAS in a range of shapes and sizes. Every kitchen boasts a PAELLERA for cooking paella and mortars for crushing garlic and saffron are very much in evidence. A feature of the well-equipped Portuguese kitchen is the assortment of molds used in preparing the popular egg-based sweets.

P *cravinhos*
S *clavos*
CLOVES

The flower buds of the clove tree, a native of the Molucca Islands, cloves were first brought to Europe and traded in the *Casa de India* in Lisbon in the mid-16th century, as a result of Vasco da GAMA's voyages of discovery and the later mercantile expansion of the Portuguese in the Far East.

Cloves were named as such because of their shape – in Portuguese, *cravinho* means "a small nail". They are much used in Portugal and Spain, since their strong aromatic flavor enhances marinades and many types of dishes generally.

---

see also   **Cream:** *see nata*

---

crema pastelaria

Confectioners' custard or pastry cream; see CREMA PASTELERA.

crema pastelera
crema pastelaria

CONFECTIONERS'
CUSTARD OR PASTRY
CREAM

Much used for cakes sold in the PASTELERIAS such as *milhojas* (layers of puff pastry sandwiched with *crema pastelera*). It is made by beating flour into hot milk and cooking until thick and smooth. Sugar, egg yolks and flavoring of lemon zest are added, and when cool, stiffly beaten egg whites are folded into the mixture. See also BARTOLILLOS and LIONESAS.

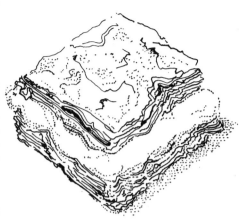

crema quemada a la catalana

BAKED CUSTARD
WITH BRITTLE
CARAMEL

A version of the very well known FLAN DE HUEVOS, this is the most popular of Catalan desserts.

---

crema quemada a la catalana (S)
baked custard with brittle caramel

Serves 6

6 egg yolks, beaten
2½ tbsp cornstarch
1¼ cups confectioners' sugar
2 cups milk
1 cinnamon stick
zest of 1 lemon
2 tbsp brown sugar

Put the egg yolks in a bowl with the cornstarch and confectioners' sugar. Simmer the milk with the cinnamon stick and lemon zest, then add the egg mixture and cook slowly, stirring to avoid lumps until the custard thickens — do not boil it. This may be done in a double boiler or in a

saucepan placed in a larger pan of simmering water. Remove the cinnamon stick and lemon zest, divide the custard between 6 3 inch ramekins, and leave in the refrigerator overnight.

Before serving, sprinkle the top with brown sugar and leave for a few seconds under a hot broiler, then cool. Do this about 30 minutes beforehand so that the caramel remains crisp.

In Spain, the sugar is caramelized with a salamandra heated on a brazier or gas flame. It is obtainable also in specialized shops in the UK and USA.

---

criadilhas

Testicles; see CRIADILLAS.

criadillas

TESTICLES

Testicles are considered a delicacy in Spain and Portugal. They are usually cut into strips and fried in seasoned flour, egg and breadcrumbs. The best are those of lamb and veal.

If Spanish and Portuguese terms differ from each other, the entry in Portuguese, in the majority of cases, is referred to its Spanish equivalent, where you will find information relevant to both countries.

S *croquetas de jamón*
HAM CROQUETTES

Served with a green or tomato salad, these croquettes, which may also be made with ground cooked chicken, flaked fish, shrimp or hard boiled eggs, make a delightful, light supper dish.

---

croquetas de jamón (S)
ham croquettes

Serves 2 (or 4 as an appetizer)

4 tbsp butter
¾ cup flour
2 cups hot milk
7 oz cooked ham, finely chopped or
*   ground (2½ cups)*
salt
pinch of nutmeg
flour, for coating
1 egg, beaten
breadcrumbs
olive oil, for frying

Melt the butter in a saucepan, add the flour and pour in the hot milk, stirring constantly. Cook for 5 minutes, then add the ham, salt and nutmeg. Continue cooking slowly for 10 minutes or until thick, then transfer the mixture to a plate and leave until cool. Shape into croquettes with two spoons or with your hands, then dredge in flour, beaten egg and breadcrumbs, and fry in hot olive oil until golden. Drain well on paper towels and serve hot, accompanied by a green salad.

S *Cuaresma*
P *Quaresma*
LENT

Lent and a regime of abstinence and fasting have traditionally been taken very seriously in Spain, though the wealthy escaped its privations by falling back on a splendid repertoire of *bacalao* (see BACALHAU) in all its guises, of which a Spanish writer remarks that the "hyperborean Norwegians and Scots (who supply the delicacy) have not the remotest idea". The fast might also be side-stepped by the acquistition for the very moderate sum of a *bula* (dispensation), enabling the purchaser to partake of meat

---

see also   ***Cumin:*** *see comino*   ***Curry powder:*** *see caril*
               Cuttlefish: *see sepia*

without the fear of being consigned to purgatory. As José Blanco White (1775–1841) remarked, Lent made little difference for the urban poor as they could not afford meat and were lucky if they ate bread and vegetables once a day.

Lent was also strictly observed in Portugal – though the chronicler of the great Monastery of Alcobaça, Frei Manoel dos Santos, has an amusing anecdote about the evasion of the fast by certain erring brothers. Flowing through the kitchens of the monastery there is a fast-running stream. Some of the food-loving brethren working in the fields drove into its upper waters a collection of pigs, lambs and calves, quickly retrieving them with exclamations of "See, brothers, what strange fish the river brings us today!" So, the chronicler adds, did gastronomy triumph over theology.

The *bula* goes back to the time of the Catholic Monarchs in the 15th century and was granted separately to Portugal at the same period. Its terms were varied over the centuries and it was promulgated in its final form by Pope Pius XI in 1928, and renewed by Pope Pius XII only on an annual basis from 1940. It was finally discontinued by Pope Paul VI in 1966.

P *Dão*
DEMARCATED WINE REGION

The Dão in central Portugal, which produces the best known of red Portuguese table wines, is situated to the northwest of Coimbra and is shut off by high mountains on its other sides. The focus of the region and of the wine industry is the old town of Viseu where some six Roman roads meet. It was also the home of the painter Grão Vasco, a master of the Primitive School, who has given his name to one of the best wines. Production is dominated by ten large co-operatives, from which the private firms buy wine, blending it and maturing it in oak barrels and selling it under their own labels. The wines are smooth, fruity and full-bodied, though without a great deal of bouquet, and extremely consistent. Smaller amounts of white wine are made. Formerly rather earthy and on occasion somewhat maderized (i.e. with a hint of madeira or sherry in the flavor), they are now being made in lighter and fresher style by cold fermentation.

S *dátil*
DATE

Thanks to the mild climate and an intricate irrigation system, the palm groves of Elche, south of Alicante, are unique in Europe, extending to some 100,000 trees. There is a large crop of excellent dates in winter, and the leaves are used for the Palm Sunday processions and for artisan work.

Dates are usually eaten as a dessert but a specialty of Elche is an omelet with dates, containing also JAMON SERRANO, sometimes prawns and a little SALSA DE TOMATE.

S *dátil de mar*
SEA DATE

You will occasionally see *sopa de dátiles* on a Spanish menu; this does not mean "date soup" but describes a delicious chowder made from a small, dark brown mussel (*Lithodomus lithophagus*) fished off the coast of the LEVANTE, especially around Peñíscola and Benicarló.

S *desayuno*

Breakfast; see HORAS DE COMIDA.

S *despojos*
VARIETY MEATS

These are cooked very widely in Spain and Portugal, where you will find special stalls in the markets selling nothing else. The Spanish and Portuguese names of the different varieties are: SESOS and *miolos* (brains), *higado* and ISCAS, *figado*, *corazón* and *coração* (heart), *riñones* and RIM, *mollejas* and *molejas* (sweetbreads), LENGUA and *lingua* (tongue), *callos* and DOBRADA or TRIPAS, and CRIADIL-

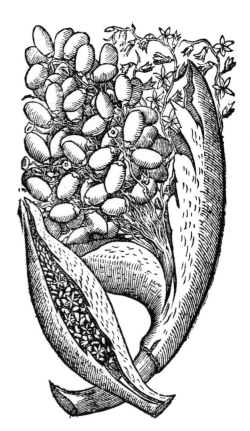

Ripening dates

LAS. Sweetbreads are cooked in exactly the same way as brains, and both make good omelets (see also ANDALUCIA).

---

see also **Date:** *see dátil*

🄿 *dobrada*

TRIPE

Tripe is known as both *dobrada* and *tripa* in Portugal. The recipe that follows is a version popular in LISBOA and the south. See also TRIPAS and TRIPAS A MODO DO PORTO.

---

dobrada à portuguesa (P)
tripe with beans

Serves 8

1 lb dried white beans, soaked overnight drained and rinsed
2 onions, peeled
2 cloves garlic, chopped
¼ lb toucinho or bacon, cut into strips
½ lb chouriço sausage, chopped
1 thyme sprig
⅓ cup dry white wine
4 tomatoes, peeled and cut up coarsely
1 cup stock, made from a cube
1 tbsp flour
½ lb presunto or ham, chopped
2 carrots, diced
2 lb tripe, cleaned, boiled and cut into strips or squares
salt and pepper
3 tbsp port wine

Put the beans in a saucepan, cover with cold water and add a whole onion. Bring to the boil and simmer for 2½ hours or more, until the beans are tender. Drain and reserve.

Finely chop the other onion and sauté it slowly with the garlic, toucinho and chouriço. No fat or oil is required since the toucinho or bacon has enough. After 10 minutes, add the thyme and white wine. Continue to fry slowly until the liquid is reduced by half, then add the tomatoes, stock, flour (previously stirred into a little cold water), the presunto (ham) and diced carrots, and cook the mixture for a few minutes.

Transfer the mixture to a stewpot and stir in the tripe and reserved beans. Season with salt and pepper and add the port. Cook slowly for a further 30 minutes before serving.

🄿 *doce de chila*

CANDIED SQUASH

In the shape of thin strands, *abóbora* (a special squash or pumpkin), candied and flavored with lemon, is to be found in every Portuguese kitchen. It is made once a year and bottled, and is obtainable from food stores or may be prepared somewhat laboriously at home by pulling out the threads, cooking them and immersing them in hot syrup. *Chila* may be used as an ingredient in many tarts and puddings and especially in egg desserts such as MORGADO and TOUCINHO DO CEU.

◀ *Doctor Thebussem*

Pseudonym of cookery writer; see CASTROY SERRANO, JOSE.

Doménech, Ignacio

EARLY 20TH-CENTURY CHEF AND WRITER

Ignacio Doménech was one of a small band of dedicated chefs and writers who, at the turn of the century, set about the uphill task of retrieving authentic Spanish recipes and restoring the tarnished reputation of the Spanish cuisine (see FRANCIA). A Catalan by birth, he was, during his long career, director of cuisine for the Dukes of Medinaceli in SEVILLA, the Marquesa de Argüelles, the Prince of Wrede and the embassies of the United Kingdom, Sweden and Norway in Madrid. Among some dozen books, his best known are the comprehensive *La nueva cocina elegante española* (New and Elegant Spanish Cookery) – a book conceived on the grand scale of *Mrs Beeton's Cookery and Household Management* – and an equally detailed and reliable manual of Catalan cooking: *Apats. Magnific manual de cuina practica catalana, adequat a tots els gustos i mas variat i seleccionat de Catalunya* (The Magnificent Manual of Practical Catalan Cooking, suited to all tasks and with the widest and most varied selection of Catalan dishes). He was also editor of the influential culinary magazine *El Gorro Blanco* (The Chef's Hat), first published in Madrid in 1906 and later in BARCELONA.

⑤ *Don Quixote*

17th-century novel; see QUIXOTE, DON.

⑤ *dorada a la sal*
GILTHEAD BREAM IN SEA SALT CRUST

Cooking fish in a crust of sea salt is a method particularly used in ANDALUCIA. During cooking, the salt hardens, sealing in all the juices without imparting a salty flavor; and the removal of the crust at the table by a waiter is something of a ceremony. Both gilthead bream and URTA are delicious when cooked in this manner.

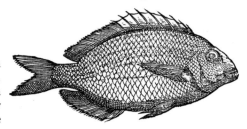
Gilthead bream

⑭ *Douro*
DEMARCATED WINE REGION

The Douro valley was delimited for the production of port by the Marquês de Pombal as long ago as 1756, but it was only in 1979 that it was demarcated for table wines. This was to take account of the fact that only about 40 per cent of production from the area, stretching from the Spanish frontier to a point rather below Regua, is of port. Red and white beverage wines account for the remaining 60 per cent. Over the last years there has been a marked improvement in the quality of these wines, of which the best are the reds. Among the most drinkable are the Vila Real reds from the makers of the famous MATEUS ROSE, "Evel" and the superior and intensely fruity wines from the Quinta do Côtto; but the star of the Douro reds is the near legendary "Barca Velha", made in very limited amounts in exceptional years, and obtainable only in Portugal itself at the best restaurants and hotels.

see also   *Doughnuts: see churros*

Douro

PORTUGUESE REGION

This is a small region centering on the city of OPORTO and bordered by the River Douro to the south. The land rises steeply to the east towards the bare granite heights of the Serras do Geres, Soajo and Marǎo. Elsewhere, the land is intensively cultivated by a host of small landholders and the fields are enclosed by hedges and climbing vines, used for making VINHOS VERDES. The port vineyards lie further east and higher up the Douro Valley.

The regional cooking has much in common with that of the MINHO bordering the region to the north. Recipes of interest include BOLA DE CARNE, BACALHAU A LISBONENSE, COELHO A MODA DE RANHADOS, CAÇÃO EM VINHO TINTO and TRIPAS A MODA DO PORTO.

Dumas, Alexandre

19TH-CENTURY FRENCH WRITER

In 1846 Alexandre Dumas, then at the peak of his literary career, undertook an extended visit to Spain, as a result of which he wrote the sparkling five volume *Paris to Cádiz*. He was vividly interested in gastronomy and the book is full of acute observations on contemporary Spanish food and eating habits.

In spite of his commendations of the drinking chocolate (see CHOCOLATE Y CACAO) and saffron soup, he was, in general, highly critical, and commented that the raw materials were first rate, but that "if people eat but poorly in Spain, it is, quite frankly, because they will not take the trouble to eat well". No mean hand in the kitchen, he would, therefore, insist on preparing the food himself in the hostelries along the way, writing of an innkeeper in Madrid that "he did me the honour of taking me for some celebrated French *maître-chef* . . . I left him with this impression, which placed me far higher in his esteem than if I had told him that I was the author of *The Three Musketeers* or of *Monte-Cristo*."

Much later in life, Dumas wrote the monumental *Le Grand Dictionnaire de Cuisine* – it was, in fact, his last work and was

see also   *Duck: see pato*

published in 1873, three years after his death. In it, his interest in Spain is reflected in the fact that out of nineteen and a half pages on *Cuisine, Cuisinier, Cuisinière*, no fewer than seventeen are devoted to Spanish cooking. Unfortunately, none of this material has been retained in the abridged English edition of Alan and Jane Davidson published by the Oxford University Press, so that the interested reader must refer to the French original.

Although Dumas' judgments on Spanish cooking were severe, he *was* impressed with what he found in Galicia (see ASTURIAS AND GALICIA) and this inspired a typical outburst: "The difference between the Castilian and the Galician is that the Castilian subsists on bread, cheese and chick-peas, and the Galician on bread made of maize or rye and on greens. We cannot say whether it is the diet or the climate which makes them so different; the Galician is straightforward, hospitable and polite, both to his own folk and foreigners; whereas the Castilian is quarrelsome, off-hand, inhospitable and proud, and has no use for the French or even Spaniards from other provinces."

Dumas, Alexandre fils

19TH-CENTURY FRENCH WRITER

Alexandre Dumas *fils* was also interested in Spain. His first visit was with his father in 1846 as a young man of 22 in the wake of his love affair with Marie Duplessis, who inspired *La Dame aux Camélias*. Later, in 1872, he returned and has left an amusing note about the drinking habits of the Aragonese: "One of the most unexpected difficulties encountered by the traveler in certain regions of Spain, especially Navarra and Bajo Aragón, is their method of drinking. It is hard to find glasses, and as it is necessary to drink, they put on the table a sort of bottle of about a litre or a litre and a half, and each member of the party must drink from it without touching it with his lips. This is most uncomfortable for the inexperienced stranger. And if he inadvertently touches the bottle with his lips, the others pour the wine over his face and load him with insults."

el aliño
DRESSING OR SEASONING

This refers to a dressing or seasoning in general and is not a recipe. In Spanish restaurants, salads are always served without dressing and the waiter will ask "¿ le aliño la ensalada?" ("Shall I dress the salad for you?"). If the answer is "si" ("yes"), he will do so, usually with oil, vinegar and salt.

embutidos
CURED MEAT AND SAUSAGES

This is the Spanish term used to describe the wide range of products made by curing pork, e.g. hams, bacon, sausages, etc. These are individually described under BUTIFARRA, CHORIZO, JAMON DE JABUGO, JAMON SERRANO, JAMON DE YORK, LOMO, LONGANIZA, MORCIL-LA, SOBRASADA and TOCINO.

Portuguese cured meats (see CHARCUTAR-IA) are listed under AZEDOS, BOCHEIRAS, CHOURIÇO, FIAMBRE, LINGUIÇA, MORCELA, PAIO and PRESUNTO. See also La MATANZA.

ementa

Menu; see MENU.

empanada gallega
SAVORY TART

One of the best-known of Galician dishes, this thick, substantial tart may contain either meat or fish, often sardines.

---

empanada gallega (S)
savory tart

Serves 6

Pastry
2⅓ cups bread flour, sifted
1 oz fresh yeast or ½ oz active dry yeast,
*   reconstituted*
¼ cup olive oil
¼ cup milk and water, mixed
1 small egg, beaten

Filling
¼ cup olive oil
1 onion, chopped
¼ lb tomatoes, peeled and chopped
2 canned red peppers (pimentos), cut in strips
½ lb cooked ham, diced
½ lb chorizo sausage, diced

Put ⅔ cup of the flour into a bowl, making a well in the center. Dissolve the fresh yeast in a little warm water or follow the instructions on the package if using dried yeast, then pour it into the flour and add the oil, milk, water and beaten egg. Knead into a smooth, elastic dough, flouring your hands and working the mixture very thoroughly until it forms a single smooth and compact whole. Cover with a clean dish towel or plastic wrap and allow to rest in a warm place for 1 hour. Ready-made puff pastry will give acceptable results if you do not wish to make your own.

Meanwhile, make the filling. Heat the oil in a pan, sauté the onion until golden and drain off the oil. Stir in the tomatoes and peppers, cook for a few minutes more, then add the ham and chorizo. Stir well and allow the mixture to cool on a plate.

Divide the dough in half and roll out each piece on a pastry board or marble slab to fit a 12 inch diameter baking tray. Use one-half to line the tray, and spread the filling on it. Place the other sheet of dough on top, cut around it, seal the edges and brush with beaten egg. Let rise for 20 minutes, then bake in a fairly hot oven (375°F) for 40–50 minutes until the pastry is golden.

---

see also

Easter: see Pascua   **Edible fungi:** see setas
Eels: see angulas   **Eggplant:** see berenjenas   **Eggs:** see huevos

S *empana-dillas valencianas*

SAVORY PASTRIES

These look rather like Cornish pasties, but the flavor is much more piquant. Both pastry and filling may be made several hours before serving.

empanadillas valencianas (S)
savory pastries

Serves 4–6

Pastry
3½ cups self-rising flour
¾ cup soft unsalted butter
pinch of salt
2 tbsp fino sherry
2 tbsp cold water

Filling
1 tbsp olive oil, plus more for frying
1 large onion, chopped
4 large tomatoes, peeled and chopped
1 green pepper, seeded and chopped
2–3 fillets smoked haddock (or similar fish), poached, skinned, boned and flaked
½ lb cooked lean ham, chopped
salt and pepper

Put the flour into a bowl, make a well in the center, and add the butter (using a little more if necessary), a pinch of salt, the sherry and water. Knead together thoroughly until elastic, adding more water if needed, then cover and leave in the bowl for 1 hour or longer. The dough may also be made in a food processor.

To make the filling, heat the oil in a frying pan, sauté the onion for 10 minutes, then remove the oil, keeping it for further use. Add the tomatoes and pepper, and cook for about 30 minutes until soft. Add the fish, ham and salt and pepper, and cook together for a further 10 minutes. Cool on a plate.

Roll out the pastry thinly on a floured surface. Place a heaping tablespoon of the filling on it, away from the edge. Cut the surrounding pastry in a 4 inch circle with a pastry cutter, leaving sufficient border to fold over in a half-moon shape, and seal the edges with a fork – this is important so that the filling does not leak out when frying. Repeat with the remaining filling and pastry, rolling out the pastry again when all the large areas have been used up. Put the turnovers on a large floured board until you are ready to fry them.

About 30 minutes before serving the empanadillas, heat about 1 inch of olive oil in a deep frying pan, and fry the turnovers, basting until golden-brown so as to avoid turning them over. With the amounts given, it will be necessary to cook them in batches. Alternatively, they may be deep fried.

Serve with a green salad.

S *empared-ados de ternera y jamón*

FRIED VEAL AND HAM

Serves 4

4 large veal escalopes
4 thin slices cooked ham
1 egg, beaten
breadcrumbs
½ cup olive oil
4 tbsp butter

Beat the escalopes until thin, cut each in two and make a sandwich with the ham, pinning it with toothpicks broken in half. Dredge in egg and breadcrumbs. Sauté the coated escalopes in oil and butter heated together until browned both sides, then reduce the heat and cook until the meat is done, turning occasionally. Increase the heat again toward the end to ensure that the escalopes are brown.

Serve with *pimientos verdes fritos*.

S *ensaimada*

A BREAD

A specialty of Majorca, *ensaimadas* are eaten at breakfast with coffee or chocolate. Light, fluffy, a little sweet – half-way between a bun and a pastry – and shaped rather like a Moorish turban, they are one of the few genuinely Majorcan things to be served in the resort hotels. It seems that they cannot properly be made except on the Islands, and large consignments are shipped to BARCELONA and other areas on the mainland.

In addition to the small breakfast *ensaima-*das, there are also much larger and more elaborate versions which are served as a sweet. These can be as much as 10 inches across and may be topped with cream or CABELLO DE ANGEL or filled with almond paste. For fiestas it is traditional to decorate them with slices of SOBRASADA and squash.

ensaladas *saladas*

SALADS

Salads are especially popular in hot countries and Spain and Portugal are no exceptions. Favorite ingredients, often in a bed of lettuce, are cooked fish, anchovies, hard-boiled eggs, shellfish as well as tomatoes, peppers, capers, radishes and cucumber. The dressing is generally a good SALSA VINAGRETA made with virgin or refined olive oil and sherry vinegar (or lemon juice in deference to wine-lovers) and with garlic and parsley. In Portugal, fresh coriander leaves are often used instead of parsley.

> CAPITALIZED *words within entries refer the reader to more information on the same subject.*

Dressing a salad

---

ensalada de pimientos encarnados o verdes (S)
red or green pepper salad

Serves 1

2 fresh red or green peppers
olive oil
salsa vinagreta (vinaigrette sauce)

Put the peppers into a frying pan with a small amount of oil, cover and fry very slowly for 1 hour until the skins are brown, turning them at intervals. Skin them on a plate so as to retain the juices, and remove the seeds and capsules. Cut the peppers into strips, add the juices and sprinkle with a little salsa vinagreta or olive oil.

Here is an alternative method. Put the peppers on a tray and bake in a very hot oven (475°F), turning them as the skins blister and blacken. This will take about 30 minutes or longer depending on the size of the peppers. Now put them in a plastic bag, secure it tightly and leave for another 30 minutes, after which time the peppers will peel very easily. Do this on a plate to collect the juices and do not wash them at this stage or you will lose much of the flavor.

ensalada manchega (S)
a salad from La Mancha

Serves 2

Salad
1 oz dried salt cod
7½ oz canned tuna, drained and flaked
2 hard boiled eggs, cut into wedges
2 large tomatoes, peeled and sliced
1 onion, thinly sliced
12 green or black olives, pitted

Dressing
¼ cup refined olive oil
2 tbsp sherry vinegar
½ tsp French mustard
1 clove garlic, chopped
salt and pepper

Soak the salt cod for 24 hours, then rinse it and remove skin and bones, and flake the fish.

Put the tuna and egg wedges into a salad bowl, then add the sliced tomatoes, onion, olives and flaked bacalao (salt cod).

Mix the dressing, pour it over the ingredients and toss well before serving.

ensalada sevillana (S)
Seville salad

Serves 4

Salad
½ cup raw rice, boiled and drained
3 canned red peppers (pimentos), drained and cut into strips
6 scallions
4 tomatoes, sliced
7 oz Seville olives, pitted
chopped parsley

Vinaigrette sauce
1 clove garlic
2 tbsp sherry vinegar
6 tbsp virgin olive oil
salt and pepper

Heap the cooked rice in the middle of a serving dish, and arrange the other ingredients, except the parsley, decoratively around it.

To make the sauce, crush the garlic in a mortar and pestle, add the other ingredients and beat well with a spoon until blended. Pour onto the salad, and garnish with a little chopped parsley.

ensaladilla rusa (S)
Russian salad

Serves 4

1 lb fresh shrimp, boiled and peeled, or ½ lb frozen shrimp, defrosted
3 oz canned tuna, drained and chopped
1 lb potatoes, boiled and diced
2 carrots, boiled and diced
¼ lb peas, boiled
1½ cups salsa mahonesa muselina (see page 267)
asparagus tips and pimentos, to garnish

Mix the shrimp and tuna with the vegetables and the salsa mahonesa muselina, then garnish with the asparagus tips and pimentos.

P *ervilhas*

Green peas; see GUISANTES.

The index, in English, is arranged by types of food — eggs, cheese, fish — kitchen equipment, cooking terms and other subjects. Consult it for recipes that make use of particular ingredients.

S P *escabechar*

COOKING METHOD

To preserve fish, game etc by steeping it in a marinade (*escabeche*) usually containing vinegar, bay leaves and other herbs, and then bottling it. See PERDIZ DE ESCABECHE.

S *escalivada*

MIXED GRILLED VEGETABLES

In CATALUÑA *escalivar* means "to grill over charcoal", and *escalivada* is a colorful mixed grill of vegetables, usually consisting of red peppers, tomatoes and eggplant. It is popular in Cataluña when the red peppers are at their peak in summer. It is also a good accompaniment to serve with grilled meat or fish, adding to the flavor if cooked at the same time.

P *escalope*

A CUT OF MEAT

A thin, boneless piece of meat, usually cut from sirloin of beef, or from pork or veal, dredged in egg and breadcrumbs and fried.

S *escudella i carn d'olla*

COMBINED SOUP AND STEW

One of the most traditional of Catalan dishes, this is served as two courses: First the *escudella*, a meaty soup containing pasta, and then the *carn d'olla*, a substantial stew made from veal, chicken, pork, blood sausage, egg, breadcrumbs and vegetables, both fresh and dried.

S *espardete*
S *pez espada*

SWORDFISH

Not to be confused with PEIXE ESPADA, the ribbon-like scabbard fish, this is the large tusked game fish. The flesh is dark colored, oily and full in flavor and perhaps at its most attractive in the *espardete fumado* or smoked swordfish from the fishing village of Sesimbra north of Lisbon.

In Spain, *pez espada* is usually cut into thin steaks, flavored with garlic, parsley and lemon juice, and grilled A LA PARRILLA. Another favorite way is to stew it slowly with white wine and onions.

Swordfish

espargos

Asparagus; see ESPARRAGOS.

S *espárragos*
P *espargos*

ASPARAGUS

Asparagus was known and appreciated by the Romans, but during the medieval period it was used mainly for its medicinal properties. Luis Solera de Avila, physician to the Emperor CARLOS V, believed that it was helpful in conditions of the liver and spleen, and up to the 17th century Spanish monks used it for stomach troubles. Because of its suggestive shape, it was also held to be a sovereign aphrodisiac, and Louis XV of France is said to have tackled the frigidity of Madame de Pompadour by obliging her to partake of asparagus, dressed with a sauce of butter, eggs and nutmeg – but by then Louis XIV had already revived its gastronomic reputation. The Spanish Bourbons had it grown in the royal gardens at Aranjuéz banked up with earth during the growing season so as to make it whiter and more tender, and, today, some of the best asparagus of all is still grown at Aranjuéz, south of MADRID and in La Rioja. Spain is, in fact, the largest cultivator of asparagus in Europe.

Apart from the white, cultivated aspara-gus, there are also wild green varieties: *espárragos amargueros* (so-called because of its more bitter taste) and *espárragos trigueros*, which springs up of its own accord in the fields of wheat (*trigo*).

In Spain asparagus is frequently served with SALSA MAHONESA. Another sauce is made with fried bread, garlic, wine vinegar and a spoon or so of the water used for cooking the asparagus. In La Mancha, a hot sauce is prepared in a BAÑO-MARIA with egg yolks, garlic, olive oil and a touch of ground cumin.

In Portugal *espargos com ovos* (asparagus with eggs) is made by boiling asparagus and cutting it into pieces about 1 inch long. Breadcrumbs and egg yolk are mixed with a little of the water used for boiling the asparagus, and the pieces are then put into it. This mixture is then poured into a frying pan containing a little hot olive oil and cooked briefly in the form of a roll. It is served with slices of CHOURIÇO and *toucinho* (belly of pork).

P *especiarias*

Spices; see ESPECIAS.

S *especias*
P *especiarias*

SPICES

Spices are used a great deal both in Spanish and Portuguese cooking. They were available in Europe – though always expensive – from very early times, being brought by caravan routes from the Far East to the Eastern Mediterranean and then shipped. When Aragón-Cataluña was Queen of the Mediterranean during the 14th century, spices formed a very important part of the commercial trade. It was not, however, until the 15th and 16th centuries when the voyages of discovery of HENRIQUE O NAVE-GADOR and Vasco da GAMA opened a direct sea route to the East that they became more generally available. Most, like cinnamon, nutmeg and cloves, were brought from the East Indies by the Portuguese, but vanilla, chili peppers and paprika were products of South America, first introduced by the Spanish CONQUISTADORES. See also under individual spices, e.g. AZAFRAN, CANELA, CARIL, NUEZ MOSCADA, PIMENTON, VAINILLA etc (see index).

A spice ship from Vasco da Gama's time, taking on supplies

P *espetada*

GRILLED MEAT

A Portuguese kebab, made with marinated chunks of beef. It originated in MADEIRA, where the farmers would break off branches of the bay tree, impale the pieces of meat and lay them on a raked-out fire to cook.

P *espigueira*

Grain storehouse, built above the ground; see HORREO.

P *espumantes naturais*

Sparkling wines; see BAIRRADA.

P *estalagem*

INN

When in Portugal, these moderately priced "inns" or small hotels are often the best places to go for regional cooking. The standard varies enormously from places like the Quinta das Torres in Azeitão near Setúbal, famous for its cuisine (see OVOS ESPECIAIS QUINTA DAS TORRES), to others where, for instance, BACALHAU is presented as plainly as the boiled potatoes accompanying it. Before visiting Portugal equip yourself with the useful *Hoteis de Portugal* available free from branches of the Portuguese National Tourist Office. This classifies all establishments from luxury hotels to *pensões* (boarding houses) according to amenities and price.

estofar / *estufar*

TO STEW

To stew food such as meat by cooking it in water or stock in a covered pot with onions, carrots etc. This was the preferred cooking method of the Moors and is popular today in both Spain and Portugal. See CHANFAINA A MODA DE BAIRRADA, COCHIFRITO, COCIDO and COZIDO A PORTUGUESA, COELHO A CAÇADORA, COELHO A CAÇADORA and COELHO A TRANSMONTANA. See also PERDICES ESTOFADAS CON CHOCOLATE.

estrellita

A PASTA

A Spanish pasta in the form of tiny stars often used in clear soups. See COCIDO CASTELLANO.

Estremadura

PORTUGUESE REGION

The Estremadura formerly marked the southern extremity of the lands reconquered from the Moors. Lying along the coast with LISBOA near the center, it takes in such charming fishing towns as Nazaré and Peniche to the north, and across the Tagus, the picturesque Arrábida peninsula and the large port of Setúbal. Further inland are Sintra with its Royal Palace, the Lines of Torres Vedras, where Wellington halted Napoleon's army, and the medieval hilltop town of Obidos, which makes the attractive Gaieras wine.

There is excellent fish and shellfish from all along the coast – the market at Cascais is one of the largest in the country – and this is the area to eat *santola recheada* (stuffed spider crab) and lobster from Cascais; *açorda de marisco* (shellfish bisque) from Ericeira; *lulas fritas* (fried squid) from Setú-

bal or the sumptuous PEIXE A MODO DA NAZARE.

The village of Azeitão in the Arrábida peninsula is the home of J.M. da Fonseca, who make the famous Moscatel de Setúbal, one of the world's classic dessert wines, and some of Portugal's pleasantest red table wines such as "Periquita", "Pasmados" and "Camarate". João Pires, once part of Fonseca, makes a fruity red "Tinto de Anfora", a "Catarina" Chardonnay, an attractive "Branco" made with Moscatel but with a dry finish and, with grapes grown in the grounds of the beautiful Moorish Quinta da Bacalhôa nearby, an excellent Cabernet Sauvignon.

P *estufar*

To stew; see ESTOFAR.

Eugenia de Montijo

19TH-CENTURY EMPRESS OF FRANCE

The daughter of the Count of Montijo, Eugenia married Napoleon III in 1853, thereby becoming Empress of France. She introduced large numbers of dishes from her native Granada to the French court, the most famous being rice *à l'impératrice*. A variety of others, after undergoing a major change at the hands of the palace chefs, became part of the standard French repertoire, being named *à l'espagnole* or *à la provençale*. Bad influence as Eugenia may have been on her husband, apparently encouraging him to embark on the Franco-Prussian War, it has been quipped that one of the few worthwhile things to survive the disaster at Sedan in 1870 was her collection of recipes.

P *Evora*

A CHEESE

Perhaps the best from the ALENTEJO, this strong and salty cheese is usually made from ewe's milk between February and June. Eaten fresh, it is creamy and piquant, and when matured for from 6 to 12 months, it becomes crumbly with real bite.

Extremadura

SPANISH REGION

The Extremadura, comprising the provinces of Cáceres and Badajoz, lies in the extreme west of Spain along the mountainous Portuguese border. It is a country of oak, beech and chestnut forests and bare upland pastures far removed from any commerce or industry, with little sign of habitation apart from the slowly wandering flocks of sheep.

Mérida, the capital of the Roman province of Lusitania, which embraced most of what is now Portugal, possesses some of the most remarkable Roman remains in Europe and Medellín and Trujillo are the birthplaces of the CONQUISTADORES, Cortés and Pizarro. The great monasteries of GUADALUPE, ALCANTARA and Yuste have been repositories of the culinary arts for many centuries.

Gastronomically, the Extremadura is best known for its EMBUTIDOS, particularly JAMON SERRANO and CHORIZOS, the prized product of the pigs which roam its oak and beech forests feeding on the acorns and other mast. It is just over the border from where the best of the very similar Portuguese

charcuterie is made. With few sophisticated restaurants, the best places to head for are the PARADORES which serve some regional dishes and wines. Those of Guadalupe, Mérida and Trujillo maintain a decent standard.

The headquarters of the charcuterie industry is the small mountain town of Montánchez, near Cáceres, which also makes a most individual wine, red in color, but growing a *flor* like SHERRY. Further south, the *Tierra de barros* (so called because its clays were used for making cooking utensils sold all over Spain) makes inexpensive wine in bulk but none of the wines from the Extremadura are demarcated. Apart from Montánchez, the best is the Cañamero, made near Guadalupe, orange colored, and also *flor*-growing with a sherry-like taste.

🇸 *fabada asturiana*

ASTURIAN BEAN STEW

This nourishing stew is one of the most famous of the rib-warming dishes of northern Spain. It is made with a basis of *alubias* (butter beans or dried white beans) – the Asturians maintain that a good *fabada* can only be made with the beans from the province – and MORCILLA, the local blood sausage.

---

fabada asturiana (S)
Asturian bean stew

Serves 6–8

2 pig's feet, blanched and split in half
1 lb brisket of beef, cubed
1 large onion, quartered
2 lb dried white beans, soaked overnight and drained
½ lb chorizo, skinned and coarsely chopped
½ lb morcilla asturiana or black pudding, cut into chunks
salt and pepper

Put the pig's feet into a large saucepan with the brisket, onion and beans. Cover with water, bring to the boil, then skim. Cover the pan and reduce the heat, simmering for 2–3 hours until the meat and beans are tender. Add the chorizo and morcilla 30 minutes before the dish is ready, and season to taste.

🇸 *faisán*
🇵 *faisão*

PHEASANT

Pheasants are available from October until the beginning of March; the female is preferred, being more tender than the male. They are served on special occasions such as birthdays or festivals.

In the south of Spain, pheasant is cooked with grapes and there are also pâtés and terrines. A specialty in CATALUÑA is the *faisán asado con manzanas braseadas* (roast pheasant with apples), the apples being cooked in the oven with lemon juice and SHERRY and served as an accompaniment. The most famous way of cooking pheasant is, however, the following recipe.

S *faisán al modo de Alcántara*

PHEASANT
ALCANTARA STYLE

Among the recipes pillaged from the Monastery of ALCANTARA by General Junot and later printed by his wife the Duchess of Abrantes in her *Mémoires*, was one for stuffing and roasting pheasant. This is of great historic (not to say culinary) interest as it demonstrates that the monks knew of the use of truffles and duck liver centuries before they were used in France. The recipe was transcribed from the *Mémoires* and reproduced by that renowned Spanish chef Ignacio DOMENECH in *La nueva cocina elegante española*. "Draw the pheasant and remove the breastbone. Make the stuffing by frying duck livers in refined pork fat, seasoning with salt and pepper and rubbing through a sieve. To this purée add truffles in large pieces, previously cooked in port. Fill the cavity with this mixture and marinate the pheasant for three days in port.

"Now season the bird with salt and pepper, put it in a casserole and roast it. Reduce the port wine used for the marinade, adding to it 14 to 16 small truffles, pour over the bird and simmer on top of the stove for 8 to 10 minutes. Place the pheasant on a serving dish, pour the sauce with the truffles over it, and carve it at the table."

P *faisão*

Pheasant; see FAISAN.

farinheira

SAUSAGE

A smoked and spiced Portuguese sausage containing rye flour as well as pork, orange juice, white wine and garlic.

fatias de Braga

EGG AND ALMOND
CANDY

These small squares made of almond paste, eggs and sugar are typical of Braga, capital of the MINHO.

If Spanish and Portuguese terms differ from each other, the entry in Portuguese, in the majority of cases, is referred to its Spanish equivalent, where you will find information relevant to both countries.

---

fatias reais

ROYAL SWEET

So called because they were a favorite of Queen Maria II, *fatias reais* are made with small squares of bread soaked in a mixture of egg yolks and sugar, flavored with lemon and cinnamon, and topped with candied squash.

favas

Broad beans; see HABAS FRESCAS.

favas à ribatejana

FAVA BEANS
RIBATEJO STYLE

From the RIBATEJO, this is a delicious way of cooking fava beans as a main course. It is important *not* to cook them in a tinned saucepan as this will blacken the beans – use a heavy non-stick pan.

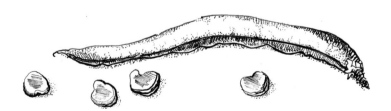

---

favas à ribatejana (P) *fava beans Ribatejo style*	*Serves 2–3* *1 medium onion, finely chopped* *1 clove garlic* *¼ lb toucinho or bacon, cut up* *1 lb fava beans, fresh or frozen* *¼ lb presunto or ham, cut into thin strips* *¼ lb chouriço sausage, chopped* *1 sprig of cilantro or parsley, chopped* *pinch of salt*	*Make the refogado: fry the onion, garlic and toucinho over a gentle heat for about 10 minutes until brown. The toucinho will supply enough fat.* *Meanwhile, cook the beans in salted water. If they are fresh they will be tender in about 10–15 minutes; if using frozen beans follow the instructions on the packet. Drain well and add to the refogado in the frying pan, together with the presunto, chouriço and cilantro or parsley. Cook slowly for another 5 minutes, stirring the mixture thoroughly. Season to taste.*

P *favas guisadas com negrito*

BROAD BEANS STEWED WITH BLACK SAUSAGE

A specialty of the BEIRA ALTA, this consists of broad beans stewed with MORCELA.

S *faves*

Lima beans; see LEGUMBRES.

P S *fiambre*

CHARCUTERIE

The Portuguese name for cold cooked ham; in Spain it refers to cold cooked meats in general.

P *figado*

Liver; see ISCAS, DESPOJOS.

P *figo*

Fig; see HIGO.

P *figo-de-inferno*

Prickly pear; see HIGO CHUMBO.

S *filetes mignon*

A CUT OF MEAT

These are cut, usually in a triangular shape, from the center fillet of the sirloin, which varies in size along its length. Always remove all sinews and skin before cooking.

S *flamear*
P *flamejar*

TO FLAMBÉ

To flambé by sprinkling food with brandy or liqueurs, either before serving or during cooking, and setting it alight. See MELOCOTONES AL RON.

Plate of cold, cooked ham

> *The index, in English, is arranged by types of food — eggs, cheese, fish — kitchen equipment, cooking terms and other subjects. Consult it for recipes that make use of particular ingredients.*

---

see also   ***Fennel:*** *see funcho*   ***Fig:*** *see higo*

---

flamejar

To flambé; see FLAMEAR.

flan de huevos
BAKED CARAMEL
CUSTARD

This "flan" or baked caramel custard is served up and down Spain, where it is probably the most popular dessert.

---

flan de huevos (S)
baked caramel
custard

Serves 6

½ cup vanilla sugar*
1 tsp water
1 pint milk
4 large eggs
pinch of salt

Heat 2 tbsp of the sugar with the water in a small saucepan until caramelized, and use to coat the base of a 1 quart soufflé dish. Allow to cool.

Meanwhile, bring the milk slowly to the boil in another saucepan. Beat the eggs in a bowl, adding the salt and remaining sugar. Once the milk has come to the boil, pour it over the egg mixture, stir well and transfer to the caramel-coated dish. Stand the dish in a pan of water and cook in a moderate oven (350°F) for about 1 hour until set. To see whether it is done, insert a skewer or knife into the custard; if it comes out clean, the custard is done, but if the egg mixture sticks to it, further cooking is necessary. Allow to cool, chill in the refrigerator and unmold on to a serving dish.

*The sugar is best flavored by keeping it in a jar with vanilla pods; alternatively, a little vanilla extract may be used.

---

flan de manzanas (S)
caramelized apple
custard

Serves 4

3 heaping tbsp granulated sugar
1 tbsp water
2 lb cooking apples, peeled, cored and coarsely chopped
3 tbsp brown sugar
1 cinnamon stick
a little grated lemon zest
3 egg yolks

First caramelize the sugar by heating it in a small saucepan with the water. Use to coat a 5 cup soufflé dish and leave to cool.

Put the chopped apples in a saucepan with 3 tbsp water, the brown sugar, cinnamon stick and lemon zest. Cook until the apple is soft, then push the mixture through a sieve or use a food processor to make a smooth purée. Beat in the egg yolks, pour into the caramel-coated mold, and cook in a water bath for about 45 minutes. This may be done either in a moderate oven (350°F) or on top of the stove. To see whether the flan is cooked, insert a cooking knife or large needle into the center; if it comes out clean, the flan is done. Leave to cool and unmold on a serving dish.

---

flan de naranja (S)
baked orange custard

Serves 6

½ cup vanilla sugar
1 tsp water
6 large eggs
grated zest and juice of 5 oranges

Heat 2 tbsp of sugar with the water in a small saucepan until caramelized, and use to coat the base of six 3 inch ramekins. Allow to cool.
   Meanwhile, break the eggs into a bowl, add the orange zest and juice with the remaining sugar and beat thoroughly. Pour the mixture into the ramekins, stand them in a pan of water and cook in a moderate oven (350°F) for about 1 hour until set. Insert a skewer or knife into the custard. If it comes out clean, it is done. Allow to cool, chill in the refrigerator and unmold on a serving dish.

S *flan de pascuas*
EASTER TART

An Ibizan specialty, this tart is made by lining a tin with *masa quebrada* (rich flan pastry) and spreading the base with thin slices of cheese. They are then sugared and eggs broken one-by-one on top and again sugared. A single egg, beaten with chopped mint, is poured over the others; more mint is sprinkled on top, and the flan is baked in the oven.

P *fogão*

Stove; see FOGON.

S *fogón*
P *fogão*
STOVE

Most old-fashioned Spanish and Portuguese stoves or ranges were fired by charcoal, and were brought to a glowing red with a fan when extra heat was required. They also provided hot water, and, in principle were very similar to the large castiron stoves so popular for country kitchens today.

   Most modern cookers are either electric or use butane gas from cylinders, as there is no natural gas in Spain except in some large cities.

S P *foie-gras*
GOOSE OR DUCK LIVER

Preparations made from the livers of specially fattened geese or ducks have been known since the earliest times. The Romans drove geese by the thousands from Gaul and, after glutting them on figs, steeped their enlarged livers in milk and honey. The epicurean taste for foie-gras was lost during the Middle Ages, and one of the first subsequent references to a goose liver pâté flavored with truffles is in the recipe book of the monks of ALCANTARA.

   Today, foie-gras of good quality is produced in Navarra and in Ampurdán near the Pyrenees by force-feeding ducks on cooked corn, thereby fattening them and greatly enlarging their livers.

P *folar doce*
SWEET BREAD

Eaten at Easter, this sweet bread is made with wheat flour, eggs, milk, olive oil or BANHA, sugar and yeast, flavored with cinnamon and herbs and with one or more hard-boiled eggs, sometimes dyed, embedded in the top. It is made in various shapes: round in the south, oval in Lisboa; and heart-shaped in some other areas.

Opposite: An 18th-century still-life by the Naples born Spanish painter Luis Melendez: this striking picture highlights the traditional austerity of Spanish still-lifes

Pages 142-143: Ripening pomegranates; also the work of Luis Melendez

Page 144: Oranges by A. Mensaque

P *folar gordo*

MEAT LOAF

This Easter specialty from TRAS-OS-MONTES, also known as *bolo de Páscoa*, is made with a dough consisting of flour, eggs, butter and olive oil, in which is baked an assortment of meats, especially pork, PRESUNTO, CHOURIÇO and SALPICAO.

P *folhas de louro*

Bay leaves; see HOJAS DE LAUREL.

Ford, Richard

19TH-CENTURY ENGLISH WRITER

Richard Ford (1796–1858) was the author of *A Handbook for Travellers in Spain*, which under its prosaic title is perhaps the most vivid commentary on Spain and its life and customs ever written in English. Ford married the beautiful Harriet Capel, daughter of the Earl of Essex and, because of her delicate health, took up residence in southern Spain for some 3 years from 1830. After installing his family in Seville and later amidst the ruined splendors of the Alhambra, he embarked on his travels, which carried him thousands of miles on horseback to every corner of the country. "Such," it has been written by Thomas Okey in the introduction to the Everyman edition of *Gatherings from Spain*, "is the magic of his pen, that even the arid facts of geography become fascinating, and the recipe for a favorite dish an absorbing theme. We are swept on by his enthusiasm, and long to sell all we have and take a wild ride through tawny Spain, to taste that *olla en grande*, fit only for bishops and abbots, those hams, transcendently superlative, with fat like melted topazes, and drink the divine ichor stored in Xerez *bodegas*."

It is surprising how much of what Ford wrote a century and a half ago remains true today. He collected much of the general information from the three-volume *Handbook*, including the fascinating chapters on food and drink, in the entertaining *Gatherings from Spain* published a year later in 1846. "I cannot," he once said, "cool my style to the tone of a way-bill; my ideas come bubbling over like a soda-water bottle, and I can't help it."

P *forno*

Oven; see HORNO

Francia

FRANCE

Depreciation of the Spanish cuisine in favor of the French began during the 17th century at the very time when French cooks were borrowing heavily from Spain and making use of the new colonial products introduced from Spanish America (see CONQUISTA-DORES). In Spain itself, a feeling of inferiority about the national cuisine appears to have spread downwards from the aristocratic court circles of the first of the Spanish Bourbons, Philip V, who left France in 1700 to be crowned King of Spain. There are echoes of this controversy in Richard FORD's *Gatherings from Spain*, when, for example, he describes how "a clever French *artiste* converts an old shoe into an *épigramme d'agneau*, or a Parisian milliner dresses up two deal boards into a fine live *Madame*." To judge from a book such as Lesage's *Gil Blas*, Spain was a barren wilderness inhabited by boorish and ignorant peasants. Again, Alexandre DUMAS, father and son, both of whom wrote accounts of their travels in Spain, were harsh in their criticism, the author of *The Three Musketeers* coming out with the dictum that "in Italy, where one has poor meals, the good inn-keepers are French; in Spain, where one finds no meals at all, the best inn-keepers are Italian . . ." And all this time Escoffier and other French chefs had been taking from Spain recipes and other ingredients such as consommé, truffles, foie gras, mayonnaise, puff pastry and chocolate.

In recent decades, Spanish chefs, especially in the elegant restaurants of MADRID, BARCELONA and Marbella, have been much influenced, as elsewhere, by NOUVELLE CUISINE. This has resulted in a welcome lightening of some of the over-substantial Catalan fare and has inspired a genuine renaissance of cooking in the Basque country: the NUEVA COCINA VASCA.

see also   *France: see Francia*

P *frango*

Chicken; see POLLO.

S *freiduría*

FRIED FISH SHOP

Cádiz is famous for its fish; *frito a la gaditana* (fried fish Cádiz style) is a name to conjure with in Spain. The establishments where it is fried, either to eat on the spot or to take away, may not be as common as they once were, but the quality remains excellent, and one cannot better this description written by that great revivalist of authentic Spanish cooking, "Doctor Thebussem" (see José CASTRO Y SERRANO), a century ago: "Fish from the *freidor* is unbeatable; it is as different from that prepared by chefs or cooks as the wine from Jerez from other wines, the sword from Toledo from other swords, and the olives from Seville from other olives. Because of the secret and special method of cutting the fish and the temperature of the oil, the aroma arising from the sole, mullet, whiting, sardines and other fish cooking in the steaming olive oil is an invitation to eat, and few suppers are more agreeable than this fried fish, washed down by half-a-dozen glasses of aromatic manzanilla."

S *freir*
P *fritar*

TO FRY

Frying is the most popular form of cooking in the southern regions of Spain and Portugal, and nowhere has the art been brought to a higher pitch than in the FREIDURIAS of Cádiz, forerunners of the homely fish and chip shop.

Food may be either shallow or deep fried, according to whether it is cooked in a thin layer of oil in a frying pan or, as for example with French fried potatoes, completely immersed in the hot oil or fat in a deep pan.

The Spaniards and Portuguese have traditionally fried in olive oil (see ACEITE DE OLIVA) rather than in expensive butter or in animal fats. Because olive oil is becoming increasingly more expensive, corn oil, sunflower or rapeseed oil is now being used as alternatives, and the Portuguese have for long made extensive use of margarine and pork fat, bought as BANHA in large cans.

Because of its pleasant aroma and flavor and also because it is healthier than animal fats, olive oil remains the best vehicle for frying most Mediterranean food.

To fry with olive oil, first cover the base of a pan to a depth of about ¼ inch and heat until really hot. A faint vapor will then rise from the surface and the heat should be reduced. If the oil is new and too strong in flavor, first fry and discard a small piece of bread. During cooking the food should be turned once or twice to cook it through and to brown it lightly on both sides. When removing it, drain off as much surplus oil as possible with a slotted spoon and blot the rest with absorbent kitchen paper. In this way the fish or meat will appear crisp and appetizing; there is no reason why properly fried food should be greasy or over rich.

The same considerations apply to deep frying, which is easier with ingredients such as whitebait or potatoes if the food is first immersed in a metal basket.

Olive oil may be used repeatedly for shallow frying by straining it into a jar and storing in a cool place; oil used for frying fish should be kept separately.

S *fresas*
P *morangos*
STRAWBERRIES

Strawberries were formerly grown in Spain on a small scale (those from Aranjuéz in CASTILLA LA NUEVA are famous). Now, however, there are large nurseries in the provinces of Huelva, Almería and VALENCIA, and also in CATALUÑA, supplying the fruit for the spring market in Europe. New varieties have been introduced giving the fruit better flavor and a longer life, together with a higher content of vitamin C, vitamin A and calcium.

Strawberries are mainly eaten fresh with fresh orange juice, white wine or sherry. Drinks made with sugar, water and strawberries are popular in Portugal; strawberry fritters and jam are made in both countries.

P *frigideira*
COOKING PAN

This is not, as might seem at first sight, the Portuguese word for a refrigerator but is a frying pan.

P *frigideiras de carne*
MEAT PASTIES

From ecclesiastical Braga in the MINHO, these are pasties of puff pastry filled with a spicy mixture of soft fried onions, minced beef, chopped PRESUNTO and white wine. They are cooked in small ovenproof earthenware dishes also known as *frigideiras* – hence the name.

P *fritar*

To fry; see FREIR.

S *fritura mixta de pescados malagueña*
MIXED FRIED FISH
MALAGA STYLE

This may be made from whatever white fish are available, provided they are small – the bigger the variety, the more contrast of flavors and the better the result. Larger fish may also be used by cutting them in pieces.

CAPITALIZED *words within entries refer the reader to more information on the same subject.*

---

fritura mixta de pescados malagueña (S)
mixed fried fish
Málaga style

Serves 4

2 lb fish, dredged with seasoned flour, and
    including some of the following:
    squid
    fresh sardines
    smelts
    perch
    whiting
2 lemons, quartered

Fry each type of fish separately in hot oil until crisp, blot off excess oil on paper towels and keep hot. Accompany with wedges of lemon and a green or roasted pepper salad.

◀ *funcho*
◀ *hinojo*
FENNEL

When an expedition despatched by HENRIQUE O NAVEGADOR discovered MADEIRA in 1419, his sailors came ashore to find the air fragrant with the smell of wild fennel and accordingly named the place where they landed Funchal. It is today the capital of the island and the center of the trade in MADEIRA wines. Fennel still grows wild in Madeira,

---

see also   **Fritters:** *see buñelos*   **Frog's legs:** *see ancas de rana*
                  To fry: *see freir*

and also on the Portuguese mainland and in Spain, and the leaves find occasional use in cooking to enhance fish dishes and sometimes veal; finely chopped, they are occasionally added to soups.

There is, however, one famous Madeiran sweet, *rebucados de funcho*, which makes unusual use of it. The stalks are boiled until very tender and then strained to make a fine purée. This is mixed with a cooked sugar syrup, cooled and shaped into strips of about 1 inch. It will keep in a closed airtight tin for about a week.

S *gacha*
CORNMEAL
PORRIDGE

A "porridge" popular in the north of Spain, made by boiling cornmeal with water and salt, and eaten with milk and sometimes honey.

P *galhina*

Stewing hen; see GALLINA.

Galicia

Spanish region; see ASTURIAS AND GALICIA.

S *gallina*
STEWING HEN

It has become difficult to find stewing hens in America in an age of flavorless, battery produced chicken, but not so in Spain and Portugal, where they are regularly for sale in the markets.

A *gallina* is a hen kept for laying eggs or hatching chickens. It weighs about 3-7½ lbs and is used for stewing.

One of the best known dishes is *gallina en pepitoria*. Chicken pieces are browned in olive oil and cooked with a sauce made with onions, garlic, parsley and wine. Before serving, a paste made of ground almonds and hard boiled eggs is mixed into the sauce.

P *Gama, Vasco da*
15TH—16TH
CENTURY EXPLORER

Following in the footsteps of HENRIQUE O NAVEGADOR, Vasco da Gama (1469–1524) succeeded in rounding the Cape of Good Hope with four ships in 1498 and continuing his voyage across the Indian Ocean to Calicut on the coast of India. This was the beginning of Portuguese supremacy in the Indian Ocean and of the *Estado de India*, with outposts east of the Malacca straits extending as far as the East Indies, China and Japan. Its main products, traded with the rest of Europe through the *Casa de India* in LISBOA, were pepper (a royal monopoly) from Malabar and the East Indies, mace and nutmeg from Banda, cinnamon from Ceylon and cloves from Ternate – quite apart from spices, silks and cotton goods, gold from China, silver from Japan, and horses and carpets from Persia and Arabia.

DOM. VASCO. LA GAMA

S P *gambas*
JUMBO SHRIMP

Shrimp are plentiful and popular in both Spain and Portugal, especially for TAPAS or ACEPIPES. To my mind, those with most flavor are from the colder waters of the Atlantic. The usual way of cooking them is on a griddle A LA PLANCHA, brushed with a little olive oil, or A LA PARRILLA with garlic. They are served with lemon wedges.

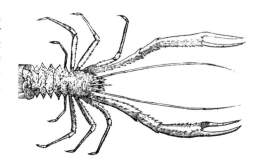

S *gambas al Jerez*
SAUTEED SHRIMP
JEREZ STYLE

An Andalucían way to cook shrimp, in which they are sautéed with diced ham and *fino* SHERRY and served with a white sauce.

Large prawn

---

gambas al pil pil (S)
shrimp with chilis

Serves 4

2 tbsp olive oil
2 lb fresh shrimp, boiled and peeled, or 1 lb
    frozen shrimp, defrosted
2 cloves garlic, crushed
2 or 3 guindillas (hot red chili peppers) seeded
    and chopped

Heat a little oil in separate small earthenware cazuelas or ovenproof dishes. Add the shrimp,

garlic and guindilla. Cook briefly over heat for 2 or 3 minutes until very hot and serve in the individual dishes so that the shrimp are piping hot when brought to the table.

Guindillas (chili peppers) are hot on the tongue; reduce the quantity by half if you find the dish too fiery.

Gambas al pil pil are served with fresh bread to dunk in the sauce.

---

gambas con gabardina (S)
shrimp fried in batter

Serves 4 (or 6 as an appetizer)

6 tbsp flour
1 tbsp olive oil
1 tbsp beer
pinch of salt
1 egg white, beaten stiff
olive oil
2 lb fresh shrimp, boiled and peeled or 1 lb
    frozen shrimp, defrosted
1 lemon, cut into wedges

Mix the flour, oil, beer and salt in a bowl with a wooden spoon to make a batter, then incorporate the egg white. Heat the oil in a deep frying pan and reduce the heat when it begins to smoke. Dip the shrimp in the batter and fry them until golden, then blot them on paper towels to remove oil. Garnish with the lemon wedges and serve in a heated serving dish.

S *Gamonedo*
A CHEESE

This semi-hard cheese, made around Covadonga, Onís and Cangas de Onís in the mountains of ASTURIAS from equal parts of cow's, ewe's and goat's milk, is similar to the famous CABRALES, though milder in taste. It is smoked for 10 to 20 days, then ripened in natural caves. The white interior, with a 33 percent fat content, is lightly veined, and the thick, brownish-yellow rind is often covered with fern fronds.

garbanzo grão
CHICKPEA

Dried chickpeas, sold by the sackful in the open market, are eaten all over Spain and Portugal, especially in COCIDOS and in COZIDO A PORTUGUESA, *cozido Alentejano, cozido Algarvia* and RANCHO A PORTA NOVA. Alexandre DUMAS wrote of them in *From Paris to Cadiz* that they "are hard, bullet-sized peas, quite beyond my powers of digestion, but if you were to begin by eating one on the first day, two on the second, and on the third day three, it is just possible that you might survive." This seems to be an invention of the enemy; the only chickpeas I have encountered to which his description might apply are those from the Indian sub-continent, which no amount of soaking would soften.

garbanzos con espinacas
CHICKPEAS WITH SPINACH

Often made during Lent (see CUARESMA), this is an appetizing, if basic soup made from soaked GARBANZOS, spinach and onion. *Bacalao* (see BACALHAU) is sometimes added or, at other times of the year, diced JAMON SERRANO.

garum
A SAUCE

Most famous of the sauces used in Roman cookery, *garum* was largely supplied to Rome by a concern with establishments along the Mediterranean coast around Cartagena. It was made in a vessel of some 6½ gallons capacity. At the bottom was put a layer of herbs, including fennel, mint, rue, basil and aniseed; next came a layer of cut-up fish, such as salmon, eel, sardines, scad and tuna; and finally a thick layer of salt. This was repeated until the receptacle was full. The mixture was left for 7 days and then stirred during 20 more, and the clear liquid that emerged was the extremely costly *garum*.

Garum is still much used in Vietnam and south-east Asia under various names and may be bought in bottles at food shops selling Asian products. A modified garum is made to perfection by that master chef Jaume Subirós at the Hotel-Restaurant Ampurdán in Figueras. This takes the form of a smooth paste of anchovies, black olives, capers and herbs, and is served as an appetizer, spread on the crusty local bread.

gaspacho

Cold soup; see GAZPACHO.

gaspacho à alentejana
COLD SOUP ALENTEJO STYLE

From the great province of the ALENTEJO in southern Portugal, this is a variant of the GAZPACHOS so popular in ANDALUCIA. It is made in the same way as gazpacho, but differs from the Spanish version in containing chopped CHOURIÇO or PRESUNTO, and the Portuguese often reduce the vegetables to a purée instead of chopping them finely.

gazpacho
ANDALUCIAN COLD SOUP

Gazpachos are ANDALUCIA's best-known contribution to gastronomy. The original *ajo blanco* was of Moorish origin and contained garlic, almonds, bread, olive oil, vinegar and salt; the use of tomatoes and peppers dates from their discovery by the CONQUISTADORES in South America.

Gazpachos always contain garlic and a little olive oil and vinegar, but may be made with a variety of uncooked vegetables, chopped or puréed. The most popular version from SEVILLA (which follows) contains peppers, tomatoes and cucumber. Other delicious versions are GAZPACHO DE ANTEQUERA; GAZPACHO DE GRANADA; GAZPACHO DE LA SERRANIA DE HUELVA; AJO BLANCO CON UVAS DE MALAGA with its whole fresh grapes; SALMOREJO CORDOBES, *sopa de almendras* (almond soup) from Granada, made with ground almonds, and SOPA FRIA GADITANA. During the winter the Andalucians also make hot *gazpachos*.

gazpacho (S)
Andalucían cold soup

Serves 6

1¾ cups canned tomato juice
2 tomatoes, peeled, seeded and chopped
1 large cucumber, peeled and chopped
2 green peppers, seeded and chopped
1 small shallot, chopped
salt
1 large clove garlic, crushed
1 tbsp pimentón dulce (sweet paprika)
1 tsp cumin seeds
3 tbsp wine vinegar
1 tbsp olive oil

Pour the tomato juice into a large bowl together with 4 measures of water from the empty can. (If using a blender or food processor, chop the vegetables in some of this liquid – but stop short of reducing them to a purée. The white foam produced by a blender should be removed with a spoon.) Put in all the chopped vegetables, then add a little salt, the garlic, and the pimentón, dissolved in a little water. Pound the cumin seeds in a mortar and add to the soup. Finally, stir in the vinegar, cover and cool in the refrigerator. Before serving, stir in the oil.

Many recipes for gazpacho include bread-crumbs, which are sometimes served as an accompaniment, together with bowls of chopped peppers, tomatoes and cucumber.

gazpacho de Antequera (S)
gazpacho from Antequera

Serves 6

3 eggs
olive oil
juice of ½ lemon
3 cloves garlic
10 almonds, blanched
salt
6 thin slices of toast

Boil the egg whites in 1 quart salted water until set, reserving the water. Strain, chop and reserve the whites. Make a mayonnaise with the yolks and olive oil, and thin with the reserved water, the chopped whites and the lemon juice. Pound the garlic in a mortar with the almonds and salt. Add some water to make a paste, then stir into the gazpacho, and add the toast. This soup may be heated, but not too hot or the mayonnaise will curdle.

gazpacho de Granada (S)
gazpacho from Granada

Serves 6

1 clove garlic
cumin seeds
salt
1 tomato, peeled (reserve blanching water)
2 red peppers, skinned and seeded (reserve blanching water)
2 tbsp olive oil
6 thin slices of bread

For best results pound the garlic, cumin seeds, salt, tomato and peppers in a large mortar or wooden bowl, or use a food processor. Add the olive oil and beat until creamy. Stir in the reserved blanching water (4 cups in all) and serve with the thin slices of bread on top.

gazpacho de la serranía de Huelva (S) gazpacho from the hills of Huelva (S)	*Serves 8* *6 cloves garlic* *2 tsp pimentón dulce (sweet paprika)* *salt* *5 green peppers, seeded* *5 tomatoes, peeled, seeded and chopped* *1 onion* *2 tbsp sherry vinegar* *olive oil* *2 cucumbers, thinly sliced* *crôutons*	*Using a large wooden bowl or a food processor, make a purée of the garlic, pimentón, salt, peppers, tomatoes and onion. Mix with about 1 quart water, transfer to a large earthenware cazuela and stir in the sherry vinegar and a little olive oil until the gazpacho resembles smooth cream. Serve very cold, accompanied by the cucumber slices and crôutons.*

gelados

Ice cream; see HELADO.

gengibre
GINGER

Ginger was one of the spices that became available as a result of Vasco da GAMA's opening up of a sea route to the Far East, but, like cloves, it is not as widely used in Portugal as cinnamon.

giraboix

Nougat; see TURRON.

glasear
vidrar
TO GLAZE

Meats are glazed by being basted with their own reduced stock and then cooked over high heat. Sweets and confectionery are first sprinkled with confectioners' sugar, then subjected to intense heat to melt it and leave them with a glossy coating.

gofio
A BREAD

This bread from the ISLAS CANARIAS has survived from the original inhabitants known as Guanches. It is made in the shape of a large ball from the flours of a number of different ingredients (wheat, barley, cornmeal and dried chickpeas) sometimes blended, but always toasted before milling, and made into a dough with water or milk.

Gorbea
A CHEESE

A semi-hard cheese from Vizcaya made from ewe's milk, with a creamy lightish yellow interior pitted with small eyes and a fat content of 45 percent. It is made in rounds of 4 to 6 inches in diameter, has a full, slightly smoky flavor, and will keep for 1 to 2 years.

grade para assar

Barbecue; see BARBACOA.

granada
romãzeira
POMEGRANATE

A native Syrian fruit, pomegranates are widely grown today in Spain in the provinces of ALICANTE and Murcia and in Majorca and also found in southern Portugal. The juice is used to flavor sweets. This fruit requires careful preparation. After

---

see also   ***Ginger:*** *see gengibre*   ***Goby, transparent:*** *see chanquetes*
 Goose: *see oca*

stripping off the skin and digging out the seeds in their gelatinous envelopes, carefully remove the bitter-tasting white connective membrane. What remains may be eaten fresh with a little sugar and sherry, but is always somewhat astringent and, of course, very gritty because of the large size of the seeds. Perhaps the best way of dealing with pomegranates is to stew the seeds with sugar and to strain off the pink juice, which goes excellently with roast lamb. In Spain, the juice is also used for making *granadina*, a dark, sweet syrup, the basis of a liqueur and also of non-alcoholic beverages.

Pomegranate tree

P *grão*

Chick-pea; see GARBANZO.

S *Grazalema*
A CHEESE

This hard cheese takes its name from the little town of Grazalema, where it is made, famous as a guerrilla outpost during the Peninsular War and high in the wild Sierra de Cádiz. It is made from ewe's milk and molded in esparto grass baskets. The taste has been compared with that of MANCHEGO, though its fat content is 51 percent and it must be eaten within 2 to 3 months unless matured in olive oil, which prolongs the life for a year.

S *grelos*
P *grelos de nave*
TURNIP TOPS

These spring greens are very popular in Galicia, where they are used for the famous LACON CON GRELOS, and in Portugal, where they are sautéed on their own in olive oil with whole cloves of garlic. The word usually refers to sprouting turnip tops, but it seems that the Portuguese also use it for other greens, such as the young shoots of a non-heading broccoli.

P *grelos de nave*

Turnip tops; see GRELOS.

S *Grosso de Macpherson, Lalo*
CHEF AND WRITER

Lalo, who is of Bostonian stock on her mother's side and of Andalusian on her father's, occupies a very special place in Spanish cooking. She bears the official titles of "Cocinera de Jerez" and "Cocinera del Rey", the second because she has special ties with the Spanish Royal Family, for whom she regularly cooks and advises on gastronomic matters. The friendship began when her husband sailed yachts with Prince Juan Carlos before he became king, and one of her books, about cooking on board ship, *Cocinar a bordo con fortuna*, is dedicated to him. There is a pun on the word "fortuna", this being the name of the royal yacht. A native of Cádiz, her most renowned book is *Los vinos de Jerez en la cocina universal*, published in English as *Cooking with Sherry*. For some years she ran a small and exquisite restaurant in Puerto de Sta. María, El Fogón, and she has also been director of cuisine for the sherry firm of Pedro Domecq.

---

see also   **Grape spirit:** *see aguardiente, bagaceira*   **Grapefruit:** *see pomelo*
                     Green peas: *see guisantes*   **Grocery:** *see mercearia*

Guadalupe, Monasterio de
GUADALUPE, MONASTERY OF

The great Spanish monasteries were famous for their kitchens and culinary standards from the Middle Ages onwards. Guadalupe, the special shrine of the CONQUISTADORES, was outstanding. The chronicler Vicente Barrantes lists the New Year's farings given to King Philip II which included six beautiful doe, three large deer, two wild boar, a hundred partridge, a hundred fowl, two hundred rabbits, a hundred ring doves, four dozen hams, an *arroba* (about 25 lb) of the best candied lemon peel, two *arrobas* of assorted confectionery, six baskets of pippins and six skins of wine from Ciudad Real.

At this period, during the 16th century, the monastery provided some 1500 meals daily for the monks and pilgrims, and the fare provided annually for the sustenance of the pilgrims ran to some 15,000 bushels of wheat; 50,000 gallons of wine; and 6–7,000 head of cattle, in addition to veal, kid, chicken and game. To this day one may still eat well in the Hospedería del Real Monasterio, which provides simple but well-cooked regional dishes for its visitors.

guarnicão

Garnish; see GUARNICION.

guarnición
guarnicão
GARNISH

These are the Spanish and Portuguese words for garnishes of all types.

guindilla

Hot red chili pepper: see PIMENTA DE GUINÉ and GAMBAS AL PIL PIL.

guisantes
ervilhas
GREEN PEAS

Peas have the highest protein content of any vegetable. In Spain, the main production areas are Murcia, Alicante, Zaragoza and Navarra, which also produce the fashionable *mange-tout* or snow peas. In both Spain and Portugal, they are used as a starter, cooked with chopped ham or chopped tomatoes and onions, and also in salads such as ENSALADILLA RUSA.

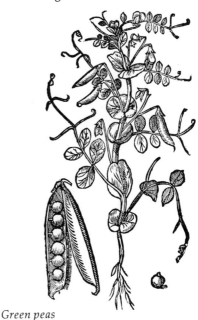

Green peas

---

guisantes a la española con jamón (S)
peas with ham Spanish style

Serves 6

4 tbsp olive oil
1 large onion, chopped
1 large carrot, grated
¼ lb cooked ham or bacon, chopped
2 lb garden peas, shelled and cooked, or 1 lb frozen peas, cooked
salt and pepper

Heat the oil in a pan and sauté the onion and carrot. When the onion is golden, add the ham, cook for about 11 minutes until browned, then stir in the peas, and season with salt and pepper.

S *habas frescas*
P *favas*
FAVA BEANS

Broad beans are very popular in Spain and Portugal and are eaten mainly in starters such as *habas salteadas con jamón* (fava beans with ham) or its Portuguese equivalent *favas à ribatejana* or in *menestras* (mixed vegetable dishes). They are dried during the hot summers and are the staple winter diet of country folk in the form of the Spanish *fabadas* (stews made with beans, pork and CHORIZO).

S *helado*
P *gelados*
ICE CREAM

Ice cream in Spain and Portugal is generally not as good as in Italy, but one or two varieties such as the HELADO DE TURRON and the famous HELADO DE PASAS CON PX are unusual and quite delicious.

Sorbets are often very good and are made with fresh fruit such as lemon, orange and tangerine and, in fashionable restaurants specializing in NOUVELLE CUISINE, with mint, celery and blackcurrant.

S *helado de pasas con PX*
RAISIN ICE CREAM WITH SHERRY

A particularly delicious ice cream from the SHERRY region, made with raisins and served by pouring sweet Pedro Ximenez sherry over it. It is a specialty of El Faro, perhaps the best restaurant in Cádiz, and of Bigote in Sanlúcar de Barrameda, famous for its fish from the Bay of Cádiz.

S *helado de turrón*
NOUGAT ICE CREAM

A superb ice cream that you will not find elsewhere as it is made with TURRON, a nougat from Jijona containing ground almonds, eggs and honey.

P *Henrique o Navegador*
15TH CENTURY PORTUGUESE EXPLORER

Henry the Navigator (1394–1460), who was a son of King João I of Portugal and of Philippa, daughter of John of Gaunt, early distinguished himself in the capture of Ceuta in 1415, but is best known for his voyages of discovery. His ships and sailors discovered MADEIRA and pushed a long way down the unknown African coast. By this and his establishment of the great navigational school at Sagres at the most westerly tip of Portugal, he paved the way for the rounding of the Cape and the voyages of Vasco da GAMA, which were to result in the Portuguese domination of the trade in spices from the Far East.

S *higado*

Liver; see ISCAS , DESPOJOS.

S *higo*
P *figo*
FIG

Figs, both green and purple, abound in Spain, Portugal and the ISLAS BALEARES, where they are eaten fresh as a delicious dessert. They are, in fact, so plentiful in southern parts of Spain that the country people feed them to their pigs and are quite bemused at their cost in northern Europe.

Both in Spain and in Portugal, but especially in the ALGARVE, figs are dried, and are sometimes ground into a paste with nuts and used in Moorish-inspired confections.

see also
Hake: see merluza
Henry the Navigator: *see Henrique o Navegador*
Herring: *see arenque*

S *higo chumbo*
P *figo-de-inferno*
PRICKLY PEAR

The prickly pear is a cactus that grows wild in the fields and by the roadside in southern Spain and Portugal, and in the Islas Baleares. Its sweet flavor somewhat resembles that of an ordinary pear – but there the similarities end. It is important to approach the glowing fruit with respect. If possible, use a pair of old gloves in picking and handling it. In any case, before removing the skin, scrape off the tufts of fine spines with a knife – otherwise they will most certainly and painfully penetrate your fingers — then peel the fruit with a sharp knife, still wearing gloves when doing this.

S *hinojo*

Fennel; see FUNCHO.

S *hojaldre*
PUFF PASTRY

The invention of puff pastry is usually attributed to the famous 17th-century French painter Claude of Lorraine (Claude Gellée) or to a chef called Feuillet, pastry cook to the house of Condé. Neither of these attributions is correct since Martínez Montiño, writing in 1611, refers to it as an ingredient long used in Spanish cooking, and it was also a novelty in Paris when the Spanish-born Maria Teresa de Austria indulged her taste for it after her marriage to Louis XIV in 1660.

In Spain, puff pastry has mostly been used for pâtisserie in confections such as *palmeras* (*palmiers*) or *milhojas* ("thousand leaves" – in fact, a layered cream cake) – but it is now much used in the elegant dishes inspired by the NOUVELLE CUISINE (see also NUEVA COCINA VASCA).

S *hojas de laurel*
P *folhas de louro*
BAY LEAVES

The *louro* (bay tree) is said to have come from Asia Minor, but was growing in all the Mediterranean countries at a very early date, and its leaves formed the laurel wreaths of emperors and athletes in Greece and Rome. Bay is an essential ingredient in many Spanish and Portuguese dishes and also in bouquets garnis.

P *horas das refeições*

Mealtimes; see HORAS DE COMIDA.

P *horas de comida*
MEALTIMES

Spaniards begin their day with *desayuno* (breakfast). This may be just a quick cup of coffee at home; others go to the nearest bar and have *chocolate con* CHURROS or coffee with a pastry.

Because breakfast is light they eat a snack, often taken from home, in the middle of the morning. TAPAS and a drink follow at 1 p.m., then home for lunch (ALMUERZO or COMIDA) around 2 p.m. The meal will probably consist of a salad, soup or vegetable dish, followed by fish and then a meat dish, with fresh fruit in season to finish. Because of the heat during much of the year, shops and offices do not open again until 4 or 5 p.m. Some people will take a siesta and others go to a café and socialize until it is time to go back to work.

MERIENDA follows between 5.30 p.m. and 8 p.m.

Between 7 p.m. and 10 p.m. it is customary to go out for TAPAS and drinks, and *cena* (evening meal), eaten between 10 p.m. and 11 p.m. will perhaps comprise soup and a light egg dish or TORTILLA, or fish, if it was not on the menu for lunch.

The Portuguese also have a light breakfast (*pequeno-almoço*) of coffee and toast or pastries. There are not many tapas here, but a mid-morning coffee or teas in a PASTELARIA.

Almoço (lunch) is earlier than in Spain, beginning about 12.30 p.m. or 1 p.m. It often

see also   **Honey:** *see mel, miel*

starts with a soup, followed by fish or meat frequently served with rice or potatoes (as in Britain or the USA, but *not* in Spain). This is followed by one of the many homemade egg sweets or tarts.

In the middle of the afternoon the PASTE-LARIAS are full of people drinking tea or coffee with slices of cake and pastries. These include school children on their way home, who stand eating the goodies in the street.

Jantar (dinner) is at about 7.30 p.m. or 8 p.m. It might consist of cold CHOURIÇO and PRESUNTO with a salad for a light meal, or fish followed by fresh fruit. In restaurants and hotels, dinner is, of course, more elaborate and very similar to lunch.

S *horchata valenciana*
VALENCIAN SUMMER DRINK

This is a refreshing summer drink, creamy white and non-alcoholic and tasting a little like coconut milk. It is, in fact, made from CHUFAS or tiger nuts. Originally available only in Valencia, where the chufas are abundant, it can now be drunk in the summer at bars all over Spain.

---

horchata valenciana (S)
Valencian summer drink

Makes approx. 1 quart

9 oz chufas or tiger nuts
1 quart water
6 tbsp granulated sugar
ground cinnamon

Wash the chufas, changing the water several times, and finally soak them for 12 hours. Wash again, drain well and purée in a food processor in batches with enough water to make a creamy drink. Macerate in a bowl for 3 hours, then strain through a cloth on top of a sieve to obtain as much of the juice as possible. Add the sugar, stirring well to dissolve it. Cool in the refrigerator and serve in tall, narrow glasses with a pinch of cinnamon on top.

S *hornazo*
SPECIAL BREAD

This is a bread made in both Old and New Castile at Easter time by incorporating in the dough chunks of cured sausage such as CHORIZO and MORCILLA, bacon and hard-boiled eggs. When it is cut, no two slices are the same.

S *horno*
P *forno*
OVEN

It is not usual in Spain and Portugal to cook roasts at home in an oven, and when, for example, you come across *en horno* on a Spanish menu or *no forno* on a Portuguese, the likelihood is that the food has been cooked in a large brick or stone oven – the Spanish and Portuguese often have recourse to the local baker when it is a question of dealing with, say, a suckling pig or turkey on special occasions.

See also A PADEIRA and ASAR.

S *horreo*
P *espigueiro*
RAISED GRAIN STOREHOUSE

These grain storehouses, built on stilts to raise them clear of the ground, are typical of the farms in the northwest of Spain and in the Portuguese MINHO, where they are known as *espigueiros*. In ASTURIAS they are usually wooden, but in Galicia and the Minho they are solid constructions of granite, resembling a small *ermita* (hermitage) or chapel with a cross on the roof at each end. Their purpose, in these damp parts, is to keep the grain dry and free from the attention of rats. Well-ventilated with the narrowest of slit windows, they are also sometimes used for maturing cheeses.

huesillos
ORANGE AND
LEMON FINGERS

These resemble cheese straws in appearance, but are flavored with orange and lemon zest and served as a sweet.

---

huesillos (S)
orange and lemon fingers

Serves 4–6

1½ cups plain flour
½ cup olive oil
½ cup milk
grated zest of 1 lemon
grated zest of 1 orange
olive oil

Make a dough with the flour, oil, milk, lemon and orange zests. Work it until smooth, then shape it, first into small balls and then into fingers with a slit along the top. Deep-fry in batches in hot olive oil until golden. Drain well.

---

huesos de santo
"SAINTS' BONES"

A confection eaten on All Saints' Day (see LOS SANTOS). It is made of a small roll of marzipan shaped like a brandy snap and filled with candied egg yolk, CABELLO DE ANGEL or jam.

huevos
ovos
EGGS

Both in Spain and Portugal, eggs are supplied to the open markets by local farmers and are free range with deep yellow yolks and a wonderful flavor.

In Spain they are much used in tortillas of all kinds (see TORTILLA ESPAÑOLA), and are hard boiled and stuffed, e.g. with tuna, then covered with SALSA DE TOMATE and decorated with anchovies and capers. They are also used in desserts such as FLAN DE HUEVOS and FLAN DE NARANJA. In Portugal eggs form the basis of many desserts (see OVOS MOLES) and include specialties such as OVOS ESPECIAIS QUINTA DAS TORRES.

huevos a la flamenca
EGGS FLAMENCA

This spicy supper dish in the cheerful colors of the Spanish flag, and so typical of SEVILLA, is served in small, individual earthenware CAZUELAS immediately after it is cooked.

---

huevos a la flamenca (S)
eggs flamenca

Serves 4

2 tbsp olive oil
4 small onions, sliced
½ lb bacon slices
4–5 tomatoes, peeled and sliced
salt and pepper
½ lb chorizo sausage, thinly sliced
1–2 eggs per person
1 lb fresh shrimp, boiled and peeled, or ½ lb frozen shrimp, defrosted
15 oz canned red peppers (pimentos), drained and cut into strips

Heat the olive oil in a pan and sauté the onions until tender, then drain off the oil. Add the bacon and tomatoes, fry for another 5 to 10 minutes until well cooked, and season with salt and pepper. Remove the mixture with a slotted spoon and divide it between four small ovenproof dishes. Arrange the chorizo around the edges, break the eggs into the middle of each dish and cook over a medium heat until the whites are set and the yolks soft. Garnish with the shrimp and pimentoes and serve at once.

S *huevos fritos a la española*

FRIED EGGS SPANISH
STYLE

Many people, having once tried fried eggs Spanish style, prefer them to the soft-fried British or American eggs.

---

huevos fritos a la española (S)
fried eggs Spanish style

For each serving

olive oil for frying
1–2 eggs

Heat the oil in a deep, heavy frying pan until it is very hot and begins to smoke, then break the eggs into it. The whites will immediately swell up and pop. Leave briefly until the whites are crispy and slightly browned and remove while the yolks are still soft.

S *huevos fritos con migas*

FRIED EGGS WITH
BREADCRUMBS

Fried breadcrumbs are traditional fare in the country districts of Spain, especially in the EXTREMADURA and ARAGON, and go well with fried eggs.

---

huevos fritos con migas (S)
fried eggs with breadcrumbs

Serves 4

½ lb stale bread (about 8 slices), crusts removed
salt
⅔ cup olive oil
2 cloves garlic, peeled
4 eggs

Crumble the bread with the fingers, put the crumbs into a bowl and moisten with a little lightly salted water. Leave for an hour or two until the crumbs are moist throughout.

Heat the oil in a frying pan, and fry the whole garlic cloves until brown, then remove and discard them. Sprinkle the breadcrumbs into the hot oil, stirring all the time so that they do not stick together, and fry until golden brown. Remove the crumbs with a slotted spoon, drain on paper towels to absorb any oil and pile them in the center of a warmed serving dish. Fry the eggs and arrange them around the edge.

CAPITALIZED words within entries refer the reader to more information on the same subject.

Opposite: Eggs form an important part of many desserts (top), Buñuelos (bottom)

Pages 162-163: The rich variety of Spanish and Portuguese fruit

Above: A selection of turrón, nougat, reflecting the many ways in which this distinctively Spanish sweet can be made

Right: This luxurious cake, known as Roscon de Reyes, is eaten throughout Spain on Twelfth Night. It is a tradition that reaches back to the 15th century and often a small prize, which is said to bring luck, is hidden somewhere in the filling

S *Ibiza*

See ISLAS BALEARES.

S *Idiazábal*
A CHEESE

One of the most delicious Spanish cheeses, Idiazábal, with a fat content of 53 percent, is made from unpasteurized ewe's milk in the Basque country. The cheeses are cylindrical in shape, weighing about 4½ lb with a semi-hard, creamy white interior and dark rind, and will keep for up to a year. Their rich flavor derives from having been smoked with hawthorn and beech wood.

P *Ilha*
A CHEESE

It is said that this cheese was introduced to the Azores by English immigrants. Firm and pale yellow in color, it certainly resembles Cheddar, mild in flavor when young and nutty when fully mature. With a fat content of 45 percent, it is much used for cooking and is sold in grated form by food stores in LISBOA.

P *iscas*
S *higado*
LIVER

The liver eaten in Portugal and Spain is mainly calf's liver. It is often cut into thin escalopes, then dipped in egg and bread-crumbs, and fried in olive oil. It is served with grilled or fried green peppers or with a sauce made by cooking a little chopped garlic and sherry vinegar with the liquid left in the pan after cooking the liver.

P *iscas à portuguesa*
LIVER LISBOA STYLE

This marinated liver, cooked with PRESUNTO and potatoes, is a specialty of LISBOA. Either calf's or lamb's liver may be used, but it is important that it is sliced thinly.

---

iscas à portuguesa (P)
liver Lisbon style

Serves 4

2 lb calf's or lamb's liver, thinly sliced
olive oil
¼ lb presunto or bacon
½ lb potatoes, peeled, boiled and sliced
1 tbsp white port wine

Marinade
¼ cup dry white wine
1 bay leaf
2 cloves garlic, peeled and chopped
freshly ground black pepper
1 tbsp wine vinegar

To prepare the marinade, mix together the ingredients in a bowl and steep the liver in this mixture for 1 hour. Reserve the liquid.
　Pat dry the marinated liver, put it into a frying pan with a little olive oil and fry briefly over high heat for 3 minutes on each side, depending on thickness, until pink inside. Add the presunto or bacon and the potatoes, and cook slowly for 5 minutes. Pour in the reserved marinade and the port, cook for another minute or two, then serve.

S *Islas Baleares*

BALEARIC ISLANDS

The coasts of the Balearic Islands – Majorca, Minorca, Ibiza and Formentera – with their sandy beaches, rocky coves and pine groves, are so well known to their millions of visitors as to need no description. What tourists in the resort hotels will not find so easily are local dishes. Based on the magnificent fish and the olives, almonds, fruit and vegetables which the Islands produce in such abundance, the native dishes are many and varied.

The best restaurant in Majorca is El Gallo in Palma de Majorca. Celler C'An Amer in Inca serves authentic Majorcan food including *frito mallorquín* (mixed fried fish), and Violet in Felanitx, with its country-house setting and beautiful garden, is also to be recommended. In Minorca, Rocamar, established some 30 years ago in Port Mahón and known for its fish and seafood, remains one of the best restaurants in the Balearics.

All the hotels do serve Majorca's answer to the *croissant,* the light and fluffy ENSAIMADA. Among the best of the vegetable dishes are TUMBET; SOPA MALLORQUINA , containing a variety of fresh vegetables; and ACELGAS CON PASAS Y PIÑONES, made with a local variant of spinach. Fish soups, including the CALDERETA DE DATILES DE MAR made from "sea dates", are numerous. Majorca has its own versions of lobster, and the mayonnaise which accompanies some of them is said to be a Minorcan invention (see SALSA MAHONESA). The Majorcan way of cooking squid (*calamares a la mallorquina*) is to stuff them with pine nuts, sultanas and other ingredients. Meat dishes, except for pork, are not so varied, but there are two excellent cured sausages, the delicate white BUTIFARRA and the soft orange-colored SOBRASADA. Another specialty is COCA MALLORQUINA, which is much like an Italian pizza.

Majorca was once a large producer of wine, but the vines were devastated by the phylloxera epidemic in 1907 and have never been fully replanted. Most of the better bottled wine is brought in from the mainland, but local wines to look out for, both red and white, are those from Bodegas José L. Ferrer. On an oenological note, Father Junípero Serra (1713–84), who introduced wine-making to California, was born in the village of Petra in Majorca.

S *Islas Canarias*

CANARY ISLANDS

The Canary Islands, of which the largest is Tenerife, lie some 500 miles into the Atlantic, nearer to North Africa than Spain. When they were taken over by the Spanish in 1402, they found the original inhabitants, the Guanches, living in the state of Stone Age man.

You will not find many of the traditional dishes in the resort hotels, but they have been jealously preserved by the islanders and may be sampled in country restaurants, such as Las Cuevas de Tacoronte on the island of the same name. One Guanche survival is GOFIO, a bread made from mixed cereal and vegetable flours. Other specialties are PAPAS ARRUGADAS; the spicy MOJO COLORADO sauce; *sopa del Teide* (a vegetable soup); *puchero canario,* in its most elaborate form known as the "stew of seven meats"; and among the desserts, the delicious

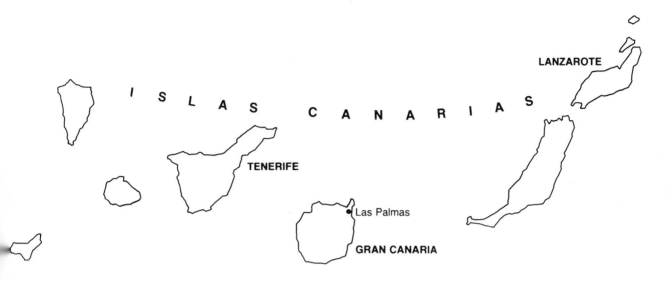

buñuelos de dátiles (date puffs) and a whole range of desserts made with the bananas for which the Islands are famous (see PLATANO).

In Shakespeare's day and for centuries afterwards, Canary was a famous dessert wine, but today the Islands produce little more than young wines for local consumption, most of the wine in the hotels being imported from the mainland. The growers labor under difficulties because the climate is so hot that without extra pruning the vines would fruit twice a year, and on the island of Lanzarote the vines have to be sunk into deep pits ringed with dry stone walls as a protection against the torrid winds from the Sahara. The best of the local wines are the white Malvasías or "Malmseys".

🆂 *jamón de jabugo*

HAM

The most sought after, tenderest and most intense in flavor of the different varieties of JAMON SERRANO. It is made from the famous CERDO IBERICO, fattened on acorns in the Sierra de Aracena some 40 miles north of Huelva.

🆂 *jamón de York*

HAM

This is similar to the boiled ham sold in the UK and USA.

🆂 *jamón serrano*

HAM

Jamón serrano is a cured Spanish ham, often eaten as an appetizer and similar to Parma or Bayonne ham; its enthusiasts maintain that it is even more intense in taste.

Before the outbreak of swine pest and the massive slaughter of domestic animals during the Civil War, the hams came almost exclusively from the native CERDO IBERICO, a dark-colored animal with leaner haunches and longer legs than the common domestic pig which roamed free, feeding on the acorns from the oak forests of Andalucía and those of the Extremadura bordering the Portuguese border. The best of all *jamón serrano* is from these pigs, but they now constitute only 5 percent of the total, and other excellent hams are made from imported white breeds or from cross-bred animals.

The pigs are killed after the fall of the acorns, which give a particularly good texture and flavor to the meat, and the rear haunches, front legs and shoulders of the animal are first covered with rock or sea salt and cured for a day or a day and a half per 2 lb of weight. The hams are then washed in warm water and dried, after which they are hung up to mature for a period of a year to a year and a half in huge cellars resembling those used for wines.

Like wines, cured hams are being awarded *denominaciones de origen* by the Spanish Ministry of Agriculture. The first two varieties to have been so recognized and controlled were the hams from Teruel in Aragón and Guijuelo in the province of Salamanca. The even better-known hams from Jabugo, Cortegana and Cumbres Mayores in the Sierra de Aracena in the province of Huelva, and those from Trévelez in the province of Granada and Montánchez in the province of Cáceres should soon be demarcated in similar fashion.

🅿 *Jantar*

Dinner; see HORAS DE COMIDA.

🆂 *jarabes* 🅿 *xaropes*

COOKED SUGAR
SYRUPS AND
CARAMEL

Spanish and Portuguese desserts often call for syrups or caramel, and these are made by boiling sugar with water. It is usual to start with about 1 quart of water per pound of sugar. The sugar should first be stirred in the hot water in the pan and dissolved completely before bringing the syrup to the boil. Use a sugar thermometer to measure the consistency, and heat rapidly to the required temperature once the sugar has been dissolved and brought to the boil. As soon as this temperature is reached, remove the pan from the heat and stand in cold water to prevent the temperature rising further and the syrup becoming thicker or burning.

---

see also

Jam: see mermelada

---

temperatures for cooked sugar	*siruposo*	syrupy	100°C	*de gran bola*	hard ball	119–122°C
	de hebra fina	fine thread	102·6°C	*de lámina*	soft crack	129°C
	de hebra gruesa	coarse thread	104°C	*de lámina*		
	de perlita	pearl	105°C	*quebradiza*	hard crack	145°C
	de gran perla	blow	110°C	*de caramelo*	caramel	175°C
	de bola blande	soft ball	110–116°C			

S *jibia*

Cuttlefish; see SEPIA.

S *judías*
P *feijão*

BEANS

Judías verdes are often cooked as a starter with a little chopped ham or with onion and fresh tomatoes, and are also used in salads with the addition of finely chopped onion and SALSA VINAGRETA.

With their high protein content, dried *judías*, similar to Great Northern beans, are the staple diet of the country folk in winter and are used for dishes such as *judías blancas guisadas*, a stew in which the beans are simmered gently for 1 to 2 hours with a head of garlic, bay leaf, CHORIZO, black pudding, onions and PIMENTON *dulce*. The famous FABADA ASTURIANA may be cooked with white beans instead of *faves* (fava beans). In Portugal they are used for *cozidos* and RANCHOS.

Judías pintas (Borlotti beans) are pale beige with pink spots and are often stewed with *panceta* (fresh pork belly), chorizo and a ham bone, which is removed before serving.

All dried beans need soaking, either overnight in cold water or, if reasonably fresh, for a shorter period in boiling water. They are ready for cooking when swollen to double their original volume.

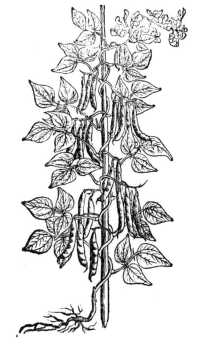

S *judías*
del barco
P *feijão*
manteiga

Butter beans; see LEGUMBRES.

S *judías*
pintas

Borlotti beans; see JUDIAS.

S *judías*
verdes

Fresh green beans; see JUDIAS.

If Spanish and Portuguese terms differ from each other, the entry in Portuguese, in the majority of cases, is referred to its Spanish equivalent, where you will find information relevant to both countries.

S *Jumilla*
DEMARCATED WINE
REGION

Lying behind the Mediterranean coast in the mountains of Murcia, Jumilla has traditionally produced some of the strongest red wines of Spain. This is both because of the heat of the long summers and because the area was never affected by that disastrous disease of the vine, phylloxera, and the Monastrell grape from which most of the wine is made is therefore grown ungrafted.

The wines are now being lightened by earlier picking of the grapes and modern methods of fermentation. Production is dominated by the huge cooperative of San Isidro, one of the largest and most up-to-date in Spain, but there are other firms making worthwhile wines, such as Bodegas Carcelén, Bleda, García Carrión and Señorío del Condestable.

K

S *kokotxas*
FISH DELICACY

Basque name for COCOCHAS.

see also   **Kid:** *see cabrito*   **Kidneys:** *see rim*   **Kitchen:** *see cozinha*

La Mancha
DEMARCATED WINE REGION

This is by far the largest demarcated wine region in Spain, producing some 35 percent of all Spanish wine. The typical grape is the thick-skinned white Airén, which flourishes in the near drought conditions of the summer. The great bulk of the wine is produced in the hundreds of cooperatives scattered over the region, which make it for direct consumption, for blending with the weaker brews of more northerly regions and also for distillation. In the past the wines have been heavy and earthy, in the Mediterranean fashion, but great strides are being made to produce attractively light, fresh and fruity wines by cold fermentation in stainless steel tanks. The adventurous Marqués de Griñón is even producing a first-rate red Cabernet Sauvignon on his estate near Toledo.

lacón con grelos
SALTED PORK SHOULDER WITH TURNIP GREENS

One of the most typical of Galician dishes, appropriate for cold winter weather, this is made by boiling the *lacón* (smoked or salted pork hocks) with the later addition of CHORIZO, potatoes and GRELOS.

lagosta

Lobster; see LANGOSTA.

---

lagosta portuguesa fria (P)
cold Portuguese lobster

Serves 2

1 lobster, boiled and split lengthwise
1 tbsp chopped cilantro
1 tbsp chopped parsley
1¼ cups molho mahonesa (mayonnaise)

Remove the lobster meat, cut it up and then return it to the half shells. Stir the chopped cilantro and parsley into the molho mahonesa (mayonnaise), and serve separately.

---

lagosta portuguesa quente (P)
hot Portuguese lobster

Serves 2

1 lobster, boiled and split lengthwise
1¼ cups molho de tomate (tomato sauce)
1 tbsp queijo da Serra or any hard cheese, grated (optional)

Remove the lobster meat and cut it up, reserving the shells. Put the meat into a saucepan, cover with molho de tomate and simmer for 5 minutes. Return the mixture to the shells. If desired, sprinkle them with grated cheese. Brown under the broiler before serving.

---

lampatana
KID OR LAMB IN RED WINE

A roast of meat prepared specially for weddings in the provinces of BEIRA ALTA and BEIRA BAIXA. See also CHANFANA A MODA DE BAIRRADA.

---

see also

Lamb: see anho, cordero

🅿 *lampreia*

LAMPREY

The eel-like lamprey, with its round jawless mouth and tooth-studded tongue, must be one of the ugliest of creatures; it is neverthe-less fished in the waters of northern Portug-al. There are two varieties: the sea lamprey, which grows to about 40 inches and the smaller freshwater lampern. They are vivid-ly described in an old English cookbook, Cogan's *Haven of Health* of 1612: "Lampreys or Lampurnes be partly of the nature of Yeeles, yet somewhat wholesomer, and less jepardous, for that they bee not so clammie and so gross as Yeeles ... After Yeeles and Lamprayes, we should drink good strong wine, as saith Arnold [Arnold of Vilanova] and generally with all kindes of fish, wine is very wholesome, for as the French man saith: 'Poisson sans vin est poison.' "

Together with the wine from the village of Amandi in neighboring Galicia, lamprey was a favorite at the table of Caesar Augus-tus and, "as every schoolboy knows" was the death of King John of England.

Lampreys, often cooked with their blood and with wine, make delicious stews, but it is safer to sample them in the restaurants of northern Portugal, since the fish contains two poisonous filaments in the back which must be removed carefully before cooking, and the recipes call for live lampreys. De-scriptions of some typical ways of cooking them follow.

Lamprey

🅿 *lampreia à modo do Minho*

LAMPREY MINHO STYLE

The lamprey is cut up, seasoned and marin-ated in white wine. It is then cooked in a REFOGADO made with onions, CHOURIÇO, the white wine and blood of the lamprey, and served with rice cooked separately in this same sauce.

🅿 *lampreia à trans-montana*

LAMPREY FROM TRAS-OS-MONTES

The lamprey is first washed in vinegar, and the roes and blood are reserved. Onions, PRESUNTO and garlic are cooked in a pan in olive oil before the lamprey is added and "sweated" over a low heat. The roes and blood are then added, the dish is seasoned with nutmeg, and the lamprey is served on fried toast.

🅿 *lampreia caseira*

LAMPREY IN RED WINE WITH RICE

In this method of cooking lamprey, from the BEIRA LITORAL, the fish is cut up and cooked briskly over heat with onions, carrots, garlic and spices. Red wine and the blood of the lamprey are then added, cooking is con-tinued, and the dish is served with boiled rice or fried bread.

🅿 *lampreia da Foz do Dão*

MARINATED LAMPREY

A method of cooking lamprey from the BEIRA ALTA. The lamprey is marinated in red wine with garlic, bay leaves, salt and pep-per. It is then cooked slowly in olive oil with onions and garlic. The blood and a little nutmeg are added during cooking, and it is served with rice.

---

see also   **Lamprey:** *see lampreia*

S *langosta*
P *lagosta*
SPINY LOBSTER

Langosta is the spiny Mediterranean lobster or sea crayfish which differs from the ordinary lobster in having a couple of long antennae instead of claws.

If you are starting with a live lobster, it must first be killed by plunging it into boiling water for a few minutes before splitting it in two lengthwise. The only inedible parts are the bitter intestinal tract, a dark line running the length of the abdomen, and a small jelly-like sac in the head. It is more likely that you will be buying a lobster already boiled by the fishmonger, so you will be spared the task and save preparation time.

In addition to the following recipe which is more akin to lobster à l'Americaine, there are a number of widely differing recipes for *langosta a la catalana*, some of them using the blood of the live lobster together with chocolate.

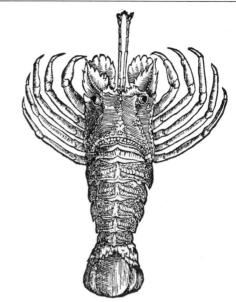

Spiny lobster

---

langosta a la catalana (S)
lobster Catalan style

Serves 4

2–4 lobsters, about 4½ lb total weight, boiled
    and split lengthwise
4 tbsp olive oil
2 small onions, grated
2 carrots, grated
2 tbsp brandy
½ lb tomatoes, peeled, seeded and chopped
salt and pepper
pinch of nutmeg

Remove the lobster meat from the shells, reserving them. Heat the olive oil in a large, deep casserole and fry the onions and carrots for 10 minutes. Add the lobster meat, stir briefly, then pour in the brandy, reduce the heat and flambé. Add the tomatoes, a little salt and pepper and the nutmeg. Cook gently for another 10 minutes, then fill the reserved shells with the mixture. Take what remains in the casserole and push through a sieve or purée in a blender to make a smooth sauce. Pour this over the half shells, place them under the broiler for 1 to 2 minutes until bubbling, and serve piping hot.

---

laranja

Orange; see NARANJA.

P *lardear*
TO LARD

Birds and meat are larded with strips of bacon or fat before being roasted. Garlic and, occasionally, cinnamon sticks are pushed into the meat during slow cooking.

> CAPITALIZED *words within entries refer the reader to more information on the same subject.*

lechazo

Baby lamb; see CORDERO LECHAL ASADO.

---

see also

Lard: see banha

S *leche*
P *leite*

MILK

Milk has often been in short supply in the hotter regions of Spain, and in MADRID it was formerly the custom to "stretch" it with water so that, according to the price, one knew exactly what one was getting! Milk is mainly used in Portugal for desserts such as TARTE DE AMENDOA, TARTE DE MAÇA and similar recipes.

S *leche frita*

A DESSERT

The quaintly named "fried milk" is one of the most popular of Spanish sweets.

---

leche frita (S)
"fried milk"

Serves 4–6

3 egg yolks, beaten
1¾ cups flour
½ cup sugar
1⅓ cups milk
1 cinnamon stick
1-2 tbsp of butter
1 egg, beaten
breadcrumbs
olive oil
ground cinnamon

Pour the yolks into a small saucepan and add the flour, sugar, milk, cinnamon stick and butter. Stir together well, then simmer slowly over a low heat, stirring all the time until the mixture is thick. Grease a large dish with butter, spread with the mixture, remove the cinnamon stick and allow to cool.

Now cut the "dough" into strips or other shapes, dredge them in the beaten egg and breadcrumbs, then fry in hot olive oil until browned (they may be fried either in deep or shallow oil; if using shallow oil, turn them over once). Dust with ground cinnamon, arrange on a serving plate and serve immediately, accompanied by warmed honey or maple syrup.

Leche frita may also be eaten cold.

S *leche merengada*

MILK SHAKE

This is a refreshing summer drink available in cafés from about mid June to September; in MADRID, it is a specialty of the Café Gijón, popular with writers and artists. It is made by bringing to the boil a mixture of milk and cream with sugar, lemon rind and cinnamon sticks, refrigerating it and then blending it with egg whites beaten with lemon juice.

Served in long glasses with chilled black coffee, it is known as *blanco y negro*.

S *legumbres*
P *legumes*

LEGUMES

Legumes (dried beans, etc.) are used a great deal in Spanish and Portuguese cooking, especially in making nourishing stews with meat, CHORIZO or CHOURIÇO and other cured sausages. Among the different types are: GARBANZOS or GRÃO; *judías del Barco* or *feijão manteiga* known as *faves* (fava beans) in ASTURIAS; *alubias*, a northern Spanish variety of butter beans used for making the famous FABADA ASTURIANA; JUDÍAS *blancas* or *feijão frade* (white beans); *judías pintas* (Borlotti beans); *fréjoles* or *feijão encarnado* (mottled Lima or kidney beans) and *lentejas* or *lentilhas* (lentils).

P *legumes*

Dried beans, peas, etc; see LEGUMBRES.

P *leitão*

Suckling pig; see COCHINILLO.

P *leitão à moda da Bairrada*

Roast suckling pig Bairrada style; see COCHINILLO.

P *leite*

Milk; see LECHE.

> If Spanish and Portuguese terms differ from each other, the entry in Portuguese, in the majority of cases, is referred to its Spanish equivalent, where you will find information relevant to both countries.

S *lengua*
P *lingua*

TONGUE

The most frequently used are small calf's tongues which need less cooking and preparation than does a large ox tongue. The cow's tongue used in Portugal must be soaked for 2 hours and simmered for almost 3 hours until it is ready to skin and trim. It is then usually cut into slices and served with a sauce made with fried onions, tomatoes or peppers, with the addition in Portugal of MADEIRA wine, and in Spain of a SALSA DE TOMATE or SALSA MAHONESA VERDE, laced with *fino* SHERRY.

S *lengua con salsa de tomate*

TONGUE IN TOMATO SAUCE

A good dish for a dinner party, since, except for the final heating, all the work can be done beforehand.

Thinly sliced cold roast beef, lamb or veal may also be served hot in the same tomato sauce.

---

lengua con salsa de tomate (S)
tongue in tomato sauce

Serves 6

1 ox tongue, soaked overnight if salted
2 onions, sliced
1 tsp mixed dried herbs or 1 tbsp chopped parsley
salt
2 cups salsa de tomate (tomato sauce)
2 tbsp fino sherry
few strands of saffron

Simmer the tongue with the onions and herbs in a large pan of salted water, skimming off the white scum that forms initially. Cover the pan and continue simmering for a total of 3–4 hours or until tender.

Place the tongue on a dish and skin and bone it. Roll it into a circular shape and put it into a bowl as nearly as possible the same size, pressing it with a flat plate and putting a heavy weight on top. Alternatively, use a tongue press.

Leave for at least 4 hours. If possible, cook and press the tongue a day before serving as it will then be much easier to carve.

Pour the salsa de tomate (tomato sauce) into a large saucepan, stir in the sherry and saffron (ground in a mortar) with a little water, slice the tongue thinly, add to the pan and simmer gently for about 10 minutes until piping hot.

Serve with plain boiled potatoes.

---

lenguado
linguado

SOLE

Sole is not of the quality of the famous English Dover sole, but is a smaller fish, more like in the US. In both Spain and Portugal the fillets are often dredged in flour and fried. The smallest are delicate and delicious but contain a large number of bones. In Galicia sole is cooked in Albariño wine with mushroom sauce poured on top.

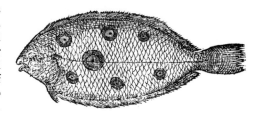

see also   **Lemon:** see *limón*

🅢 *lenguados con almendras*

SOLE WITH ALMOND SAUCE

This is an attractive way of baking fillets of sole with potatoes and almond sauce. The base of an ovenproof dish is lined with fried potatoes and the fish is placed on top together with fried onions. The sauce is prepared with a mixture of ground almonds, garlic, parsley and wine. This is stirred and poured over the fish, which is then baked in the oven for 15 minutes.

🅢 *Lentejas*
🅟 *Lentilhas*

Lentils; see LEGUMBRES.

🅢 *León*

A CHEESE

A mellow, semi-hard cheese with a close-textured white interior and a fat content of 52 percent. It is made with cow's milk and found only around Oseja de Sajambre.

> *If Spanish and Portuguese terms differ from each other, the entry in Portuguese, in the majority of cases, is referred to its Spanish equivalent, where you will find information relevant to both countries.*

Levante

SPANISH REGION

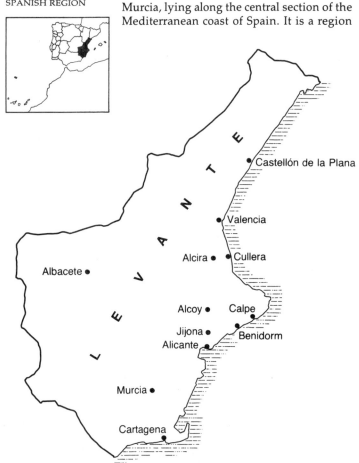

The Levante comprises the four provinces of Castellón de la Plana, Valencia, Alicante and Murcia, lying along the central section of the Mediterranean coast of Spain. It is a region of mild winters and hot summers with violent rainstorms in the autumn. Semi-tropical crops such as rice and sugar cane flourish in the rich soils of the coastal plain. Valencia and Castellón are islanded amidst the orange and lemon groves. The *huertas* (market gardens) are particularly fertile and produce several crops of vegetables each year. In Almería further south, even more prodigious yields are achieved in huge plastic greenhouses – see VERDURAS.

The cooking of the Levante and its capital, VALENCIA, is dominated by rice dishes: first and foremost, of course, PAELLA, originally made with the rice and eels from the marshes of the great lagoon of Albufera on the outskirts of the city. Other rice dishes are ARROZ ABANDA, *arroz a la marinera* and *arroz con pescado* (both made with rice and fish) and ARROZ MURCIANO. Vegetable dishes include the spicy *mirichones picantes* from Murcia (lima beans with CHORIZO and chili peppers) and *faves al tombet* (fava beans Alicante style). There is Mediterranean fish and shellfish in abundance; among less familiar varieties are the ugly *rascasio* (*rascasse*, or scorpion fish used to such good effect by the French in *bouillabaisse*) and the DATIL DE MAR which makes such beautiful chowders. Jijona, in the hills behind Alicante, makes the famous TURRON, most delicious of nougats. One restaurant with a country-wide reputation is the Rincón de Pepe in Murcia; another is the Eladio in Valencia with its reputation for seafood.

The coastal area between Valencia and

Alicante is well known for its Moscatel grapes, used both for winemaking and for eating, and until the Civil War, there was a British community in the port of Denia engaged in exporting raisins. There are four demarcated wine regions in the Levante. These are ALICANTE, JUMILLA, VALENCIA and YECLA.

The index, in English, is arranged by types of food — eggs, cheese, fish — kitchen equipment, cooking terms and other subjects. Consult it for recipes that make use of particular ingredients.

P *limão*

Lemon; see LIMON

S *limón*
P *limão*

LEMON

Like bitter oranges (see NARANJA), lemons were first introduced to Iberia by the Moors; in Spain they are grown extensively in the provinces of VALENCIA and Castellón de la Plana, and in Portugal in the ALGARVE and the Setúbal peninsula south of LISBOA. In both countries lemons are stuffed with mixtures of cooked fish and served as appetizers. Cut in wedges or slices, lemons are used for garnishing fish dishes; they are preserved and also, of course, used for making lemonade or adding to drinks such as SANGRIA.

An attractive Portuguese dish is *amêndoas cobertas com vidrado de limão* (almonds glazed with lemon). A lemon syrup is made and mixed with roasted almonds. This is cooked and spread on a baking sheet, and the almonds are separated and left to cool and dry.

P *lingua*

Tongue; see LENGUA.

P *linguado*

Sole; see LENGUADO.

 linguiça

A SAUSAGE

A type of CHOURIÇO, long and thin, containing finely chopped pork, garlic and paprika. It may be eaten uncooked, but is most often used in COZIDOS.

lionesas

PROFITEROLES

These are soft golden cream puffs filled with CREMA PASTELERA. They are always bought in PASTELERIAS.

Lemon tree

Lisboa

LISBON

Lisbon, the capital of Portugal since 1255, when it replaced Coimbra, was founded about 1200 B.C. by the Phoenicians, who called it the "serene harbor". Its history has been dominated by its superb natural anchorage and its port, still one of the largest in Europe. The city became enormously prosperous as a result of the opening up of sea routes to the Far East by the Portuguese, together with the trade in spices, silver, ivory, silks and precious stones.

see also **Lisbon:** *see Lisboa*

Built on seven low hills, like Rome, it is a place of wide avenues and open spaces and very much the center of Portugal in gastronomic matters as in others. Apart from its own specialties such as the *caldeirada à fragateira de Lisboa* (fish soup); *pescada cozida de Lisboa* (boiled hake); *santola à moda de Lisboa* (crabmeat); ISCAS and DOBRADA, one can find dishes from all the different regions in the smaller restaurants and, of course, "international cooking" in the larger and sophisticated ones.

Among the most elegant restaurants in the grand style are Avíz, Tégide and Tavares, and specially noted for their cooking are Gambrinus, Conventual and Casa de Comida. For an evening's entertainment the *fado* places in the Alfama and Bairro Alto quarters, often with very reasonable food and wine, are to be recommended. *Fado* and its haunting songs apart, there are dozens of tiny restaurants in the Alfama – the old Moorish quarter – serving individually cooked native dishes such as PEIXE ESPADA.

P *lombo de vaca*

A cut of meat; see SOLOMILLO.

---

lombo de porco à camponesa (P)
roast loin of pork
Portuguese style

Serves 4

2 lb pork loin roast, rolled and tied
1⅓ cups dry white wine
2 carrots, chopped coarsely
2 cloves garlic, cut in half
1 bay leaf
juice of 1 lemon
1 tsp colorau doce (sweet paprika)
1 tbsp chopped parsley
salt and pepper
6 potatoes, parboiled for 10 minutes
6 onions, sliced
4 tbsp banha (lard)

Put the meat in a glass dish and leave for 24 hours in a marinade made of the white wine, carrots, garlic, bay leaf, lemon juice, colorau doce, parsley and salt and pepper.

Next day, remove the meat from the marinade, pat dry, and transfer to an ovenproof dish. Place the potatoes and sliced onions around it, dot with banha (lard), and place in a hot oven (425°F) for 10 minutes. Lower the temperature to fairly hot, (375°F) and roast for 30 minutes per lb until golden brown.

S *lomo*

A SAUSAGE

Lomo is cured pork loin made into a thick sausage. It is produced by marinating the pork, preferably from the CERDO IBERICO, in a solution of salt with garlic and bay leaves. After some 10 days it is taken out and allowed to dry, then smeared with olive oil and PIMENTON, put into large sausage skins and hung up to dry for several months.

Lomo is also used to describe fresh loin of pork.

---

see also

Liver: *see iscas*   **Lobster:** *langosta*

lomo a la naranja (S) pork loin with orange	Serves 4	
	2 lb pork loin roast, tied 4 tbsp olive oil 1 onion, cut into rings 1 large carrot, cut into julienne strips 2 tsp arrowroot 2 tbsp fino sherry 2 oranges, zest removed, segmented and chopped	*Brown the roast in the olive oil in a large heavy pan, then add the onion and carrot, cover with the lid and cook slowly for about 1 hour or until tender. Remove the meat. Slice it thinly and keep warm on a serving dish.* *Meanwhile, purée the contents of the pan in a food processor or blender, or push through a sieve, then return them to the pan. Stir the arrowroot with the sherry, add to the pan and cook gently for a few minutes until smooth and creamy. Add the orange zest and chopped segments, and cook together for 5 minutes longer until heated through and smooth, then pour over the meat.*

longaniza
A SAUSAGE

A thin Spanish sausage, one of the products of La MATANZA, made from minced and marinated pork. The *longaniza* from Navarra and Aragón is usually fried or broiled and sometimes served with eggs for breakfast in country hotels; *longaniza de pascua* from VALENCIA, containing both pork and veal, is eaten without cooking.

Los Reyes Dia de Reis
TWELFTH NIGHT

In Spain and Portugal, children receive their presents, not at Christmas but on Twelfth Night, when, instead of delivery being made down the chimney by a nordic Santa Claus, they are brought by the three Magi on their journey from the East.

A special sweet bread, ROSCON DE REYES (*Bolo-rei* in Portugal), containing candied fruit, is baked for the festival and contains a coin or figurine bringing luck to the person who finds it. Another sweet bread eaten at this time is PÃO DOCE.

Los Santos Todos os Santos
ALL SAINTS' DAY

All Saints' Day (1 November) was instituted by the Roman Church in 835 to overshadow the pagan ceremonies of Halloween the preceding night, which marked the beginning of winter when the souls of the dead were abroad. There is, therefore, none of the ducking for apples – the survival of an old rite for divining the future – but All Saints' Day is a most important date in the religious calendar in Spain and Portugal and all over Europe generally. It is a public holiday and people go to the cemetery to lay flowers. In Spain, they make a special confection, HUESOS DE SANTO – "Saint's Bones", and a little reminiscent of bones in appearance! PANELLETS are a special marzipan typical of CATALUÑA.

In Portugal it was – and still is, in country places – the practice to go in groups from door to door on 2 November, the *Dia de Finados*, asking for *pão por Deus* ("bread for God"). The callers are given dried figs, walnuts, chestnuts, pine nuts, apples and also *bolinhos*, to be distributed to the poor. These are a form of fancy bread made from dough containing flour, egg yolks, sugar and cinnamon, fried in olive oil, decorated with squash and coated with syrup.

louro

Bay tree; see HOJAS DE LAUREL.

S *lubina*
P *robalo*
SEA BASS

With its silver skin and delicate white meat, this is a delicious and expensive fish. It is particularly valued by the Spanish if caught by rod and line. *Lubina* may be stuffed with mushrooms and cooked in a green sauce with fresh herbs.

S *lubina "Albufera"*
SEA BASS IN ALMOND SAUCE

A dish from the LEVANTE made by cooking a mixture of mint, garlic, parsley and ground almonds with a touch of PIMENTON in olive oil. The fish is either baked in the oven or cooked over heat with the sauce poured over it.

Albufera refers to the great lagoon outside VALENCIA, which was the source of the rice first used for making PAELLA. After Marshal Suchet captured Valencia for Napoleon in 1812, he took the title of Duke of Albufera, and it was from this period that the French began calling sauces "Albufera". They are, however, in no way similar to the Spanish "Albufera" sauce made with almonds and garlic.

S *Luján, Nestor*
WRITER AND GASTRONOME

Nestor Luján is one of the most respected and authoritative of contemporary Spanish gastronomic writers. He is especially knowledgeable on the cuisine of his native CATALUÑA and BARCELONA.

P *lulas*

Squid; see CALAMARES.

P *lulas grelhadas*
GRILLED SQUID

A dish made by grilling the smallest and tenderest squid and serving them with a tomato sauce, boiled potatoes and slices of lemon.

P *maça*

Apple; see MANZANA.

P *maçapão*

Marzipan; see MAZAPAN.

SP *macerar*
TO MACERATE

To steep fruits or other foods in wine or liqueurs with sugar and spices so that they are softened and impregnated with flavor.

> *If Spanish and Portuguese terms differ from each other, the entry in Portuguese, in the majority of cases, is referred to its Spanish equivalent, where you will find information relevant to both countries.*

Madeira
PORTUGUESE ISLAND

Madeira was discovered in 1419 by an expedition despatched by HENRIQUE O NAVEGADOR after his sailors, blown off course while exploring the Guinea coast, had sighted what they thought to be "vapors rising from the mouth of hell". It is an odd first description of this island paradise with its balmy climate and lush, semi-tropical vegetation.

When the Portuguese first landed, the island was even more densely wooded than it is today ("*madeira*" means "wood" in Portuguese), and the settlers set fire to the trees and began clearing the ground for planting sugar cane, the predominant crop until it became cheaper to produce it in

Brazil. Nowadays, the most important crops are vines for making the famous wines (see separate entry below), bananas, exotic fruits and spring vegetables.

There are deep water fish in abundance – the island is volcanic and rises a sheer 4 miles from the ocean bed – including ESPARDETE; *atum* (see ATUN) and PEIXE ESPADA, which in Madeira is often served with fried bananas; there is also good lobster, crab and prawn. A meat dish very typical of the island is ESPETADO, a form of kebab served in all the restaurants, but most of the dishes are those of the mainland – fish soups, *leitão* (see COCHINILLO), BACALHAU, *pudim flan* (the same as FLAN DE HUEVOS except that the Portuguese use more egg yolks). The so-called "Madeira cake", a sort of pound cake, is a purely British invention designed to go with a glass of madeira at tea-time; true Madeira cake as made on the island is rich and spicy, like gingerbread and made with molasses (see BOLO DE MEL).

The capital, Funchal, possesses a number of restaurants of good standard and many hotels, one of which, Reid's, with its 10 acres of tropical garden cascading down to the waterfront and standards of service harking back to less hurried times, is quite outstanding.

MADEIRA

● Funchal

madeira
A WINE

Madeira ranks with vinho do PORTO and SHERRY as one of the world's great fortified wines. Winemaking began with the arrival of the first Portuguese settlers in the 15th century, but the style of the wines as they exist today was established during the 18th century with the settlement in Madeira of

numerous British wine merchants.

The four main styles of madeira take their names from those of the grapes used for making them. The driest is Sercial, drunk like *fino* sherry as an aperitif. Verdelho is slightly sweeter, but may still be drunk before a meal or with a slice of Madeira cake

---

see also

Madeira cake: *see bolo de mel*

during the morning or at tea-time. Bual and Malmsey are rich, sweet dessert wines, intense and fruity, for after dinner drinking. Good madeiras are the longest lasting of all wines, and Sir Winston Churchill once held up his glass of Bual at a banquet, booming: "Do you realize that this wine was made when Marie Antoinette was still alive?"

Although not much used for cooking in Madeira itself or in Portugal, madeira has wide applications in the kitchen. Sercial or Verdelho improve almost any soup and are essential for turtle soup (this is made with turtle flippers braised in madeira wine). Sercial is the best accompaniment to rich avocados, and sauces for chicken and game are all transformed by the addition of a little madeira. The luscious Bual and Malmsey come into their own in making sweets, cakes and jellies and with desserts – try pouring a little over fresh strawberries.

Madrid
SPANISH CITY

"The townspeople think Madrid the 'envy and admiration' of mankind: they talk of it as the capital of *Spain*, and thus the world, for *Quien dice España dice todo*. There is but one Madrid, *No hay sino un Madrid:* unique, like the phoenix, it is the *only* court on earth, *Solo Madrid es corte*. Wherever it is mentioned the world is silent with awe, *Donde está Madrid calle el mundo*. There is but one stage from Madrid to *La Gloria*, or paradise, in which there is a window for the angels to look down on this counterpart heaven of earth . . ." So said Richard FORD in ironical vein – nevertheless, since the Spanish court removed there from Valladolid in 1607, it has increasingly been a magnet for *forasteros* (new inhabitants) from all over Spain. This is as true in the culinary sphere as in others, and while there have always been the typical TABERNAS and unpretentious eating places serving the fare of CASTILLA LA NUEVA, the best restaurants have always been started by foreigners or new arrivals, usually from the Basque country and the north. Thus the first restaurant of any elegance and sophistication was Lhardy, founded by an Italian in 1839 – and still maintaining good standards. Of the present top-flight establishments, by far the oldest, Horcher, was founded by an Austrian, while most of the others owe their cuisine and their success to *nuevos madrileños* (new inhabitants of Madrid) such as Clemencio Fuentes at Jockey, Benjamín Urdiain at Zalacaín, Ramón Ramírez at El Amparo and Pedro Larumbe at Cabo Mayor.

Elegant restaurants such as these have been much influenced by the NOUVELLE CUISINE, but there are others which specialize in authentic regional cooking, such as Alkalde, Guria or Jai-Alai (Basque); Horno de Sta. Teresa (Asturian); O'Pazo (Galician); Las Cumbres (Andalucían); La Panocha (Murcian) – and these are just a very few – so that the cooking of any part of the country may be sampled in Madrid. For dishes typical of Madrid itself and Castilla la Nueva, it is best to head for the simpler and less expensive restaurants in Old Madrid around the Puerta del Sol and the magnificent arcaded Plaza Mayor or in the Calle Ventura de la Vega or the Calle Echegaray, off the main Alcalá and near the Prado Museum.

S *Mahón*
A CHEESE

Made in the ISLAS BALEARES, particularly Minorca, this is a soft cow's milk cheese with a fat content of 45 percent and moulded in cloth in characteristic squares of 4½–9 lb. It is matured for 2 months and smeared with olive oil to help preserve it, and may be eaten all year, the creamy white interior becoming harder and darker with age.

S *maíz*
P *milho*
CORN

It has been suggested that corn was brought to Spain from Asia by the Moors in the 13th century. However, it seems a good deal more likely that the plant was native to the tropical regions of South America, where it had been extensively cultivated at the time of Columbus, and was first introduced to Europe by the CONQUISTADORES.

---

see also   *Majorca: see Islas Baleares*

Corn is much grown in the north of Spain and Portugal, as food for humans and animals. It was first introduced to the Asturias in 1604 by Gonzalo Méndez de Cancio, governor of Florida. It was not cultivated in Galicia until the beginning of the 18th century and only caught on as a foodstuff after the dreadful famines of 1812. It is very popular in the form of a "porridge" known as GACHA.

S *Málaga*
A CHEESE

A semi-soft goat's milk cheese made around Málaga. The interior is compact and creamy with a light pungent taste, and has a fat content of 58 percent. Ripened for 5 days, it should be eaten fresh.

S *Málaga*
DEMARCATED WINE REGION

Málaga has been famous for its rich dessert wines since Roman times. Their heyday was in late Victorian times, and you will still come across silver wine labels inscribed "Mountain", referring to the location of the vineyards in the hills around the city. Two factors have contributed to a decline in their production and consumption: a current fad for dry wines and the invasion of Málaga and its vineyards by tourists and property developers. At its glorious best, when it is neither sticky nor unduly sweet (as in the wonderful Scholtz Solera 1885), Málaga is one of my favorites for an after-dinner tipple – and nothing else comes near it for drinking with Christmas pudding.

The seal for the Málaga demarcated wine region

S *Manchego*
A CHEESE

Made in the broad plains of Don Quixote's La Mancha, this is the most famous of Spanish cheeses, being to Spain what Cheddar is to England. Produced in large, thick rounds, patterned with the esparto grass in which it is pressed and aged for not less than 2 months, it has a firm texture with a few holes towards the center, a yellow rind and a fat content of 50 per cent. It is sold in three grades: *fresco*, sold and eaten as soon as it is mature, with an elastic ivory-colored interior; *curado*, the most commonly found type, kept for a further 13 weeks before being sold, and with a firm interior of a deeper yellow; *añejo*, matured for six months to a year, sometimes in jars of olive oil. With ageing it becomes much darker in color and harder, and acquires a sharp bite, and is often served as an appetizer.

Manchego cheese is sometimes cubed, dredged in egg and breadcrumbs, then fried and served as *queso frito*. In grated form it is used very widely in cooking in the same way as Parmesan and other hard cheeses.

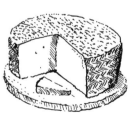

🇸 *manjar blanco*
SWEET CHICKEN

An historic Spanish sweet dish traditionally served *before* a meal. At the historic University of Salamanca, the statutes required every student during the period of examinations to offer supper to the doctors and masters, placing in front of each diner "a round wooden box and a large porcelain bowl with a lid, the first containing sweetmeats and the second *manjar blanco*.

"The professors and graduates sit at table and are served by six students chosen for the task. After the above preliminaries, each diner is served with a roast bird, often turkey. . . ."

Cooked chicken breasts are simmered with milk, sugar, cloves, a little rice flour and sometimes strips of orange zest, until thick. The flavorings are removed and the mixture placed on small earthenware discs and baked in a very hot oven until brown.

🇵 *manjar-branco*
MILK PUDDING

Evidently of common origin with MANJAR BLANCO, this popular Portuguese dessert from the BEIRA ALTA is today made by creaming *fecula* (a local starch), wheat flour, sugar and milk together with cloves, and simmering the mixture until thick. The cloves are removed and the dough browned in the oven. It is served with cream.

🇵 *manjericão* 🇸 *albahaca*
BASIL

Although basil is not much used for cooking in Portugal or Spain, it is the custom in Lisboa on St. Anthony's Day (12 June) for young people to give small pots of the herb to their sweethearts. It is in the narrow streets of the Alfama, the ancient Moorish quarter of Lisbon, where Santo Antonio, the patron saint of lovers, was born, that the festivities are at their most picturesque.

🇵 *manteiga*

Butter; see MANTEQUILLA.

🇵 *manteigas compostas*
SAVORY BUTTERS

In Portuguese restaurants, savory butters, sometimes a proprietary brand called Tartex, are often put on the table before a meal to be eaten with bread or on small squares of toast as an appetizer. The danger is to blunt one's appetite by eating too much!

They are all made very simply by mixing soft, unsalted butter with a savory flavoring. Either a sieve or a food processor may be used to make the butters.

manteiga de anchovas (P) anchovy butter	*4 oz canned anchovies, drained and soaked in milk for 10 minutes* *freshly ground black pepper* *10 tbsp unsalted butter, softened*	*Rinse and rub the anchovies through a fine sieve and grind a little pepper over the purée. Mix thoroughly with the softened butter, using a wooden spoon. Put the mixture into small pots, cover with foil and chill.*
manteiga de atum (P) tuna butter	*5 oz fresh or canned tuna, drained* *a little lemon juice* *freshly ground black pepper* *12 tbsp unsalted butter, softened* *If the tuna is fresh, first poach it in a little salted water until tender, then drain, skin, bone*	*and flake it. Either push cooked, fresh or canned tuna through a fine sieve or use a food processor to purée it. Season with lemon juice and freshly ground pepper. Mix thoroughly with the softened butter, using a wooden spoon. Put the mixture into small pots, cover with foil and chill.*

manteiga de camarão (P) shrimp butter	*5 oz shrimp, cooked and peeled* *freshly ground black pepper* *6 tbsp unsalted butter, softened*	*Rub the shrimp through a fine sieve or use a food processor, season with pepper, then mix with the softened butter, using a wooden spoon. Put the mixture into small pots, cover with foil and chill.*
manteiga de pimentos (P) pimento butter	*6 oz canned red peppers (pimentos), drained* *salt and pepper* *6 tbsp unsalted butter, softened*	*Push the peppers through a sieve or purée in a food processor, season with salt and pepper, then mix with the softened butter, using a wooden spoon. Put the mixture into small pots, cover with foil and chill.*

mantequilla *manteiga*
BUTTER

Butter is made only in the north of Spain and Portugal and is not much used in cooking or provided with bread or rolls except in the more expensive restaurants and hotels, where it is served sparingly in small individual portions in foil.

manzana *maça*
APPLE

The region of Spain best known for its apples is the province of ASTURIAS on the Atlantic north coast, where they are grown both for eating and for making cider. The orchards lie in the coastal strip between the mountains and the sea. The other main production areas are Lérida, Alicante, VALENCIA and Murcia.

manzanilla
CAMOMILE, CAMOMILE TEA, TYPE OF DRY SHERRY, SMALL OLIVE

Camomile tea is popular in Spain and is an infusion of the flowers of the camomile plant, which grows wild all over Spain. The word *manzanilla* is also used to describe a very light and dry type of SHERRY made in Sanlúcar de Barrameda, probably so named because both the tea and the sherry are highly aromatic. In a bar it is as well to be quite definite about what one wants, because I have on occasion ordered a sherry and been served with the tisane! The word is also used to describe a variety of small olive, and here too confusion may arise. In his book *Sherry*, Julian Jeffs relates how ''a prominent sherry shipper sent a small barrel of them, preserved in brine, to one of his customers. A very worried wine buyer telephoned and complained diffidently that his present of manzanilla had been tampered with: the wine tasted strongly of salt and it was full of foreign bodies.''

María Teresa de Austria
17TH-CENTURY CONSORT

The daughter of Philip IV of Spain, María Teresa married Louis XIV of France in 1660 and was ridiculed at Versailles for various culinary innovations (see CHOCOLATE Y CACAO). A special object of attack was her Spanish serving maid, ''La Molina'', who, in the words of Mlle de Montpensier's *Mémoires* ''assuaged the hunger of her poor mistress by giving her cold pasties, prepared with minced meat, highly seasoned and enveloped in *feuilleté* pastry''. This pastry, which La Grande Mademoiselle goes on to denigrate, was in fact nothing other than HOJALDRE, the original puff pastry, invented in Spain.

marinar

Cooking method; to marinate, see ADOBAR.

---

see also   **To marinate:** *see adobar*

S *mariscada a la plancha con salsa romesco*

MIXED GRILLED
SHELLFISH

A dish from CATALUÑA in which an assortment of fresh shellfish is grilled in the shell A LA PLANCHA, on a hot plate griddle brushed with olive oil, and served with the spicy SALSA ROMESCO.

S P *marisco*

SHELLFISH

This is the word used in Spain and Portugal to describe shellfish in all its wide variety. There is excellent shellfish from all along the Spanish and Portuguese coastlines, some of the best being from the Atlantic waters of the Bay of Cádiz and the ALGARVE, and from the northern shores of Portugal, Galicia (see ASTURIAS AND GALICIA) and the Basque region. Demand for shellfish in Spain outstrips supply, and substantial amounts of scampi and lobster fished in the cold waters of the North Sea are sent from Scotland.

S *marmelada*

A PRESERVE

A stiff quince paste. There is a story that marmalade was first concocted by the Spanish doctor of Mary Queen of Scots as a cure for sea sickness and hence called *mer alade*, but it seems much more probable that it took its name from Portuguese MARMELADA. As we know it today, it certainly originated in Dundee, Scotland, when a ship with a cargo of bitter oranges took shelter in the harbor, and James Keiller bought a large quantity, only to find that the fruit was too bitter to re-sell. His thrifty Scots wife converted the oranges into a jam, for which there was a runaway demand, and in 1797 the firm of James Keiller & Sons was established to make and market it.

Ninety-five percent of the orange crop from SEVILLA is exported to Britain for making marmalade, either as fresh oranges or a processed pulp. Firms like Frank Cooper's consider that the best results are obtained by carrying out the first boiling and subsequent cooking of the oranges in Sevilla as soon as the fruit is picked. The cooked fruit is left to mature for some months and is then despatched in barrels to Britain for the addition of sugar and for final cooking and maturation.

see also   *Market: see mercado*

marmelada (P) **membrillo (S)** *quince paste*	2 lb ripe quinces, wiped with a damp cloth, but not washed or peeled 1½ lb granulated sugar zest of 1 lemon in a single piece 1 cinnamon stick	for another 30 minutes until a purée or pulp is obtained. Remove the zest and cinnamon stick. Strain the pulp through muslin tied up at the four corners and supported in a large sieve, with a bowl underneath to collect the juice – this can be used to sweeten other fruit desserts. After 20 minutes and before it has time to cool completely, spoon the pulp into a glass dish and leave to set.
	Cut up the quinces, removing seeds and cores, and put into a heavy pan. Cover with cold water, bring to the boil and simmer gently for 1 hour until tender. Remove with a slotted spoon and push through a sieve or purée in a food processor, then return to the pan with the sugar, lemon zest and cinnamon stick. Simmer	*In Spain, membrillo is usually shaped like a meat loaf, and in Portugal, marmelada has a domed shape. Leave to cool, then cut into thin slices to serve with cheese.*

P S marmelo membrillo

QUINCE

Marmelo in Portuguese and *membrillo* in Spanish mean "quince". The paste made from the fruit is known as MARMELADA in Portugal and *membrillo* in Spain. It may be eaten either as a jam or sweetmeat, or served with cheese, which it accompanies very well. *Membrillo* was a favorite of the last of the Antipopes, Pedro de Luna, and during his last years, in the early 15th century, when he took refuge in the citadel of Peñíscola, it was by dosing it with arsenic that his Papist enemies made an unsuccessful attempt to kill the indestructible old man.

S marmitako

COOKING UTENSIL

Basque name for MARMITE.

S marmite

COOKING UTENSIL

This large pot used by Basque fishermen and known here as *marmitako*, is concave in shape to prevent the contents from slopping over when cooking on board a boat. It has given its name to a famous dish made by stewing BONITO with onion, garlic and potatoes. In this part of the world it is held that a *marmite* never tastes so good as when made at sea and, during the bonito season, members of the *cofradías* or SOCIEDADES GASTRONOMICAS who have fishermen friends count themselves very lucky.

S marrons glacés

Glazed chestnuts; see CASTAÑA.

masa massa

PASTRY

The main types of pastry used in Spain are *masa quebrada* (rich pie pastry), *masa de* HOJALDRE, *masa sablée* (short pastry), *masa con almendras* (a rich pastry incorporating ground almonds) and *petisú* (choux pastry). Directions for making pastry are given in individual recipes.

Puff pastry is known in Portugal as *massa folhada*, and pastries used for sweets as *massas de pastelaria*. They include *massa de amêndoas* (an almond pastry made with ground almonds, sugar and egg white), *massa areada* (short pastry) of which basic ingredients are flour, butter, sugar, eggs and egg yolks, lemon zest or vanilla, *massa de profiteroles* (choux pastry) of which basic ingredients are flour, BANHA and butter in equal parts, water and eggs.

See also MASSA PARA EMPADAS for savory pastries.

see also	*Marzipan: see mazapán*

S *masa con almendras*   Almond pastry; see MASA.

S *masa sablée*   Sablée pastry; see MASA.

P *massa*   Pastry; see MASA.

P *massa areada*   Sablée pastry; see MASA.

P *massa de amêndoas*   Almond pastry; see MASA.

P *massa de profiteroles*   Choux pastry; see MASA.

P *massa folhada*   Puff pastry; see HOJALDRE.

P *massa de empadas*

PASTRY FOR SAVORY TARTLETS

These attractive pastry cases may be used to hold a variety of fillings – for example, *molho bechamel* (see SALSA BESAMEL) blended with minced chicken, fish or shrimps. To make them you will need the individual molds about 2–2½ inches in diameter, available in great variety at any ironmonger in Portugal or from kitchen shops at home. They are similar to muffin pans.

---

massa de empadas (P)
pastry for savory tartlets

2¾ cups self-rising flour
⅔ cup butter or margarine
1 egg, beaten
salt

Sift the flour into a bowl and make a well in the center. Add the butter and work with the hands until smooth. Add the egg, season with salt, then flatten the dough, adding a little water, if necessary. Continue working it until thoroughly kneaded, then cover with a dish-towel and leave to rest for an hour or two. Dust a table top or pastry board with flour and roll out the dough. Cut circles of appropriate size, then press these into lightly greased molds to line the insides. Add the appropriate filling, then cover the molds with smaller circles of dough, well pinched around the side so that they are securely sealed. Bake in a hot oven (425°F) until the pastry is golden brown.

Before serving, gently ease out the tartlets with a knife.

P *massa vinhe*

BATTER

This is a batter used for coating and frying fish, meat and vegetables. When using it for desserts, add a tablespoon of sugar to the other ingredients.

massa vinhe (P) batter	1¾ cups flour ¼ cup olive oil salt 2 tbsp beer water 2 egg whites 1 egg yolk	Sift the flour into a large bowl and make a well in the center. Pour in the oil, a pinch of salt, the beer and a little water. Mix the batter thoroughly until smooth, then add the yolk and stir with a wooden spoon. Alternatively this can be done in a food processor. Leave to rest for 2 hours. Beat the egg whites with a pinch of salt until stiff and fold into the batter. Use as soon as possible.

massapão

Marzipan; see MAZAPAN.

Matança, A

Butchering of the pig; see MATANZA, LA.

Matanza, La

THE BUTCHERING OF THE PIG

The hams and many varieties of cured pork and sausage (see EMBUTIDOS) seen hanging from the ceiling in any Spanish or Portuguese grocer's or pork butcher's shop (see CHARCUTARIA) are all products of this annual butchering rite.

Richard FORD, the early 19th-century traveler and acute observer of all things Spanish, describes how in Spain "pigs pervade the provinces" and along the Portuguese border "when the acorns are ripe and fall from the trees, the greedy animals are turned out in legions from the villages, which more correctly may be described as coalitions of pigsties."

Once a year their owners invite friends and relatives to *La Matanza*, which traditionally takes place on 10 or 11 November on the day of St. Andrew or St. Martín, hence the proverb "every man and pig has his St. Martín or his fatal hour, *a cada puerco su San Martín*." As Ford continues, "it is the duty of a good pig to get fat as soon as he can and then to die for the good of his country."

After the man of the house has killed it, the women folk set to. The legs are cut off for curing; and everything else is salted, smoked, marinated, stuffed into casings and hung up to dry to provide rations for the winter months ahead. The sweet hams of the Alpujarras near Granada are salted only sparingly and buried in the snow to cure.

The ritual of *La Matanza* continues in small villages, but the production of hams and CHORIZOS is now big business. Pigs are now killed under strict supervision in slaughterhouses while the hams are hung up to cure by the thousands in vast underground cellars. See also JAMON SERRANO.

P *Mateus Rosé*

A WINE

"Mateus Rosé", one of the world's largest selling and most popular wines, was the creation of the late Fernando van-Zeller Guedes, who founded the SOGRAPE wine company to make a somewhat sweeter pink wine along the lines of the gently sparkling Portuguese VINHOS VERDES. By 1951 the British author Sacheverell Sitwell was writing that it was "the most delicious vin rosé that I have ever tasted ... Mateus is delicious beyond words; and since I am told that it will travel and is exported to Brazil, it is a pity that one cannot buy it here."

Mateus, in its distinctive flagon-shaped bottle, has long since achieved huge sales all over the world. It is made by allowing the skins of the grapes to stand in contact with the fermenting must for a short time so as to withdraw coloring matter, and the sparkle is achieved by pumping in carbon dioxide gas under pressure. The plants used by SOGRAPE, and by J.M. da Fonseca Internacional (see ESTREMADURA) for making the competitive "Lancers", are among the largest and most sophisticated in the world.

S *Mató*

A CHEESE

This popular cheese from CATALUÑA is made from goat's milk boiled with lemon juice or other vegetable rennet. It is a soft white cheese, resembling cottage cheese that is not matured and must be consumed fresh within a week. Eaten with honey as *mel y mató*, it is a favourite Catalan dessert.

S *mazapán*
P *maçapão, massapâo*

MARZIPAN

The origins of marzipan, widely made both in Spain and Portugal, have been much debated. It has been related to the *panis martius*, or March bread of Roman antiquity offered up during the Spring rites and later incorporated into the Christian liturgy. There is an Italian legend that *marzipane*, or St. Mark's bread, was made in Venice at some indeterminate time when bread was in short supply, while there is a strong and very similar tradition that it was invented in

see also

Mayonnaise: *see salsa mahonesa, salsa mahonesa muselina, salsa mahonesa verde*

Toledo by the nuns of the Convent of San Clemente in 1212, when supplies of flour had been cut off during hostilities between the Moors and Alfonso VIII of Castile. The nuns hit upon the idea of using their stocks of almonds and sugar, by making a paste with the almonds and blending it with the sugar, the name being derived from *maza* (a mallet) and *pan* (bread). Molds for making marzipan in the form of figures and religious images and dating from a very early period still exist in the convent. Marzipan has always been linked with religion and is today much eaten in Spain on *Nochebuena* (Christmas Eve), when it is sold in all sorts of different shapes – geometrical, animal, fish and human. Similarly in Portugal, where it is made of almonds from the groves of the ALGARVE first planted by the Moors, it is the basis of a whole range of confectionery and is sold in the CONFITERIAS in Spain and PASTELARIAS in Portugal modeled in marvelous detail.

mazapán (S) marzipan	1 lb almonds, blanched and skinned ½ tsp almond extract 1 lb vanilla sugar (see page 297) 2 egg whites confectioners' sugar, flavored with 2–3 drops orange flower water	*Pound the almonds finely in a mortar and pestle with the almond extract and the sugar, slowly adding the egg whites and mixing well with the confectioners' sugar, using a spatula or wooden spoon. Leave to stand for 10 minutes, then roll out the paste ¼ inch thick. Cut it into shapes with fancy pastry cutters, place them on a baking sheet and leave until dry in a low oven (300°F).*

P *medalhões*

A CUT OF MEAT OR FISH

This is generally cut into a round or oval shape.

S *medallones*

A cut of meat; see TERNERA.

meia-desfeite de bacalhau

BACALHAU WITH CHICKPEAS

One of the many ways of preparing the dried, salted cod so popular in Portugal. This version from LISBOA is cooked with chickpeas, onion, parsley and garlic, and garnished with slices of hard boiled egg.

The index, in English, is arranged by types of food — eggs, cheese, fish — kitchen equipment, cooking terms and other subjects. Consult it for recipes that make use of particular ingredients.

mejillones
 mexilhões

MUSSELS

Mussels are used for TAPAS by boiling and opening them and serving them with SALSA VINAGRETA; they may also be removed from their shells, dredged in egg and breadcrumbs and fried in olive oil. In the north, they are popular served in scallop shells as *conchas de mejillones*. The mussels are cleaned and opened as described in the following recipe and a little chopped onion is added. They are then removed from their shells and placed in scallop shells or ramekins before being topped with SALSA BESAMEL made with the addition of egg yolks. A little grated cheese is added and they are then browned under the broiler. Mussels are also widely used in dishes such as PAELLA and ZARZUELA.

see also   **Mealtimes:** *see horas de comida*

mejillones en salsa verde (S) mussels in green sauce	*Serves 4* 48 mussels ⅓ cup dry white wine 4 shallots, finely chopped 2 tbsp olive oil 2 cloves garlic, crushed 2 tbsp chopped parsley salt and pepper to taste *Soak the mussels in cold water for 5 to 10 minutes. Scrape the shells with a knife and scrub them with a brush until thoroughly clean. Discard any that are open. Put them in a large saucepan with the wine and bring to the boil, when the mussels will open. Leave for a minute*

or two, then remove with a slotted spoon and transfer to a plate – any which have not opened must be discarded, as they are not fit to eat. Strain and reserve the wine stock. Remove the mussels from their shells, keeping enough of the half shells for serving the mussels later. Meanwhile, make a sauce: sauté the shallots in hot olive oil, then add the garlic, parsley and finally the reserved wine stock. Season, place the mussels in the reserved half shells and spoon the sauce over them. Eat with the fingers by sucking the contents from the shells.

P **mel**

HONEY

In Portugal, *mel* is used to describe real honey (*mel de abelhas*) and molasses (*mel da cana*), both much used for cakes and confectionery. See MEXIDOS DO NATAL.

P **melão**

Melon; see MELON.

S **meloco-tones**
P **pessegos**

PEACHES

In recent years there has been a large expansion in the production of peaches. The type most common to Spain is the cling, with firm flesh and tight adhesion to the stone. Nectarines are also being grown in large quantities.

melocotones al ron (S) peach soufflés with rum	*For each serving* 1 egg white, beaten until stiff with a pinch of salt 1 tsp sugar 2 tbsp rum 2 peach halves, peeled if fresh

Mix the beaten egg whites with the sugar and half the rum. Put the peach halves in a 4½ inch diameter individual ovenproof dish and heap the meringue mixture onto them with a fork. Bake in a very hot oven (450°F) for 2–3 minutes until the mixture is browned on top.

Warm the remaining rum and pour it around the peaches. Set alight and bring to the table when flaming.

S *melón*
P *melão*

MELON

Melons were known to the ancient Romans, but were at that time only the size of oranges; they were introduced to Spain by the Moors and have long since become a staple part of the diet, being an almost obligatory dessert from July to September, often eaten with JAMON SERRANO as an appetizer. Different varieties are, in fact, available all year round, beginning with the *Ogen* or early melon in April, soon followed by the well known canteloupe. In mid-June there is a *melón reticulado* (a "reticulated melon"), so called because of the network of white lines on the skin. Honeydew melons appear in July and, finally in October, there are the Tendral or Elche melons with thick, furrowed skins that will keep fresh and juicy when properly stored until the following March.

The digestibility and therapeutic properties of the melon were the subject of heated controversy among the royal physicians of the 16th century, an echo of which survives in the Spanish proverb: *El melón en ayunas es oro; al mediodia, plata; y por la noche, mata* (the melon at breakfast is gold; at midday, silver; and at night, it kills).

S *membrillo*

Quince; see MARMELO AND MARMELADA.

S *menestra a la Riojana*

MIXED VEGETABLES
FROM RIOJA

From the famous wine district of the RIOJA, this is made from whatever vegetables are in season – the larger the variety the better.

The recipe is from the kitchens of the Marqués de Riscal and was given to me by the renowned Petri.

---

menestra a la Riojana (S)
mixed vegetables from the Rioja

Serves 4 (or 6 as an appetizer)

1 lb fresh peas
1 lb green beans
½ lb carrots, cut into strips
4 leeks, white part only, cut into chunks
½ lb artichoke hearts
1 small cauliflower, divided into florets after boiling
5 tbsp olive oil
1 large onion, chopped
¼lb jamón serrano (ham)
flour, for dredging
1 egg, beaten
olive oil
1 clove garlic
few strands of saffron
2 hard boiled egg yolks
salt to taste
2 hard boiled eggs, cut into wedges
1½ tbsp chopped parsley

Bring about 2 inches salted water to the boil in a large saucepan. Add the peas, beans, carrots, leeks, artichokes and cauliflower, cover and boil for 15 minutes so that they are not overcooked, then remove with a slotted spoon and reserve. (In the Rioja the different vegetables are sometimes cooked separately.)

Heat the oil in a large, heavy casserole, sauté the onion until soft, then stir in the jamón serrano (ham). Add the peas, beans, carrots and leeks, and cook for 2–3 minutes. Remove from the heat and set aside.

Dredge the artichokes and cauliflower florets with flour and beaten egg, fry in hot oil in another pan until brown, then remove and add to the vegetables in the casserole. Mash the garlic, saffron and hard-boiled yolks in a mortar, stir with 1 tbsp hot water and add to the casserole. Season to taste. Place the casserole uncovered over a gentle heat for 10 minutes, shaking (but not stirring) from time to time so that the contents do not stick to the bottom. Garnish with the wedges of hard boiled egg and chopped parsley.

---

see also

Melon: see melón

S *Méntrida*

DEMARCATED WINE
REGION

Located to the southwest of Madrid in the province of Toledo and lying alongside the much larger region of LA MANCHA, Méntrida produces robust red wines for everyday drinking.

S *menú*
P *ementa*

MENU

Apart from the ordinary à la carte menu, most Spanish restaurants have a *menú del dia* (menu of the day), known as *menú do dia*, *ementa do dia* or *pratos do dia* in Portugal, and varying according to what is most attractive in the market. The top-flight and most expensive Spanish restaurants often offer a *menú de degustación* with some eight recommended dishes (served, of course, in small portions). This is a convenient way of sampling their specialties. It is not at all common to find a *menú de degustación* in Portugal. What is accepted and frequently done is for three persons to order three different dishes and the restaurant to divide each dish between the three persons. This is possible even in expensive restaurants.

S **P** *mercado*

MARKET

All Spanish and Portuguese towns have large central markets which remain thronged and popular despite the encroachment of the supermarkets or SUPERMERCA-DOS. Some of these markets are vast in size but all are organized in the same way: with rows of individual stalls clustered together according to whether they sell fruit, vegetables, fish, meat, charcuterie, groceries, spices or whatever. There is a simple satisfaction in seeing the profusion of vegetables fresh from the fields, the sacks of dried beans or barrels of salted herring, the hams and cured sausages hanging in serried rows, and, above all, the almost entire absence of prepackaged commodities. Spanish and Portuguese homemakers, or those who do not go out to work – and also the best of the restaurateurs – still plan their meals according to what is fresh and in season at the market, and this leads to a welcome and very sensible variation of menus throughout the year.

See also MERCAMADRID.

S *Merca-madrid*

A WHOLESALE MARKET

Mercamadrid is the huge and spotlessly hygienic wholesale market built at Vallecas on the outskirts of MADRID to replace the old Mercado Central de Legazpi – where it is said that during its last days the rats were so numerous and fierce as to frighten even the cats and dogs. It rivals the central market in Paris in size and amenities, the six halls dealing with fruit and vegetables alone extending to 76,000 square yards and handling some 428,000 tons of produce annually. The new fish and vegetable markets are among the largest in Europe – the *madrileños* (inhabitants of Madrid) are nicknamed *gatos* (cats) and one explanation for this is their predilection for fish. The market's statistics are interesting evidence of the tastes: in order of sales, the most popular fish are whiting, sardines, *gallo* (a small, oval flat fish), fresh anchovies, hake and red mullet; the most popular shellfish are mussels, cockles, prawns, crab, clams, sea crayfish, sea snails; and the biggest-selling frozen fish are hake, prawns, squid, whiting, octopus, sea crayfish, sole and fresh anchovies. Some 40 percent of the fish is supplied from Galicia (see ASTURIAS AND GALICIA) followed by ANDALUCIA and the Basque coast.

P *mercearia*

Grocery; see ULTRAMARINOS.

S *merienda*

AFTERNOON SNACK

In Spain, the time between *almuerzo* (lunch) and *cena* (evening meal), usually eaten at 10 p.m. or 11 p.m., is so long that Spaniards fit in an extra light meal called *merienda*. Children are usually given a BOCADILLO, a substantial sandwich of CHORIZO, JAMON SERRANO or TORTILLA, on their return from school, while their parents may go out a little later at 7 or 8 p.m. to trifle with pastries and chocolate at a CONFITERIA.

S
P *merluza pescada*

HAKE

Hake is particularly plentiful in Spain where the smaller fish are known as *pescadillas* and are usually dusted with flour and fried until crisp in olive oil with their tails in their mouths. In its various forms such as MERLUZA A LA VASCA, MERLUZA CON MAHONESA Y SALSA DE PIMIENTOS and MERLU-ZA A LA GALLEGA, hake is the favorite fish of most Spaniards. It may also be cooked more simply in a *court bouillon* with white wine, and served with SALSA MAHONESA or SALSA VINAGRETA, a method which brings out all its delicate flavor.

S *merluza a la gallega*

HAKE GALICIAN STYLE

A Galician way of cooking hake or similar firm white fish. Fish steaks are baked in individual earthenware CAZUELAS with highly seasoned potatoes cooked with onion, garlic and paprika.

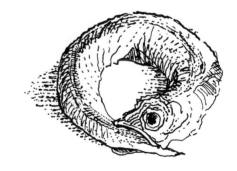

S *merluza a la vasca*

HAKE IN GREEN
SAUCE WITH
ASPARAGUS TIPS

This is one of the best-known dishes from the Basque region and also one of the very few of which the origin and date are known. In his *Viaje por las cocinas de España* ("Journey through the kitchens of Spain"), Luis Antonio de Vega recounts how he came upon a letter written during the first week of May 1723 by Doña Plácida de Larrea of Bilbao to a namesake living in Navarra. Doña Plácida specified that the hake must be caught from a boat by hook and line. She went on to describe how she stewed it in an earthenware CAZUELA and served it in a green sauce made from parsley and with a garnish of asparagus, a present from friends in Tudela.

---

merluza a la vasca (S)
hake in green sauce
with asparagus tips

Serves 4

4 hake or cod steaks, about 1 in thick
flour
4 tbsp olive oil
2 small onions, chopped
2 cloves garlic, crushed
1 tbsp flour
1⅓ cups fish stock
1 tbsp chopped parsley
½ lb fresh peas, shelled and cooked
4 small potatoes, peeled, boiled sliced
salt and pepper
8 asparagus tips
1 hard boiled egg, cut into wedges

Dredge the fish in flour, then fry in hot olive oil until browned. Place in a large ovenproof dish or in four small ovenproof dishes.

Using the same olive oil and adding a little more if necessary, sauté the onions until golden, then add the garlic and flour. Cook gently for 10 minutes, stirring in the fish stock and parsley. Pour this sauce over the fish, add the peas, potatoes and a little salt and pepper, then cook in a moderate oven (350°F) for 20 minutes until the fish is cooked through.

Garnish with asparagus tips and wedges of hard boiled egg.

---

merluza con mahonesa y salsa de pimientos (S)
hake with mayonnaise and pimiento sauce

Serves 4

2 lb hake or halibut, in one piece
1 onion, finely chopped
1 tbsp chopped parsley
¼ cup dry white wine
2 tbsp olive oil
1⅓ cups salsa mahonesa (mayonnaise)

Pimento sauce
1 tbsp chopped parsley
1 clove garlic, crushed
2 shallots, finely chopped
15 oz canned red peppers (pimentos), drained
pinch of salt

Put the fish in an overproof dish with the onion, parsley, wine and oil. Bake for about 30 minutes in a fairly hot oven (400°F) until the flesh easily comes off the bone. Remove and discard the backbone and skin, then return the fish to the ovenproof dish and set aside.

Meanwhile, make the pimento sauce. Push the parsley, garlic, shallots and peppers through a sieve or purée the ingredients in a blender or food processor. Season to taste with salt. Pour first the salsa mahonesa and then the pimiento sauce over the fish, then return it to the oven for 10–15 minutes to heat through.

S *mermelada*

JAM

Mermelada in Spanish means jam or *confiture*, and not marmalade. Most *mermeladas* are cloyingly sweet to the American taste but *not* to the Spanish, and if you want marmalade you should ask for *mermelada de naranja amarga*.

P ***mexidos do Natal***

CHRISTMAS DESSERT

A Christmas dessert from the MINHO made by boiling together a lump of butter, port wine, lemon rind, cinnamon, honey and sugar in water. To this are added pine nuts, walnuts and raisins and, as cooking continues, cut-up bread soaked in water. This is all boiled together with careful stirring to avoid lumps and then put into a glass dish and eaten cold.

P ***mexilhões***

Mussels; see MEJILLONES.

S ***miel***

HONEY

In Spain, as in the UK and USA, there are many different varieties of honeys, among the most fragrant being those from the orange blossom of the LEVANTE and the heather of the Sierra de Francia between Salamanca and the Portuguese border. There are even narcotic and poisonous honeys (like that from the oleander), but these do not reach the market.

One of the most unusual thick honeys, a dark mahogany color and robust in taste, is that made by bees in La Alberca near Ciudad Rodrigo. The acorns of the evergreen oak on which these bees feed are still green and on the tree.

One of the best-known dishes is *mel y mató* (honey and cream cheese) which comes from CATALUÑA.

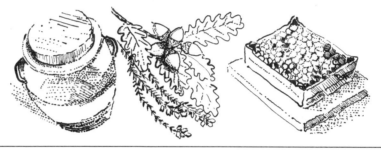

S ***migas***

FRIED BREADCRUMBS

Serves 4

4 tbsp olive oil
2 cloves garlic
½ lb chorizo sausage, skinned and sliced
¼ lb tocino or unsmoked bacon, rind removed and chopped
7 oz stale white bread (about 7 slices), crusts removed and soaked in water
1 tsp pimentón dulce (sweet paprika)

Heat a little olive oil in a frying pan, cook the garlic until browned and discard it. Add the chorizo and tocino, and fry for about 10 minutes until brown. Squeeze the bread dry on paper towels, sprinkle it with pimentón, and crumble into the pan. Fry until golden brown and serve with fried eggs.

P ***milho***

Corn; see MAIZ.

P ***milho frito***

BREAD

A bread made with cornmeal, which is traditionally served fried with the Madeiran specialty *carne de vinho e alhos* (pork marinated with garlic and white wine before cooking).

CAPITALIZED *words within entries refer the reader to more information on the same subject.*

see also   ***Milk:*** *see leche*

Minho

PORTUGUESE
REGION

The Minho is the most northerly of the coastal regions of Portugal, bounded by the Minho river, with Galicia to the north and the DOURO to the south. The most striking geological feature is the presence of granite, used for building, paving, for fencing in the form of flat slabs and for the pillars used to support the high-growing vines.

With its chestnuts and oak trees, its groves of eucalyptus, wild roses and

hydrangea lining the country roads, this is one of the most scenic areas of Portugal. As in the Douro, the landscape is a patchwork of fields and vineyards owned by small-holders who often grow the tall green *couves* beneath trellised vines. There are few towns of any size, the largest being Braga, once the seat of the Primate of All Spain and still strongly ecclesiastical in character – there is an old saying which goes; "Lisbon plays, Coimbra studies, Braga prays and Oporto works."

Gastronomically, the Minho is first and foremost famous for its CALDO VERDE made from the tall, dark green *couve* or Portuguese cabbage grown everywhere. As in other coastal areas, the fish is first rate, and LAMPREIA, stewed, roasted or served with rice is a specialty. Pork is popular and is prepared in various ways, for example, *lombo de porco assado à minhota* (roast loin); *costeletas* (cutlets); ROJÕES A MODA DE MINHO and *bucho de porco com todos os matadores* (elaborately stuffed pig's stomach). The capital – Braga – provides FRIGIDEIRAS DE CARNE and sweets such as FATIAS DE BRAGA. A Christmas specialty of the region is MEXIDOS DO NATAL.

It is, of course, in the Minho that the famous *pétillant* VINHOS VERDES are made.

S *Minorca*

See ISLAS BALEARES.

P *miolos*

Brains; see SESOS.

P *Modesto, Maria de Lourdes*

WRITER AND
BROADCASTER

Maria de Lourdes Modesto is the best-known of contemporary Portuguese food writers. Her book *La Cozinha Tradicional Portuguesa*, first published in 1982, has been reissued many times since. It is a treasury of

traditional Portuguese recipes from the different regions of the country, and she regularly conducts cooking programs on Portuguese television.

S *mojama*

Dried salted tuna fish; see ATUN.

S *mojo colorado*

PIQUANT CHILI
SAUCE

A piquant sauce from the ISLAS CANARIAS containing garlic, olive oil, PIMENTON *picante*, chili peppers and cumin seeds. It is used to accompany fish and also the famous PAPAS ARRUGADAS.

> *If Spanish and Portuguese terms differ from each other, the entry in Portuguese, in the majority of cases, is referred to its Spanish equivalent, where you will find information relevant to both countries.*

P *molejas*　　Sweetbreads; see DESPOJOS.

P *molho bechamel*　　Béchamel or white sauce; see SALSA BESAMEL.

P *molho de tomate*　　Tomato sauce; see SALSA DE TOMATE.

---

molho de tomate (P)
tomato and wine sauce

Makes approx. 2 cups

2 onions, chopped
2 cloves garlic, chopped
olive oil
1 cup dry white wine
1 lb tomatoes, peeled, seeded and chopped, or 1 lb canned tomatoes
2 tbsp tomato paste
2 tsp flour
a little meat stock or water
salt and pepper
1 tbsp chopped parsley

Sauté the chopped onions and garlic slowly for 10 minutes in hot olive oil, then drain off the excess oil. Add the white wine and reduce a little, then stir in the tomatoes, flour, dissolved in a little meat stock, and the tomato paste. Season with salt and pepper and add the chopped parsley. Cook until very soft. Use, for example, with roupa-velha and ameijoas fritas.

P *molho espanhola*　　Sauce espagnole (brown sauce); see SALSA ESPAÑOLA.

P *molho mahonesa*　　Mayonnaise; see SALSA MAHONESA.

P *molho vinagreta*　　Vinaigrette sauce; see SALSA VINAGRETA.

P *molhos*　　Sauces; see SALSAS.

mollejas　　Sweetbreads; see DESPOJOS.

Montilla-Moriles
DEMARCATED WINE REGION

The hill town of Montilla and the village of Moriles, lying to the south of Córdoba in one of the sunniest and hottest parts of Spain, have given their name to wines much resembling SHERRY – in fact, until the region was demarcated in 1944, a lot of Montilla found its way to Jerez de la Frontera for blending. The vines are grown in a very similar chalky soil and, like sherry, undergo

The seal of the Montilla-Moriles demarcated wine region

---

see also　　**Monkfish:** *see rape*

continuous blending in a SOLERA. They are, however, made from the Pedro Ximénez grape rather than the Palomino and traditionally vinified in large earthenware *tinajas* – resembling the large jars in which Ali

Baba hid. Although they are made in all the styles of sherry, the most typical is the light and bone dry fino (sold abroad as "Montilla Dry"), a prime favorite in the TABERNAS of Córdoba as an apéritif.

P *morangos*

Strawberries; see FRESAS.

P *morcela*

A SAUSAGE

A Portuguese blood sausage, akin to the British black pudding and much used in making stews and vegetable dishes.

P *morcelas de Arouca*

A SAUSAGE

A sweet black pudding from the DOURO made with pork loin, almonds, sugar, breadcrumbs and aromatic spices.

Morcilla

S *morcilla*

A SAUSAGE

A Spanish blood sausage much used in cooking stews such as FABADA ASTURIANA and akin to the Scots black pudding. Unlike black pudding, it is, however, made not with oatmeal but with savory rice and onions.

S *morcilla dulce*

A SAUSAGE

A version of MORCILLA prepared with cinnamon, other spices and a little sugar. Although somewhat sweet, it is usually eaten as an appetizer.

> CAPITALIZED *words within entries refer the reader to more information on the same subject.*

P *morgado*

CANDY

A term used to describe a range of candies from the ALGARVE made with a basis of ground almonds, to which are added a variety of other ingredients, such as chocolate, eggs (see OVOS MOLES) and shredded

figs. These are kneaded into a stiff paste and flavored with lemon and cinnamon, then molded into small hens, rabbits, sausages and other motifs typical of the Algarve.

S *Morón*

A CHEESE

From the town of Morón de la Frontera in the province of SEVILLA, this is a soft creamy cheese made from a mixture of cow's and ewe's milk, or sometimes from goat's milk.

It is normally ripened for only 24 hours, but a firmer and spicier version is made by maturing it in olive oil and rubbing it with PIMENTON.

Moros, Los

THE MOORS

The Moorish invasion of Spain took place in 711, and within three short years, the Arabs and their Berber auxiliaries had extended the boundaries of Islam deep into Europe, sweeping through Spain and what is now Portugal and across the Pyrenees into

France. Even today their shadow lies heavy across the land, with remains such as the Great Mosque at Córdoba, the Alhambra in Granada and the Alcázar and Giralda in SEVILLA.

The Moors introduced many new crops

---

see also   ***Moors:*** *see Moros, Los*

and plants to Spain and Portugal, including spices such as saffron, nutmeg and black pepper. They also planted sugar cane in the LEVANTE and almonds, bitter oranges, lemons and grapefruit in ANDALUCIA and the ALGARVE. Perhaps the most important surviving account of agriculture in Moorish-occupied Spain or al-Andalus is the calendar compiled in 961 by the Mozarab bishop Recemundus. His entry for March reads: "Fig trees are grafted in the manner called *tarqi*; the winter corn grows up; and most of the fruit trees break into leaf. It is now that the falcons of Valencia lay eggs on the islands of the river and incubate them for a month. Sugar cane is planted. The first roses and lilies appear. In the kitchen garden, the beans begin to shoot. Quails are seen; silkworms hatch; grey mullet and shad ascend the rivers from the sea. Cucumbers are planted, and cotton, saffron and aubergines sown. During the month the government sends orders for horses to agents in the provinces. Locusts appear and must be destroyed. Mint and marjoram are sown. Peacocks, storks, turtle-doves and many other birds mate . . ."

Possibly because of a shortage of fuel in their North African homelands, the Moors' favorite method of cooking was stewing rather than frying, and the OLLA, a meat and vegetable stew resembling the French *pot-au-feu*, was the prototype of the many PUCHEROS, COCIDOS (or *cozidos* in Portugal) and RANCHOS cooked up and down the peninsula. Another Arabic survival is the cold soup or GAZPACHO so popular in Andalucía, and also, as *gaspacho*, in the Algarve. The small cakes and sweets, made in such profusion in regions formerly occupied by the Moors, often with a basis of ground almonds and egg yolks, reflect their widespread planting of almond groves. After the Reconquest, the Moorish confections were, ironically enough, perfected and sold by the nuns, and to this day their sale constitutes a valuable source of revenue to the religious orders (see also CONFITERIA, PASTELARIAS and BOLOS DE D. RODRIGO).

The consumption of wine was forbidden by the Koran to Believers; in deference to its prohibition many vineyards were rooted up or abandoned, but by the 11th century the sophisticated Moorish sovereign of Sevilla,

Moorish aqueduct near Morella in Maestrazgo

al-Mu'tamid, could write:
As I was passing by
A vine, its tendrils tugged my sleeve,
"Do you design," said I,
"My body so to grieve?"

"Why do you pass," the vine
Replied, "and never greeting make?
It took this blood of mine
Your thirsting bones to slake."

P *morteiro*

Mortar; see MORTERO.

S *mortero*
P *morteiro*

MORTAR

Before the days of the blender and food processor, mortars, some of them 18 inches or so wide, were extensively used – for example in crushing the vegetables for a GAZPACHO. A small mortar is still an essential item of kitchen equipment for crushing such things as garlic, almonds and saffron filaments, used in quantities too small for a blender.

S *morteruelo*

MEAT PATE

This is a dish with a very long history, since the word "morteruelo" first occurs in the *Arte Cisoria* of 1423 by Enrique de Villena, the first book to be written in Castilian on the art of cooking. An even earlier French book, *Le Viander* by Guillaume Tirel, printed between 1373 and 1380, contains a recipe for "morterel", made from pheasant, partridge, capon, giblets of kid, breadcrumbs, ginger and saffron. The 1520 edition of the *Llibre del Coch* of RUBERT DE NOLA contains a recipe corresponding closely to the *pâté foi manchego* as *morteruelo* is known today. This is made from pork and chicken liver, spices, fresh breadcrumbs and garlic in the form of a smooth paste.

P *mouros*

A SAUSAGE

A variety of Portuguese blood sausage.

see also

Mushrooms: *see setas* **Mussels:** *see mejillones*
Mutton: *see carneiro*

S *naranja*
P *laranja*

ORANGE

Bitter oranges were introduced to Spain and Portugal by the Moors some two centuries before the returning Crusaders brought the first specimens to Sicily and Italy from the Near East. They are nowadays grown widely around SEVILLA, large quantities going to Britain for making MARMALADE.

Sweet oranges originated in China and were introduced to Europe much later by the Portuguese after they had opened up the sea route to the Far East. Portuguese oranges are of the best, sweet and very juicy, and they are grown as far north as OPORTO. In Spain, the large navel oranges are grown on a very large scale in the provinces of VALENCIA and Castellón de la Plana, as are tangerines and CLEMENTINAS. As a general rule, the fruit grown in Europe is juicier and less fleshy than that from the southern hemisphere.

---

*naranjas
acarameladas (S)*
caramelized oranges

Serves 4–6

6 oranges
1¼ cups water
1 cup sugar
1 cinnamon stick or vanilla bean

Remove the zest from the oranges with a zester or use a potato peeler and cut into julienne strips.

Bring the water to the boil in a small saucepan with the sugar and cinnamon stick or vanilla bean. Add the zest, reduce the heat, *then simmer for about an hour until the liquid thickens and the zest caramelizes.*

Meanwhile hold each orange over a bowl to collect the juice, and cut away and discard the white pith and inner skin with a sharp knife. Still holding the skinned orange over the bowl, cut between the segments to separate the skin from the flesh. Remove any seeds.

Arrange the segments in a serving dish, and sprinkle the caramelized zest on top together with the juice from the bowl. Refrigerate and serve chilled.

P *nata*

CREAM

Cream is not used a great deal in Spain and Portugal; until recently it was difficult to obtain fresh cream in Spain, most of it being of the canned variety from the Nestlé factory in Santander.

Natal

Christmas; see NAVIDAD.

Navarra

Spanish region; see ARAGON AND NAVARRA.

Navarra

DEMARCATED WINE
REGION

This region borders the RIOJA to the north and east and makes its wines from the same grape varieties: the red Tempranillo, Garnacha, Mazuelo and Graciano, and the

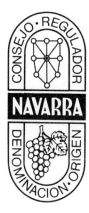

The seal of the Navarra demarcated wine region

white Viura, Malvasía and Garnacha blanca. Its strong red wines were favorites of Catherine the Great of Russia in the 17th century, and it is best known for its fruity reds and rosés, which have come to the fore with the establishment of a new oenological station, EVENA, to help and advise the growers.

S *Navidad*
P *Natal*

CHRISTMAS

From the time when Pope Julian I decreed in the 4th century that Christmas should be celebrated on 25 December, the most popular Christmas dish in Mediterranean countries was the capon, and it was apparently the Jesuits who domesticated it. In latter years a variety of birds, including the guinea fowl, goose and turkey have been traditional in Spain and Portugal as Christmas fare (see also OCA and PAVO). The Portuguese have an original way with turkey, putting it in a large dish, smearing it liberally with lard and olive oil and covering it with a thick layer of coarse salt. This hardens into a crust in the oven, thus sealing in all the juices of this somewhat dry bird, and is of course removed before serving. Traditions vary throughout the country: for example, in BEIRA BAIXA, turkey and main dishes are served, not on Christmas Day, but after Mass on Christmas Eve, and in MADEIRA pigs are killed the day before to provide the midday meal on Christmas Day.

In Portugal, it is traditional all through the Christmas period to place little baskets of walnuts, pine nuts, almonds and raisins on the table, and also ALETRIA DOCE. Before the *missa do galo* (midnight mass) on Christmas

Guinea fowl; game birds are an important dish at Christmas in both Spain and Portugal

Eve, *bacalhau com todos os matadores* (a dish of dried cod) is served, and after mass the company partake of *vino quente*, a hot mulled wine made with honey, cinnamon, pine nuts and egg yolks. Tradition requires that, on retiring, the food is left on the table, to be enjoyed during the night by the dead of the family.

In most parts of Portugal, Christmas Day lunch is ROUPA-VELHA, or the leftovers from the previous day, served with fried eggs. The main meal is in the evening, consisting of chicken, ducks, *cozido* (meat and vegetable stew), or *peru assado* (roast turkey).

Christmas dinner in Spain is eaten late on Christmas Eve. Traditionally an elaborate meal of four to six courses, *what* is eaten varies greatly from one place to another, the only course common to all parts of the country being the final one of turrones, MAZAPANES, dried and crystallized fruits etc, which are always bought by the head of the family. The meal is sometimes interrupted for midnight mass, and these fruits and sweets eaten with a glass of wine on the return of the family from church.

Fish, especially BESUGO is popular everywhere, and this may be preceded with a soup and in Bilbao and the Basque country by ANGULAS. In country districts *bacalao al pil pil* (cooked in *cazuela* with chili peppers and garlic) sometimes follows the soup, followed in turn by *gallo* (rooster) fattened on corn for the occasion. OCA CON PERAS is a favorite with the Catalans, while in NAVARRA, *perdiz* (partridge) and CORDERO ASADO are much eaten. Turkeys have tended to be the preserve of the better off. Whereas in Portugal they are given a swig of brandy, in Bilbao they were for some weeks beforehand fed with walnuts, honey, *guindillas* (chili peppers) and sometimes, fried sardines.

In these parts, it is traditional for groups of villagers to go singing to the houses, in the manner of North American carolers, where they are given dried and crystalized fruits and a glass of wine or cider.

see also

New Castile: *see Castilla la Nueva*
New Year's Eve: *see Nochevieja*

S *níscalo*

Mushroom; see ROBELLON.

S **P** *Nochevieja*
NEW YEAR'S EVE

It is usual to eat out in Spain on New Year's Eve, and the custom is for the restaurant to provide a dozen grapes, which must be swallowed on the chimes of twelve o'clock, often relayed by radio.

The Portuguese swallow raisins – but not fresh grapes – on New Year's Eve. Like the Spaniards they down twelve, one for each month of the year, on the twelve strokes of the clock. In some parts of Portugal, pomegranate seeds take the place of raisins.

nouvelle cuisine
COOKING STYLE

The *nouvelle cuisine* has much influenced chefs in the more sophisticated Spanish restaurants, especially those in CATALUÑA and the Basque country (see also NUEVA COCINA VASCA). Indeed, that master chef, ARZAK, has gone on record as saying: "Ten years ago the Catalans, quite without reason, had a heavy cuisine. Now it has changed completely."

Or has it? Spanish cooking has traditionally relied on the strong flavors of native ingredients such as red peppers and chili peppers, and Spaniards generally are hearty eaters, unlikely to be satisfied by those dainty little plates of steamed vegetables – five French beans, three broccoli spears, three tiny potatoes and the same number of miniature carrots, served *au naturel* and forlorn, and appearing on the table with the inevitability of the cutlery and the glass.

Unruffled by the winds of change, most restaurants continue to serve the full-blooded dishes of tradition: thick Spanish potato omelets, the saffron colored paella with its assortment of fish and garnish of peppers, chicken and lamb in the spicy CHILINDRON sauce and the rest. To do anything else would be to court bankruptcy. And indeed no less than Paul Bocuse himself has paid tribute to such homespun dishes. When, in 1979, he was invited to cook for the centenary celebrations of the Compañía Vinícola del Norte de España (CVNE), he brought all the provisions from France in a refrigerated caravan; but he and his helpers sat down to an early lunch prepared by Pilar Grandival, the *bodega's* regular cook. Commenting on the PATATAS A LA RIOJANA, Bocuse, according to newspaper reports, said frankly: "Are you out of your minds? This is much better than anything I shall serve later."

Sophisticated restaurants in Cataluña have, nevertheless, undoubtedly benefited. A solution adopted by many establishments with a reputation for good cooking has been to serve traditional Spanish dishes and examples of the *nouvelle cuisine* in parallel.

noz

Walnut; see NUEZ.

noz moscada

Nutmeg; see NUEZ MOSCADA.

nueva cocina vasca
COOKING STYLE

When Paul Bocuse launched the NOUVELLE CUISINE, among his most talented disciples were a group of chefs from the north of Spain. In 1976 they founded the *Grupo de la Nueva Cocina Vasca*. This was dedicated to cooking the best prime ingredients in such a way as to bring out their natural flavors to the full. Juan María ARZAK, Pedro Subijana, Josep Mercador, Víctor Merino, Ramon Roteta and Jesús María Oyarbide (who migrated to MADRID to open Zalacaín, arguably the best restaurant in Spain) are now famous beyond their homeland; and the movement that they started has swept the country.

Nevertheless, Arzak and his colleagues in the Basque country, much as they admired and were influenced by Paul Bocuse and Raymond Oliver, were never slavish imitators of the *nouvelle cuisine*. Rather, they

---

see also

Nougat: see Turrón

---

welcomed it as a bold step in breaking loose from the set forms and complications of Escoffier's *La Guide Culinaire* or *La Repertoire de la Cuisine*, and in reverting to simpler methods of cooking which enabled them to make the most of the splendid fish and vegetables of Spain's north coast.

The attitude of the Basque chefs who have spearheaded this renaissance of Spanish cookery is perhaps best put by Pedro Subijana of the renowned Akelarre in SAN SEBASTIAN, two of whose best dishes are *lubina a la pimienta verde* (sea bass *au poivre*) and *rodaballo relleno al hojaldre* (stuffed turbot in puff pastry): "People go to France, or to Japan if necessary, and in most cases they simply copy recipes to the last possible detail. This, as I see it, is profoundly wrong; the important thing is to understand why things are done and to know how to adapt them without losing one's own personality. . . ."

He goes on to define the aims of the *nueva cocina vasca* as: ". . . the return to simple cookery and the respect for tradition and its rehabilitation. You therefore have on your menu: old dishes, some included more for nostalgic reasons than for their flavor; traditional dishes, but very carefully cooked, and, finally, some new ones."

S *nuez*
P *noz*

WALNUT

The first walnut trees were planted in Spain and Portugal by the Romans, and the Spaniards in turn introduced the tree to California. Spanish production of walnuts has always been limited, and in recent decades there has been a danger that it would cease altogether because of the demand for walnut wood and widespread felling of trees. However, thanks to extensive planting of nursery-grown trees in CATALUÑA and the EXTREMADURA, it is hoped that production of walnuts will in time return to its previous level. Walnuts are used in confections and desserts, such as the Catalan POSTRE DE MUSICO.

S *nuez moscada*
P *noz moscada*

NUTMEG

Nutmeg is the dried fruit of a tree native to Indonesia and the Philippines and was known in Europe even at the time of Chaucer, who refers to it as "note muge". It did not become generally available until the discovery of the Spice Islands by the Portuguese in 1512, after which it came into great demand. Despite this, it is today used a good deal more in Spanish cooking than in Portuguese, generally as an alternative to cinnamon in desserts and stews.

---

see also   *Nutmeg: see nuez moscada*

S *oca*

GOOSE

Goose is a favorite Christmas dish in CATA-
LUÑA where it is served with pears. In the
Ampurdán region of Cataluña near the
Pyrenees, the geese range at will. Small,
with dark gamey meat, they are eaten all
year round.

---

oca con peras (S)
roast goose with
pears

Serves 6

1 goose of about 7½–10 lb, trussed
1 lemon, cut in half

Stuffing
1 onion, finely chopped
½ lb bacon, chopped
2 sticks celery, finely chopped
2 tbsp olive oil
the goose liver, chopped
5 cups fresh breadcrumbs
2 cloves garlic, finely chopped
2 eggs, beaten
2 apples, diced
4 oz pine nuts, ground
1 tbsp chopped parsley
salt and freshly ground pepper
juice of ½ lemon

Gravy
giblets of goose
bouquet garni
2½ cups water
2 tsp cornstarch
2 tbsp oloroso sherry
salt and pepper

Garnish
6 pears, peeled and cored, stalks left on the
   pears
1⅓ cups dry white wine
1¼ cups sweet oloroso sherry
1¼ cups sugar
1 cinnamon stick

Rub the outside of the goose with the lemon,
then prick it and place on a rack in a shallow
roasting pan. Put in a fairly hot oven (400°F)
and roast for 15 minutes, when the fat will
begin to run out. Discard the fat, or reserve as
required – I use it for roasting potatoes. Repeat
the operation; the goose is now ready for
stuffing.

To make the stuffing, sauté the onion with
the bacon and celery in hot olive oil until
transparent. Add the goose liver and cook a
little longer, leaving the inside of the liver pink.
Mix well with the remaining ingredients, and
use to stuff the goose through the neck cavity,
securing with a thin skewer. Return to a fairly
hot oven (400°F) for 15 minutes, then reduce
the heat to 325°F and cook for 20 minutes a
pound – slow roasting makes the goose juicier
and more succulent.

To make the gravy, cook the giblets with the
bouquet garni and water, reducing the liquid by
half and reserve. Skim what fat remains in the
roasting pan, add a little cornstarch, stirring
well, and moisten with the reserved giblet stock
and the oloroso sherry. Cook for 1–2 minutes,
until well blended and heated through, and
season with salt and pepper to taste.

Meanwhile, make the garnish by gently
simmering the pears for about 40 minutes with
the wine, sherry, sugar and cinnamon stick
until transparent. Drain, reduce the syrup,
pour it over the pears and arrange them around
the bird on a serving dish.

Serve with roast potatoes and peas.

---

see also

Octopus: *see pulpo*
Olive: *see aceitunas*   **Olive oil:** *see aceite de oliva*

S *olla*

COOKING UTENSIL,
STEW

A large stewpot, made either of earthenware or iron, narrower at the top than the bottom and with handles. The word is also used for the stews habitually eaten for the main meal of the day in many parts of Spain and made with chickpeas, meat and pork belly.

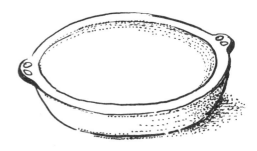

S *olla podrida*

MEAT AND
VEGETABLE STEW

The full name for the stews made in an OLLA. They are so called because *podrida* in Spanish means "overripe", and the vegetables and meat are cooked very slowly for long periods until very soft.

Oporto

PORTUGUESE CITY

Oporto, which lies on the DOURO not far from the open Atlantic, is Portugal's second city and bears to LISBOA much the same relationship as BARCELONA to MADRID.

On the culinary front, Oporto is above all famous for one dish, tripe (see TRIPAS A MODA DO PORTO). It is not necessary – or advisable – to go to expensive restaurants for the tripe. One of the best places is the modestly priced Abadia or, of course, there is Tripeiro, where they serve little, if anything, else.

Probably the most soigné of Oporto's restaurants, serving excellent and expensive shellfish and steaks, is Portucale at the top of a tower with panoramic views across the city and the river.

---

see also   **Omelet:** *see tortilla*   **Onion:** *see cebola*

S *Orduña*

A CHEESE

A hard ewe's milk cheese from the Basque country with a fat content of 49 percent, pressed after being steeped in brine for 24 hours. It is made in rounds of 5 to 6 inches diameter and some 4 inches thick and possesses small irregularly spaced eyes. It is sometimes eaten fresh in the summer, but is usually kept for 2 years, after which it gains in piquancy.

P *orégão*
S *orégano*

OREGANO

Oregano, or wild marjoram, is more pungent and peppery when grown in Spain and Portugal than in colder and wetter climates. It is used a good deal in the Portuguese ALENTEJO to season meats, soups and vegetables.

S *Oropesa*

A CHEESE

Also known as *queso de la Estrella*, this is made around Oropesa in the province of Toledo. It is a hard ewe's milk cheese of excellent quality with a fat content of 46 percent. Matured for some 4 months and then kept in olive oil, it much resembles MANCHEGO, but the rounds are smaller in size.

S *orujo*

A SPIRIT

This is the name by which AGUARDIENTE *de orujo*, distilled from grape skins and seeds and very popular in Spain, is sold in bars.

P *ostión*

Portuguese oyster; see OSTRA.

> *If Spanish and Portuguese terms differ from each other, the entry in Portuguese, in the majority of cases, is referred to its Spanish equivalent, where you will find information relevant to both countries.*

S *ostra*

OYSTER

The traditional source of the best Spanish oysters, of the species *Ostrea edulis*, was the RIAS of Galicia (see ASTURIAS AND GALICIA). As long ago as 1797, José Cornide, a Galician writer, issued a warning as to overfishing them: "In our Galicia there is an abundance of them in the *rías* of Vigo, Arosa and El Ferrol, but I am afraid that the greed and persistence with which they pursue them will finish them, as has already happened in the Ría del Burgo, next to this city."

What Cornide foresaw has now come true. There are virtually no oysters in any of the *rías* of Galicia. Determined efforts have been made to start new oyster beds with spat or oysters from Arcachón and Britain but, with rare exceptions, to no avail because of disease and other causes. Most of the oysters now on sale in Galicia are sent in barrels from Salonica in Greece and refreshed in salt water for a few days before being put on sale in the markets.

The Portuguese oyster (*Ostrea angulata*), is also fished in the Bay of Cádiz, where it is known as *ostión* and often used in fish soups and stews (see SOPA AL CUARTO DE HORA). It is smaller than the Spanish oysters. Most of those on sale in Portuguese markets are bought up by the restaurants.

By far the most popular way of eating oysters is chilled and raw, with a squeeze of lemon juice. *Ostras rebozadas* (fried oysters) are oysters dredged in egg and breadcrumbs, fried in olive oil and served with lemon wedges. The Portuguese *sopa de ostras à lisboeta* (oyster soup Lisbon style) is made by cooking together tomato paste, onion, fish fumet and white wine, then adding the oysters and some crôutons.

---

see also　　　*Orange: see naranja*　　*Oregano: see orégão*　　*Oven: see horno*

P *ovos*

Eggs; see HUEVOS.

P *ovos especiais Quinta das Torres*

EGGS QUINTA DAS TORRES

These eggs from the enchanting Quinta das Torres in the Setúbal Peninsula, an ESTA-LAGEM installed in a small 16th-century palace, are a specialty indeed, and knowing *Lisbonenses* make the journey across the great suspension bridge just to taste them.

Crisp and brown on the outside of their nest of white sauce and soft in the middle, they pose as much of a mystery as the fully rigged schooner inside its bottle. One of the secrets is to start with small and very fresh eggs.

---

ovos especiais Quinta das Torres (P)
eggs Quinta das Torres

6 small eggs
olive oil
1¼ cups freshly made molho bechamel (white sauce)
2 tsp grated cheese, preferably Parmesan or Queijo da Serra
1 egg, beaten
dry breadcrumbs

First fry the eggs in hot olive oil, making sure that the yolks remain soft, then place them on a marble slab or cold flat dish.

Mix the hot molho bechamel with the grated cheese, and leave to cool – without putting it in the refrigerator. Coat the outside (but not the bottom) of the eggs with the sauce, and leave for about 10 minutes in the refrigerator until you are ready to serve them. Trim off the irregular edges, dredge in the beaten egg and breadcrumbs, and deep fry in hot olive oil until crisp and brown. Serve immediately.

P *ovos moles*

EGG CREAM

This cream of egg yolks and syrup, cooked until set, is the basis for many of the numerous Portuguese egg desserts. See FATIAS DE BRAGA, FATIAS REAIS, FLAN DE HUEVOS, MORGADO, PÃO-DE-LO, TOUCINHO DE CEU. Others are *ovos queimados* (made by stirring beaten egg yolks into sugar, melted and browned in a frying pan), *pudim de ovos*

Guimarais (a traditional sweet from Guimarais, made with egg yolks, sugar and port) and *pudim de ovos Coimbra* (in which yolks, butter and sugar are baked in the oven). In Aveiro, *ovos moles* are cooked by boiling a little rice in water, then discarding the rice and using the water to make the syrup.

---

see also   *Oyster: see ostra*

S *pacharán*
A LIQUEUR

A characteristic liqueur from NAVARRA made with sloeberries.

P *padaria*

Bakery; see PANADERIA.

P *padeira*

A baker; see A PADEIRA.

The index, in English, is arranged by types of food — eggs, cheese, fish — kitchen equipment, cooking terms and other subjects. Consult it for recipes that make use of particular ingredients.

S *paella*
RICE DISH

Paella is one of the great Spanish contributions to gastronomy – though one might not think so faced with the sloppy concoctions of rice and fish that have usurped the name in many foreign restaurants. It is now served in restaurants the length and breadth of Spain – for some reason, Thursdays and Sundays used to be the days when it was always to be found on their menus. It originated in VALENCIA and is still best made with the short-grained rice from the region. In his classic *Guía del buen Comer español* (Guide to Good Food in Spain), Dionisio PEREZ says of the original dish that in addition to rice: "The true *paella*, the authentic, genuine and traditional, contains only eels, snails and green beans. It is the *paella* from the shores of the Albufera [the salt water lagoon outside Valencia] and it must be made in a saucepan with a slightly convex bottom placed on a wood fire. It should be eaten, not with bread, but with spring onions. Nevertheless, failing the classical ingredients, every locality in the Kingdom of Valencia and every village in the province has put into its *paella* all kinds of meat, fish, shellfish and vegetables; and everything goes well with the magnificent rice."

The secret of a good *paella* is indeed in the cooking of the saffron-flavored rice, whose grains, though tender, must remain individual when the dish is brought to the table. For this purpose it is essential to start with short-grained Spanish or Italian rice – the long-grained Indian or American varieties make excellent rice pilaf or curry, but not *paella*. The amount of water used in cooking it is all important. The traditional method was to put the rice with a little water in the PAELLERA and to heat it over a high flame, meanwhile adding more water gradually and stirring with a wooden spoon. To begin with, the spoon will stand upright in the mounded rice. When it begins to slump under its own weight, it is a sign that sufficent water has been added. Heating should be steady, otherwise the grains will disintegrate; and once all the water has either evaporated or been absorbed, the *paella* must be removed from the fire and left to stand for some minutes so that the moisture penetrates to the heart of the grains and softens them all through. An easier method of gauging the correct amount of water is by measuring two cupfuls to each cupful of dry rice, as described in the recipe that follows.

Chicken pieces, small sausages and pieces of meat may all be used for a *paella*; I myself prefer a *paella marinera*, made entirely from shellfish, and a most important ingredient for the flavor is CALAMARES – even those alarmed by things with tentacles will never know if it is cut up. *Paella* is most simply cooked in a large round, two-handled metal PAELLERA made for the purpose and available anywhere in Spain or at specialist cookware shops elsewhere; when not in use it should be lightly wiped with olive oil to prevent rusting. Failing this, use a very large frying pan; you will have to deploy either over two gas or electric burners.

paella valenciana (S)
RICE DISH

Serves 6–8

2½–3 lb chicken pieces
flour
olive oil
1 lb small squid, cleaned and sliced
  (see page 79)
24 mussels, soaked, scraped, scrubbed and
  opened (see page 192), using water instead of
  wine
2 cloves garlic
¾ cup per person Spanish or Italian round rice
few strands of saffron
salt
shellfish, such as shrimp, crayfish, lobster or
  crab, boiled
15 oz canned red peppers (pimentos), drained
  and cut into strips
green or black olives, pitted

Dredge the chicken pieces with flour, brown lightly in hot oil and put aside. Fry the squid in hot oil for about 10 minutes and reserve. Remove the mussels from their shells, keep the best half shells for decoration and strain and reserve the stock.

Heat 2 tbsp olive oil in a paellera or large frying pan and fry 1 garlic clove, cut in two or three slices until they begin to brown. Discard them and add the rice, cooking gently until it begins to yellow. Meanwhile, crush together the remaining garlic and the saffron in a mortar and pestle, scatter the mixture over the rice and season with salt.

The liquid for boiling the rice is made up of the strained mussel stock with as much additional water or fish stock as is required; it must be hot. The total amount should be 1½ cups per person, i.e. exactly twice the volume of dry rice. Add to the rice, cooking over fairly high heat and stirring for 5 minutes as it begins to boil and bubble. If necessary, use two gas or electric burners, turning and shaking the paellera so that the contents boil evenly. Stir in the squid and place the pieces of chicken around the edge. Allow the rice, squid and chicken to cook together for 15 minutes uncovered, then garnish the top with the other ingredients: first the shellfish, then the strips of red pepper and finally the olives. Last of all, replace the mussels in their half shells and garnish the dish with them.

Remove the pan from the heat and cover it with a clean dish-towel for about 10 minutes before serving.

A well made paella is a most colorful and decorative sight, and one of the advantages of using a paellera is that it may be brought to the table.

S *paellera*
COOKING UTENSIL

A metal pan of large diameter with two handles used for cooking PAELLA. This is how this utensil is commonly known in Spain and is what to ask for in a *ferretería* (ironmonger's), but there is a school of thought that the pan is properly described as a *"paella"* and that this is how the dish received its name.

At any rate, whatever you call it, keep it from rusting when not in use by wiping it with a clean rag moistened with olive oil.

Opposite: Fresh vegetables at a market

P *paio*
A SAUSAGE

A type of CHOURIÇO, containing larger pieces of pork loin.

Pages 214-215: An afternoon picnic or merienda

S *pan*
BREAD

The bread in Spain is generally of very good quality, crusty, substantial and with real flavor. This is because of the type of flour which is used and because there is no cutting of corners in the high-speed mixing of dough or in the rising, and also because it is baked in the traditional brick ovens. Spanish bread is usually baked with wheat flour as *baguettes* of different sizes; in smaller country places in the north, corn and rye flour is sometimes blended with wheaten, and heavier, coarser-textured rounds are made, such as the Catalans use for their *pan con tomate y jamón* (country bread smeared with olive oil, rubbed with tomato and garlic, and served with ham). Spanish bread is made to be eaten fresh and quickly goes stale; the Spanish household will, therefore, buy bread twice a day, and if yesterday's bread is used for breakfast, it is always toasted.

In large hotels, and even in some of the PARADORES, there has, however, been a tendency to serve cotton-like rolls. This appears to be a regrettable repercussion of the tourist invasion and of Gresham's Law – that the bad drives out the good.

S *pan de costra al ajo*
CRISP BREAD FROM MALAGA

A savory bread from Málaga, served at mealtimes like the Catalán *pan con tomate y jamón* (country bread smeared with olive oil, rubbed with tomato and garlic, and served with ham). It is made by pounding garlic in a mortar with a little PIMENTON *dulce* and salt, then stirring in orange juice and oil to make a thin paste. This is spread over the bread, which is warmed in the oven before serving.

pan dulce
SWEET BREAD

A Spanish fruit loaf, rather like a coffee cake, made by beating egg yolks with sugar, folding in the beaten whites, flour, raisins and candied peel, and baking the mixture in a buttered baking pan in a moderate oven.

pan integral
WHOLEWHEAT BREAD

In spite of the generally good and natural quality of Spanish flour, Spaniards, like the rest of the world, have become increasingly health conscious, and are eating *pan integral* made from wholewheat flour.

panadería padaria
BAKERY

The *panaderías* and *padarias* in the villages and small towns of Spain and Portugal are alike in baking crusty bread of real flavor and substance in the traditional brick bakers' ovens. This they do several times a day, as the Portuguese and Spanish insist on eating their bread really fresh. In small towns the bakers also oblige their customers by roasting joints of meat for them – there is nothing like COCHINILLO (*leitão* in Portugal) straight from a baker's oven.

These bakeries make and sell only regular bread and rolls in a variety of shapes and sizes; fancy breads, cakes and pastries are sold in the PASTELERIAS and PASTELARIAS.

Opposite: Fresh sardines (top) and cooked salt cod in a tomato sauce (bottom)

P *panar*

Cooking method; see REBOZAR.

S *panceta*

Fresh pork belly; see JUDIAS.

S *panecillo*

Roll; see PÃOZINHO.

S *panellets*
CATALAN PETITS
FOURS

A Catalan sweet made with almonds or pine nuts, sugar and eggs in the form of a marzipan. It is traditionally eaten on All Saints' Day (see LOS SANTOS).

---

panellets (S)
Catalan petits fours

Makes approx. 2 lb

Basic dough
2¼ cups sugar
½ cup water
pinch of cream of tartar
1 lb almonds, blanched, skinned, dried and
    ground (can be done in a food processor)
3 eggs

Make a hard ball syrup (see page 169) with the sugar, water and cream of tartar.
    Put the almonds into a large bowl and pour the syrup over them very slowly, mixing constantly with a spatula or wooden spoon until smooth and well blended. Now slowly add the 3 unbeaten eggs and continue to mix until the mixture is very smooth. Pour on to a marble slab and leave to cool for about 10 minutes, then work it with the hands for another 10 minutes.

panellets al piñón (S)
panellets with pine kernels

Take small portions of the basic panellet dough and shape in the hands like walnuts. Paint with unbeaten egg white. Stick pine nuts on top and bake in a moderate oven (350°F) for about 10 minutes until the nuts are browned.

panellets al limón (S)
lemon panellets

These are made in the same way as panellets al piñón but lemon zest is substituted for the pine nuts.

P *pão*
BREAD

More or less all that has been said about Spanish bread (see PAN) applies to the Portuguese. It is similarly made by small bakers in brick ovens and is crusty, firm and full of character – in a word, worth eating in its own right. Descriptions of breads from the different regions follow.

P *pão de broa*
A BREAD

A bread baked with mixed rye and wheat flours and made to perfection at Avintes near OPORTO.

P *pão de centeio*
RYE BREAD

A bread made in rounds with a high proportion of barley flour, popular in the country districts of Portugal.

P *pão de forma*

RICH BREAD

Made from a stiff dough which holds its shape – hence the name – this bread from the Portuguese ALENTEJO is richer than the ordinary PÃO since it contains butter and sugar, and milk instead of water.

P *pão-de-lo*

SPONGE CAKE

Portuguese sponge cake contains a high proportion of egg yolks and is deep yellow in color. Cut into small squares, the cake is topped with a variety of creams and fruits (often soaked in wine or liqueurs). This comprises a whole range of sweets, most often made and consumed in PASTELARIAS.

P *pão do Minho*

MINHO STYLE BREAD

The country bread of northern Portugal, made from wheat flour and rather rougher in texture than the ordinary bread.

P *pão-doce*

SWEET BREAD

A sweet bread, containing eggs and butter, and sometimes almonds or candied fruit, usually eaten in Portugal at holiday times and at festivals such as Easter and Twelfth Night (see PASCOA and LOS REYES).

> *The index, in English, is arranged by types of food — eggs, cheese, fish — kitchen equipment, cooking terms and other subjects. Consult it for recipes that make use of particular ingredients.*

P *pão preto*

A BREAD

A dark-colored Portuguese bread made with rye flour.

P *pãozinho*
S *panecillo*

ROLL

The rolls in Portugal are quite delicious. Unlike the ubiquitous and insubstantial "French bread" which so quickly converts itself to chewing gum, they are made from an honest-to-goodness dough and baked in a traditional brick baker's oven.

P *papa laberça*

WINTER SOUP

A soup from the BEIRA LITORAL, similar to CALDO VERDE but made with cornmeal instead of potatoes.

S *papas*

Potatoes; see PATATA.

S *papas arrugadas*

NEW POTATOES CANARY ISLANDS STYLE

A potato dish from the ISLAS CANARIAS made by boiling new potatoes in their skins in sea water, then baking them and serving with the spicy MOJO COLORADO sauce.

S *papas de milho*

Cornmeal porridge; see XEREM.

S *papas de sarrabulho*

SAVORY PORRIDGE

A dish of porridge-like consistency from the MINHO made with pork liver, lungs, throat and heart, stewing hen, beef, pig's blood and cornmeal.

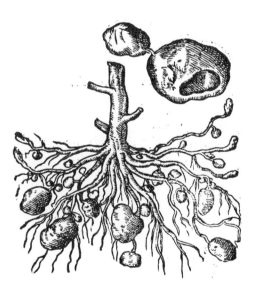

Potato plant

---

see also   **Paprika:** *see pimentón*

§ *Parador*

GOVERNMENT-RUN
HOTEL

The first of the government-run Spanish Paradores was opened in 1928 and represented a new idea in hotels – to provide comfortable accommodation for motorists, often in meticulously restored castles and monasteries, in areas of scenic or historic interest where no facilities had previously existed.

The word "parador" has been derived from the Arabic *waradah*, a "halting place". Writing in 1846, Richard FORD emphasized the oriental character of the Parador of his day when he described it as "a huge caravansary for the reception of waggons, carts and beasts of burden" and further recounted how travelers brought their own provisions and that the assembled company would settle around the kitchen fireplace with repeated invitations to join in their severally prepared meals.

The first Paradores were situated in magnificently restored buildings suitably furnished in period, such as the Castles of Ciudad Rodrigo on the remote Portuguese border and of Oropesa on the highroad from MADRID to LISBOA, and the former Convento, de Jesús in Roman Mérida. In addition to the Paradors, the government opened less elaborate Albergues (only a few of which survive) on main routes for the convenience of motorists and also a few Hosterías, such as El Estudiante installed in the ancient Colegio Trilingue in Alcalá de Henares outside Madrid, which serve meals but have no accommodation. More recently, a number of modern seaside Paradors have been built, especially in the ISLAS CANARIAS where there was a shortage of hotel accommodation, and in all there are now above 80 Paradors and associated establishments.

It would be unrealistic to expect the same culinary standards throughout a chain of this size, but the Paradors make a genuine effort to serve a selection of regional dishes

The parador at Monzon de Campos, Palencia

and wines. The food is always palatable and the service by waitresses, some dressed in local costume, is unfailingly friendly. If, for example, you wish to share a plate of Parador *entremeses* (hors d'oeuvres), prover-bial for their size and variety, they will smilingly bring an extra plate. Some of the Paradors, like that at Mérida, have won culinary awards and others from time to time mount medieval-style banquets.

S *Pardo de Figueroa, Mariano*

19TH-CENTURY WRITER

Joint author with José CASTRO Y SERRANO, under the pseudonym of *El Doctor Thebus-sem y un cocinero de S.M.*, of a series of articles, which from 1885 onwards did much to revive the national cuisine.

> *The index, in English, is arranged by types of food — eggs, cheese, fish — kitchen equipment, cooking terms and other subjects. Consult it for recipes that make use of particular ingredients.*

S *parrilla*

Grill; see A LA PARRILLA.

---

parrillada de marisco (S)
mixed grilled fish and shellfish

Serves 6

6 sea bass steaks (about ¾ in thick)
6 hake steaks (about ¾ in thick)
6 jumbo shrimp, in the shell
6 scampis, in the shell
6 mussels, in the shell, well scrubbed and washed in cold water
12 clams, in the shell, well scrubbed and washed in cold water
salt
olive oil

Sprinkle the fish and shellfish with salt, brush with olive oil and grill over a charcoal fire for 5–6 minutes until brown on both sides.

S *pasas corinto*

RAISINS

A Spanish term for seedless raisins. See also UVAS PASAS.

S *Pascua*
P *Páscoa*

EASTER

Easter marks the end of Lent (see CUARESMA) and a long regimen of fish; in the culinary calendar it is the beginning in Spain of the season for the delicious CORDERO LECHAL, or milk-fed baby lamb. In Portugal, *borrego* (baby lamb), CABRITO and *lombo de boi* (loin of ox, also known as *boi de Páscoa*) are all popular at Easter time.

Also thoroughly typical of Easter in Portugal are the round breads known as *folar*. These are of two types, the sweet FOLAR DOCE in the south and the meat-filled FOLAR GORDO in TRAS-OS-MONTES and the north.

PÃO-DOCE is another specialty.

Eggs have been a symbol of life and regeneration all over the world, not least in the Christian community. Their consump-tion during Lent was formerly forbidden by the Church in Portugal, and eggs painted in bright colors, especially vermilion, are cen-tral to the Easter ceremonies.

The favorite Easter candy in Spain and Portugal is almonds coated with a smooth, hard layer of colored sugar, known in Spain as ALMENDRAS GARRAPIÑADAS.

---

see also   *Parsley: see perejil*   *Partridge: see perdiz*

S *pasiego sin prensar*

A CHEESE

A soft white cheese from the Santander region made with cow's milk and with a fat content of 8 percent. It is unpressed and shaped into small rounds by hand. As it is not matured and will not keep for more than a week, it is eaten fresh and also used for the well-known cheesecake from Santander known as *quesada*.

SP *pasta*

PASTA

Pasta is made in a large range of shapes and sizes in Spain. The smaller ones, used in soups, include: *maravilla, cus-cus, estrellas* (stars), *piñones* (pine nut-shaped), *alpiste, letras* (letters), *anillos* (rings), *pistones* and *fideos finos* (vermicelli). Among larger sizes, served with a meat, fish or tomato sauce, are: *plumas* (feathers), *macarrones* (macaroni), *tiburones* (shells), *tallarines* (strips) and spaghetti. One may also obtain stuffed pasta, such as ravioli and tortellini, and other types enriched with eggs and vegetables, such as spinach and tomatoes.

Spanish CANALONES are thin wafers of dough for wrapping around the filling.

Pasta is eaten in Portugal as all over the world, but there is nothing particularly individual about it (but see ALETRIA DOCE) and rice is much more popular.

P *pasteis de bacalhau com arroz do mesmo*

BACALHAU FRITTERS WITH RICE

From the RIBATEJO, this is one of the scores of ways of cooking BACALHAU, in this case, in the form of *beignets* (fritters) served with rice.

> CAPITALIZED *words within entries refer the reader to more information on the same subject.*

P *pastelaria*

PASTRY SHOP

The Portuguese equivalent of the Spanish PASTELERIA or CONFITERIA, where you may buy cakes, chocolates and liqueurs, and often take coffee or tea.

S *pastelería*

PASTRY SHOP

Literally a "pastry shop", there is no difference between this and a CONFITERIA; both sell cakes and pastries, confectionery and liqueurs, and sometimes provide tables where you may enjoy freshly brewed coffee and sample their wares.

S *pata de mula*

A cheese; see VILLALON.

S *patata*
P *batata*

POTATO

Potatoes grow wild in Chile and Peru, but the Spaniards first found them under cultivation in the neighbourhood of Quito in what is now Ecuador. In the *Crónica de Perú* of 1553, Pedro de Creça describes the potato under the name of *battata* and *papa* (*batata* is the Portuguese for potato, and they are still called *papas* in South America and occasionally in Spain itself as with the PAPAS ARRUGADAS of the ISLAS CANARIAS). It is said that potatoes were first introduced to Spain by a monk, Hieronymus Cardan, and were first grown, at the suggestion of the Catholic Monarchs, in the region of Málaga. From

Sweet potato

---

see also   **Pastry:** *see masa*

there they passed to Italy, and then to Belgium and the rest of Europe.

Potatoes are very widely eaten in Spain and Portugal, often as a dish on their own to begin a meal (see, for example, PATATAS A LA RIOJANA, PATATAS CASTELLANAS or TORTILLA ESPAÑOLA). The Spanish and Portuguese version of potato chips, *patatas* or *batatas fritas,* is very popular as an accompaniment to aperitifs.

More substantial than in the US, they are made by slicing potatoes thinly in a special machine and frying them in hot olive oil. They are made daily and in Spain may be bought hot from the *churrería.*

patatas a la riojana

POTATOES RIOJAN STYLE

A piquant starter on cold days, in a deep orange-colored sauce, this potato dish is a favorite with the *bodegueros* (winery owners) of the RIOJA and has been much commended by Paul Bocuse.

---

patatas a la riojana (S)
potatoes Riojan style

Serves 4

½ cup olive oil
2 lb potatoes, peeled and coarsely cubed
5 oz chorizo, sliced
1 lb onions, chopped
1 lb tomatoes, peeled, seeded and chopped
3 red peppers, fried or roasted, seeded and cut into strips
salt and pepper
4 cups chicken or meat stock

Heat the oil in a deep casserole, reduce the heat when hot and sauté the potatoes, chorizo and onions for 10 to 15 minutes until the onion is soft but not brown. Add the tomatoes and peppers, cook for another 5 minutes, season with salt and pepper, then add the stock. Cover and simmer gently for about 15 minutes until the vegetables are very tender and much of the stock has been absorbed. Serve very hot.

---

patatas castellanas

POTATOES CASTILIAN STYLE

These potatoes, spiced with paprika, are often served as an appetizer in Castile; they may also be eaten with meat.

---

patatas castellanas (S)
potatoes Castilian style

Serves 6

4 tbsp olive oil
1 onion, chopped
1 clove garlic, chopped
4½ lb potatoes, peeled and cut up coarsely
1 tsp pimentón dulce (sweet paprika)
1 tbsp flour
salt and pepper
1 bay leaf

Heat the oil in a saucepan and fry the onion and garlic until golden. Add the potatoes and pimentón dulce (sweet paprika), cook briefly until colored, then mix in the flour and stir with a wooden spoon until the potatoes begin to brown. Cover with boiling water, add a little salt and pepper and the bay leaf, and cook slowly for another 30 minutes until the potatoes have absorbed most of the liquid and are so soft as to be almost melting.

Ⓢ *patatas con chorizo*

POTATOES WITH CHORIZO

A spicy dish made by sautéing potatoes with CHORIZO and bacon.

ⓈⓅ *pato*

DUCK

The best time to eat duck is from September to February. It should be about 4 months old and roasted for 20–25 minutes per pound. Older birds are stewed as with PATO A LA SEVILLANA, PATO CON ANANAS and PATO GUISADO A RIBATEJANA. In Spanish restaurants usually only the breasts are served; the legs and carcass are used for making the accompanying sauce together with oranges and olives. The Portuguese often prick the duck and simmer it in water to get rid of most of the fat, then when tender brown it in the oven together with rice.

Ⓢ *pato a la sevillana*

DUCK WITH OLIVES

A delicious way of cooking duck from SEVILLA. All the ingredients are from the region: duck from the marshes of the Guadalquivir river, olives from the groves surrounding the city and SHERRY from neighboring Jerez de la Frontera. In some restaurants the duck is first roasted, then cut into quarters or carved and served with a sauce containing the olives and sherry.

---

pato a la sevillana (S)
duck with olives

Serves 4

4 tbsp olive oil
1 duck of about 4½ lb, trussed
1 onion, chopped
2 carrots, coarsely chopped
1 tbsp plain flour
2 cups chicken stock
2 tbsp fino sherry
1 parsley sprig
salt and freshly ground black pepper
8 oz large green olives, pitted

Heat the oil in a heavy casserole large enough to turn the bird during cooking. Add the duck, onion and carrots, and brown the duck until golden, taking care not to rupture the skin. Remove from the casserole and transfer to a plate with the onion and carrots.

Stir the flour into the oil remaining in the casserole, cook it until browned, then pour in the stock and sherry. Return the duck and vegetables to the casserole, add the parsley and a little salt and black pepper. Heat until the liquid begins to boil, then reduce the heat, cover and cook very slowly for 2 hours or until tender, laying the bird on its side from time to time so as to cook the legs.

Meanwhile, put the olives into a small saucepan, pour boiling water over them and cook over high heat for 5 minutes. Remove, dry and reserve them.

Take the duck from the casserole and put it on a serving dish. Heat the olives for a minute or two in the sauce, at the same time scraping the base and sides of the casserole. Finally, arrange the olives around the serving dish, skim off excess fat and either pour the sauce over the duck or serve it separately in a sauce boat.

Ⓟ *pato com arroz de cabidela*

DUCK WITH WINE

A dish from the Bairrada region. Some of the duck's blood is used in the sauce, which is made with garlic, onions, parsley, bay leaves, salt, pepper, tomatoes, red wine and a little vinegar, and it is served with rice.

P *pato con ananás*

DUCK WITH
PINEAPPLE

In this dish from Macau, the duck is cut up and cooked gently in a casserole with a little BANHA, onions, pork belly, lemon zest and fresh pineapple chunks. A little salt and pepper and some water are added, and the duck is simmered until the stock is reduced and the meat is very tender.

---

pato guisado à ribatejana (P)
stewed duck
Ribatejo style

Serves 4

1 onion, chopped
2 tsp olive oil
1 duck of about 3½–4½ lb, cut in pieces
fresh thyme
2 cups dry white wine
2 cups giblet stock
salt
2 tsp flour
3 tbsp madeira or port
2 carrots, grated
1 banana, sliced
1 tangerine, segmented

Sauté the onion in hot olive oil for about 10 minutes until soft but not brown, then transfer the contents of the pan to a large casserole. Add the pieces of duck, together with the thyme, and continue frying until browned. Add the white wine and stock, and simmer for 2 hours, covered, until tender. Season to taste with salt.

Stir the flour into a little water, dissolving well, add the madeira or port and the grated carrots, and cook this mixture slowly in a small pan for some minutes until completely blended and smooth. Add the sliced banana and the tangerine segments, and cook for a further 10 minutes until heated through. Transfer the stewed duck to a serving dish and pour the sauce over it before bringing it to the table. Serve with arroz de manteiga (buttered rice).

---

pavo
peru

TURKEY

Turkeys are so called because of a mistaken belief that they came from Turkey, but all the different species of the bird are native to North or South America, and turkeys were first introduced to Europe by the Spaniards. They were domesticated by the Mexicans and Peruvians, hence the Portuguese name *peru*. In Spain and Portugal, as in other countries, they are roasted and are a favorite for Christmas (see NAVIDAD).

In Portugal it was the custom – and still is in country districts – to make the turkey tipsy on brandy before killing it. This was done neither for sentimental reasons nor as part of the seasonal celebrations, but with the strictly practical object of making the meat whiter and more tender.

In the Portuguese ALENTEJO turkey is marinated for a day or two before being cooked in salted water containing orange and lemon slices. It is then stuffed with chopped CHOURIÇO, *toucinho* (see TOCINO), olives, veal and pork.

---

see also **Peaches:** see melocotones **Peas:** see guisantes

S *Pedroches*

A CHEESE

A semi-hard ewe's milk cheese with a fat content of 52 percent made in large amounts over an area stretching from Córdoba to Ciudad Real in La Mancha. Rather piquant in flavor and cylindrical in shape, the cheeses will keep for up to a year.

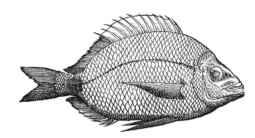

P *peixe à modo de Nazaré*

FISH STEW NAZARE STYLE

The fish in the charming little fishing town and resort of Nazaré is of the most fresh, and a favorite way of cooking it is in steaks in a REFOGADO of onions and tomatoes.

P *peixe espada*

SCABBARD FISH

Brilliantly silver in color, long like an eel but more ribbon-like, and upwards of 3 feet in length, this fish is common in the markets of the ALGARVE, Cádiz (where it is known as *pez cinto*) and the Atlantic islands. Rich and rather oily, it is chopped into diagonally cut steaks at the market and is best cooked by marinating them in lemon juice, seasoning with salt and pepper, smearing with a little olive oil and cooking under the broiler.

P *peixe na cataplana*

FISH COOKED IN CATAPLANA

This recipe is included for those who are intrigued enough to acquire a CATAPLANA and to experiment with it.

---

peixe na cataplana (P)
fish cooked in cataplana

Serves 4

2 lb firm white fish, cleaned, boned and cut into
    8 pieces
½ lb presunto or bacon, thinly sliced
5 medium onions, sliced
1 lb ripe tomatoes, quartered
3 green peppers, seeded and cut into strips
olive oil
1 cup dry white wine
2 cloves garlic, chopped
salt and pepper
colorau doce (hot paprika)
3 bay leaves, coarsely crumbled
dry breadcrumbs
piri-piri
chopped parsley

Lay a first layer of the fish on the base of the cataplana. On top of this place some of the thinly sliced presunto, sliced onions, tomato quarters and strips of green pepper. Moisten with olive oil and wine, and sprinkle with some of the chopped garlic, salt, pepper, colorau doce, bay leaves, breadcrumbs, piri-piri and parsley.

Repeat this operation, making further layers, until you have used up all the ingredients.

Fit the other half or "lid" of the cataplana, both dome-shaped halves are in fact the same, and cook over a moderate heat for 10 minutes until done. Turn over the cataplana and cook for another 10 minutes until done.

Remove the upper section and serve piping hot from the cataplana.

If using an oven dish, preheat the oven to hot (425°F), insert the tightly closed dish, reduce the heat and cook in a fairly hot oven (375°C) for 30 minutes, or until the fish is done.

---

⑤ *Penedès*

DEMARCATED WINE
REGION

Lying southwest of BARCELONA along the Mediterranean coast, this is the most important wine region in CATALUÑA and makes some of the best Spanish wines. It is here that 80 percent of CAVA is produced, the industry centering on the little town of San Sadurni d'Anoia, hollow with cellars and the home of scores of wineries. The Penedès also produces first-rate still wines, both red and white, for which the most important grapes are the Parellada, Macabeo (or Viura) and Xare-lo for the white, and the Ull de Llebre (Tempranillo), Monastrell, Cariñena and Garnacha tinta for the red. The largest producer of still wines is Miguel TORRES. Villafranca del Penedès, where many of the leading *bodegas* (wineries) are located, is also the home of the best wine museum in Spain, housed in a 13th-century palace of

The seal of the Penedès demarcated wine region

the Kings of Aragón, with exhibits illustrating winemaking from the earliest times, including examples of presses, barrels and winemaking equipment, drinking glasses and *porrones* (see PORRON), and a bar where the end product can be sampled.

② *pequeno-almoço*

Breakfast; see HORAS DE COMIDA.

⑤Ⓟ *percebe*

GOOSE BARNACLE

A large barnacle found along the northern coasts of Spain and Portugal. It resembles a detached clump of lobsters claws, the edible part being the meat inside the rubbery lower sheath, which is stripped away. It is eaten cooked as an appetizer, and the taste is fresh and very much of the sea.

Ⓟ *perdiz*

PARTRIDGE

Partridge is plentiful in both Spain and Portugal (see CAZA, LA) and is best eaten when very young. In the BEIRA ALTA it is stewed in white wine, olive oil, onion and PRESUNTO, and is also roasted. In Spain the most famous and delicious way is that which follows: partridge cooked with chocolate.

perdices estofadas con chocolate

STEWED PARTRIDGES
WITH CHOCOLATE

This intriguing recipe from Navarra dates possibly from the introduction of cocoa beans from South America.

perdices estofadas con chocolate (S)
stewed partridges with chocolate

Serves 2

1–2 partridges per person, depending on size, trussed
1 onion, cut up coarsely
1 head garlic, skinned
3–4 cloves
1 bay leaf
4 tbsp olive oil
8 fl oz dry white wine
1 tbsp sherry vinegar
salt and pepper
1 oz semisweet chocolate, grated
fried potato slices

Put the partridge in a casserole with the other ingredients apart from the chocolate and potato slices, inserting the cloves into the head of garlic. Bring to the boil, cover and simmer for 45 minutes–1 hour, shaking the casserole at intervals and adding a little more wine, if necessary.

Remove the partridge and place on a serving platter. Add the chocolate to the contents of the casserole, cook for 5 minutes, then rub the sauce through a sieve with a wooden spoon or process in a blender or food processor.

Arrange the slices of fried potato around the partridge then pour on the sauce so that it completely covers the birds.

P *perdiz à montemor*
ROAST PARTRIDGE ALGARVE STYLE

Partridge are often cooked in the ALGARVE by wrapping them in strips of *toucinho* (pork belly – see TOCINO), roasting them in the oven, then carving the birds and serving the slices in a sauce made with onion, tomatoes, bay leaf, parsley and a little port wine.

P *perdiz de escabeche*
MARINATED PARTRIDGE

A method of serving partridge from the ALENTEJO, in which they are stewed in a pan with olive oil, onions, bay leaf, black pepper or parsley, lemon zest, vinegar, salt and meat stock. They are then put on a dish and when cool, transferred to the refrigerator to marinate for 2 or 3 days before serving cold.

S *perejil*
P *salsa*
PARSLEY

In the UK and USA, curly-leaved parsley is grown almost to the exclusion of the flat-leaved type more common elsewhere, which is considerably milder in flavor.

Flat-leaved parsley is said to be the most used herb in Spain and Portugal and is given away free in the markets with a purchase of vegetables or fruit. It is used for garnishing and a sprig is often added to hot food to release flavor.

Parsley

Pérez, Dionisio

WRITER

In 1929 Dionisio Pérez published his *Guía del buen comer español* ("Guide to Good Food in Spain") which remains the best account of the history of Spanish cooking and of the traditional dishes of the different regions. He was Honorary President of the Professional Association of Chefs of CATALUÑA, and, under the pseudonym of Dr Thebussem, wrote *Prólogo y glosario de el libro de guisados de Rubert de Nola* ("Prologue and Glossary for Book of Stews of Rubert de Nola") and *Documentos pars la história de la cocina española* ("Documents Relating to the History of Spanish Cooking"). See also CASTRO Y SERRANO, José and RUBERT DE NOLA.

S Perilla

A cheese; see TETILLA.

P peru

Turkey; see PAVO.

> CAPITALIZED *words within entries refer the reader to more information on the same subject.*

peru recheado com castanhas (P)

turkey stuffed with chestnuts

Serves 10

1 lb toucinho or bacon slices
½ lb pork, ground
½ lb veal, ground
2 sticks of celery, finely chopped
½ cup walnuts, ground
1 tbsp fresh mixed herbs
1 tbsp fresh breadcrumbs
pinch of nutmeg
1 large egg, beaten
1 cup tawny port or Portuguese brandy
salt and pepper
1 lb chestnuts, boiled, peeled and puréed
1 turkey of 10–12 lb, trussed
2 tbsp dry white wine

Put all but 6 slices of the toucinho or bacon into a heavy pan and fry slowly for 10 minutes to render the fat. Add the pork and veal and fry for another 10 minutes until the meat is pale brown. Transfer to a bowl and mix with the celery, walnuts, herbs, breadcrumbs, nutmeg, egg and port. Season to taste, add the chestnut purée, mix well and use to stuff the turkey. Cover the top with the remaining toucinho and roast in a hot oven (425°F) for 25 minutes per pound. When the bird is done, place it on a carving dish. Remove the fat from the roasting pan, deglaze with the wine and serve in a sauce boat, accompanied by roast potatoes and a vegetable.

pescada

Hake; see MERLUZA.

pescada à Romariz

BOILED HAKE
DOURO STYLE

Boiled hake served with a sauce made from egg yolks, lemon juice, vinegar and parsley.

pescada lusitana

BAKED HAKE WITH
MASHED POTATOES
BEIRA ALTA STYLE

Hake cooked in the style of the BEIRA ALTA by baking it in the oven and serving with mashed potatoes.

S *pescadillas*

Small hake; see MERLUZA.

P *pessegos*

Peaches; see MELOCOTONES.

S *pestiños andaluces*

ANIS AND HONEY COOKIES

These soft cookies from ANDALUCIA are made by frying the skin of a whole lemon in olive oil, adding a little ANIS, then straining and mixing the oil with white wine and flour so as to make a stiff paste. This is rolled out and cut into squares, which are fried. The *pestiños* are briefly put into a honey syrup and are then dusted with confectioners' sugar.

S *pestiños madrileños*

ANIS-FLAVORED PASTRIES FROM MADRID

Typical of MADRID, these are anis-flavored choux pastries which puff up when fried and are then dipped in honey and served with confectioners' sugar.

S *petisú*

Choux pastry; see MASA.

S *pez cinto*

Scabbard fish; see PEIXE ESPADA.

S *pez espada*

Swordfish; see ESPARDETE.

Choux pastry

S *picada*

CATALAN SAUCE

This is one of the five basic Catalan sauces (see CATALUÑA). It is made from almonds, a few strands of saffron, hazelnuts or pine nuts and other ingredients in the form of a smooth paste, to which is added a little of the broth of the dish for which it is to be used. Ingredients can be varied to some extent. *Picada* is used in ZARZUELA DE MARISCOS A LA CATALANA and RAPE EN SALSA DE ALMENDRAS.

---

picada (S)
Catalan sauce

For a recipe serving 4–6

4 fingers white bread
olive oil
½ cup roasted almonds and/or hazelnuts, skinned
few strands of saffron
2 large cloves garlic, peeled

First fry the fingers of bread in hot olive oil, then pound all the ingredients in a mortar to a smooth paste. This is diluted with a spoonful of liquid from the dish for which it is intended (whether fish, shellfish or game) and stirred together well. Picada is usually added during the last stages of cooking.

P *Pico*

A CHEESE

There are two varieties of this cheese from the island of Pico in the Azores. There is a low fat white cow's milk type known as "Cheese of the North" and a richer, creamier and more piquant "Cheese of the South" made from a blend of cow's and goat's milk.

---

see also

Pheasant: see faisán

P *pimenta da Guiné*
S *guindillas*
CHILI

Chili peppers, known as *guindillas* in Spain, are small and very hot red peppers, hotter even than Cayenne. They originated in Mexico and were brought to Spain by the CONQUISTADORES.

Soak the chili peppers in hot water for 5-10 minutes. Remove the seeds unless you want them *very* hot and keep the flesh for use in recipes. Wash the hands well in soapy water after touching chilis or use rubber gloves to prevent irritation of the skin. It is particularly important not to carry hands to the eyes after touching chilis.

P *pimento*

Bell pepper; also preserved red pepper; see PIMIENTO.

S *pimentón*
PAPRIKA

Pimentón corresponds to the Hungarian paprika and is made by drying and milling a special red pepper that is shaped like a top. According to the type of pepper used, either the sweet *pimentón dulce* or pungent *pimentón piquante* is obtained. The Spanish product is usually more of a vermilion color than the deeper red Hungarian paprika. It should be used generously and is essential for making many Spanish dishes, as well as CHORIZO and other cured sausages. In Portugal, the hot pepper of this type is known as COLORAU and the sweet as *colorau doce*.

S *pimiento*
P *pimento*
BELL PEPPER

Peppers were unknown outside South America until the CONQUISTADORES brought back specimens to Spain, and all of the peppers domestically cultivated today are derived from them. There is no clear cut botanical distinction between the fiery chili peppers and the fleshy sweet peppers used as a vegetable, and in the countries where they grow, there are peppers of all shapes and sizes, both sweet and hot.

Red and green peppers are much used both in Spain and Portugal for making sauces and also they are roasted and eaten cold as a salad.

S *pimientos rellenos*
STUFFED PEPPERS

It is often thought that only fresh peppers can be stuffed, but with care, the canned variety may be used, and the results are equally good – indeed, some Spanish restaurants use them by preference. Make sure that the can specifies that the peppers are *whole*, as is almost always the case with Spanish produce but not with peppers from other countries.

pimientos rellenos de gambas (S)
peppers stuffed with shrimp

Serves 4

½ cup raw rice, boiled and drained
1 lb fresh shrimp, boiled and peeled, or ½ lb
    frozen shrimp, defrosted
6 tomatoes, peeled, seeded and chopped
1 clove garlic, crushed
salt and pepper
4 large red peppers or 8 canned red peppers,
    drained
1⅓ cups salsa de tomate (tomato sauce)

Mix the rice in a bowl with the shrimp, tomatoes, garlic and a little salt and pepper.

Method for fresh peppers
First blanch the peppers, then cut around the tops and remove them, discarding the seeds but keeping the tops. Fill with the prepared mixture, replace the tops and stand upright in an ovenproof dish. Pour on the salsa de tomate (tomato sauce) and cook in a moderate oven (350°F) for 45 minutes to 1 hour until tender, depending on size.

Method for canned peppers
Hold each pepper in the palm of the hand and carefully stuff with the mixture, ensuring that it does not disintegrate. Secure at the end with a wooden toothpick, then lay the stuffed peppers in an ovenproof dish just large enough to hold them comfortably. Pour the salsa de tomate (tomato sauce) on top, cover and cook over gentle heat for about 20 minutes until very soft.

pimientos verdes fritos (S)
fried green peppers

olive oil
1 pepper per person

Heat a tablespoon of olive oil in a non-stick pan, then turn down the heat, put in the washed and dried peppers, cover and cook very slowly for 45 minutes to 1 hour. Turn them occasionally, taking care, as they spatter violently. Remove when the skins are black and the peppers very soft. Cut around the core and remove scraping out the seeds with a teaspoon. Skin over a plate, leaving the peppers in one piece, and pour the juices from the plate on top.

⬛ pinchos morunos
LAMB AND KIDNEY KEBAB

Small kebabs made with highly spiced pieces of lamb, kidney, mushrooms and bacon, skewered and grilled over charcoal. Popular as TAPAS.

Opposite: The Douro valley near the Spanish frontier (top). In this region of Portugal the vineyards are used to grow grapes for making port. Harvested grapes (bottom)

Pages 234-235: The port lodges, with the river Douro and Oporto in the background

Page 236: Boats like the one shown here, known as Barcas velhas, were formerly used to transport the young wines from the vineyards to the port lodges

see also   **Pine kernel:** see piñón   **Pineapple:** see ananás

▣ *pinhão*

Pine nut; see PIÑON.

⊠ *piñón*

PINE NUT

Archaeological discoveries suggest that pine nuts formed a part of man's diet both in Europe and America as early as the Mesolithic Age, some 12,000 years ago.

In Spain, the kernels are produced from the Royal Pine Nut tree or *piñonero* (*Pinis pinea L*). The pine cones are gathered between November and March and left to dry in small heaps until the summer, when they open and release the nuts. From every ton of cones only about 85 lb of nuts are obtained, and they are the most expensive of nuts and, indeed, of all agricultural products, apart from saffron and truffles.

Pine nuts are very popular in Spain. They are sold in their shells in small paper cones outside the MADRID Métro stations and at street corners, and provide endless diversion in extracting the minute nuts. They are also used a great deal for soups and desserts, for other dishes such as the famous Catalan ACELGAS CON PASAS Y PIÑONES and for making TURRONES. They are known as *pinhão* in Portugal, and are used mainly for making tarts or decorating cakes.

⊠ *piperada vasca*

BASQUE OMELET

Popular on both sides of the Pyrenees, this dish with its aromatic fragrance of peppers is more akin to scrambled eggs than an omelet proper.

---

piperada vasca (S)

Basque omelet

Serves 2

2 tbsp olive oil
1 very large or 2 medium onions, chopped
2¼ lb back bacon, jamón serrano or Bayonne ham, rind or skin removed, cut up coarsely
4 tomatoes, peeled, seeded and chopped
8 oz canned red peppers (pimentos), cut into strips (liquid reserved)
salt and pepper
2 eggs

Heat the oil in a frying pan, sauté the onions until soft, then stir in the bacon or ham and cook slowly for another 5–10 minutes. Add the tomatoes and peppers, together with the liquid from the can, season with salt and pepper, and cook uncovered for another 20 minutes on the lowest possible heat until the mixture is soft. Break the eggs into the pan and stir well with a fork until all the ingredients are blended and the eggs are cooked but still soft.

Piperada vasca is best served with a green salad and French bread.

If desired, the basic cooking of the bacon and vegetables can be done in advance so that all that is required is to reheat and add the eggs before serving.

◄ *pipirrana jaenera*

SALAD FROM JAEN

A salad containing tomatoes, green peppers, ham, hard boiled eggs and tuna.

P *piri-piri*
A SAUCE

This is a Portuguese sauce used in small quantities for seasoning and is made by half filling a small bottle with olive oil, scraping off the upper part of a few small red chili peppers and immersing them in the oil. It should be left for a couple of months before use, but will then keep indefinitely. *Piri-piri* is also available as a prepared powder. Alternatively, Tabasco sauce can be substituted.

The index, in English, is arranged by types of food—eggs, cheese, fish— kitchen equipment, cooking terms and other subjects. Consult it for recipes that make use of particular ingredients.

S *pisto*
MIXED VEGETABLE DISH

Pisto, resembling the French *ratatouille*, goes well with roast veal or lamb. With eggs broken into it as cooking finishes, it may also be eaten as a dish on its own.

---

pisto (S)
mixed vegetable dish

Serves 4

4 tbsp olive oil
1 onion, sliced into rings
1 lb green or red peppers, de-seeded and cut in rings
½ lb potatoes, peeled and finely sliced
1 lb small zucchini, peeled and cut in strips
1 tbsp tomato paste
2 cloves garlic, chopped finely
bunch of mint, parsley and basil, chopped, or a pinch of dried herbs if fresh are not available
salt and pepper

Put the oil into a heavy casserole and sauté the onion slowly for 3-4 minutes. Add the peppers and potatoes and cook for another 2-3 minutes before adding the zucchini. Stir in the tomato paste, season with the garlic, herbs, pepper and salt, and simmer slowly for 1 hour until very soft.

S *plancha*

Flat metal griddle; see A LA PLANCHA.

S *Plasencia*
A CHEESE

A semi-hard cheese from Plasencia in the EXTREMADURA, made from pasteurized goat's milk and high in fat. The cheese is matured for up to 45 days and is red in color and entirely individual in taste because it is smeared with PIMENTON during this period. It is especially suitable for frying in olive oil.

S *plátano*
BANANA

The ISLAS CANARIAS are famous for their small, sweet bananas, though, in fact, the plantations are of relatively recent origin. They were planted to replace the prickly pears (see HIGO CHUMBO) used for rearing the cochineal insect, widely used for making a red dye before the introduction of coal tar dyes in the late 19th century. The Islanders use bananas to good effect in desserts, sometimes fried, or with other ingredients such as pineapple, semolina, eggs and liqueurs (see ARROZ CANARIO). Bananas are also preserved by stewing them in a syrup flavored with kirsch.

Bananas are an important crop in MADEIRA. In recent years when there have been disastrous failures in the wine harvest because of appalling floods, there has been a tendency to root up vines and replant with bananas, and the government has instituted subsidies to the wine growers to reverse this tendency and to protect production of the famous wines. An example of the use of bananas in cooking is PEIXE ESPADA, served in Madeira with fried bananas.

S *platos combinados*
COMBINED DISHES

These are quickly served dishes typical of the CAFETERIAS in Spanish cities. Identified by numbers on the menu, each is a meal in itself, comprising in different combinations such items as veal escalopes, sausages, fried fish, eggs, tortilla and salads. They are usually well cooked and appetizing.

S *pochas Riojanas*
RIOJAN BEAN STEW

A traditional dish from the RIOJA made by stewing a local variety of haricot beans, allowed to fatten in the pod but not to dry, with CHORIZO. This gives it a rich orange color and piquant flavor.

S *pollo*
P *frango*
CHICKEN

It is still possible in Spain and Portugal to buy free range chickens. Brought to the open markets by the local farmers, they are often fed on corn and the skin is very yellow. During cooking it becomes very crisp and there is no fat between the skin and the meat. Most of the chicken dishes in both countries are cooked in a casserole, the meat frequently being cut up and cooked with tomatoes, onions and peppers. Wine and herbs are also used and, of course, garlic, as in the following dish.

S *pollo al ajillo*
CHICKEN FRIED WITH GARLIC

A dish cooked up and down Spain, in which a chicken is cut into small pieces and cooked in a heavy pan with olive oil and garlic.

S *pollo con higos*
CHICKEN COOKED WITH FIGS

A Catalan recipe for cooking chicken in a casserole with ham, white wine and olive oil mixed with a syrup made from fresh figs and flavored with cinnamon.

S *pollo con piñones*
CHICKEN WITH PINE NUTS

Chicken stewed with onions, bay leaves, olive oil and pine nuts.

P *polvo*

Octopus; see PULPO.

Figs; a syrup made from fresh figs is used in pollo con higos

---

see also   *Plum: see ameixa*

---

§ *polvorones*

A CONFECTION

A powdery confection, wrapped in twists of paper and often eaten in ANDALUCIA with SHERRY or ANIS at eleven in the morning or in the afternoon. *Polvorones* are made with a basis of confectioners' sugar and ground almonds, but may be flavored with choco-late or *anís*. Estepa, on the main road from Córdoba to Málaga, is the principal center of production, and you will be served a glass of sherry if you stop to sample its wares. *Polvorones* are also made in Jijona, the home of the best TURRON.

§ *pomelo*
℗ *toranja*

GRAPEFRUIT

Grapefruit were introduced to Spain and Portugal by the Moors, together with bitter oranges and lemons, and are grown in the Valencian region of Spain and mainly in the ALGARVE in Portugal.

℗ *ponche*

A LIQUEUR

A speciality of Jerez de la Frontera, *ponche* is a blend of brandy with orange and herbs, sweeter than brandy, but much fresher and less sticky than most liqueurs. It was first produced by the sherry firm of José de Soto in 1888, whose brand is still one of the best. Another popular brand is that of Luis Caballero; both stand out on the shelves of a bar because they are presented in brilliantly silvered bottles.

§ *porrón*

DRINKING BOTTLE

This long-spouted drinking vessel, like the leather BOTA, now a mainstay of the souvenir shops, is still used in small TABERNAS, where a party of friends can enjoy their wine without the need for glasses. The best description is that of Richard FORD. "[The Catalans] are . . . given to wine, which they often drink after the fashion of Rhytium and the phallo-vitrobolic vessels of antiquity; they do not touch the glass with their lips, but hold up the *porrón*, or round-bellied bottle with a spout, at arm's length, pouring the cooled liquid into their mouths in a vinous parabola; they never miss the mark, while a stranger generally inundates his nose or his neckcloth."

℗ *Porto,*
**   *vinho do***

FORTIFIED WINE

Port is one of the world's great fortified wines and, as with SHERRY, the British had a great deal to do with its evolution. In the early 17th century, when Britain and France were at loggerheads, there was every reason to import Portuguese wine in place of claret. However, the DOURO valley wine with which the shippers tried to replace it was made so inexpertly and fermentation proceeded so fast and furiously that most of the flavor bubbled away, and it was left without a trace of sugar to soften it. The solution turned out to be to brandy the wine before fermentation was finished, so killing the yeasts and leaving some of the grape sugar in it. This, in effect, is how port has been made ever since.

The grapes are grown high up the Douro valley in steeply terraced vineyards overlooking the river. It is here that the wine is made and brandied, and it is then transported to the old red-roofed Lodges of Vila Nova de Gaia opposite OPORTO on the other side of the river, to begin its long maturation in oak, mahogany and chestnut casks.

According to the quality and blend of the grapes and the way in which the wine is matured, it emerges in the following main styles:

Vintage port: This is the aristocrat of the wines, made exclusively from wine of the same year from the best vineyards. It spends 2 years in cask and is thereafter matured in bottle, but it may well be 20 years before it reaches its peak. Vintage port throws a heavy deposit and must be decanted.

Late bottled vintage port also consists entirely of wine of the same year, but is kept longer in wood than vintage port, usually for 5 years before bottling.

Tawny port is a blend of different vintages matured for long periods in cask. As a result it is a paler and very aromatic wine with less body than vintage port. Fine old tawnies like the 20-year-old Ferreira "Duque de

---

see also   **Pomegranate:** *see granada*   **Pork:** *see cerdo carne*

Bragança'' are expensive wines and do not improve with age once bottled.

Wood port: This is a blend of younger wines matured in cask until ready for drinking; the popular *ruby port* is a wine of this type.

White port: These are made in the same way as other ports, but from white rather than black grapes. The dry types are drunk as an apéritif and are improved when chilled and served with a twist of lemon.

postre de músico

PLATE OF MIXED NUTS AND DRIED FRUITS

Often served in CATALUÑA as a dessert, this is a mixed plate of almonds, raisins, walnuts, hazelnuts, figs and other dried fruits.

Pousada

GOVERNMENT- RUN INN

The network of Portuguese Pousadas was inaugurated in 1940 by Antonio de Oliveira Salazar, then dictator of Portugal. The Pousadas were patterned on the PARADORES, which had proved so successful in Spain, and are controlled by the state tourist agency ENATUR. Smaller and more intimate than the Paradores, many of them are accommodated in castles, monasteries and old houses, while new buildings have been constructed along the coasts and in the mountains. In all there are now about thirty, and all have their individual attractions: the marvelous mountain panorama at Marvão; the intimacy of the nine-room Pousada housed in the 15th-century castle of Obidos; and the atmosphere of the Pousada Dos Lóios in Evora with its interior court, the magnificent staircase and rooms recalling the monastic cells of its former occupants. The star as regards cuisine is undoubtedly Elvas on the Spanish frontier, to which Spaniards flock across the border to sample dishes such as the CARNE DE PORCO A ALENTEJANA, *arroz de pato à pousada* (roast duck with rice) and *favas guisadas à caseira* (fava bean stew).

---

see also　　　　　**Potato:** *see patata*

ℙ *presunto*

A CURED MEAT

A cured ham from Portugal very similar to the Spanish JAMON SERRANO. The best *presunto* comes from Chaves and Valpaços in the Province of TRAS-OS-MONTES, the most northerly in Portugal, and has a sweetness derived from the acorns on which the pigs feed – though this, unfortunately, is a practice which is dying out. Monchique, in the mountains of the ALGARVE, also makes a good *presunto*.

The starting point for *presunto* is a fresh leg of pork. It is impregnated all over with coarse salt, much in the same way as small fragments of garlic may beneficially be inserted into a leg of lamb prior to roasting. It is left for 3 months, then washed repeatedly with water and white wine. Once dry, it is coated thickly with a paste made of sweet paprika and olive oil and hung for a further 3 months.

𝕊 *Priorato*

DEMARCATED WINE REGION

This small region in the mountainous hinterland of TARRAGONA takes its name of "Priory" from that of the great monastery of Scala Dei, now abandoned and ruined. It makes full-blooded red wines, reminiscent of some of those from California in their intense fruity flavor, their body and high degree of alcohol.

Provincias Vascas

BASQUE PROVINCES

Some of the best and most varied cooking in Spain is to be found in the Basque provinces, flanking the Bay of Biscay (see also SAN SEBASTIAN and BILBAO). Good cooking stems from the quality of the materials; and the Basque country is blessed with dairy produce, vegetables and fruit from its green meadows and mountain pastures, and splendid fish from the cold waters of the Bay of Biscay.

The headquarters of Spain's steel-making and ship-building industries and many of the important banks, it is a prosperous area. Given excellent materials and the wherewithal to indulge a taste for good cooking, which the Basques share with the Gascons across the French border – both names come from the Latin *Vascones* – it is hardly surprising that they should be pre-eminent, that many of the leading Madrid restaurateurs are Basques, or that it was here that chefs were first influenced by the *Nouvelle Cuisine* (see NUEVA COCINA VASCA).

Among traditional dishes from the Basque country are MERLUZA A LA VASCA; *kokotxas* (strips cut from the "cheek" of the hake – see COCOCHAS); ANGULAS; BACALAO A LA VIZCAINA and PIPERADA VASCA.

The restaurants in San Sebastian and Bilbao are among the best in Spain and the area is famous for its gastronomic societies (see SOCIEDADES GASTRONOMICAS).

Because of the high rainfall and mountainous terrain, the region makes no wine except for small amounts of CHACOLI, a *pétillant* young wine in the style of the Portuguese VINHOS VERDES.

P *púcara*

COOKING VESSEL

An earthenware jug used in Portugal for cooking poultry and game, as with the *frango na púcara* (jugged chicken).

S *puchero*

COOKING UTENSIL, STEWS

A large stewpot of earthenware or enameled iron similar to an OLLA. The word is also used for a stew made in such a pot.

P *pudim de pão*

BREAD PUDDING

From the BEIRA ALTA, this bread pudding is made by softening bread in hot milk flavored with lemon and vanilla, then pushing it through a sieve to make a purée and combining it with whole eggs, egg yolks and beaten egg whites. The mixture is then poured into a greased mold, cooked in a BAÑO-MARIA, allowed to set, unmolded and served with cream.

Púcara

S *pulpo*
P *polvo*

OCTOPUS

Octopus is most popular in northern Spain and Portugal. A great feature of *fiestas* in Galicia is the outdoor cooking of octopus in large copper cauldrons by *pulpeiras*, who travel from one fiesta to another. The octopus is first boiled and served as *pulpo a feira* (stewed octopus) with a sauce of olive oil, garlic and PIMENTON. One of the largest of such celebrations, the Fiesta del Pulpo, is held in Carbanillo in the province of Orense on the second Sunday of August.

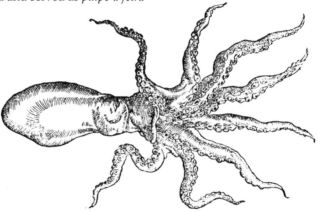

purrusalda

SALT COD AND VEGETABLE SOUP

A favorite soup in the Basque country, made with *bacalao* (salted and dried cod – see BACALHAU), leeks, garlic, olive oil and potatoes.

puzol

A CHEESE

A soft, mild and fresh white cheese from the Valencian area, which must be eaten within 2 days of making.
It has a fat content of 50 percent.

> *If Spanish and Portuguese terms differ from each other, the entry in Portuguese, in the majority of cases, is referred to its Spanish equivalent, where you will find information relevant to both countries.*

P *Quaresma*

Lent; see CUARESMA.

P *queijo da serra*

A cheese; see SERRA.

P *queijo de amêndoas e ovos*

ALMOND CUSTARD PUDDING

This is not a cheese, as the name implies, but a stiff custard with a topping of almond paste. The recipe is from J.M. da Fonseca Internacional, makers of "Lancers" rosé, who serve it at lunches in their beautifully decorated arched cellars, encompassing one of the finest collections of old *azulejos* (polychrome tiles) in the country.

---

queijo de amêndoas e ovos (P)
almond custard pudding

Serves 8

Custard
12 egg yolks, well-beaten
2¼ cups sugar
¾ cup + 2 tbsp water

Topping
1 lb ground almonds (about 3½ cups)
2¼ cups sugar
1 cup water

Make a custard with the yolks, sugar and water, and cook in a double boiler until thick. Transfer to a serving bowl and leave to cool.
  Meanwhile, prepare a syrup with the almonds, sugar and water, simmering for about 5–10 minutes until thick. Cool a little, then spread the syrup on top of the cooled custard as with a fondant icing. Serve cold – it is very rich.

P *queijos*

PORTUGUESE CHEESES

Most Portuguese cheeses, except for the hard and Cheddar-like ILHA from the Azores, are made from ewe's milk. The most famous is the full-flavored *queijo da* SERRA, runny when young, but firm when ripened and matured. There are fresh cream cheeses, such as AZEITAO, and also large amounts of Dutch Edam type, bright red and shaped like a ball. Different cheeses are individually described.
  Some soft cheeses such as Azeitão are eaten before a meal as an appetizer but in general cheese is served at the end and on its own with a knife and fork. If you want bread or butter with it, you must ask. Crackers are not served.

P *queijo de ovelha*

A CHEESE

A soft and salty ewe's milk cheese from Castel Branco.

P *queijo fresco*

A CHEESE

These fresh, moist and creamy cheeses are made in farms all over Portugal, most often from ewe's or goat's milk. They are usually produced and eaten during the winter, some of the best coming from around Sintra and Mafra.

The index, in English, is arranged by types of food — eggs, cheese, fish — kitchen equipment, cooking terms and other subjects. Consult it for recipes that make use of particular ingredients.

---

see also

Quail: see codornices

P *queijo seco*

A CHEESE

A semi-soft fresh cheese, grey and crumbly, and cured in brine.

S *queimada*

HOT TODDY

Queimada is a Galician word describing a drink made by setting alight the potent AGUARDIENTE or *marc*. This is sometimes done simply by pouring the aguardiente into a small white porcelain bowl and setting fire to it; when the blue flame playing over the surface finally dies out, the liquid is stone cold.

For Christmas and other festivities, a more elaborate version is made by pouring half a bottle (failing aguardiente, use the Portuguese BAGACEIRA or French *marc*) into a large round earthenware CAZUELA, adding roasted coffee beans, slices of lemon and maraschino cherries and setting alight the potion. Be sure to do this *well clear* of anything that might catch fire, and use a ladle to fill the glasses.

P *Queluz, Palacio de*

PALACE AND RESTAURANT

The royal palace of Queluz near LISBOA, inspired by Versailles and built between 1758 and 1794, is one of the most graceful in Portugal. Installed in the splendid old kitchens is one of the best restaurants in the country, Cozinha Velha, officially rated five star. Among its specialities are smoked swordfish, BACALHAU, lobster, liver and steaks to choice.

S *quesos*

SPANISH CHEESES

If you ask for cheese in a Spanish restaurant, it is a near certainty that you will be served with MANCHEGO. This is a pleasant enough hard cheese along the lines of Cheddar or Parmesan, also often used in cooking. There are, however, scores of other worthwhile cheeses, usually made from ewe's milk, except in the north with its lush pasturage where cow's milk cheeses are also available. They are not more widely available because they are often made from unpasteurized milk by individual farmers and can be obtained only locally.

With the appearance of magazines devoted to gastronomy and an increasing awareness on the part of the Spanish public, sophisticated restaurants are beginning to serve very interesting cheese boards, and it is certainly worth asking for cheeses such as CABRALES, IDIAZABAL, SAN SIMON and RONCAL, which are among the many separately described. Cheeses are eaten, generally, at the end of a meal as in Portugal (see QUEIJOS).

queso añejo de Huelva

A CHEESE

A lightly pressed goat's cheese with a fat content of 52 percent from the province of Huelva. Semi-hard and very piquant with a penetrating odor, it may be eaten fresh or ripened for some 3 months.

queso fresco valenciano

A cheese; see CERVERA.

queso de la estrella

A cheese; see OROPESA.

Quixote, Don

17TH-CENTURY NOVEL

There are many interesting sidelights in *Don Quixote* on the culinary habits of 16th-century Spain. Thus, Cervantes begins his immortal narrative with: ''In a place of La Mancha, whose name I do not remember, there lived not long ago one of those gentlemen who boasts a wooden lance and old buckler, a scraggy horse and a greyhound for coursing. An *olla* [stew] containing more cow's meat than mutton, scratch fare most nights, grief and bickering on Saturdays, lentils on Fridays and perhaps

see also   *Quince: see marmelo*

a pigeon on Sundays consumed three quarters of his substance. . . ."

Cervantes could be surprisingly up-to-date in his comments. In this present day and age when almost all that we eat and drink has been condemned for containing fat, sugar, cholesterol, alcohol etc, Sancho Panza's plea to the learned doctor who snatched away each dish before he could taste it, strikes an all-too-familiar note: " 'I am dying with hunger; and to deny me my victuals, though it be against the grain of signor doctor [*sic*, the translation is Charles Jarvis's of 1809], and though he should say as much more against it, I say is rather the way to shorten my life than to lengthen it . . . That great dish smoking yonder, I take to be an olla podrida, and, amidst the diversity of things contained it, surely I may light upon something both wholesome and toothsome.' – '*Absit*,' quoth the doctor; 'far be such a thought from us: there is no worse nutriment in the world than your olla podridas: leave them to the prebendaries and rectors of colleges . . .'.''

Rabacal
A CHEESE

A soft cheese with a fat content of 45 percent made around Coimbra with blended ewe's and goat's milk. It is eaten fresh, often for breakfast, and may be ripened in the sun for a month or so, when it firms up and the flavor becomes much stronger.

raia

Monkfish; see RAPE.

ramo de cheiros
BOUQUET GARNI

This is a Portuguese version of the French bouquet garni, varying according to what is being cooked. It always contains garlic, parsley, bay leaf and sometimes leek, fennel and celery.

rancho
STEW

A form of the Portuguese *cozido*, made in the same way but less elaborate.

rancho à Porta Nova
CHICKPEA STEW

This variation of COZIDO A PORTUGUESA is from the small Porta Nova restaurant in the historic old town of Barcelos in the MINHO, famous for its pottery cocks. The legend as to their origin is too good not to repeat. A pilgrim on his way to Santiago de Compostela was falsely accused of theft, but condemned to be hanged. Invoking St. James and noticing that his judge was supping off a roast cock, he declared that the bird would stand up and crow in proof of his innocence – which it did – and he was thereupon released (it is of interest that a live descendant of this same cock may be found in the Cathedral of Santo Domingo de la Calzada in the RIOJA).

---

rancho à Porta Nova (P)
chickpea stew

Serves 4

½ lb grão (or dried chickpeas), soaked overnight
1 lb pork shank, cut into large chunks
1 lb stewing beef or fresh brisket (in Portugal a cut from the cow), cut into large chunks
salt and pepper
1 cup macaroni
1 onion, finely chopped
olive oil
pinch of piri-piri powder or a few drops piri-piri extract
pinch of cumin seeds, ground in a mortar
few strands of saffron

Drain and rinse the soaked chickpeas, put them into boiling water and simmer for 2–3 hours until tender.

Cover the pork and beef with cold water in another pan, bring to the boil slowly, then skim off the white foam before seasoning with salt and pepper. Simmer for 1–1½ hours, or until tender. Boil the macaroni separately in salted water for 15 minutes. Put the chickpeas, meat and macaroni into the same large pot and stew together for 30 minutes until everything is well mixed and tender. Meanwhile, sauté the chopped onion in hot olive oil for 10 minutes, drain off the excess oil, then add a little piri-piri, the ground cumin seeds and the saffron mixed with a little hot broth, and stir well. Add this mixture or refogado to the pot, stir together and simmer for another 30 minutes until the stew resembles a thick soup.

---

see also   **Rabbit:** *see coelho*

S *rape*
P *raia*

MONKFISH

The monkfish is large (32 to 60 inches long) and ugly. The tail makes good eating and its flavor has been compared with that of lobster, especially when cooked and served cold with chopped raw onions, parsley and

shellfish in a SALPICON DE MARISCOS.

RAPE EN SALSA DE ALMENDRAS, of which the recipe follows, is another gastronomic delight.

---

rape en salsa de almendras (S)
monkfish in almond sauce

Serves 4

4 monkfish steaks 1 in thick
salt and pepper
3 tbsp olive oil
1 slice bread about ½ in thick
1 clove garlic, chopped
1 sprig parsley, chopped
⅓ cup almonds, blanched and chopped
few strands of saffron
1 onion, chopped
1 lb tomatoes, peeled, seeded and chopped

Put the fish in an ovenproof dish, sprinkle with salt and pepper and leave until needed.
  Meanwhile, heat the oil in a pan and fry the

bread, garlic, parsley and almonds for a few minutes until golden brown. Remove with a slotted spoon and reserve the oil. Transfer the mixture to a mortar, add the saffron and crush to a paste, then dissolve in a little hot water. In the oil remaining in the pan, fry the onion and tomatoes for 10–15 minutes, and make a purée either by pushing the vegetables through a sieve or putting in a blender or food processor. Mix this with the paste from the mortar, season with salt and pepper, and daub on top of the fish. Bake in a fairly hot oven (375°F) for 20 minutes until the fish is done. Serve from the ovenproof dish.

S *rebozar*
P *panar*

COOKING METHOD

To dredge food in beaten egg and breadcrumbs or flour before frying it.

CAPITALIZED *words within entries refer the reader to more information on the same subject.*

P *refogar*

To braise; see BRASEAR.

S *refogado*
P *sofrito*

BASE FOR STEWS AND SAUCES

Refogado and *sofrito* are chopped and lightly sautéed vegetables that are used to enrich food for a variety of dishes. They consist of chopped onion and garlic and can be varied by the addition of tomatoes, peppers and

PIMENTON and fresh herbs. The ingredients are usually sautéed in olive oil. *Refogado* and *sofrito* can be prepared at the start of cooking or the cooked vegetable may be added at the end.

P *requeijão*

A CHEESE

A soft, fresh and very mild cheese low in fat, made by boiling the whey from the production of ewe's milk cheeses and draining the coagulated solids in a small straw basket. It

will not keep for more than 5 days and is eaten both for breakfast or as a dessert, sprinkled with cinnamon and sugar.

S *requesón*

A CHEESE

A cream cheese made all over Spain and very similar to the Portuguese REQUEIJÃO.

---

see also   **Red mullet:** see salmonete

Rías Bajas, Las

TIDAL RIVERS

From somewhat south of Cape Finisterre to Vigo, the northwest coast of Spain is penetrated by a series of deep inlets. Separated by mountain spurs, and with water which is often the darkest of blues, they can perhaps best be described as fjords. The Rías are among the richest sources of shellfish in Spain and have been described as a giant natural vivarium or nursery. Some of the shellfish is dug from the beaches and other varieties fished from deep water; while, opposite the port, in the Ría de Vigo, there are what at first sight appear to be flotillas of houseboats. These are, in fact, *mejilloneras*, or floating platforms for fishing cultured mussels.

There is a long history of exporting shellfish from the Rías (much of it is now flown to MADRID). From the end of the 16th century small barrels of oysters containing five dozen each were regularly shipped to England, and it was these that Dr Johnson and Boswell enjoyed in London taverns. A major development in the fishing industry took place in the second half of the eighteenth century, when some 17,000 Catalan fishermen, who had learnt from the Provençales how to use a new and effective type of dragnet, descended on the region. Their descendants remain there today.

There are numerous restaurants and *marisquerías* (shellfish bars) in the area, where all this magnificent seafood can be enjoyed. Among them the famous Chocolate near Cambados; O'Arcos, also in Cambados; and on the quayside of Villagarcía de Arosa on the Ría de Arosa, Loliña, where the shellfish at its magnificent best – oysters, clams, scallops, langoustines, lobsters and SANTIAGUIÑOS – is served within hours of being caught. Try also the *marisquería* in the splendid grounds of the PARADOR Nacional Conde de Gondomar at Bayona.

Ribatejo

PORTUGUESE REGION

The region takes its name from *"riba de Tejo"* or "bank of the Tagus", and lies just to the northwest of LISBOA on both sides of the river. The hills bordering the north bank are intensively cultivated with vast stretches of vegetables, olives, fruit trees and vines; to the south lie marshes and paddy fields, giving way to empty expanses scattered with olives and cork oak, resembling the adjacent ALENTEJO. At the center of the area, overlooking the wide Ribatejo plain, lies Santarém, much fought over by Christian and Moor, while the great monastery at Tomar was once the stronghold of the Knights Templar.

The Ribatejo is well known for its game, with dishes such as *lebrada* (hare stewed in red wine) and PATO GUISADO A RIBATEJANA. Other typical dishes include *ovos de sável à pescador* (shad roes); *costeletas de cabrito* (kid cutlets), FAVAS A RIBATEJANA and *pudim de cenouras* (carrot pudding).

With its vast expanses of vineyard, the Ribatejo is a main supplier of everyday drinking wine to Lisbon, from areas such as the Cartaxo. The best known wine firm in the Ribatejo is Carvalho, Ribeiro and Ferreira, makers of the popular and very drinkable red and white "Serradayres" and also of some first-rate old red *garrafeiras* (select vintage wines with long bottle aging).

S *Ribeiro*

DEMARCATED WINE
REGION

The largest of the wine regions in Galicia (see ASTURIAS and GALICIA) to the far north-west of Spain, the Ribeiro is the wettest, and the grapes are grown well clear of the ground on trellises and in arbors as in the Portuguese MINHO. The wines are *pétillants* (slightly sparkling) like the VINHOS VERDES, and visitors find the light and refreshing whites with their flowery nose easier drinking than the brusque and tart reds. The best known and most frequently encountered are those made by the large Bodega Cooperativa del Ribeiro and labelled as "Pazo".

The seal of the Ribeiro demarcated wine region

S *Ribera del Duero*

DEMARCATED WINE
REGION

VEGA SICILIA, east of Valladolid, had been a legend for almost a century before the demarcation some years ago of this region lying along the valley of the Duero (the Portuguese Douro). The area as a whole is now making first-rate, very fruity red wines from the Tinto fino grape (a cousin of the Riojan Tempranillo). So impressed was the famous American wine taster and writer Robert Parker with the wines from the tiny Pesquera *bodega* (winery) that he rated them with those of Château Petrus – with the result that they are now very expensive and difficult to come by.

Other worthwhile and more accessible red wines from the region are those of the co-operative at Peñafiel and from Bodegas Peñalba López and Bodegas Mauro and the "Viña Pedrosa" from Pérez Pascuas.

P *rim*
S *riñones*

KIDNEYS

Lamb's, pig's and calf's kidneys are the most popular in both Portugal and Spain. (Ox and sheep's kidneys are never used because they are tough and smell of urine.) They must be soaked in cold water with a little vinegar or lemon juice, washed well, sprinkled with salt and left for 20 minutes, then rinsed in running water for 10 minutes, turning them until all the salt has been removed.

In addition to the recipes which follow, kidneys may also be grilled A LA PARRILLA.

---

rim salteado com porto (P)
kidneys sautéed in port

Serves 4

*2 lb calf's or lamb's kidneys
vinegar
olive oil
2 or 3 shallots, chopped
1 cup white port wine
¼ lb mushrooms, chopped
salt and pepper*

Stand the kidneys in cold water acidulated with a little vinegar for 20 minutes. Drain, rinse for 10 minutes, then remove the skin and membranes and cut them into small pieces. Heat the olive oil in a pan and sauté the kidneys briskly for 10 minutes until browned on the outside and slightly pink inside, then drain in a colander and place them on a plate. Heat a little more oil in a clean pan and sauté the shallots for 5 minutes. Pour in the port and reduce a little before adding the chopped mushrooms. Cook slowly for a further 10 minutes. Stir the kidneys into the sauce, season with salt and pepper, and simmer for about 10 minutes until tender.

Serve with triangles of fried bread or, if you prefer, with arroz de manteiga (buttered rice).

---

see also   *Rice: see arroz*

riñones

Kidneys: see RIM.

---

riñones al Jerez (S)

kidneys in sherry

Serves 4

2 lb lamb's kidneys
vinegar
salt and pepper
½ cup olive oil
1⅓ cups salsa de tomate (tomato sauce)
⅔ cup fino sherry
1 tbsp pine nuts
1 hard boiled egg yolk

Stand the kidneys for 20 minutes in cold water acidulated with vinegar. Drain, rinse for 10 minutes, remove skin and membranes, and cut into thin slices. Season with salt and pepper. Heat the oil in a pan and sauté the kidneys briskly for 5 minutes. Drain them in a colander and transfer to a plate.

Heat the salsa de tomate (tomato sauce) in a saucepan, add the sherry and reduce a little. Meanwhile, crush the pine nuts in a mortar with the hard boiled egg yolk. Add to the pan, stir well, then add the kidneys and cook for about 5 minutes until piping hot. Serve with boiled rice.

Rioja, La

DEMARCATED WINE REGION

The Rioja, on the borders of the Basque country in northern Spain, makes the best-known Spanish table wines. The region has been making wine at least since the Roman occupation of Spain, but in their present form the wines date from the late 19th century when the phylloxera epidemic devastated the French vineyards, and shippers and growers moved in from Bordeaux to buy and make wines. The Rioja makes more red than white wine, from the native Tempranillo, Garnacha, Mazuelo and Graciano grapes; the traditional reds from *bodegas* (wineries) such as the Marqués de Murrieta, López de Heredia and La Rioja Alta, with long maturation in cask, and nose and flavor compounded of oak and fruit, are typical of the Bordeaux wines of that period.

To obtain *denominación de origen*, all the better red Rioja must spend at least 1 year in 50 gallon oak casks, but the present tendency is to cut down this period of time in favor of longer bottle ageing so as to make fruitier, more claret-like wines such as, for example, those from the Marqués de Cáceres, Martínez Bujanda and Bodegas El Coto.

Most of the white wine is now made by cold fermentation in stainless steel vats without maturation in wood, so as to produce light and flowery wines in the style of

The seal of the Rioja demarcated wine region

Alsace or the Loire. However, there are connoisseurs who prefer the traditional and characterful oaky whites, such as the beautiful Murrieta and "Tondonia" (from López de Heredia) or the rather less oaky "Monopole" from the Compañía Vinícola del Norte de España (CVNE).

P *rissóis*

RISSOLES

The Portuguese *rissóis* resemble small turnovers to the extent of being round and soft and fried in egg and breadcrumbs, but there the similarity ends. They contain an inner filling consisting of *molho bechamel* (see SALSA BESAMEL) mixed with, for example, BACALHAU or shrimps and an outer coating of MASSA DE PROFITEROLES. They may be eaten hot or cold and are excellent as an appetizer or for picnics.

---

rissóis (P)
rissoles

Serves 4

1¾ cups water
1½ tsp salt
½ cup butter
2¾ cups flour
6 oz shrimp, boiled and peeled; or bacalhau (salt cod), cooked and flaked; or veal, cooked and ground
1¾ cups freshly made molho bechamel (white sauce)
1 egg, beaten
dry breadcrumbs
olive oil

Bring the water to the boil in a saucepan with the salt and butter, then stir in the flour. Reduce the heat and continue stirring with a wooden spoon until the mixture comes away from the sides of the pan and a ball is formed.

Leave to cool. Dust the table or pastry board with flour and work the dough until smooth, finally shaping it into a flattish lump and rolling it out until thin.

Stir the shrimp, bacalhau or veal into the hot white sauce, then leave to cool before chilling in the refrigerator until stiff.

Shape portions of the stiff mixture between two spoons and place on the rolled-out pastry. Using a pastry wheel or sharp knife, cut around each spoonful of mixture in the shape of a wide half moon, then fold over the pastry and seal it. Continue until all the pastry and filling have been used up.

Place the rissóis in a large floured plate or on a board as you make them. Finally, dredge them in beaten egg and breadcrumbs and fry in hot olive oil until golden brown.

P *robalo*

Sea bass; see LUBINA.

S *robellón*

WILD MUSHROOM

Also known as *níscalo*, this large, orange-colored, mushroom-like fungus of the genus *Lactarius deliciosus* is particularly popular in CATALUNA. It grows in pine woods and is sometimes called *seta pino* or pine mushroom. It is most often fried in an earthenware CAZUELA with a little olive oil and garlic.

P *Rodrigues, Domingos*

17TH-CENTURY CHEF/COOKERY WRITER

Domingos Rodrigues, who in 1680 published the first Portuguese cook book, the *Arte de Cozinha*, was born near Lamego in 1637 and was successively master of cuisine to the Marquises of Valença and Gouveia, and King Pedro II of Portugal. He was a man of lively intellect, well versed in languages, mathematics and philosophy and he possessed a magnificent library. Among its books was a treatise on cooking written in 1611 by the Spaniard Francisco Martínez Moriño, by whom he was much influenced.

The full title of his book was (in translation) *The Art of Cookery Divided into Two Parts. The first treats of the cookery of every*

Opposite: Blending sherry in a jarra

Pages 254-255; Vineyards in La Rioja Alta (left). Hand-bottling an old 'reserva' wine at the bodegas of CVNE (right)

---

see also   **Rissoles:** *see rissóis*   **To roast:** *see asar*

Above and left: Tapas are unique to Spain. These appetizing snacks, served in bars and cafés, are usually accompanied by a glass of sherry. Tapa literally means lid, after the custom of covering a wine glass with a plate of olives, tortilla, etc. It is not uncommon for more than thirty dishes to be on offer, ranging from boiled potatoes garnished with parsley, mayonnaise and garlic to baby eels boiled in oil with cayenne

sort of meat, & of making conserves, pastes, tarts and pies. The 2nd treats of fishes, shellfish, fruits, herbs, milk dishes, conserves and sweets, and banquets appropriate to every season of the year. It was reprinted a dozen times, the last edition being that of 1844. It is of interest that the great bulk of the recipes are for meat rather than fish; this is because fish was very little eaten in 17th-century Portugal except on days of fast and during Lent (see CUARESMA). The only vegetables to be mentioned are cardoons, eggplant, artichokes, asparagus and carrots. The recipes do not read attractively today, as they include such things as a meat stew bathed with egg yolks, sugar and cinnamon or stewing hen with honey, but the book was a landmark in the history of Portuguese gastronomy.

rojões à moda do Minho
PORK SAUSAGES

Cubes of pork, pork liver, onions, carrots, garlic and olives stewed together. The mixture is then stuffed into casings to make a form of sausage and served hot with roast potatoes.

ARTE DE COZINHA
DIVIDIDA
EM DUAS PARTES.

A PRIMEYRA TRATA DO MODO de cozinhar varios pratos de toda a casta de carne; & de fazer conservas, pastéis, tórtas, & empadas.

A SEGUNDA TRATA DE PEYXES, marisco, frutas, nervas, òvos, lacticinios, cōfervas, & doces : com a fórma dos banquetes para qualquer tempo do Anno.

COMPOSTA.

Por DOMINGOS RODRIGUEZ Cozinheyró do Conde do Vimioso : & dedicada ao mefmo Senhor.

LISBOA.
Na Officina de JOAŌ GALRAO.

Com todas as licenças neceffarias Anno de 1680.

The title page of 'The Art of Cookery Divided into Two Parts' by Domingos Rodrigues

Romanos, Los
THE ROMANS

The Romans first moved into Spain some 200 years BC during the First Punic War, and a century later most of the Iberian Peninsula was under Roman control. During the centuries that followed, the whole area was pacified and colonized. Innovations in agriculture were not so much in the introductions of new crops but in more fruitful use of the land and improvements in the cultivation of existing staples such as cereals, olives and vines; olive oil and wine were exported to Rome in large amounts. As in Gaul a century later, the most important innovations in the culinary sphere were the replacement of animal fats for cooking by olive oil and the widespread use of garlic.

It is evident from the book *De Coquinaria*, attributed to Apicius, the famous Roman gastronome, that very many of the vegetables, fruits, spices, fish and meat eaten in Spain and Portugal today were known to and enjoyed by the Romans, and Spain was the main supplier of the sauce most widely used in Roman cookery (see GARUM).

romãzeira

Pomegranate; see GRANADA.

Roncal
A CHEESE

One of the best Spanish cheeses, with a fat content of 43 percent, this is made from ewe's milk in the Valley of Roncal in Navarra during June and July. It is a hard cheese with a smoky, piquant flavor, ivory-colored interior and dark, hard rind. Much of the production goes to France, where it is also greatly appreciated.

S *ropa vieja*

LEFTOVERS IN TOMATO SAUCE

The Spanish equivalent of the Portuguese ROUPA-VELHA, made from leftovers of meat, often from COCIDOS. It is cut up finely (never ground) and warmed with SALSA DE TOMATE.

S *roscón de Reyes* P *bolo-rei*

TWELFTH NIGHT CAKE

Makes 2 large rings

1 oz compressed yeast
⅔ cup warm water
½ cup butter
½ cup sugar
pinch salt
2 eggs, beaten
1 tbsp brandy
⅔ cup milk
pinch of ground cinnamon
3¾ cups self-rising flour
4 oz candied fruit peel
glacé cherries, pineapple, etc, for decoration
confectioners' sugar

In a warm bowl dissolve the yeast in warm water. Cream the butter, sugar, salt and one of the beaten eggs, then add the brandy, milk, the dissolved yeast and a pinch of cinnamon. Gradually mix in the flour, working with a spatula or wooden spoon to obtain a soft and somewhat sticky dough. Add the candied fruit peel and knead on a cool, floured working surface, adding a little flour if necessary, until the dough is soft and elastic. Put it into a plastic bag and leave to rest for 2 hours in a warm place until about doubled in size. Test the dough by pressing with a floured finger; when properly risen, it will spring back. Now insert a silver coin or other small object for good luck.

Shape the dough into two large ring molds outer diameter 9 inches, inner 5 inches – and decorate with the glacé fruit, pressing it lightly into the dough. Leave to rise further in a warm place for another hour. Brush with the other beaten egg, sprinkle with confectioners' sugar and bake in a moderate oven (350°F) for about 40 minutes, or until golden brown. Allow to cool on a rack before serving.

P *roupa-velha*

LEFTOVERS OF MEAT

Literally "old clothes", this is used of any Portuguese dish often made (like the English shepherd's pie) of leftovers of meat from COZIDOS and warmed up with MOLHO DE TOMATE Y PIMENTOS.

Rubert de Nola

15TH-CENTURY CHEF/COOKERY WRITER

The publication of the *Llibre de Coch* by Maestre Rubert de Nola, written in Catalan and first printed in BARCELONA in 1477, was an event of major importance in the history of Spanish cooking. In the gastronomic sphere, Spanish commentators have compared it to Don QUIXOTE – and certainly it was to run to a great many more editions during the 16th century than Cervantes' masterpiece in the next. Its author was reputedly chef to the conqueror of Naples – Alfonso the Magnanimous of Aragón-Cataluña – for whom he is said to have cooked during the Italian expedition. In recent years, doubts have been cast on his identity – it has, for example, been pointed out that Nola is a town near Naples, hence giving rise to the suggestion that the famous Rubert or Robert was Italian rather than Catalan. He remains a shadowy figure, but there is nothing vague about the detailed and sophisticated recipes, running to 243 in later Castilian editions, or the precise instructions for carving meat or for household management, of which the following is typical: "There are three officials in noble houses, who are never at peace: the carver, the steward and the chef. If the steward brings the meat without properly breaking the bones or provides meat of poor quality, the chef says that he does not know how to buy and that he is a poor steward, and at times they quarrel. Similarly the carver tells the chef that his food is uneatable and that he has no talent for cooking, because the meat is overdone and impossible to carve, with the result that the master loses patience

and it is he who is blamed for it. This is the reason why these three officials are never at peace, and if they are to settle their differences among themselves, it is essential that the steward is a good cook and carver, that the chef is a good carver as well as cook, and that the carver is a good steward and chef. . . .''

Rueda

DEMARCATED WINE REGION

This small region to the southwest of Valladolid centers on the village of Rueda. It makes only white wines, mainly from the Verdejo grape. The traditional wines grow a *flor* and are matured, like SHERRY, in a SOLERA or in partially stoppered glass carboys. However, Rueda is turning increasingly to the production of fresh young table wines of which some of the best are made by the famous RIOJA firm of the Marqués de Riscal in a modern *bodega* equipped with temperature-controled stainless steel fermentation tanks.

The seal of the Rueda demarcated wine region

ruivo

Gurnet; see CALDEIRADO.

S *sábalo*   Shad; see SAVEL.

P *safio*   Conger eel; see CALDEIRADA.

S *sal*   Both Spain and Portugal with their long sea coasts and sunny climate have been large producers of sea salt from the earliest times. In the 14th century, Portugal traded salt from Setúbal and Aveiro with the English, part of it being shipped back in the form of BACALHAU, as popular then as now.

SALT

    At that period almost all of the salt commercially available was produced by the evaporation of sea water, and there are many today who prefer it to rock salt, as in addition to sodium chloride it contains other mineral salts and trace elements. It is made by running the sea water into *salinas* (shallow pans). After precipitation of the less soluble material, the concentrated brine is crystallized in further pans and graded according as to whether it is to be used for table salt, chemical manufacture or for salting fish. In addition to some 96 percent of sodium chloride, a good quality sea salt might contain 1 percent of calcium sulphate, 0·2 percent magnesium sulphate, 0·2 percent magnesium chloride, plus 2·6 percent of water and a trace of iodine.

P *saladas*   Salads; see ENSALADAS.

---

*salada à
Almonda Parque
(P)*
Almonda Park salad

Serves 4

2 sprigs watercress
3 slices presunto or ham, cut into strips
3 hard boiled eggs, sliced
3 tomatoes, sliced
4 potatoes, boiled and sliced
3 shallots or scallions
molho vinagreta (vinaigrette sauce)

Mix together the watercress, ham, sliced eggs, tomatoes, potatoes and shallots, and pour the molho vinagreta (vinaigrette sauce) on top.

---

*salada à
andaluza (P)*
Andalucían salad

Serves 4

a little mustard
2 cloves garlic, crushed
molho vinagreta (vinaigrette sauce)
6 tomatoes, sliced
2 canned red peppers (pimentos), drained and
    cut into strips
1 cup boiled rice

Stir the mustard and garlic into the molho vinagreta (vinaigrette sauce), then mix it with the other ingredients.

---

see also   **Saffron:** *see azafrán*   **Salad:** *see ensaladas, saladas*

***salada à lisbonense* (P)** Lisbon salad	Serves 4 3 Belgian endives, cooked, cut into julienne strips 4 tomatoes, sliced 3 carrots, cooked, cut into julienne strips 3 beets, cooked, cut into julienne strips 2 hard boiled eggs molho vinagreta (vinaigrette sauce)	*Put the endive in the center of a large serving dish and around it arrange alternate slices of tomato, heaps of carrot and beetroot. Separate the egg whites and yolks and push the yolks through a sieve. Sprinkle the carrot with the chopped egg whites and the beets with the yolks. Pour the molho vinagreta (vinaigrette sauce) over the salad before serving it.*

***salada à sevilhana* (P)** Seville salad	Serves 4 ¼ cup rice, cooked 2 canned red peppers (pimentos), drained and cut into strips 2 tomatoes, peeled, seeded and chopped 2 oz cooked ham, cut into strips molho vinagreta (vinaigrette sauce)	*Mix together the rice, peppers, tomatoes and ham, and pour the molho vinagreta (vinaigrette sauce) over the salad before serving it.*

***salada portuguesa* (P)** Portuguese salad	Serves 4 leaves of 1 Boston lettuce 1 small bunch of watercress 1 large tomato, sliced 1 onion, cut into rings 12 olives, stuffed with anchovies molho vinagreta (vinaigrette sauce)	*Mix the lettuce, watercress, tomato slices, onion rings and olives, and toss in a bowl with molho vinagreta (vinaigrette sauce) before serving.*

salamandra
COOKING UTENSIL

Aptly named, this is a heavy metal disc mounted on a long handle, which is heated until red hot over a fire or gas ring and used for caramelizing the surface of desserts such as CREMA QUEMADA A LA CATALANA. It is not the easiest of operations, and the alternative is to put the dish briefly under the grill.

salchicha blanca asturiana
A SAUSAGE

A sausage from the north of Spain made by filling a casing with ground lean pork and herbs into a casing and hanging it up to dry for 2 days. It is usually served fried for breakfast.

salchichas
SAUSAGES

Fresh pork sausages for frying or stewing. They are often used in rice dishes such as some forms of PAELLA.

> *The index, in English, is arranged by types of food — eggs, cheese, fish — kitchen equipment, cooking terms and other subjects. Consult it for recipes that make use of particular ingredients.*

S *salmón*

SALMON

In times past, salmon abounded in the rivers of northern Spain from the Bidasoa on the French border to the Miño, dividing Galicia from Portugal, in the far west. Although the fishing rights were a royal prerogative in medieval times, granted to the nobility and monasteries, salmon were so plentiful that in the 17th century the choristers of the Church of Santa María in Tolosa complained that they were glutted with it, while in the Asturias the miners staged one of the most unusual strikes on record as a protest against the habitual inclusion of salmon in their rations. In more recent times, overfishing and the positioning of fixed nets to trap the fish as they swim upstream in the spring has unfortunately led to their virtual extinction. Although salmon fishermen can still be seen on rivers such as the remote Deva, which flows down from the Picos de Europa to the Atlantic, most of the salmon now eaten in Spain is farm bred fish from other countries.

---

salmón empanado (S)
spiced broiled salmon

Serves 4

4 salmon steaks, about 1 in thick
salt and pepper
juice of 2 lemons
2 tbsp olive oil
2 cups fresh breadcrumbs
2 oz cooked ham, ground
1 clove garlic, crushed
4 tbsp chopped parsley

Marinate the salmon steaks for about 30 minutes with a little salt and pepper, the lemon juice and oil. Meanwhile, mix together the breadcrumbs, ham, garlic and parsley. Remove the salmon from the marinade and roll it in the mixture until both sides are coated. Put the salmon under a preheated broiler and cook for about 5 minutes on each side or a little longer until cooked through.

S **P** *salmonete*

RED MULLET

This handsome fish with its vermilion markings and fine white flesh is a great favourite in Spain and Portugal. It is usually broiled or fried, and there is an intriguing version from Setúbal in the Portuguese ESTREMADURA in which it is grilled with bitter oranges.

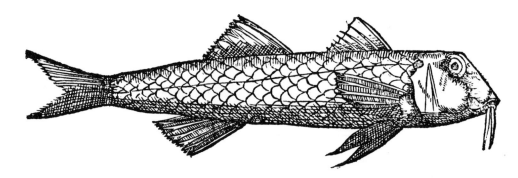

S *salmorejo*

A SAUCE,
A COLD SOUP

The word is used to describe a sauce made from water, vinegar, olive oil, salt and pepper. It is also the name of a variety of GAZPACHO from ANDALUCIA in which the vegetables are reduced to a purée (see following recipe).

salmorejo cordobés (S) cold soup from Córdoba	Serves 8 3 cloves garlic salt 1 green pepper, seeded and coarsely chopped 3 tomatoes, peeled and coarsely chopped 1 lb bread, cubed, moistened and squeezed dry olive oil 2 tbsp sherry vinegar 1 quart water 3 hard boiled eggs, chopped 3 oranges, peeled and chopped	*Put the garlic, a little salt, the pepper, tomatoes and moistened bread into a large wooden bowl, and work into a paste. Gradually stir in olive oil as if making a mayonnaise until a stiff cream forms, then thin it to the consistency of a purée with the vinegar and water. Add the chopped eggs and oranges, and serve with toasted bread crusts.*

salmorejo de perdiz

PARTRIDGE WITH CUSTARD

An unusual dish from Toledo in which a baked custard is made, incorporating partridge stock and a paste made from the wings and legs, and flavored with nutmeg. This is turned out on to a serving dish and surrounded by roasted partridge breasts covered in a sauce made from the giblets, shallots, white wine and herbs.

Saloio

A CHEESE

A soft fresh white cheese from the LISBOA area, usually made with cow's milk. It has a fat content of 45 percent, the flavor is a little sour, and it is usually eaten in restaurants, where it is served as an appetizer.

salpicão

CHARCUTERIE

A Portuguese spiced and smoked tenderloin of pork.

salpicón de mariscos

COLD BOILED SHELLFISH IN SAUCE

An assortment of cold boiled shellfish, often including lobster, shrimp and scampi, served with a *salpicón* sauce made with olive oil, capers, hard boiled eggs and parsley.

salsa

Parsley; see PEREJIL.

salsas molhos

SAUCES

Sauces are much more widely used in Spain and Portugal than in the UK and the USA, where the meat, in particular, is so often served plain roasted or broiled.

The base most frequently used is *sofrito* and its Portuguese equivalent REFOGADO, both of which are used in almost all stews. Other well known sauces include CHILINDRON, MOLHO DE TOMATE, SALSA ESPAÑOLA, PICADA and SALSA ROMESCO.

Of cold sauces, the best known are SALSA

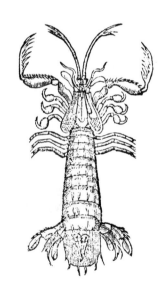

Large prawn; an ingredient in salpicón de mariscos

MAHONESA and ALIOLI, the garlic sauce from CATALUÑA.

salsa al vino blanco (S)
white wine sauce for fish

Makes approx. ¾ cup

4 shallots, chopped
¾ cup dry white wine
3 egg yolks
6 tbsp butter
salt
lemon juice

Simmer the shallots with the wine in a small saucepan until the liquid is reduced by half, then cool and push through a sieve. Add the egg yolks one at a time, beating them into the mixture. Pour into a baño-maria or stand the small saucepan in a larger pan of simmering water and continue beating until the sauce thickens. Remove from the heat and, still beating vigorously, add butter by tablespoons, a little salt and a few drops of lemon juice until smooth.

Suitable for poached or baked fish, it also goes well with asparagus.

S salsa besamel
P molho bechamel
WHITE SAUCE

This is the basic recipe for white sauce, which is made thicker or thinner by the use of less or more milk. It can be modified in endless ways – for example, by the addition of grated cheese or stock. In its thickest form it is the basis for *croquetas* (croquettes) made with meat, chicken or fish (see CROQUETAS DE JAMON).

The index, in English, is arranged by types of food — eggs, cheese, fish — kitchen equipment, cooking terms and other subjects. Consult it for recipes that make use of particular ingredients.

---

salsa besamel (S)
molho bechamel (P)
white sauce

Makes approx. 1⅓ cups

2 tbsp butter
3 tbsp flour
salt and pepper
pinch of nutmeg
1⅓ cups hot milk

Melt the butter in a small saucepan and stir in the flour. Cook carefully over a low heat until blended but not browned. Remove the pan from the heat, and season with salt, pepper and a pinch of nutmeg. Over a low heat, add the hot milk, and cook until thick, stirring all the time to avoid lumps forming.

---

salsa de almendras (S)
almond sauce

Makes approx. 1⅓ cups

12 medium tomatoes, peeled and seeded
½ cup olive oil
20 almonds, blanched and peeled
salt and pepper

Put all the ingredients into a blender or food processor and purée until smooth. Suitable for poached or baked fish, escalopes of veal and pork chops.

salsa de patatas para pescado (S)
potato sauce for fish

Makes approx. 1⅔ cups

9 oz potatoes, peeled and coarsely cubed
olive oil
2 fresh red peppers, fried, peeled, seeded and
    cut into strips, or 2 canned peppers
    (pimentos), drained and cut into strips
¾ lb tomatoes, peeled and seeded
salt
a few cumin seeds
1 bay leaf

Sauté the potatoes in hot olive oil until golden, then add the peppers and tomatoes and cook for another 10 minutes. Add the salt, cumin seeds and bay leaf, together with 1⅓ cups water or a little more if necessary, and simmer for another 10 minutes until the potatoes are soft. Finally, push the mixture through a sieve or put into a blender or food processor.

    This sauce is served with any fried, baked or poached white fish.

salsa de pimientos encarnados

RED PEPPER SAUCE

This sauce is delicious as an accompaniment to lamb or other broiled or roast meat.

salsa de pimientos encarnados (S)
red pepper sauce

Makes approx. ⅔ cup

1 small onion, finely chopped
2 tbsp olive oil
1 clove garlic, crushed
15 oz canned red peppers (pimentos), drained
    and cut up coarsely
salt

Slowly sauté the onion in hot olive oil for about 10 minutes until soft but not brown. Drain off any oil, add the garlic and peppers, cook for another 10-15 minutes until very soft, then purée the mixture using a blender, food processor or sieve and season to taste.

salsa de tomate

TOMATO SAUCE

A sauce with numerous uses. The first recipe overleaf is somewhat akin to *sofrito* (see REFOGADO), but differing from it in containing red peppers.

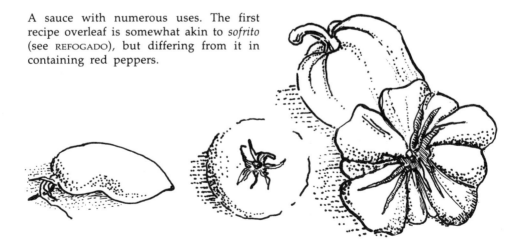

salsa de tomate I (S)
molho de tomate I (P)
tomato sauce

Makes approx. 1⅓ cups

3 tbsp olive oil
2 large onions, chopped
2 red peppers, seeded and chopped, or 2 canned red peppers, drained and chopped
1 lb tomatoes, peeled and chopped, or 15 oz canned tomatoes
small bunch fresh mint, parsley and basil
1 clove garlic, crushed
salt and pepper
2 tbsp fino sherry

Heat the oil in a large skillet, and sauté the onions gently until soft. Add the peppers, if fresh, cover and continue slow frying for about 20 minutes until they are tender, then drain off any oil. Add the tomatoes, herbs and the peppers, if canned, and fry slowly, uncovered, until the ingredients form a pulp, finally adding the garlic and seasoning with salt and pepper. Purée the mixture using a sieve, blender or food processor, and stir in the sherry.

salsa de tomate II (S)
molho de tomate II (P)
tomato sauce

Makes approx. ⅔ cup

2 tbsp olive oil
1 large onion, chopped
1 lb tomatoes, skinned and chopped
1 clove garlic, crushed
1 tbsp chopped parsley
salt

Put the oil into a deep frying pan and fry the onion until golden. Add the tomatoes, garlic and lastly the parsley and season to taste. Cook uncovered for 30 minutes until very soft.

salsa española (S)
molho espanolha (P)
brown sauce

Makes approx. 3 cups

3 tbsp pork fat or olive oil
¾ lb beef bones
¾ lb beef trimmings without fat
½ lb ham bone with meat
2 onions, quartered
2 large carrots, coarsely chopped
2 large leeks, split lengthwise
2 sticks of celery
1–2 bay leaves
pinch each of dried rosemary, thyme and oregano
freshly ground black pepper
2 cloves
3 large tomatoes
salt
4 peppercorns
6 sprigs parsley
3 quarts water
¼ cup dry oloroso sherry

Put the pork fat or olive oil, the beef bones, beef trimmings and knuckle of ham into a heavy ovenproof casserole, and brown in a fairly hot oven (400°F) for 1 hour or a little longer. Add the vegetables, seasoning and herbs, and return to the oven for another hour or longer, until everything is nicely browned. Transfer to a large heavy pot and add the water. Deglaze the juices in the casserole with the sherry, add to the pot, cover and simmer gently for 2½ hours, removing the scum from time to time until the broth is clear.

Strain twice through a sieve and leave overnight in the refrigerator. Next day, remove the hard layer of fat on the surface with a slotted spoon.

Salsa española is added to many dishes as a stock and is sometimes served with meats.

salsa mahonesa (S)
molho mahonesa (P)
mayonnaise

Makes approx. 1⅓ cups

2 egg yolks
1 tsp dry mustard
1 tsp salt
1 clove garlic, crushed (optional)
1⅓ cups approx. olive oil
juice of 1 lemon
salt, to taste

Method with a blender or food processor
Put the yolks, mustard, salt and garlic into the blender and mix at medium speed. With the motor running, trickle in the olive oil until the mayonnaise has thickened, then add the lemon juice and salt and blend at the highest speed for a few seconds.

Method without a blender
Break the egg yolks into a large bowl and beat with the garlic, salt and mustard. Add the oil little by little, beating with a wooden spoon until the mayonnaise thickens. If it shows any signs of curdling, beat in another yolk. Once it has thickened, trickle in the lemon juice and stir well. This mayonnaise may be stored in the refrigerator in a screw-top jar for up to a week and used as required.

salsa mahonesa muselina (S)
fluffy mayonnaise

Makes approx. 1⅓ cups
Proceed as described in the previous recipe for salsa mahonesa, but add the whites of 2 eggs, beaten until very stiff, after the basic mayonnaise has thickened. This mayonnaise is particularly suitable for ensaladilla rusa.

salsa mahonesa verde (S)
green mayonnaise for fish

Makes approx. 1⅓ cups

½ cup spinach, chopped
½ cup watercress, chopped
⅓ cup tarragon, chopped
⅓ cup chervil, chopped
⅓ cup parsley, chopped
olive oil if required
salt
1⅓ cups salsa mahonesa (mayonnaise)

Boil all the vegetables and herbs together for 8 minutes or cook them in a pan for the same time with a little olive oil, adding a little salt. Drain well and push through a sieve or purée in a blender or food processor to obtain a smooth paste. Leave until cold, then add to the mayonnaise and stir well with a wooden spoon.

salsa para pescado (S)
sauce for fish

Makes approx. ⅔ cup

7 oz canned red peppers (pimentos), drained
    and coarsely chopped
1 large clove garlic, peeled
1 small chili pepper (optional), seeded
1 tsp pimentón dulce (paprika)
3-4 tomatoes, peeled, seeded and chopped
salt
3 tbsp olive oil
3 tbsp wine vinegar

Crush the peppers in a mortar and pestle with the garlic, chili pepper (if used), pimentón (paprika), tomatoes and a little salt to make a fine paste. Alternatively, this may be done in a blender or food processor. Finally, stir in the oil and wine vinegar.
    This sauce makes a delicious accompaniment to fish or shellfish, including lobster.

S *salsa romesco*

ROMESCO SAUCE

This famous sauce takes its name from a variety of small, dried and very hot red pepper used for making it in its native CATALUÑA. It goes well with fish, vegetables and broiled meat.

---

salsa romesco (S)
romesco sauce

Makes approx. 1 cup

3 dried romesco peppers or dried chili peppers, seeded
10 toasted almonds
3 cloves garlic, crushed
3 medium tomatoes, peeled, seeded and chopped
1 slice bread, fried and crumbled
white pepper
½ cup virgin olive oil
½ cup wine vinegar
salt

Soak the peppers or chili peppers in tepid water for 30 minutes, then drain and crush them in a mortar and pestle with the almonds, or use a blender or food processor. Blend the paste with the garlic, tomatoes, fried breadcrumbs and pepper, and transfer the mixture to a bowl. Gradually add the oil, stirring with a wooden spoon as if making mayonnaise. Alternatively, a blender or food processor may be used. Continue with the addition of the vinegar and a pinch of salt. Cover the bowl and leave for 2 hours in the refrigerator, checking the seasoning before serving.

---

salsa vinagreta (S)
molho vinagreta (P)
vinaigrette sauce

Makes ½ cup

1 clove garlic
2 tbsp sherry vinegar
6 tbsp virgin olive oil
salt and pepper
chopped parsley

Crush the garlic in a mortar and pestle, add the vinegar, olive oil and seasoning, and beat well with a spoon until well combined.

After pouring the sauce over the salad, it should be garnished with a little chopped parsley.

---

salsa vinagreta para pescados cocidos (S)
vinaigrette sauce for poached fish

Makes approx. 1 cup

2 anchovies, drained
2 tbsp finely chopped onion
1 tbsp chopped parsley
a little tarragon, chopped
3 hard boiled egg yolks
⅞ cup olive oil
2 tbsp vinegar
salt and pepper
1 tbsp capers

Crush the anchovies in a mortar and pestle, add the chopped onion, parsley and tarragon, and blend into a smooth paste. Mix in the egg yolks, then push the mixture through a sieve into a bowl. Slowly drip in the olive oil, stirring with a wooden spoon, as if making mayonnaise. Once the sauce begins to thicken, drip in the vinegar, and continue stirring. Season with salt and pepper, then add the capers.

---

see also

Salt: see sal *Salt cod: see bacalhau*

saltear
corar
TO SAUTÉ

To sauté, i.e. to cook food in a small amount of hot oil or fat over a high heat, regularly turning it.

San Sebastián
SPANISH CITY

San Sebastián, with its beautiful bay and curving beach of La Concha fringed by the old houses of the aristocracy, is the most elegant of Spanish seaside resorts. Times have, however, changed since the members of the court took up residence there during the summer, and the well-to-do from Madrid now often head for Marbella.

It is a great gastronomic center with its Academy of Gastronomy and a selection of some of the best restaurants in the country. Like BILBAO, it is also known for its SOCIEDADES GASTRONOMICAS, a peculiarly Basque institution.

Among many first-rate restaurants, pride of place must go to Arzak, run by the famous Juan María ARZAK, one of the founders of the NUEVA COCINA VASCA. This is exemplified in such dishes as *ensaladas de verduras con aceite de avellana* (mixed greens dressed with walnut oil) and *magret de pato con hojaldre y peras* (breasts of duck with pastry and pears). Scenically located on the slopes of Monte Igueldo overlooking the sea is Akelarre, the creation of Pedro Subijana, another great exponent of the New Basque Cooking. Specialties here are the *endivias con manzanas y nueces* (endive salad with apple and walnuts), *medallón de ternera con foi-gras y champiñones* (escalope of veal with foie gras and mushrooms) and the *sorbetes de limón cava* (sorbets of lemon and champagne). Nicolasa is a thoroughly good and traditional Basque restaurant, where one is welcomed with a glass of CHACOLI and can choose from hearty and delicious fare such as *calamares pescados con anzuelo* (line-caught squid), *huevos revueltos con cangrejos de río* (scrambled eggs with sea crayfish) and *capón asado con puré de castañas* (roast capon with chestnut purée).

San Simón
A CHEESE

This most individual cheese from Galicia is made from the milk of a cow called the "rubia gallega" by a somewhat elaborate process in which it is pressed in special wooden molds and finally smoked with birch wood. Creamy, with a fat content of 40 percent and with a most individual smoked flavor, it is unfortunately becoming increasingly difficult to find.

Sancho Panza

See QUIXOTE, DON.

sangría
WINE PUNCH

Most refreshing in summer, this Spanish wine punch – also drunk in Portugal – is made by pouring red wine into a large pitcher with twice the amount of sparkling lemon drink, then adding plenty of ice cubes and orange and lemon slices, and a dash of Spanish brandy.

santiaguiño
A SHELLFISH

This is a large crayfish (*Scyllarus arctus*) fished in the RIAS BAJAS of Galicia (see ASTURIAS AND GALICIA). Appropriately enough – and hence the name – it bears a distinctive marking on its head resembling the cross of St. James (Santiago).

> *If Spanish and Portuguese terms differ from each other, the entry in Portuguese, in the majority of cases, is referred to its Spanish equivalent, where you will find information relevant to both countries.*

santola

Spider crab; see CENTOLLA.

---

see also   *Sandwich: see bocadillo*

P *São Jorge*

A CHEESE

A hard cheese with a fat content of 45 percent made with unpasteurized cow's milk from the island of São Jorge in the Azores. It is ripened for 2 or 3 months, and is piquant and crumbly like Cheddar.

S *sardinas*
P *sardinhas*

SARDINES

Fresh sardines in season are among the cheapest fish in Spain and Portugal and, for the foreign visitor at least, one of the most attractive. They are widely available in Portugal, and probably for this reason they are not served in sophisticated restaurants. They are, however, popular in seaside places like the charming fishing town of Nazaré, where they sprinkle the fish with coarse salt and grill them over charcoal in the open air.

On the beaches of the Basque coast of Spain, sardines are also grilled in the same way during the summer tourist season, and they are most delicious, with their smoky, somewhat charred flavor.

Some other variations, both for fresh and canned sardines follow. The canned fish, large and luscious, from Santoña on the Basque coast and from northern Portugal, is the best obtainable.

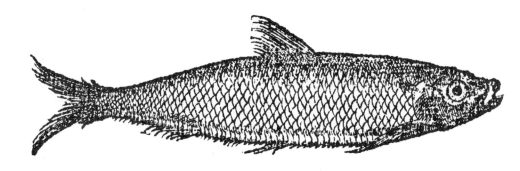

sardinas fritas
(S)
fried fresh sardines

fresh sardines
salt
1 egg, beaten
flour or dry breadcrumbs
garlic, crushed
olive oil

Split the sardines along their length, remove heads, guts and backbones, and open them flat. Season with salt, then dip in beaten egg, dredge in flour or breadcrumbs mixed with the crushed garlic, and fry in very hot olive oil until golden brown.

Alternatively, the sardines may simply be cleaned, dredged in seasoned flour without filleting them and crisply fried.

P *sardinhas*

Sardines; see SARDINAS.

P *sardinhas em leque*

SARDINES IN A FAN

This is a decorative way of serving canned sardines as a starter. The sardines are drained and arranged in a fan on the serving dish. Around them are arranged halved and scooped-out hard boiled eggs filled with cooked and chopped green beans. The yolks are then pushed through a sieve and sprinkled on top.

see also

Sardines: see sardinas

---

sardinhas no forno (P)
baked sardines

Serves 4

2 lb fresh sardines
salt
olive oil
2 onions, cut into rings
chopped parsley

Sprinkle the sardines with a little salt, then lay them in an ovenproof dish. Pour in a little olive oil and cover with the onion rings and a sprinkling *of chopped parsley. If necessary, place a second layer of sardines, onions and parsley on top. Bake in a fairly hot oven (375°F) for 20 minutes until crisp and golden brown.*

Serve with a salad of freshly sliced tomatoes and molho vinagreta (vinaigrette sauce), garnished with cilantro.

---

sardinhas pamplinas

FRIED FRESH
SARDINES WITH
TOMATO SAUCE

This is another attractive and decorative way of serving fresh sardines. They are first filleted and marinated in lemon juice, then dipped in egg and breadcrumbs, fried in hot olive oil and arranged around the edge of a serving dish, with a freshly made tomato sauce poured into the center.

sauce espagnole

BROWN SAUCE

This is, of course, the French translation of *salsa española*, the famous brown sauce of which Richard FORD wrote that: "It has been said of our heretical countrymen that we have but one form of sauce – melted butter – and a hundred different forms of religion, whereas in orthodox Spain there is but one of each, and, as with religion, so to change this sauce would be little short of heresy . . . Its brown *negro de hueso* color is the livery of tawny Spain, where all is brown from the *Sierra Morena* to duskier man. Of such hue is his cloak, his terra cotta house, his wife, his ox, his ass, and everything that is his. This sauce has not only the same color, but the same flavor everywhere; hence the difficulty of making out the material of which any dish is composed . . . It puzzles even a Frenchman; for it is still the great boast of the town of Olvera that they served up some donkeys as rations to a Buonapartist detachment. . . ."

Sauce espagnole is one of the classics of fine cooking for which, despite its obvious origins, the French were later to claim credit. Thus, in his *Cuisinier parisien*, written at the beginning of the 19th century, Carême refers to "*our* Espagnole and *our* Allemande (we underline the personal pronoun to emphasize that these sauces are entirely French in origin)." Chauvinism can go no further!

The sauce is always made with a basis of meat stock cooked with bacon and vegetables, but there is also considerable variation. A typical recipe is given under SALSA ESPAÑOLA.

sável
sábalo

SHAD

Shad is obtainable in Spain and Portugal in the spring, when as described in writings dating back to the time of the Moors, the fish swim up the rivers from the sea.

For the following Portuguese recipe, fresh cod or halibut may be substituted.

CAPITALIZED *words within entries refer the reader to more information on the same subject.*

---

see also   **To sauté:** *see saltear*   **Sauces:** *see molhos, salsas*

---

sável de escabeche (P)
marinated shad

Serves 4

2 lb shad, skinned, boned and cut into strips
flour
olive oil

Marinade
½ cup white vinegar
1⅓ cups dry white wine
½ cup water
1 tsp salt
pepper
2 carrots, finely grated
2 onions, cut into rings
2 cloves garlic, chopped
1 tbsp chopped parsley
½ cup virgin olive oil
1 bay leaf

Dredge the shad in flour, shake to remove excess flour, and fry in hot olive oil until golden. Transfer to an ovenproof dish with a lid.

If using other fish, it is simpler to cut it into thin slices.

To make the marinade, simmer all the ingredients in a saucepan for 15 minutes and pour the mixture, while still hot, over the fish. Cover and leave to marinate for 3 days in the refrigerator. Serve cold.

P **sazoar**

To season; see SAZONAR.

S **sazonar**

TO SEASON

Salt and garlic (see AJO) are the universal Spanish and Portuguese seasoning agents. Additionally, more piquant spices such as PIMENTON in Spain, CARIL in Portugal and AZAFRAN in both countries, are all regular features of many recipes.

The Spanish and Portuguese prefer to grind their condiments freshly using a mill, rather than use the prepackaged varieties, and to use a mortar and pestle for pounding garlic, saffron, etc.

S **sepia**

CUTTLEFISH

The *sepia*, also known as *jibia*, is very similar to a small squid, but the body is rounder and the tentacles shorter. It is cleaned in the same way (see CALAMARES) and is delicious when grilled whole A LA PARRILLA.

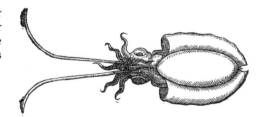

S **Serena**

A CHEESE

A first-rate hard ewe's milk cheese from Badajoz made only by individual farmers. With a fat content of 52 percent, the interior is creamy and somewhat bitter in flavor, but highly appreciated by its *aficionados*.

Opposite: A traditional omelet or tortilla española

---

see also

Scallops: *see vieiras*   **Sea bass:** *see besugo*

Opposite: Gilded Spanish wine decanters from the 18th century; these were used only on formal occasions

Above: A still-life of salmon and cooking pots by Luis Melendez

Left: An 18th-century sprinkler

P *Serpa*

A CHEESE

One of the best Portuguese cheeses, this has been made at Serpa in the ALENTEJO since Roman times. It is made from ewe's milk, has a fat content of 45 percent and is generally similar to SERRA, being eaten either in the spring, when it is soft and runny, or matured for long periods, becoming hard and much stronger in flavor. This ageing is carried out in caves and the cheese is brushed with a mixture of olive oil and paprika to give the rind an orange color.

P *Serra*

A CHEESE

This most famous of Portuguese cheeses, with a fat content of 45 percent, is made from the milk of sheep which graze in the heights of the Serra da Estrela, dividing the ALENTEJO from the Dão – the area has, in fact, been demarcated for cheesemaking. It is made between October and April or May and ripened for 4 to 6 weeks. When young, it is soft and buttery, and the flavor has been compared with that of Brie. Some of the cheese is, however, ripened for another 5 months until firm and pungent, when it is sold as *Serra velho*. The factory made "Tipo Serra" is hard and not of the same quality and should be avoided.

S *sesos*
P *miolos*

BRAINS

Brains are eaten all over Spain and Portugal. They must be carefully cleaned and prepared before cooking. Soak them in water with a little vinegar for about 20 minutes depending upon size – calf's brains require a little longer than lamb's. Remove membranes and skin and wash gently with cold water until completely white and no blood remains. In Portugal, brains are sometimes blanched (by pouring boiling water over them) before cleaning, especially when making *molho de miolos* (brain sauce).

Spanish dishes include *buñuelos de sesos* (brain fritters) and *sesos con salsa de tomate* (brains with tomato and cheese sauce). In the Portuguese Cabo Verde islands, brains are puréed with beaten eggs, cooked onion, butter and lemon juice to make *miolos da ilha do Fogo* (brain paté).

---

sesos a la romana (S)
crisp fried brains

Serves 4

4 calf's brains
2 tsp vinegar
salt and pepper
2 bay leaves
pinch of thyme
beaten egg
flour
olive oil
1 lemon, sliced
1 tbsp chopped parsley

Soak the brains for 20 minutes in cold water to cover, adding the vinegar. Remove the skin and membranes and wash the brains. Cover them with water in a saucepan, and add salt and pepper, bay leaves and thyme. Simmer slowly for 15 minutes. Discard the water and cut the brains into small pieces; leave until cool. Dredge in egg and flour, and fry in hot oil until golden brown. Garnish with lemon slices and chopped parsley.

Sweetbreads may be cooked in the same way, but soak them for 1–2 hours, changing the water several times, and then cook, as above in salted water, substituting lemon juice for the herbs.

Opposite: Regional specialties (top) and goose with pears (bottom), a favourite Christmas dish in Cataluña.

ⓢ *setas*
WILD MUSHROOMS

Although there are hundreds of varieties of edible wild mushrooms in Spain, it is only in the north of Spain that any but a few are eaten. A Spanish mycologist reports the following conversation with a country-woman in Aragón about a specimen of BOLET (*Boletus edulis*): "We call them mushrooms here and they are very poisonous, in spite of which they are eaten by the sheep."

"How very strange," said Calduch.

Without registering the irony, the woman added: "Ah, but the Catalans eat them, too!"

In Castile, only two varieties are commonly eaten: the *níscalo* (or *robellón*) and the *champiñón silvestre*. In CATALUÑA and the Basque country, the picture is entirely different. In spring and in the autumn the markets are overflowing with colorful fungi which make more cautious visitors, confined to the field mushroom, blanch. Some, like the delicious *perrechico*, fetch as much as 4,000 ptas or about $35 per lb, while in a sophisticated restaurant quite half the cost of the meal may be accounted for by some rare and delicate variety.

Among the most sought after are, in the spring: the *seta de marzo*, *perrechico* and *colmenilla* (known as the *rabassola* in Cataluña), and in the autumn, the *setas de chopo*, *sisas amarillas*, *hongo negro* and *oronjas* (*Amanita caesarea*). The last is so named because the flavor is so exquisite that it was at one time reserved for the Roman emperors; there are, however, a number of quite deadly *amanitas*, and it is on record that the Emperor Claudius was poisoned by his wife, who included one of a poisonous variety in a plate of *oronjas* served to him.

This underlines the fact that "mushrooms" should not be picked unless one is thoroughly familiar with them; but they may be safely bought in Spanish markets or, of course, eaten in restaurants.

The choicer and rarer types of *setas* are cooked either by sprinkling with a little olive oil, garlic and parsley and putting under the broiler or by greasing a frying pan with olive oil, heating very briefly, then moistening with olive oil and seasoning with garlic and parsley. CHAMPIÑONES are cooked as elsewhere by sautéing in hot olive oil and are also used in the normal way in sauces, omelets and stews etc.

"Mushrooms" (or *cogumelos*) are not often eaten in Portugal except in sophisticated restaurants.

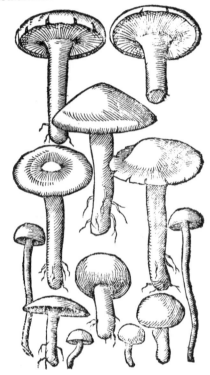

The index, in English, is arranged by types of food — eggs, cheese, fish — kitchen equipment, cooking terms and other subjects. Consult it for recipes that make use of particular ingredients.

ⓟ *Setúbal*
DEMARCATED WINE REGION

One of the world's best sweet dessert wines, this is made in the Arrábida peninsula south of LISBOA, by steeping the skins of the Moscatel grapes in the young wine, thus giving it an exceptionally fruity and luscious flavor. The best of it is made by the long-established firm of J.M. da Fonseca, who sell it either 6 or 25 years old.

Sevilla
SPANISH CITY

Sevilla, on the river Guadalquivir, is the capital of ANDALUCIA. Although it is ringed with factories and ramparts of ugly high-rise apartments, at its heart are many of the great architectural treasures of Spain. The old Jewish quarter is interspersed with narrow alleys, small squares and hidden patios, and inviting little restaurants and TABERNAS.

Sevilla is surrounded by olive groves, and its large green olives are everywhere served as an appetizer and used extensively in cooking, as in the ENSALADA SEVILLANA or the PATO A LA SEVILLANA and *ternera a la sevillana* (veal with olives). Other typical dishes are GAZPACHO, HUEVOS A LA FLAMENCA, *menudo gitano* (poultry offal with SOFRITO) and *cocido sevillano*, a variant of the OLLA which contains stoned olives and endives and is quite distinct from *cocido andaluz* (stew made with chickpeas, honeycomb tripe, ham bone, CHORIZO, garlic, salt and PIMENTON), see also MARMELADA.

What many visitors find most enticing are the TAPAS, for which the bars and tabernas of La Triana, the gypsy quarter on the west side of the Guadalquivir, are famous. When in Sevilla, it is well worthwhile getting hold of a copy of Juan Carlos Alonso's book *Guía*

del Tapeo en Triana, published by the municipality of Seville, which lists small places well known for their tapas and which also suggests itineraries. Among larger and more comfortable places with good standards of cooking are San Marcos, El Rincón de Curro, Paco Ramos in Triana facing the bridge, and Rio Grande with terraces overlooking the Guadalquivir. The Alfonso XIII Hotel in Moorish style is one of the most majestic in Spain, but not to be recommended for its food.

Sherry
FORTIFIED WINE

Sherry is, of course, the classic Spanish wine and has close ties with the United States: Columbus carried it on his three voyages. During the 18th and 19th centuries many English, Scottish and Irish merchants settled in Jerez de la Frontera to set up the famous houses that bear their names today.

The sherry grape *par excellence* is the white Palomino, grown in the white *albariza* soil of an area centering on the town of Jerez, to the north of Cádiz. Sherry, unlike other wines, is matured in casks with partial access to air under a protective layer of *flor*, a spontaneously growing yeast. The wines also differ from most others in that they are aged in SOLERA by a continuous process, in which the older wine is "refreshed" or blended with younger wine of the same type. The tiered casks in which this is done are housed by the thousand in lofty arched *bodegas*, which have been described as "sherry cathedrals".

The main styles of sherry are:

Fino: The lightest, driest and most delicate of sherries, drunk chilled as an apéritif before meals. Once opened, a bottle should be consumed within a week.

Manzanilla: A crisp and very dry *fino* from Sanlúcar de Barrameda on the coast, whose enthusiasts find in it a tang of the sea air.

Amontillado: Amber-colored with a dry, nutty flavor, these are *finos* which have undergone further ageing. They are also drunk as an apéritif.

Oloroso: This is a darker, fuller-bodied and very fragrant sherry that may contain more than 20° (percentage by volume) of alcohol. In their natural state, *olorosos*, like the "Rio Viejo" from Pedro Domecq, are completely dry and are drunk before a meal – they are especially welcome in cold weather.

Cream sherry: The dark, luscious variety, like "Bristol Cream", is made by sweetening

see also   **Shad:** *see sável*   **Shellfish:** *see marisco*

an *oloroso* and is usually drunk after a meal.

Pale cream is also sweet, but is a lighter sherry made from a *fino* and drunk chilled.

The use of sherry in cooking is a vast subject, which has been covered admirably by Lalo GROSSO DE MACPHERSON in a definitive book, translated into English under the title of *Cooking with Sherry*. In an introductory note, Jan Read summarizes its uses: "There can be few cooks who are unaware of the culinary uses of sherry – most would like to use more, but fight shy of raiding their husbands' precious bottles! It is no more profitable to use a cheap sherry-type wine for delicate cooking than to employ a rough *vin ordinaire* for making *boeuf bourguignonne*, when one has spent so much on the other ingredients. In general, it is always more sensible to use a little genuine sherry than to bathe the food in a cheap substitute. And with the prices of meat and fish as they are, a modicum of decent sherry is not such an extravagance.

"The individual styles of sherry have their different uses in the kitchen. A dash of *fino* will improve most consommés and sauces. The *olorosos* come into their own

Jerez-Xérès-Sherry
Manzanilla-Sanlúcar de Barrameda

The seal of the demarcated Sherry region

with more fully flavored foods – try adding a little to the gravy from a roast; while a trifle or fruit salad is hardly the same without a libation of cream sherry. But this is only the beginning, and few can have experimented more widely than Sra de Macpherson in matching the variegated flavors of the wines to the foods in the recipes which follow. . . ."

🅂 *sidra*

HARD CIDER

The best Spanish cider is from the apple orchards of ASTURIAS. It is made from a blend of three different types of apple: one rich in malic acid, one in tannin and the third in sugar.

In times past cider was drawn from the barrel, but on the commercial scale it is now bottled and slightly aerated. The best-known brand, "El Gaitero", is not inexpensive, costing about the same as a medium-priced bottle of wine.

When Asturian enthusiasts talk of cider, it is, however, of the natural uncarbonated variety, and small groups, usually of six

people, gather regularly in the *chigres* (as cider-making establishments are called in Asturias) to enjoy it. There is a set ritual. The *escanciador* pours the cider from a bottle held above his head to a depth of two fingers (two *culinos*) into a large glass held in his other hand at knee level. This is handed to the first of the company, who drinks, but leaves a little of the cider to rinse the rim before the glass is recharged and handed to the next participant. An expert *escanciador* will pour exactly six *culinos* to the glass.

🅂 *sobado*

A cheese; see ARMADA.

🅂 *sobrasada*

A SAUSAGE

Although made in other parts of Spain, *sobrasada* is typical of the ISLAS BALEARES, especially Majorca. It is a thick sausage made from minced lean pork and TOCINO spiced with PIMENTON.

There are two varieties. The hard sausage may be eaten uncooked or fried with eggs; the soft makes a tasty spread on bread or may be dissolved in sauces.

sociedades gastronómicas

GASTRONOMIC SOCIETIES

The Spanish gastronomic societies, also known as *cofradías*, are especially typical of the Basque country and of BILBAO and SAN SEBASTIAN. Like the old London clubs, they are exclusively male organizations. Men have always cooked in this part of the world, and the societies are an extension of the 19th-century *sidrerías* (cider bars) where groups of male friends would get together in the evenings – women at that time being confined to the home and their children. The clubs now own their own premises, with a well equipped kitchen, a well stocked bar and cellar, and spacious dining room. On any particular Friday night, one or two of the members will see to the preparation of the meal, while the others look after the setting of the tables. Basic foods are kept in stock and the costs of the ingredients are shared among the members, who also pay an annual subscription for belonging. Membership is limited and there is a long waiting list to join the better-known societies, but they are anything but snobbish and membership ranges from workers in the local steel mills to professional people and civil servants. The rule against women has now been relaxed to some extent. In some of the most traditional clubs, their presence is countenanced twice a year, but in the majority they may be invited on any occasion – with the strict proviso that they do not set foot in the kitchens.

sofrito

Base for stews and sauces; see REFOGADO.

Sogrape

WINE FIRM

SOGRAPE, Portugal's largest wine firm, was founded in 1942 by the late Fernando van-Zeller Guedes, the creator of MATEUS ROSE. Having established it as one of the world's biggest selling wines, Guedes widened the company's scope, establishing a winery in Viseu to make the excellent "Grão Vasco" Dão, and marketing well bred VINHOS VERDES from the family's estate at Aveleda and good table wines from the DOURO and BAIRRADA.

solera

A system of adjacent casks used for the fractional blending and maturation of wines such as SHERRY, MONTILLA-MORILES and MALAGA. Wine is periodically drawn from the bottom row of casks – the *solera* proper – for bottling or shipping, and it is replenished from a series of casks containing younger wine of the same type.

solomillo lombo de vaca

A CUT OF MEAT

This corresponds to the American tenderloin or English sirloin. Like the French *filet*, it is the undercut of the sirloin. This word is used for meats generally, not simply beef.

solomillo all-i-pebre

TENDERLOIN COOKED IN A GARLIC AND PEPPER SAUCE

All-i-pebre is a Catalan description of dishes cooked in a garlic and pepper sauce. *Solomillo all-i-pebre* is tenderloin of beef pot-roasted in a heavy pan with olive oil, onions, garlic, pepper and parsley.

Solomillo all-i-pebre

sonhos de alperce

APRICOT FRITTERS

These "apricot dreams" are made by cutting open the apricots, removing the stones and marinating them with a little sugar, brandy and lemon zest. They are then lightly coated in batter (see MASSA VINHE), fried in hot olive oil and served hot with a dusting of confectioners' sugar.

---

see also

Sole: see lenguado

P *sonhos de morangos*

STRAWBERRY
FRITTERS

These "strawberry dreams" are made by marinating the strawberries in PORT or MADEIRA with a little sugar and then proceeding as for SONHOS DE ALPERCE.

S P *sopa*

SOUP

Spaniards and Portuguese alike are fond of starting a meal with soup. In the summer months, GAZPACHOS (*gaspachos* in Portugal) of all sorts are served throughout both countries. In the winter there are the nourishing soups made with eggs and bread, like the Portuguese AÇORDAS or Spanish *sopa de ajo* (garlic soup) and, of course, fish soups such as SOPA DE MEJILLONES or SOPA DE PESCADO MEDITERRANEA. Other popular thick soups are *sopa de hortaliça* (vegetable soup) and *sopa de puré de batata* (potato soup).

S *sopa al cuarto de hora*

QUARTER-OF-AN-HOUR SOUP

This rich Andalucían soup, containing vegetables, ham and fish, is so named because of the quarter-of-an-hour for which it is finally cooked. It is best made from *ostiones*, fished from the Bay of Cádiz and akin to Portuguese oysters, but cockles or clams are a satisfactory alternative.

---

sopa al cuarto de hora (S)
quarter-of-an-hour soup

Serves 4

½ lb clams, well scrubbed and washed in cold water
1 tbsp olive oil
1 small onion, chopped
2 oz cooked ham
½ lb tomatoes, peeled, seeded and chopped
1 tsp pimentón dulce (paprika)
¼ lb hake fillets
¼ cup shelled fresh peas or frozen peas, defrosted
2 tbsp Spanish or Italian rice
salt and freshly ground black pepper
croûtons of bread
2 hard boiled eggs, cut into wedges
½ lb fresh shrimp, boiled and peeled, or ¼ lb frozen shrimp, defrosted

Cover the clams with cold water and heat for a few minutes in a covered saucepan until they are open. Discard those which remain shut and remove the rest from the shells, setting them aside on a plate. Strain the water in which they have been boiled first through a sieve, then through a cloth to remove sand, and reserve.

Heat a little oil in a pan and fry the onion until golden. Drain off any oil, then add the ham and cook for another minute or two before stirring in the tomatoes and pimentón dulce (paprika). Pour in the reserved liquid, adding water, if necessary to make 1½ quarts, and add the hake, peas and rice. Season with salt and freshly ground black pepper, and gently cook over moderate heat for exactly a quarter of an hour (this will cook the fish and allows the flavors to mingle).

Meanwhile, put some croûtons in a preheated tureen, together with the egg wedges, cockles and the shrimp. When the quarter of an hour is up, pour the soup on top and serve.

sopa de mejillones (S)
mussel soup

Serves 4

4½ lb mussels, well scrubbed and washed
   in cold water
1⅓ cups dry white wine
2 tbsp butter
4 shallots, finely chopped
1⅓ cups light cream
1 tbsp chopped parsley

Discard any mussels that are open and bring the remaining ones to the boil in a saucepan with a little of the wine until they open. Reject any that do not open. Remove the meat from the shells and set aside.

Melt the butter in a saucepan and slowly sweat the shallots for about 10 minutes without browning. Add the cream and mussels, stir and simmer over a low heat until heated through. Pour a little wine into each soup cup, add the mussels in their sauce, season to taste with salt and sprinkle with parsley.

sopa de pescado mediterránea (S)
Mediterranean fish soup

Serves 6

4 tbsp olive oil
2 onions, chopped
2 tomatoes, skinned
1 clove garlic, crushed
½ lb mussels, well scrubbed and washed in cold
   water
2 lb mixed white fish (cod, hake or bream)
½ lb shrimp, boiled and peeled
⅓ cup rice, boiled
few strands of saffron
salt

Put a little oil into a deep pan and sauté the onions until soft, then add the tomatoes and garlic. Discard any mussels that are shut and boil the remaining ones in 1 quart of water, rejecting any that do not open. Strain the liquid through muslin to remove grit, and reserve. Remove the mussels from their shells and put to one side. Simmer the white fish in the reserved stock for ten minutes, then remove with a slotted spoon and bone and skin it. Add to the cooked vegetables in the pan, with the stock, mussels, shrimp and rice. Crush the saffron in a mortar, dissolve in a little hot stock and add to contents of the pan. Heat through, and season to taste.

sopa fría gaditana (S)
cold soup from Cádiz

Serves 6

3 cloves garlic
pinch cumin seeds
1 small onion, chopped
3–4 slices bread, moistened and squeezed dry
1½ lb tomatoes, peeled, seeded and chopped
salt and pepper
pimentón dulce (paprika)
2 cucumbers, peeled and chopped
2 green peppers, skinned, seeded and chopped
olive oil
2 tbsp sherry vinegar
½ cup salsa mahonesa (mayonnaise)

Crush the garlic, cumin seeds and onion in a large mortar or wooden bowl, add the moistened bread and 1 lb of the tomatoes. Continue pounding until smooth, then season with salt, pepper and pimentón dulce (paprika) and add water to make a thin purée.

Put the remaining tomatoes, the cucumbers and peppers into an earthenware cazuela, sprinkle with salt, mix with 2–3 tablespoons olive oil and leave for an hour or two. Mix together the two preparations, adding a little more water, the sherry vinegar and salsa mahonesa (mayonnaise).

S ***sorbete de turrón***

TURRÓN SORBET

An ice made with TURRON de Jijona or Alicante.

S ***Soria***

A CHEESE

A soft goat's cheese from Soria with a smooth and somewhat salty white interior, it has a fat content of 55 percent and must be eaten fresh because it keeps for only 8 days.

S ***suizos***

ROLLS

These sweet, sugar-topped buns are often served at Spanish hotels in a basket of assorted breads for a Continental breakfast.

S **P** ***super-mercado***

SUPERMARKET

Although large central markets with individual stalls continue to flourish in Spain and Portugal and are the best source of fresh vegetables, fish and meat (see MERCADO), supermarkets have, as elsewhere, become increasingly common and are the main providers of food and household goods in the new housing developments.

S ***suquet***

CATALAN FISH STEW

A stew containing mussels, different types of white fish, white wine, olive oil, garlic, saffron, fresh bread, peas and parsley.

---

see also

Soup: *see sopa*   **Spices:** *see especiarias*   **Spider crab:** *see changurro*
Squid: *see calamares*   **To stew:** *see estofar*   **Strawberries:** *see fresas*
Sugar: *see azúcar*

Moorish tiles from the Spanish Levante. A hare or liebre (above) and a sole or lenguado (left). Overleaf: A wild boar or jabali (top) and a bull or toro (bottom).

taberna

TAVERN

We for a certainty are not the first
Have sat in taverns while the tempest
  hurled
Their hopeful plans to emptiness, and
  cursed
Whatever brute or blackguard made the
  world.

               A.E. Housman

Before the invention of the bar, the *taberna* was the place where friends would meet to celebrate or to commiserate with one another. There are still *tabernas* the length and breadth of Spain – known colloquially as *tascas* by their habitués; in general they are simpler than bars and do not serve spirits, and sometimes there are no seats, only a bar with barrels of wine behind it.

MADRID is famous for its *tabernas*, many of them in Old Madrid, cavernous establishments with tiled walls, where it is traditional to serve the wine, often from VALDEPEÑAS, from large square bottles. TAPAS are available, but they are usually simple, as people do not make a meal at a *taberna*, but move on from one to another.

tachos de barro

COOKING UTENSIL

These earthenware casseroles, excellent for cooking, and resembling Spanish CAZUELAS, may be bought cheaply in Portuguese markets in a whole range of shapes and sizes.

> If Spanish and Portuguese terms differ from each other, the entry in Portuguese, in the majority of cases, is referred to its Spanish equivalent, where you will find information relevant to both countries.

tamboril

Frog fish; see CALDEIRADA.

tapa

APPETIZER

In its original sense the word *tapa* means a "cover" or "lid", and it seems that it came to be used for an apéritif or appetizer because in the bars of ANDALUCIA it was the custom to cover a glass of wine or SHERRY with a small plate containing a few olives, cubes of tortilla or small portions of JAMON SERRANO; these came with the compliments of the house. Today *tapas* are rarely free, and in many bars there is a whole array of dishes, both cold and hot, displayed along the counter. They range from mussels in marinade, Russian salad, CALAMARES crisp-fried in rings or cooked in their own ink, fried BOQUERONES, stuffed peppers and assorted shellfish. In fact, *tapas* have now come to mean almost any dish served in small portions and eaten informally in a bar or *tasca* (see TABERNA) either as an appetizer or as a light meal.

Tarragona

DEMARCATED WINE
REGION

Tarragona is the largest of the demarcated regions in CATALUÑA and makes massive quantities of wine, most of it for everyday consumption in Spain, for bulk export, blending or distillation. Its most famous wines are the *clásicos*, sweet dessert wines containing upwards of 20° (percentage by volume) of alcohol. It was a cheap *clásico* which was once popular in London pubs as "Tarragona" or, less politely as "red biddy". The genuine old SOLERA-made *clásicos* from a firm such as de Muller are wines of superb quality, reminiscent of old *oloroso* SHERRY, MALAGA or PORTO, vinho do.

The seal of the Tarragona demarcated wine region

P *tarte de amêndoa*

ALMOND TART

There are various versions of this favorite Portuguese sweet, of which I give two. The first recipe is from Dona Angela Pombo, the inspired cook of the beautiful Renaissance Quinta Palacio da Bacalhôa near Setúbal, lovingly restored by the mother of its American owner, Tom Scoville. In its grounds he grows the Cabernet Sauvignon for one of Portugal's best table wines.

Dona Angela makes a cake rather than a tart, and covers it with crunchy, toasted almonds.

---

tarte de amêndoa I (P)
almond cake

Serves 8

⅔ cup margarine or butter
1¼ cups sugar
2 eggs
1¾ cups self-rising flour, sifted
2 tbsp milk

Topping
⅔ cup unsalted butter
⅔ cup sugar
⅓ cup milk
1 cup blanched, slivered almonds

Put the margarine or butter (Dona Angela uses margarine) into a mixing bowl with the sugar, and beat for about 5-6 minutes until fluffy. Add the eggs one at a time and continue beating with a wooden spoon. Add the sifted flour all at once, fold into the mixture and add the milk.

Transfer the mixture to an 11 inch greased cake pan, smoothing the top with a spatula or the back of a spoon. Bake on a middle shelf in a preheated fairly hot oven (375°F) for 35-40 minutes, or until well risen and golden brown (the cake should spring back when lightly pressed).

Meanwhile, make the topping by warming the butter, sugar and milk in a non-stick saucepan and stirring with a wooden spoon. When melted, add the almonds and cook gently for about 10 minutes, until slightly syrupy but not brown.

Smooth the almond mixture on the cake, then return to the oven for 20-30 minutes, or until it becomes brown, light or dark according to taste.

The cake may be eaten hot or cold and may successfully be reheated the next day.

---

tarte de amêndoa II (P)
almond tart

Serves 6

6 eggs
1 cup sugar
½ lb almonds, blanched, then finely chopped or grated
1¼ cups self-rising flour
1 tbsp brandy

Beat the eggs with the sugar, then add the grated almonds, flour and the brandy. Mix well with a spatula and pour the mixture into a 10 inch removeable-bottom tart pan lined with pastry. Bake in a fairly hot oven (375°F) for 25–30 minutes until golden-brown. This tart is often served with meringue on top.

P *tarte de maça*

APPLE TART

This is another of Dona Angela Pombo's recipes from the Quinta Palacio da Bacalhôa.

tarte de maça (P)
apple tart

Serves 8

Rich pastry
1 cup self-rising flour
¼ cup sugar
⅓ cup margarine or soft butter, cut into cubes
1 egg
1 tsp active dry yeast

Filling
2½ cups milk
grated zest of 1 lemon
1 cinnamon stick
¾ cup sugar
2 tbsp self-rising flour
2 eggs
2 egg yolks
4 large eating apples (use Reineta in Portugal),
    peeled, cored, quartered and thinly sliced

To make the pastry, place the flour on a marble slab or clean working surface, make a well in the center, add the sugar, margarine, egg and yeast, and work with your hands and fingers until well blended. Knead until smooth, then leave in a bowl to rest while you make the filling.

Bring the milk to the boil in a pan with the lemon zest and cinnamon stick and simmer for 5 minutes. Pour the boiled milk into another pan, add the other ingredients apart from the sliced apples, and bring gently to the boil. Cook until creamy.

Smooth the pastry into a greased 11 inch pastry case, pour in the creamy filling, stack the slices of apple around the edges and bake in a hot oven (425°F) for 30 minutes or until golden brown.

tasca

Tavern; see TABERNA.

Tenerife

See ISLAS CANARIAS.

ternera
VEAL

The veal from calves not more than 3 or 4 months old, pinkish white and very digestible, is the best and most tender. In Portugal a favorite method of cooking it is *no espeto* (on the spit), painting it with a parsley or coriander twig moistened with olive oil. ESCALOPES are cooked with a sauce containing lemon and garlic. Turnedos or *medallones* (MEDALHOES) are dusted with flour and fried in olive oil until golden. They are then sprinkled with a little white wine or sherry and left for a few minutes for the alcohol to evaporate, leaving a mellow flavor.

tetilla
A CHEESE

A well known Galician cheese made entirely from cow's milk and also known as *perilla* because of its flattened pear shape derived from the wooden mold in which it is made. The paste is soft with a clean, salty taste and has a fat content of 40 percent.

tigela
COOKING VESSEL

A small earthenware baking dish, similar to a Spanish CAZUELA, and used for making *tigelada*, a browned egg custard of almost sponge-like consistency.

tocino
toucinho
A CURED MEAT

Tocino or *tocino entreverado* is fresh or salted pork belly. It is used in stews and may be fried with eggs for breakfast. Until fairly recently it was the nearest equivalent to North American-style bacon that is now served in hotels and sold in supermarkets.

see also

Tavern: *see taberna*   **Tea:** *see chá*

S *tocino de cielo*

Egg dessert; see TOUCINHO DO CEU.

P *Todos os Santos*

All Saints' Day; see LOS SANTOS.

P *Tomar*

A CHEESE

These small white ewe's milk cheeses are made around Tomar, the former stronghold of the Knights' Templar, north of LISBOA. Ripened for 2 or 3 weeks, they have a fat content of 45 percent and are semi-hard and crumbly with small holes and a nutty taste.

S **P** *tomate*

TOMATO

Tomatoes, now a staple of cooking world-wide, were unknown outside South America before the CONQUISTADORES brought them to Spain. Here, they soon became popular, but in Europe, generally, they were at first regarded with suspicion – and even thought to be poisonous.

Very wide use is made of tomatoes, both in Spain and Portugal. They are used in salads, stuffed with tuna or other things as an appetizer, and for the Catalan *pan con tomate* (country bread rubbed with fresh tomato and garlic and sprinkled or smeared with olive oil). They are also used extensively in many Spanish and Portuguese bases and sauces such as REFOGADO and *sofrito*, SALSA and MOLHO DE TOMATE and SALSA ESPAÑOLA.

P *toranj*

Grapefruit; see POMELO.

P *tornedos*

A cut of meat; see TURNEDOS.

S *Torres, Miguel*

WINE FIRM

An old family firm dating from the 17th century, Torres is the largest and best known maker of still wines in CATALUÑA and probably the largest exporter in the country – shipments to the USA alone amount to several million bottles annually.

The brilliant young French-trained oenologist Miguel A. Torres Riera was the first to introduce the cold fermentation of white wines in stainless steel to Spain and has acclimatized a variety of noble foreign vines to the PENEDES, including the Cabernet Sauvignon, Pinot Noir and Chardonnay. From the inexpensive white "Viña Sol" to the prize-winning red "Gran Coronas Black Label", all the Torres wines are well made and offer good value.

S *torta de Burzago*

CHESTNUT TART FOR EASTER

An Easter tart from León filled with a paste made with a mixture of powdered dried chestnuts and milk.

S *torta del Casar*

A CHEESE

Like all the cheeses from Cáceres, this is made from ewe's milk, which is of particularly good quality in the EXTREMADURA.

The cheese is ripened for 2 to 3 weeks, and the interior is soft and golden with a very full flavor.

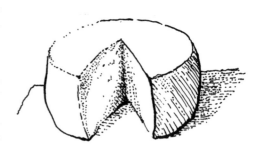

Torta del Casar

see also

Tomato: see tomate   **Tomato sauce:** *see salsa de tomate*
Tongue: see lengua

tortilla española
SPANISH OMELET

The authentic Spanish omelet bears no resemblance to the thin pancake with embedded vegetables sometimes served in foreign restaurants, but is a thick cake, always containing potatoes and sometimes onion, which makes it juicier. Eaten cold between crusty bread in the form of a BOCADILLO, it is what the shepherds and farm workers take with them for their midday meal.

---

tortilla española (S)
Spanish omelet

Serves 4

1⅓ cups olive oil
6 large potatoes, peeled and thinly sliced
2 onions, cut into rings
salt
6 large eggs, beaten

Heat the oil in a large non-stick frying pan. Mix together the potato and onion slices, and add to the pan with a little salt. Cover and cook over a low heat for about 20 minutes until soft. Remove the mixture with a slotted spoon and stir well into a bowl with the eggs, retaining any surplus oil for further use. Return a little oil to the pan, heat until it begins to smoke, then pour in the egg mixture and cook for 2–3 minutes uncovered. Cover the pan with a plate and invert the half-cooked omelet on to it. Slide the omelet back into the pan; the uncooked side will now be downwards. Cook for another few minutes. The final result should be golden brown and about 1 inch thick, with the inside still juicy.

Serve with a green salad as the main dish of an informal supper.

---

tortillitas de bonito con tomate y besamel (S)
stuffed tuna omelet in two sauces

Serves 4

1 cup grated cheese
1⅓ cups freshly made salsa besamel (white sauce)
7 oz canned tuna or salmon, drained, or smoked haddock, poached and flaked
2½ cups salsa de tomate (tomato sauce)
4 tbsp butter
6 eggs, beaten

Stir the cheese into the salsa besamel (white sauce) and pour half over the base of a shallow ovenproof dish. Mash the tuna, salmon or haddock with a tablespoon or two of salsa de tomate (tomato sauce).

Heat the butter in a frying pan until it is smoking. Add 1 tbsp of the beaten egg and as it spreads and cooks, put on top of it 1 tbsp of the prepared fish. Spread it out, then fold the finished omelet like a pancake and place it in the cheese sauce in the ovenproof dish. Make as many small omelets as the quantities of egg and fish mixture will allow. It is best to make a single layer of omelet in the sauce, but if necessary they can be laid carefully on top of one another.

Pour the remainder of the cheese sauce over the top, then spoon the remaining salsa de tomate between the small omelets so that it forms a criss-cross pattern in red across the whole surface. Pour the rest of the sauce around the edge of the dish, and cook in a fairly hot oven (400°F) for 15 minutes until the surface of the sauce browns.

---

toucinho
Charcuterie; see TOCINO.

P *toucinho do ceu*

EGG DESSERT

The name of this dessert is exactly the same as that of the equally well-known Spanish *tocino de cielo* – and I have seen translations as grotesque as "Little pigs from heaven" (in a book by a well-meaning American lady) and "Salt Pork Sky" (in the menu of a Spanish restaurant). The name *is* puzzling, because *toucinho*, or TOCINO in its Spanish form, means belly of pork. It has been suggested that at one time pork fat may have been used in making it, and Portu-guese recipes do use butter, though basical-ly the dessert is made by blending an egg mixture with a vanilla flavored syrup, some-times with the addition of ground almonds. The mixture is poured into individual molds which are either steamed or cooked in a BANHO MARIA and then turned out into small dishes for serving. The texture is smooth and glossy, and the Portuguese with their sweet tooth sometimes sprinkle on confectioners' sugar.

Trás-os-Montes

PORTUGUESE REGION

The name means "beyond the mountains," and the province, a region of high, barren plateaux and deeply cut valleys, including that of the DOURO, lies beyond the Marão and Geres ranges in the extreme northwest of Portugal, bordering Spain.

This is one of the least populated areas of Portugal with remote villages built of granite or shale, many of whose inhabitants have emigrated to OPORTO or further afield. Around Chaves the valleys are planted with fruit trees, vegetables, corn and vines, but basically the inhabitants are dependent on sheep and pigs for their mainstay. The people from around Chaves and Valpaços are famous for producing the best cured hams in Portugal (see PRESUNTO).

Typical dishes include *sopa da castanha* (chestnut soup); *sopa seca do Douro* ("dry soup" made from bread, cabbage, salt pork and bacon, and cooked in the oven); BACALHAU A TRANSMONTANA; BOCHEIRAS (highly spiced sausage); *bola de carnes de Bragança* (a light dough filled with stewed veal and chicken, bacon, PRESUNTO and SALPICÃO and cooked in a baker's oven); *folar de carnes de Chaves* (bread baked with eggs, assorted meats and game); *lombo de vitela no espeto* (loin of veal on the spit); *orelhas de porco no grelho* (charcoal grilled pig's ears); *leitão assado* (roast sucking pig); *nogado* (nougat made with nuts, honey, eggs and breadcrumbs) and a variety of confec-tions made with almonds and eggs.

Trás-os-Montes produces some good red table wines, which are winning an increas-ing reputation abroad (see DOURO), but is known above all for the famous port vineyards in the terraced valley of the Douro (see PORTO, VINHO DO).

S *Tres Madres*

"Three mothers"; see COCHIFRITO.

S **P** *trinchar*

TO CARVE

Roasts are best carved if left for 10 minutes or so in a warm place after they have been removed from the oven. This prevents the meat from crumbling.

P tripas
S callos

TRIPE

In LISBOA the name for tripe is DOBRADA but in Oporto, which has given its name to the most famous version, it is known as *tripas*.

In Europe and elsewhere, butchers wash and blanch the tripe; in Portugal you may have to do this yourself.

**tripas (S)
callos (P)**
tripe

To clean and boil 2 lb tripe
coarse salt
juice of 1 lemon
a few cloves
fresh thyme
1 onion
1 carrot

First scrape the tripe with a knife, clean it with coarse salt and lemon juice, then wash it in changes of cold water and finally in hot water.

Place in a saucepan with cold water, bring to the boil and continue boiling for 5 minutes, removing the foam with a spoon. Discard the water, replace with fresh water and bring to the boil again, removing any further foam. Add salt, cloves, thyme, onion and carrot and simmer over moderate heat for 2–3 hours until tender.

When using washed and blanched tripe, it is only necessary to carry out the final cooking with the other ingredients.

P tripas à modo do Porto

TRIPE OPORTO STYLE

OPORTO has been famous for its tripe since HENRIQUE O NAVEGADOR despatched his sailors on their voyages of discovery in the 15th century. The people of Oporto built his ships and supplied them with prime meat from their herds, leaving little to eat for themselves except the tripe and so gained the nickname of *tripeiros* (tripe eaters) – or

so the legend goes.

The tripe from Oporto differs from the DOBRADA from further south, and one of the restaurants best known for it is appropriately called Tripeiro. Its chef, who gained first prize at a *concurso* held in Bordeaux for the express purpose of cooking tripe, has supplied the recipe that follows.

**tripas à moda do
Porto (P)**
tripe Oporto style

Serves 8

1 cup dry white beans, soaked overnight and
    drained
3 onions
2 lb tripe, cleaned, boiled and cut into strips or
    squares
1 pig's foot, blanched
½ lb chicken pieces
½ lb chouriço, sliced
¼ lb touchinho or pork belly, coarsely chopped
½ lb presunto, ham or bacon
cumin seeds, crushed in the mortar
powdered cloves
1 tbsp curry powder
salt and pepper

Cover the beans with water, add an onion and simmer for 1–2 hours until tender.

Meanwhile, put the tripe, pig's foot, chicken and chouriço in a pot, bring to the boil, skim until no more foam appears, then simmer for 1 hour, or until the meat is tender. Take out the pig's foot, remove bones and return to the pot.

Chop the remaining onions and fry with the touchinho and ham or presunto for 10 minutes, then drain off the excess fat. Add the cumin seeds, cloves, curry powder and salt and pepper. Add this refogado to the pot together with the beans. Stir well and season with salt and pepper to taste. Simmer a little longer before serving to allow the flavors to mingle.

---

see also   **Tripe:** *see tripas*

S *Tronchón*
A CHEESE

This semi-hard cheese from ARAGON, with a fat content of 45 percent, is made mainly with ewe's milk, sometimes mixed with a little goat's milk.

The taste is mild but pleasant. The small cheeses are eaten fresh, but the larger ones may be kept for up to a month.

S *trucha*
P *truta*
TROUT

Spain is criss-crossed with mountains, and almost every region considers the trout from its streams to be the best. Ernest Hemingway swore by those he fished from the cold streams of the Pyrenees, when staying at the little inn at Burguete, near the Pass of Roncesvalles. Trout is frequently served sandwiched with ham, a dish often, though mistakenly, described as *trucha a la Navarra* because of the popularity of trout in this region.

In Portugal the best trout are fished from the mountain streams of the MINHO and TRAS-OS-MONTES in the north.

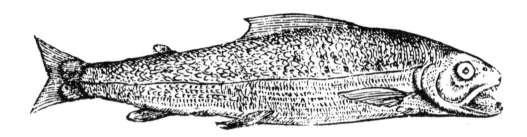

S P *trufa*
TRUFFLE

Probably the first person to write about truffles was the Greek philosopher, Theophrastus of Lesbos, who described them as "a rootless vegetable, engendered by autumn rains when accompanied by thunder and lightning." They were relished both by the Greeks and Romans, and much later the famous Brillat-Savarin was to call them "the diamonds of cuisine."

Since the Périgord truffle fields have become almost exhausted by over-exploitation, Spain has been sending an annual 30 to 40 tons of truffles to France for eating or re-export in the form of pâté or foie gras.

Truffles are usually found some 5 to 12 inches underground beneath oaks, hazels and pines. Because they can smell them out, sows have traditionally been used to root them up, but are so greedy that it is almost impossible to stop them eating the truffles. In Spain, specially trained truffle dogs are, therefore, used instead.

Truffles are produced over a wide area in northeastern Spain, some of the main centers being Olot (Gerona); Solsona (Lérida); Vich (Barcelona); Morella (Castellón) and Navaleno (Soria), where semi-clandestine markets are held for them during the season from the end of November until the end of March – the object being to keep secret where the precious commodity has been found.

At a very early date the monks of the monastery of ALCANTARA were well aware of the gastronomic virtues of truffles but the variety which they used was the *criadilla de tierra* (earth sweetbread), which has little in common with the most highly esteemed Spanish black winter varieties: *Tuber melanosporum* and *Tuber brumale*. Truffles are today used in sophisticated restaurants in Spain but not in Spanish cooking generally, and some 90 per cent of the crop goes to France. They are not common in Portugal and, therefore, not much used, though they are to be found in the ESTREMADURA.

P *truta*

Trout; see TRUCHA.

---

see also   **Trout:** *see trucha*   **Truffle:** *see trufa*

---

tumbet

MAJORCAN EGG
AND VEGETABLE PIE

Serves 4

olive oil
½ lb potatoes, peeled and sliced into rounds
½ lb red peppers (pimentos), seeded and
    coarsely chopped
½ lb onions, cut into rings
½ lb sliced zucchini
2½ cups salsa de tomate (tomato sauce)
4 eggs, beaten

Fry separately in hot olive oil the potato rounds, chopped peppers, onion rings and sliced zucchini. Drain and reserve on separate plates. Lay a first layer of the cooked vegetables on the base of a large greased ovenproof dish, cover with salsa de tomate (tomato sauce) and the beaten eggs, and continue with alternate layers of vegetables, salsa de tomate (tomato sauce) and beaten egg until all the ingredients are used up. Bake in a moderate oven (350°F) for 1 hour or until crisp and golden.

S *turrón*

NOUGAT

*Si la reina saber
lo que es giraboix
a Jijona vendris,
a llepar el boix.*

[If the queen knew
Turrón and its taste,
She'd go to Jijona to
Eat it in haste.]

So goes an old rhyme about *turrón*, or *giraboix* as it was called in the little hill town of Jijona near Alicante, where it is made. This most famous of Spanish nougats was formerly packed in small wooden boxes and sold at Christmas, but the market for it has so grown that it can now be bought at CONFITERIAS all year round, and it is packed in plastic and sent all over the world.

Jijona, with its 40 or so small factories, is devoted entirely to making *turrón* and is fragrant with the smell of toasted almonds and hot honey. There are two sorts. The *turrón de Alicante* is a hard, brittle tablet made of toasted and coarsely chopped almonds, honey and egg whites while the *turrón de Jijona* is softer and contains ground almonds, ground pine nuts, sugar, coriander seed and egg yolks. Neither may be made with any success at home, but chestnut nougat, for which a recipe follows, presents no difficulties.

turrón de castañas (S)
chestnut nougat

Makes 1½ lb

1 lb chestnuts, boiled and peeled
⅓ cup unsalted butter, softened
3 oz semisweet black chocolate, grated
6 tbsp vanilla sugar (see page 297)

Push the chestnuts through a sieve while still warm, and mix with the butter, chocolate and sugar. Beat together thoroughly. Alternatively, process the ingredients in a blender or food processor. Smooth the mixture into a 6 × 4 inch cake pan with a removeable base and place in the refrigerator overnight. Remove from the tin and slice thinly before serving.

see also   **Tuna fish:** *see atún*   **Turkey:** *see pavo*

S **Ulloa**

A CHEESE

A soft cheese from Galicia made with cow's milk and with a fat content of 45 percent. It is pressed lightly by hand in muslin bags or in a cloth-lined wooden mold and matured briefly in an HORREO, after which it keeps for 5–6 months. The interior is white, soft and mild, and the rind yellow and springy.

S **ultramarinos**
P **mercearia**

GROCERY

Apart from the usual groceries, Spanish and Portuguese grocers always sell a wide range of cured meats such as CHORIZOS and JAMON SERRANO. They are also the best place to go for wines, spirits and liqueurs, which they stock in great variety.

S **urta**

A FISH

This ugly-looking but delicious fish (*Dentex dentex*) is fished only in the waters of the Bay of Cádiz off Rota. It feeds off shellfish, which gives it a particularly gamey flavor. See also DORADA A LA SAL.

S **urta a la roteña**

URTA ROTA STYLE

The traditional way of cooking URTA is in a rich sauce containing tomatoes, peppers, onions and garlic.

S **Utiel-Requena**

DEMARCATED WINE REGION

Utiel-Requena lies at the western extreme of the province of VALENCIA in the foothills of the great central plateau of Spain. The wines, made from some 90 per cent of the black Bobal grape, are mainly red and rosé. The rosés, made as a by-product of the powerful *vino de doble pasto* used for blending, are pale onion-skin in color, light, fragrant and delicate, and among the best of the type from Spain.

The seal of the Utiel-Requena demarcated wine region

S **uvas pasas**

RAISINS

Spain produces large amounts of raisins, the best being produced around Málaga and Denia, up the Mediterranean coast, by sun-drying Moscatel grapes. In his *Handbook for Travellers in Spain* of 1845, Richard FORD remarks that: "The *Huerta* [of Denia] is covered with vines, olives, fig and almond trees; the great traffic is in the *Denias* or coarse Valentian raisins, which are so much used in England for puddings, being inferior to those of Malaga; the latter are dried in the sun, while the former are cured in a lye, whence they are called *Lexias.*" The scale of the trade in the 19th century may be judged by a note in Cyrus Redding's *A History and Description of Modern Wines*, reporting that "In 1829, eight million pounds of Muscatel and bloom raisins, and 30,000 arrobas [750,000 lbs] of *lexias* in casks, were exported from Malaga." Today, raisins are used in a variety of ways as in ice cream (see HELADO DE PASAS CON AL PX) and with nuts (see POSTRE DE MUSICO).

vainilla
baunilha
VANILLA

Vanilla was introduced to Spain, Portugal and Europe by the CONQUISTADORES. It is the bean of a climbing orchid, native to South America, where it was used, as it is today, by the Aztecs to flavor chocolate. The beans are picked when yellow and unripe, and develop their fragrance only after curing.

Vanilla beans, though expensive, are much better than the extract for flavoring. They may be steeped in custards and creams and reused after washing, but it is simpler to keep a few beans in a jar of the sugar used for making desserts. The jar may repeatedly be refilled with sugar and the vanilla beans will continue to perfume it.

Valdeorras
DEMARCATED WINE REGION

One of two demarcated regions in Galicia (see ASTURIAS AND GALICIA), Valdeorras lies to the east of the province of Orense along the mountainous valley of the River Sil. The vines, unlike most of those in Galicia, which grow high, are pruned low in normal Spanish fashion. The best of the wine is made by the Cooperativa del Barco de Valdeorras, which markets a clean, bone dry red and a refreshing white.

Valdepeñas
DEMARCATED WINE REGION

Valdepeñas is the most southerly of the wine regions of the great central plateau of LA MANCHA, bordering ANDALUCIA to the south. It has for centuries been famous for its red wines, and its *aloques*, made from a blend of black and white grapes, were great favorites with CARLOS V. Valdepeñas was also the mother's milk of Cervantes' Sancho Panza, who declared: *"Bebo cuando tengo gana, cuando no la tengo y cuando me lo dan, por no parecer melindroso o mal criado"*. [I drink it when I have the taste and also when they give it to me and I do not, so as not to seem offhand or bad-mannered.] It is still the staple wine of the TABERNAS in MADRID.

The wine has traditionally been made in 10 feet high *tinajas*, fabricated of local clay and so reminiscent of Roman amphorae, and there was a mystique about fermenting it in the town of Valdepeñas itself, where there are still no less than some eighty *bodegas* (wineries). The larger and more modern establishments have moved with the times and are now making the wine in temperature-controlled stainless steel vats. Again, the tradition was to drink the wine young, and it was sold as a two-year-old from the *tinaja* in which it was fermented. A few of the *bodegas* have now begun ageing the wines in oak casks – using for this purpose red wines made with 100 per cent of the black Cencibel, rather than the traditional blend of Cencibel and white Airén – with excellent results in the case of wines such as the fruity *Reserva* and *Gran Reserva* from the Señorío de los Llanos.

Valencia
SPANISH CITY

Valencia, or Valencia del Cid as it is sometimes called in memory of the famous warrior who liberated it from the MOORS, is the Queen of the LEVANTE, surrounded by orange and lemon groves and its fertile *huerta* (garden), producing vegetables all year round. A great deal of old Valencia was destroyed during the Napoleonic and Civil Wars; one fine old building to have survived is the Baroque palace of the Marqués de dos Aguas, which now houses the best ceramic museum in Spain. One of its features is a traditional Valencian kitchen tiled with the *azulejos* (polychrome tiles) made in the region and complete with cooking vessels and utensils.

Valencia, with the paddy fields of the Albufera on its outskirts, is the home of PAELLA and rice dishes. It is the major port in Spain for the export of wines, which the surrounding regions produce in large amount (see following entry).

Among the best of its restaurants, Eladio, named after its gifted *maître de cuisine*, Eladio Rodríguez Blanco, specializes in fish and seafood such as hake, monkfish, sea bass and *suprême* of turbot roes. Las Graelles is well known for regional cooking and rice dishes such as *paella*, ARROZ ABANDA, *rosexat* (rice, chickpeas, broth and leftover COCIDO with MORCILLA, tomatoes and garlic) and *arroz amb fessols naps* (rice with turnips and beans).

S *Valencia*
DEMARCATED WINE REGION

Valencia is best known as a large scale exporter of inexpensive beverage wine. It is the headquarters of huge concerns such as VINIVAL and Schenk, some half of all foreign shipments of Spanish wine pass through its *grao* (port). Of the wine pro- duced in the demarcated region of Valencia, probably the best is the luscious Moscatel; the sub-region of Alto Turia in the cooler and hillier northwest of the province makes some fresh and fruity white wines with a greenish cast from the Merseguera grape.

S *Vega Sicilia*
WINE

Founded in 1864, Bodegas Vega Sicilia in the Duero valley near Valladolid make one of the most prestigious – and certainly the most expensive – of Spanish table wines. Made from a blend of French and native grapes, the wine (all of it red) is aged for 10 years in 50 gallon oak casks before being bottled, and is deep in color, oaky and splendidly fruity and complex in flavour with a long finish.

It is obtainable only in the best Spanish restaurants and hotels and very little is shipped abroad. There are many stories – or legends – about it. Sir Winston Churchill, encountering it for the first time at a banquet, is reputed to have said: "My vote goes to this unknown claret." Then there was the joke current in Spain that its maker, Don Jesús Anadón, approached by Buckingham Palace about wine for the Prince of Wales' wedding, replied: "With pleasure – I can spare you two cases."

S P *verduras*
VEGETABLES

Spain and Portugal are famous for the profusion and quality of their vegetables. In the Spanish LEVANTE there are two crops a year and output has been increased still further in Almería by growing them out of season on the sandflats in the Campo de Dalias to the west of the city.

These are now covered by mile upon endless mile of vast plastic canopies prop- ped up by tall eucalyptus supports. Seen in the distance, with the sun glinting on the plastic, they look like an inland sea. The vegetables, grown all year round and watered from artesian wells, supply a large part of the European demand – and this is why, for example, Europeans may now buy peppers in or out of season. The industry has caused a social revolution. Peasant farmers, who once found it hard to scratch a living, are now employed by international companies or are members of large coopera- tives, and spend their lives amidst the luxuriating vegetation of an artificial en- vironment, earning sums of money pre- viously undreamt of. Meanwhile, a whole community of botanical advisers, plastic manufacturers, plant hirers, well-drillers, seedsmen, pipe-layers, insurance agents, government inspectors and haulage contrac- tors has sprung up alongside.

As a result of all this frenetic activity and biological engineering, Almería can now

---

see also   ***Veal:*** *see ternera, vitela*   ***Vegetables:*** *see verduras*

---

produce vegetables to almost any specification – tomatoes "made to measure" in any desired size and weight, red peppers with thick skins and large cavities for stuffing or lettuces without coarse outer leaves which look green even under the fluorescent lighting of hypermarkets. In order of sales, the vegetables in most demand are: peppers, winter tomatoes, eggplant, runner beans, zucchini, melons and lettuces.

In Spain, vegetables are always served on their own as a separate course, usually as an appetizer. In the evenings especially, when a light *cena* (evening meal) is served, the Spaniards often begin with a vegetable dish.

In Portugal, the custom is different. Vegetables, especially potatoes of which they are excessively fond, are served *with* the main dish.

vidrar

To glaze; see GLASEAR.

vieiras
SCALLOPS

Galicia (see ASTURIAS AND GALICIA) is famous for its scallops. Their shells were worn as a badge by the medieval pilgrims to the shrine of St James in Santiago de Compostela, hence the name for one of the recipes for cooking them: CONCHAS DE PEREGRINO. See also SANTIAGUIÑOS.

---

vieiras fritas a la gallega (S) *fried scallops* *Galician style*	*Serves 4* 8 scallops, cleaned juice of 1 lemon salt and pepper 2 tbsp flour ¼ cup butter 4 tbsp chopped parsley	*Soak the scallops in half the lemon juice for 30 minutes. Remove, season with salt and pepper and dredge in flour. Heat the butter in a frying pan and fry the scallops slowly for 5 minutes on either side (or for a little longer depending on their size) until pale brown. Add the remaining lemon juice and the parsley, and serve at once.*

Vilarinho de S. Romão, Visconde de
19TH-CENTURY AGRICULTURALIST/ WRITER

Like his mother, who introduced potatoes to TRAS-OS-MONTES in 1798, Antonio Lobo de Barbosa Texeira Girão, Visconde de Vilarinho de S. Romão, was a person of great ability, distinguishing himself in politics, literature and agricultural studies. He wrote an important book on the Port Wine Company and viticulture in the Douro and in 1841 published one of the most influential of Portuguese cooker books, *A Arte do Coinheiro e do Copeiro* ("The Art of Cooking and Serving Food"). His ideas were idiosyncratic and positive: he considered the only healthy cooking vessels to be those of earthenware and he warned against eating mushrooms in any shape or form because of the existence of poisonous varieties. He commented scathingly on the Portuguese predilection for dried cod from remote waters: "Instead of buying *bacalhau* to the annual value of 3,500,000$00 cruzados . . . the worth of 29,166 fat and healthy bullocks, we should rear these bullocks on our empty pastures and obtain a dispensation for eating them."

Ⓢ *Villalón*
A CHEESE

Also called *pata de mula,* this is a soft ewe's milk cheese from Valladolid, hand-pressed and steeped briefly in brine. With a fat content of 54 percent, it has a mild salty taste and is usually eaten fresh, but may undergo further ripening.

Ⓢ Ⓟ *vinagre*
VINEGAR

Vinegar is made by the bacterial oxidation of alcoholic liquids such as wine, beer and cider in the presence of *Mycoderma aceti* (mother of vinegar).

Since it contains acetic acid, vinegar is always acidic, but the color and flavor vary greatly. Malt vinegar is yellowish and slightly bitter, resembling the beer from which it is made. Wine vinegars are somewhat sweeter and fruitier in taste, with aromas resembling those of the wines from which they are made. Fruitiest of all is sherry vinegar – it is a disaster for the *bodeguero* (winemaker) if his casks are infected, but they make the very best quality vinegar.

Vinegar has numerous uses in cooking, for example in marinades, and in Spain and Portugal, wine or sherry vinegar is the preferred type. But a word of warning: vinegary food destroys the taste of an accompanying wine, and if you plan to drink wine, it is generally better to use lemon juice.

Ⓟ *vinhos verdes*
DEMARCATED WINE

Such is the importance of the *vinhos verdes* or "green wines" of Portugal, which account for some 25 per cent of the country's production, that in Portuguese restaurants the wine list is divided into two parts: *vinhos verdes* and *vinhos maduros* ("mature" wines made in the normal fashion).

The name refers not to the color, but to the youth and freshness of the wines, which are slightly *pétillant,* leaving a prickle on the tongue. They are made in the north of Portugal, mainly in the MINHO. The vines are trained high and well clear of the ground because of the damp climate, and are festooned along a line of trees, in trellises or on T-shaped uprights of wood or concrete, known as *cruzetas.* Grown in this way, the grapes contain a high amount of the tart malic acid found in unripe fruit and undergo a prolonged secondary or malo-lactic fermentation to eliminate it; and it is as a result of this that the incipient bubble is generated.

Most of the wines are made in one of 21 cooperatives from grapes grown by smallholders. An association of private producers of estate-grown wines, APEVV, has also been formed, and their wines are among the best, though in limited supply. The single most famous producer is the Palacio de Brejoeira in the sub-region of Monção, of which the wines, made from the Alvarinho grape, without bubble and rather stronger than the others, have long been the most sought after from the whole area.

Some 60 percent of production is of red wines, which are not much exported, as foreign wine drinkers find them overly harsh and dry. Nevertheless, they do complement rich or oily dishes, such as grilled sardines, RANCHO, or kippers. The whites are most refreshing as an apéritif, go well with fish and light food, and drivers will be interested to know that they contain only 8·5–11·5 percent alcohol by volume.

Ⓟ *vitela*
VEAL

What is usually served as veal in Portugal is, in fact, baby beef from a weaned calf, the meat being red rather than pale pink.

see also   ***Vinaigrette:*** *see salsa vinagreta*   ***Vinegar:*** *see vinagre*

The Spanish and Portuguese alphabets do not contain the letter W, except where foreign words have been adopted. English cross-references beginning with this letter can be found at the bottom of the page.

xaropes

Syrups and caramel; see JARABE.

xerém ou papas de milho com sardinhas

PORRIDGE

Xerém is the Arabic name for porridge, and this Portuguese version, also known as *papas de milho,* is a creamy cornmeal porridge served either with sardines cooked with a sauce of olive oil, tomatoes and onions or with *toucinho* (see TOCINO) or fried CHOURIÇO.

see also   **Walnut:** *see nuez*   **Water:** *see agua*

⑤ *Yecla*

DEMARCATED WINE REGION

Situated in the province of Murcia in the hills behind ALICANTE, Yecla produces strong, full-bodied red wines from Monastrell grapes, often grown ungrafted, since the region was little affected by phylloxera. The great bulk of the wine is made in the Cooperativa la Purísima, one of the largest in Spain.

⑤ *yemas de coco*

COCONUT CANDIES

Round candies made with a sugar and brandy syrup to which chopped coconut is added. It is left overnight and then shaped into small balls. These are served with hot chocolate poured over them.

⑤ *yemas de Santa Teresa*

CANDIED EGG YOLKS

This famous candy is named after Santa Teresa of Avila, the 16th-century Carmelite nun whose reforms did much to prevent the spread of Protestantism to Spain.

A soft ball syrup is made (see JARABES) with the addition of a cinnamon stick. This is removed and beaten egg yolk and lemon zest are added to the syrup. It is cooked over a gentle heat, then turned on to a flat greased sheet or waxed paper and allowed to cool. The candies are shaped to look like egg yolks and are then put into individual paper cups.

Opposite and overleaf: Traditional, decorative panels from two bakeries

PASTISSERIA
* DEL PUIG *

zanahorias

Carrots; see CENOURAS.

zarzuela de mariscos a la catalana

SHELLFISH STEW
CATALAN STYLE

Zarzuela means a variety show in Spanish, and you may vary as you wish on this magnificent fish stew, provided that any white fish used is firm and does not disintegrate in cooking.

---

zarzuela de mariscos a la catalana (S)
shellfish stew
Catalan style

Serves 6

12 clams or 24 mussels, well scrubbed and
    washed in cold water
½ cup olive oil
1 onion, chopped
½ lb squid, cleaned and
    cut up (see page 79)
½ lb sea bass or hake, sliced
½ lb angler fish, sliced
½ lb shrimp in shell, boiled
8 scampi in shell, boiled
2 tbsp Spanish brandy
1 clove garlic, crushed
1 tbsp tomato paste
¼ cup dry white wine
salt and pepper
1 tbsp chopped parsley
4 fingers fried white bread, without crusts
few strands of saffron
12 roasted almonds, skinned

Bring the clams to the boil in water, leave them until they open, then drain and reserve them together with the stock.

Heat the olive oil in a large, deep casserole, fry the onion for 10 minutes, then add the squid, sea bass or hake, angler fish, the shrimp and scampi, and fry together until brown. Pour in the brandy and flambé. Add the garlic, tomato paste, wine and reserved stock. Season with salt, pepper and parsley, stir together well and cook slowly for 20 minutes, uncovered, adding a little hot water if necessary. Ten minutes before removing from the heat, add the clams. Crush the fried bread, saffron and almonds to a paste, dissolve with a little of the stock, and stir this picada into the stew. Serve immediately.

BIBLIOGRAPHY

Alonso, Juan Carlos. *Guía del tapeo en Triana*. Ayuntamiento de Sevilla, Sevilla 1985.

Anderson, Jean. *The Food of Portugal*. Robert Hale 1987.

Anne Mary Louise [D'Orléans], Duchesse de Montpensier. *Mémoires* de Mademoiselle de Montpensier, fille de Gaston d'Orleans, frère de Louis XIII. Nouv. éd., 8 tom., Amsterdam 1746.

Apicius. *De Re Coquinaria*. Translated by Flores Samantana, Primitiva & Torrego Salcedo, Esperanza. Ediciones Generales Anaya, Madrid 1985.

Arias de Apraiz, Elvira. *Libro de cocina*. 14th edn. Vitoria 1930.

Arnaut, Salvador Dias. *A Arte de Comer em Portugal na Idade Média*. Introduction to *O Livro de Cozinha da Infanta D. Maria de Portugal*. Coimbra University Press 1967; Lisbon 1986.

Arrazandi, Telesforo. *Setas u hongos del País Vasco*. 1857.

Ballard, Sam and Jane. *Pousadas of Portugal*. Harvard Common Press, Boston 1986.

Bardají, Teodoro. *El Gorro Blanco* (periodical). Madrid & Barcelona 1906 continuing.

Bardají, Teodoro. *Indice culinario*. Madrid 1915.

Bardají, Teodoro. *La salsa mahonesa*. Madrid 1928.

Boletín de la Cofradía Vasca de Gastrónomia. Año V, Gráficas Colón, San Sebastián 1970.

Belo, Antonio Maria de Oliveira (Oleboma). *Culinária Portuguesa*. Lisbon 1936.

Bernard de Ferrer, Genoveva. *Cocina vasca*. Barcelona 1974.

Bernard de Ferrer, Genoveva. *Los entremeses*. Biblioteca Ama de Casa, Barcelona 1962.

Bernard de Ferrer, Genoveva. *Nuevas recetas de pescados y mariscos*. Biblioteca Ama de Casa, Barcelona 1962.

Bernard de Ferrer, Genoveva. *Platos regionales españoles*. Biblioteca Ama de Casa, Barcelona 1960.

Bettónica, Luís, Ibáñez i Escofet, Manuel and Vallsi Grau, Josep. *Un home de Cadaqués, Portbou i Figueres* (Josep Mercader). Privately printed, Gerona 1985.

Bettónica, Luís. *Cuisine of Spain*. W.H. Allen, London 1983.

Borrow, George. *The Bible in Spain*. London 1843.

Bradford, Sarah. *The Englishman's Wine – The Story of Port*. New edn. Christie's Wine Publications 1983.

Brillat-Savarin. *Physiologie du goût*. 1st edn. 1826. Reprint: Hermann, Paris 1975.

Calera, Ana Ma. and Repollés, José. *Cocina española*. De Gasso Hnos., Barcelona 1973.

Camba Julio. *La casa de Lúculo o el arte del buen comer*. 7th edn. Espasa-Calpe, Madrid 1968.

Casas, Penelope. *Tapas*. Pavilion 1987.

Casas, Penelope. *The Foods and Wines of Spain*. 3rd edn. A.A. Knopf, New York 1983.

Cass, Elizabeth. *Spanish Cooking*. André Deutsch 1957.

Cossart, Noel. *Madeira – the island vineyard*. Christie's Wine Publications 1984.

Davidson, Alan. *Mediterranean Seafood*. Penguin 1972.

Delegación Nacional de la Sección Femenina. *Manual de cocina*. 20th edn. E. Almena, Madrid 1969.

Delgado, Carlos. *Diccionario de gastronomía*. Alianza, Madrid 1985.

Dioscorides. *De medicina materia*. Lyons 1550.

Doménech, Ignacio. *La nueva cocina elegante española*. 7th edn. Quintilla y Cardona, Barcelona n.d.

Dumas, Alexandre. *From Paris to Cádiz*. Translated by A.E. Murch n.d.

Dumas, Alexandre. *Le Grand Dictionnaire de Cuisine*. Reprint: Edition Henri Veyrier, Paris 1978.

Enciclopedia del vino. Orbis, Barcelona 1987–1988.

Escobar, Julio. *Itinerarios por las cocinas y las bodegas de Castilla*. Ed. Cultura Hispánica, Madrid 1968.

Escoffier, Auguste. *Le Guide Culinaire*. Paris 1902. Reprint: Editions Flammarion, Paris 1985.

Ferreira, Manuel. *A Cocinha Ideal*. 4th edn. Oporto 1959.

Ford, Richard. *A Hand-book for Travellers in Spain and Readers at Home*. John Murray 1845. Reprint: Centaur Press 1966.

Ford, Richard. *Gatherings from Spain*. John Murray 1846. Reprint: Everyman's Library n.d.

Forti, Fransesc. *Del yantar y del comer*. Fransesc y Albino Forti, Argentona 1982.

Franco Cañero, Juan de Dios. *Diccionario gastronómico multilingua*. Aries, Madrid 1978.

García Corella, Laura. *Guria. Cocina vascongada*. 3rd edn. Editorial Cantábrica. Bilbao 1973.

Hilgarth, Mary. *Spanish Cookery*. International Wine and Food Society 1970.

Jeffs, Julian. *Sherry*. 3rd edn. Faber, London 1982.

Junot, Lauré (Duchesse d'Abrantes). *Memoirs*. Translated London 1832.

Laboratorio de Estudos Mercadotécnica. *Restaurantes de Portugal, Roteiro gastronomico*. Lisbon pub. annually.

Larousse Gastronomique. English edn. 10th imp. Hamlyn 1971.

Libre de Sent Sovi (fourteenth and fifteenth century Catalan recipes). Translated by Rudolf Grew, Editorial Barcino, Barcelona 1979.

L'Obel, Matthias de. *Plantarum historia*. Antwerp 1576.

Lobo de Barbosa Texeira Girão, António Visconde de Vilarinho de S. Romão. *A Arte de Coinheiro e do Copeiro*. Oporto 1841.

Luján, Néstor and Perucho, Juan. *El libro de la cocina española Gastronomía e historia*. 2nd edn. Danae, Barcelona 1974.

Macpherson, Lalo Grosso de. *Cocinar a bordo con Fortuna*. Espasa-Calpe, Madrid 1986.

Macpherson, Lalo Grosso de. *El vino de Jerez en la cocina universal*. Espasa-Calpe, Madrid 1982. Translated by Maite Manjón. *Cooking with Sherry*. Espasa-Calpe, Madrid 1983.

Manjón, Maite. *The Home Book of Portuguese Cookery*. Faber 1974.

Manjón, Maite and O'Brien, Catherine. *Spanish Cooking at Home and on Holiday*. Pan 1973. Enlarged edn. Book Club Associates 1976.

March, Lourdes. *El libro de la paella y de los arroces*. Alianza, Madrid 1985.

Mestayer de Echague, María. *Enciclopedia culinaria*. 6th edn. Madrid 1949.

Michelin Green Guide *Espagne*. Michelin 1985.

Michelin Green Guide *Portugal, Madeira*. Michelin 1980.

Michelin Red Guide *Espagne, Portugal*. Michelin Pub. annually.

Ministerio de Agricultura, Dirección General de Ganadería. *Catálogo de quesos españoles*. Madrid 1969. Instituto Nacional de Denominaciones de Origen (INDO). *Denominaciones de origen of Spain, Wine, Olive oil, Cured Ham, Cheese*. 2nd edn. Madrid 1984.

Ministerio de Información y Turismo. *Guía gastronómica de La Mancha*. Madrid 1975.

Modesto, Maria de Lourdes, *La Cozinha Tradicional Portuguesa*. 6th edn. Verbo, Lisbon 1986.

Ortega, Simone. *1080 recetas de cocina*. 13th edn. Alianza, Madrid 1986.

Ortega, Simone. *Quesos españoles*. Alianza, Madrid 1987.

Pérez, Dionisio. *Guía del buen comer español*. Sucesores de Rivadeneyra S.A. Madrid 1929.

Quitério, José. *Livro de Bem Comer*. Assirio & Alvim, Lisbon 1987.

Read, Jan. *Sherry and the Sherry Bodegas*. Sotheby 1988.

Read, Jan. *The Moors in Spain and Portugal*. Faber 1974.

Read, Jan. *The Wines of Portugal*. 2nd edn. Faber 1987.

Read, Jan. *The Wines of Spain*. 2nd edn. Faber 1986.

Read, Jan and Manjón, Maite. *Flavours of Spain*. Cassell 1978.

Read, Jan and Manjón, Maite. *Paradores of Spain*. Macmillan 1977.

Read, Jan, Manjón, Maite and Johnson, Hugh. *The Wine and Food of Spain*. Weidenfeld 1987.

Ripoll, Luis. *Cocina de las Baleares*. 2nd edn. Palma de Mallorca 1974.

Rodrigues, Domingos. *Arte de Cozinha*. (1st edn. 1680), 13th edn. Lisbon 1844.

Rondelet, Guillaume. *De piscibus marinis*. Lyons 1554.

Ruperto de Nola [Rubert de Nola]. *Libro de Guisados, Manjares y Potajes*. Valladolid edn. of 1529. Reprint: Editorial Artes Gráficas, Madrid-Palma de Mallorca 1968.

Selecções do Reader's Digest. *Tesouros da Cozinha Tradicional Portuguesa*. Reader's Digest. Lisbon 1984.

Serra, Victoria. *Tía Victoria's Spanish Kitchen*. Translated by Elizabeth Gili. Nicholas Caye 1963.

Stobart, Tom. *Herbs, Spices and Flavourings*. 3rd edn. Penguin 1987.

Sueiro, Jorge-Victor. *Comer en Galicia*. Penthalion, Madrid 1981.

Torres, Marimar. *The Spanish Table*. Ebury Press 1987.

Valente, Maria Odette Cortes. *Cozinha Regional Portuguesa*. 1st edn. Lisbon 1962.

Vega, Luís Antonio de, *Viaje por las cocinas de España*. Editorial Fareso, Madrid 1960.

Vega, Luís Antonio de. *Guía gastronómica de España*. 3rd edn. Editorial Nacional, Madrid 1970.

Gastronomic periodicals

Spain
Bouquet (Barcelona)
Club de Gourmets (Madrid)
Comer y Beber (Barcelona)
Gourmetour (Madrid)
Mesa y Más (Barcelona)
Sobremesa (Madrid)

Portugal
A Boa Mesa (Lisbon)
Banquete (Lisbon)

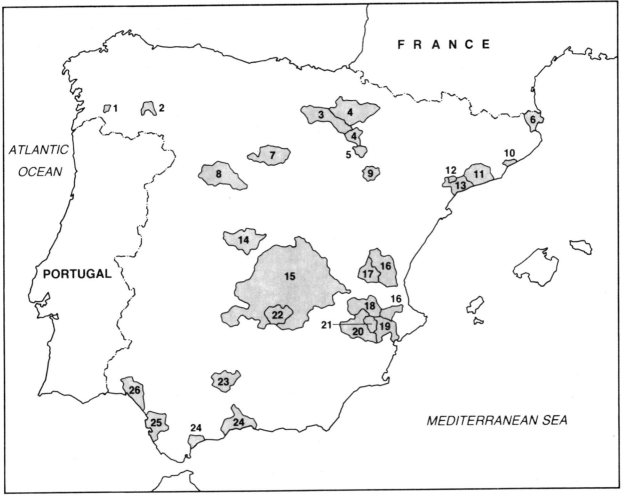

Major Wine Producing Regions in Spain

1. Ribeiro
2. Valdeorras
3. Rioja
4. Navarra
5. Campo de Borja
6. Ampurdán – Costa Brava
7. Ribera del Duero
8. Rueda
9. Cariñena
10. Alella
11. Penedès
12. Priorato
13. Tarragona
14. Méntrida
15. La Mancha
16. Valencia
17. Utiel – Requena
18. Almansa
19. Alicante
20. Jumilla
21. Yecla
22. Valdepeñas
23. Montilla – Moriles
24. Málaga
25. Sherry
26. Condado de Huelva

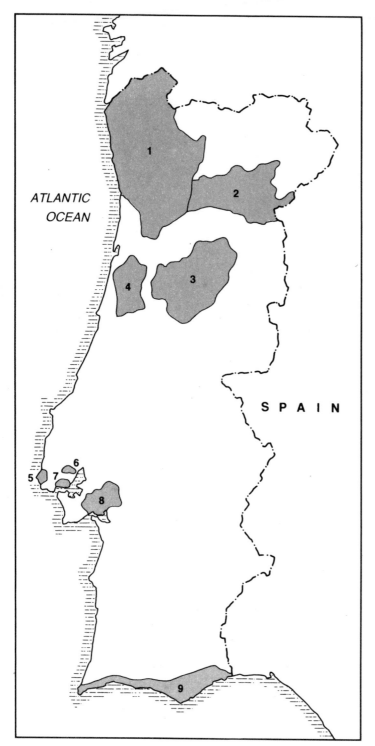

Major Wine Producing Regions in Portugal

1. Vinhos Verdes
2. Port and Douro
3. Dão
4. Bairrada
5. Colares
6. Bucelas
7. Carcavelos
8. Setúbal
9. Algarve

ATLANTIC OCEAN

SPAIN

INDEX

PICTURE CREDITS

Corning Museum of Glass, New York: 275b; Foods from Spain: 20t, 20b, 32t, 32b, 105t, 105b, 161, 213, 233, 303; Gourmetour: 161; ICEX: 30-31, 49, 52t, 52b, 69, 72, 164, 216t, 256t, 256b, 273, 276t; Museo del Prado, Madrid: 275t; Oronoz/Museo a Decorativas, Madrid: 108; Oronoz/Museo del Prado, Madrid: 19, 50-51, 141, 142-143, 162-163, 214-215; Oronoz/Museo Romantico, Madrid: 144; Jan Read: 1, 2, 29, 70-71, 106-107, 164b, 216b, 233t, 234-235, 236, 253, 254, 255, 276b, 285t, 285b, 286t, 286b, 304; Maureen Thompson Ltd: 274

Madeleine David; 22, 35, 36, 42, 43, 47, 55, 63, 64, 66, 74, 83, 84, 96l, 100, 103, 109, 119, 137, 138, 148, 169, 178, 183b, 188, 190, 197, 199t, 201, 208t, 218, 229, 230, 232, 265, 281, 284, 290, 305; John Freeman & Co.: 149; Jan Read: 17, 28, 37, 38, 59, 60, 87, 93, 101, 115, 120, 125, 129, 132, 146, 183t, 186, 194, 199b, 200, 203, 220, 225, 227t, 241, 243t, 250, 251, 257, 259, 279, 280, 287, 296, 298; University of St Andrews Library/Jan Read: 18, 21, 24, 25, 26, 34, 37, 39, 41, 45, 53, 54, 79r, 79l, 81, 84, 85, 86, 95, 96r, 99, 113, 114, 122, 124, 131, 136, 149, 150, 154, 157, 172, 173, 175, 177, 180, 204, 206, 207, 219, 222, 227b, 228, 231, 239, 243b, 262, 263, 270, 272, 278, 294, 299